In memory of Norbert Elias
&
for Anna, Pat, & Liv Jorunn

Contents

Notes on Contributors

Eric Dunning is professor of sociology at the University of Leicester, England. A native Londoner, Eric is a graduate of the Universities of London and Leicester and has taught extensively in America and continental Europe. With Norbert Elias, he is one of the pioneers of the sociology of sport, having worked in the field since 1959. His publications include *Barbarians, Gentlemen and Players* (1979, with Ken Sheard), *Quest for Excitement* (1986, with Norbert Elias), *The Roots of Football Hooliganism* (1988, with Pat Murphy and John Williams), and *Sport and Leisure in the Civilizing Process* (1992, with Chris Rojek).

Eric is divorced and has two children, Michael and Rachel. Formerly an active soccer centre-half and opening batsman at cricket, his main sporting involvements now are watching Leicester City's and his son's soccer teams.

Dr. Joseph Maguire completed his doctorate in sociology at the University of Leicester, England. He has lectured in the USA, Canada, and Norway and has published articles on violence, the emotions, and globalization in various sport journals. Joe is coauthor with John Bale of *The Global Arena: Sports Talent Migration in an Interdependent World* (in press). He is a member of the extended board for the International Committee for the Sociology of Sport and the editorial boards of the *Sociology of Sport Journal* and the *International Review for the Sociology of Sport*. Joe lectures in the Department of Physical Education, Sports Science, and Recreation Management at Loughborough University, England. He remains a keen soccer player.

Bob Pearton is head of the Department of Sport Science at Canterbury Christ Church College of Higher Education, Kent, England. He has been lecturing in the sociology of sport in British universities since 1963, and his paper (with Dr. Stanley Parker) at the annual conference of the British Sociological Association in 1972 was the first BSA conference paper on sport. Bob's research has been principally in the area of sport-related violence; his most recent publication is in *Sport and Social Theory*, edited by C. Roger Rees and Andrew W. Miracle (1986, Human Kinetics Publishers). Bob has had an active sporting career since childhood, including soccer, volleyball, marathon running, downhill skiing, and golf.

Joseph L. Arbena is professor of history at Clemson University, South Carolina. In addition to compiling *An Annotated Bibliography of Latin American Sport* (1989), he has written at length on the interrelationships of sports, social change, and national identity in the Latin American realm. He maintains a similar interest in music as a dynamic and entertaining expression of human creativity and as contested social terrain.

Robert Beamish is an associate professor jointly appointed to the Department of Sociology and the School of Physical Education at Queen's University, Kingston, Ontario. Rob's main academic interests are in sociological theory and sport as work. In addition to *Q: What Do You Do For a Living? A: I'm an Athlete* and numerous articles on sport and labour relations, Beamish has recently published *Marx, Method and Division of Labor* and is putting the finishing touches on *Drugs and Sport: After the Ben Johnson Affair.*

Allen Guttmann, after publishing several books in American studies, turned to sport history. The best-known of his six contributions to this field is *From Ritual to Record* (1978). *The Games Must Go On: Avery Brundage and the Olympic Movement* (1984) was named Olympic Book of the Year by the USOC, and the North American Society for Sport History honored *Women's Sports: A History* (1991) with its yearly book prize. Guttmann teaches at Amherst College, Amherst, Massachusetts.

Richard Gruneau teaches media and cultural studies in the Department of Communication at Simon Fraser University in Vancouver, British Columbia. His previous publications include *Canadian Sport: Sociological Perspectives* (1976 with John Albinson), *Sport, Culture and the Modern State* (1982 with Hart Cantelon), *Class, Sports and Social Development* (1983), and *Popular Cultures and Political Practices* (1988).

Jennifer Hargreaves is reader in the politics and sociology of sport at the Roehampton Institute, London, where she works in the sports studies department teaching history and the sociology of sport. She has published widely in books and journals, has edited a collection entitled *Sport, Culture, and Ideology* (1982), and is completing a book on women and sport. Jennifer lectures frequently in England and other countries and has been a consultant for the BBC and the Open University. In 1992 she was a visiting professor at the University of Hamburg.

Dr. Klaus Heinemann is a professor at the University of Hamburg, Germany, whose main areas of research include the sociology of economics, organizations and sport, the economy of sport, and the sociology of unemployment. He is chairman of the Scientific Advisory Board of the German Sport Association and editor-in-chief of the *International Review for the Sociology of Sport.*

Alan G. Ingham is an associate professor in the Department of Physical Education, Health, and Sport Studies at Miami University, Oxford, Ohio. He graduated from Carnegie College/University of Leeds, earned an MS in physical education at Washington State University, and a PhD in sociology at the University of Massachusetts. Alan has contributed many articles and book chapters in various areas of scholarly inquiry, among them experimental social psychology, sport history, social history, sport sociology, and cultural studies. He is on the editorial board of the *International Review for the Sociology of Sport* and was president of the International Committee of the Sociology of Sport from 1984 to 1987.

Grant Jarvie is a senior lecturer at the University of Warwick in England. He is the author of a number of sociological and historical books on sport and leisure. He is currently working on *Scottish Sport in the Making of the Nation* (Leicester University Press, 1993) and *Sport and Leisure in Social Thought* (with Joe Maguire, Routledge, 1993).

Peter McIntosh holds degrees in classics and history from the Universities of Oxford and Birmingham. He has been a teacher and researcher at universities in Britain, New Zealand, and Canada. He has also been senior inspector of physical education for London for 14 years and served on the Sports Council for Great Britain for 9 years. Peter is the author of *Sport in Society* (1963, revised in 1987).

Dr. Bero Rigauer studied sociology at the Main Institute for Social Research in Frankfurt, Germany, and sociology and physical education at the University of Frankfurt. He is a professor in the Department of Sportwissenschaft at the University of Oldenburg, Germany, where he teaches courses in the sociology of sport, the social and cultural history of sport, general theory of sport, and methodology of sciences. Bero is still an 'elder sportsman' who enjoys skiing, basketball, volleyball, and Chinese pa tuan chin.

James Riordan is a professor of Russian studies and head of the Department of Linguistics and International Studies at the University of Surrey, England. He is the author of several books and articles on Communist sport. Jim's most recent book is *Sport, Politics and Communisim* (Manchester University Press, 1991).

Preface

We are pleased and excited at the publication of *The Sports Process*. Its appearance, we feel, provides compelling evidence of the strides that have been made in recent years in a comparatively new area of academic endeavour, a field that can be variously described as the 'historical', 'comparative-developmental', or 'process-sociological' ('figurational') study of sport. It is, in general, a lively field, full of engaged and interesting controversy and debate. It is this combination of progress, engagement, controversy, open discussion, and debate that makes the field so stimulating for teachers, students, and researchers.

It was our aim as we organised *The Sports Process* to create a volume that would serve not only as a reference but also as a viable text for Sociology of Sport courses.

The book is divided into three main parts: 'Perspectives on the Making of Modern Sports'; 'Aspects of the Diffusion and Development of Modern Sports'; and 'Comparative and Developmental Studies of Modern Sports Cultures'. It begins with an Introduction in which we (a) define what we take the principal aims and parameters of this emerging field to be; and (b) introduce the reader to some of the main controversies that have grown up among its practitioners. Each section is preceded by introductory comments where we summarise the existing level of knowledge in the relevant subfield and locate particular chapters in that context. These 'specific' introductions also contain summaries of the chapters, together, where appropriate, with critical comments. At the end of each section, we have added lists of questions that will stimulate class discussion and debate, lists of research tasks for students to carry out, and guides to further reading.

In putting *The Sports Process* together, we have tried as far as possible to strike a balance between the different perspectives—mainly Weberianism, figurational/process sociology, and various forms of Marxism—that have so far contributed to the field. In other words, even though two of the editors—Dunning and Maguire—are strongly committed to the figurational/process sociological approach, we have sought not to privilege that position. We are acutely aware in saying this that we have failed in at least one respect to achieve the sort of balance that we would, ideally, have desired: The book contains only one piece by a feminist writer. The excellence of Hargreaves's contribution in chapter 3 helps only marginally to make up for our disappointment that—unavoidably at present it seems to us—our reader reflects the large measure of continuing male dominance in the sociology of sport as a whole.

Thanks are due to the authors for agreeing to contribute to *The Sports Process* and, in some cases, for complying with our editorial requests and suggestions in double-quick time. Thanks are also due to Pat Murphy and Ivan Waddington for their critical reading of the Introduction and to Dianne Swift for her typing and word-processing help in producing the manuscript. Finally, thanks are due to George McKinney and Rodd Whelpley of Human Kinetics Publishers. They have never been anything short of constructive, supportive, and helpful in their dealings with us, and we are very grateful to them.

Credits

1. 'Sociology of Sport in the Ancient World' by Peter C. McIntosh originally appeared in *Handbook of Social Science of Sport* (pp. 25-48) by Günther R.F. Lüschen and George H. Sage (Eds.), 1981, Champaign, IL: Stipes Publishing Co. Copyright 1981 by Stipes Publishing Co. Reprinted by permission.

2. 'Sport in the Civilising Process: Aspects of the Development of Modern Sport' by Eric Dunning originally appeared as 'Sport in the Civilizing Process: Aspects of the Development of Modern Sporting Forms,' 1988, *Centring Smaskrifter*, **nr. 4**, in the series *Centring Smaskrifter*. Copyright 1988 by Eric Dunning. Portions of the text have also appeared in 'The Figurational Approach to Leisure and Sport' by Eric Dunning in *Leisure for Leisure* (pp. 36-52) by Chris Rojek (Ed.), 1989, Houndmills, Basingstoke, Hampshire, and London, England and NY: Routledge, The Macmillan Press Ltd. Copyright 1989 by Chris Rojek. Adapted by permission.

3. 'The Victorian Cult of the Family and the Early Years of Female Sport' by Jennifer Hargreaves is adapted from 'Victorian Familism and the Formative Years of Female Sport' by Jennifer Hargreaves in *From "Fair Sex" to Feminism: Sport and the Socialization of Women in the Industrial and Post-Industrial Eras* (pp. 130-144) by J.A. Mangan and Roberta J. Park (Eds.), 1987, London, England and Totowa, NJ: Frank Cass & Co. Ltd. Copyright 1987 by Frank Cass & Co. Ltd. Adapted by permission.

4. Some sections of 'The Critique of Sport in Modernity: Theorising Power, Culture, and the Politics of the Body' were presented in less-developed form as a keynote address entitled 'Sport and l'esprit de corps' at the International Symposium, *Sport: The Third Millennium*, Quebec City, Canada, 20-25 May, 1990.

5. 'The Diffusion of Sport and the Problem of Cultural Imperialism' by Allen Guttmann is adapted from ' "Our Former Colonial Masters": The Diffusion of Sports and the Question of Cultural Imperialism' by Allen Guttmann, 1988, *Stadion*, **14**(1), pp. 49-63. Copyright 1988 by Academia Verlag Richarz. Adapted by permission.

6. An earlier version of Joseph Arbena's 'International Aspects of Sport in Latin America: Perceptions, Prospects, and Proposals' was presented at the annual conference of the North American Society for the Sociology of Sport, Denver, CO, November 7-10, 1990.

7. 'American Football, British Society, and Global Sport Development' by Joseph Maguire is adapted from his essay 'More Than a Sporting Touchdown: The Making of American Football in England 1982-1990' September, 1990, *Sociology of Sport Journal*, **7**(3), pp. 213-237. Copyright 1990 by Human Kinetics Publishers, Inc. Adapted by permisison.

8. 'Sport and the Economy: A Developmental Perspective' by Bero Rigauer has been translated from the original German by Eric Dunning.

Introduction

Sports in Comparative and Developmental Perspective

In March 1990, as part of their marketing of the 1991 Rugby Union World Cup, the Rugby Football Union (RFU) invited the media to witness a staged reenactment of the supposed 'first act' in the making of rugby football. The event took place at Rugby School and involved a present-day Rugby pupil emulating the alleged feat of William Webb Ellis, who in 1823 supposedly inaugurated the distinctive rugby way of playing football. Because the trophy that the competing nations were about to play for is named after this nineteenth-century 'Old Rugbeian', it is hardly surprising that the RFU should have adopted such a strategy. What is perhaps surprising is that rugby administrators and players in late twentieth-century Britain should take the Webb Ellis story as being historically accurate. It is, in fact, a myth. It was constructed in the 1890s, some 70 years after the alleged deviant/innovative act of Webb Ellis is supposed to have taken place (Dunning & Sheard, 1979).

Comparable examples of origin myths in the field of sport include the belief that baseball originated in the United States in 1839 as a result of the intervention of General Abner Doubleday in a game played in a cow pasture in Cooperstown, New York (Gardner, 1974). Sometimes, myths of this kind postulate a collective rather than an individual origin for a particular sport or sports. An example is the belief that modern sport, in particular the Olympic Games, is the continuation of an ancient Greek tradition (Elias, 1986).

Whether the reference is individual or collective, it is easy to see that these origin myths serve psychological and social functions of various kinds. The Webb Ellis myth, for example, was invented just when a process of professionalisation was splitting rugby into two versions—Union and League. It started partly as a celebration by the game's original elite of the public school[1] credentials of rugby football, and partly as an expression of their desire to exclude outsiders and preserve control exclusively for themselves. The Doubleday myth was invented to celebrate the idea that baseball is a specifically American product, completely distinct from the English game of 'rounders', a children's game played especially by girls, from which it is sometimes said to have sprung and with which it is sometimes disparagingly compared.

Understandable though the origins and persistence of myths of these kinds may be, they are simply not sustained by the available evidence. They grossly oversimplify and distort the complex social processes that are involved in the development of sports. In fact, they are a kind of sports equivalent of the belief in the tooth fairy or Father Christmas. They indicate a degree of naivete on the part of those who believe them and are a sign that such people, however mature and sophisticated

1

they may be in other respects, are in some ways 'cultural dopes'. Many people involved in sports—whether athletes, coaches, managers, trainers, administrators, journalists, sports analysts, or fans—lack the kinds of understanding that are, we believe, essential for coping realistically with the diverse and complex range of problems and difficulties with which the world of sports is currently beset. The comparative and developmental approach to the sociological study of sport embodied in the present reader is intended as a remedy to this situation. Such an approach does not pretend to offer easy solutions or quick fixes for the manifold problems and difficulties of sports today. On the contrary, it holds out the prospect of a hard and complex route by means of meticulous, theory-guided research. At present, the comparative and developmental sociology of sport is in and remains in its infancy. Let us begin to explore the current 'state of play'.

Most sociologists of sport agree that studies of sports that are not also studies of the societies where the sports are played are studies out of context. The proponents of some perspectives, however—functionalism and symbolic interactionism are examples—tend to engage solely in studies of sports in the present (Loy, McPherson, & Kenyon, 1978; Fine, 1986). Valuable sociological descriptions of sports are obtainable in this manner. So, too, is knowledge of the ways in which sports are affected by social environments and social institutions of varying kinds, and vice versa, of the impact of sports on their social settings. However, 'synchronic', 'hodiecentric' (Goudsblom, 1977), solely present-centred studies like these are un-able to tell us anything about the origins and development of sports or about the ways in which they are changing. Proponents of the perspectives represented in this volume—principally feminism, Weberianism, figurational sociology, and some of the varieties of Marxism—believe that static sociological approaches, which are not focused on the *processes* at work in sport and society, are at best severely limited and at worst fundamentally flawed.

Let us undertake a brief critical review of some of the most useful work concerned with the social processes in and involving sport. We shall start by looking at some recent work by Marxists. Although we shall be more or less critical of aspects of what they have to say, it is our opinion that all the authors we have singled out for comment have made important contributions to the sociology of sport.

Writing of leisure in capitalist Britain, Clarke and Critcher (1985, p. 215) percep-tively suggested that 'the leisure of the individual needs to be understood within the patterns of the whole society and both require an historical analysis of the dynamics of social structure'. Earlier, they had expanded on the first side of this equation in the following terms:

> Just as we need the horizontal axis of history, so we need the vertical axis of the individual and the society. Their inter-connectedness is that between 'the personal troubles of the milieu' and the 'public issues of the social structure'. Understanding how personal issues come to be experienced as disconnected from public issues, and the individual's milieu from any sense of social structure, is one step in the analysis. The second is to restore a sense of connection, to establish that private troubles are public issues as experienced by individuals,

public issues the sum of those private troubles and their location in the social structure. (Clarke & Critcher, 1985, p. 214)

The emphasis here on the interconnectedness of personal and social issues and on the need for an historical approach is welcome. It is based on the work of C. Wright Mills (1959) and is fully consistent with the idea of 'the sociological imagination' that led us to construct this reader. However, while Mills called for an integration of substantive research and theory, Clarke and Critcher produced what seems to us to be a largely descriptive text concerned solely with one society. As such, despite its considerable sociological value, it fails to live up to the promise that Mills saw in a comparative and historical approach. For Mills (we shall elaborate on our own position later), a theory-guided comparative and historical approach represents the core of sociology, the only way of securing an advance of knowledge in the field.

If it is right to describe the 1985 work of Clarke and Critcher as representative of a kind of empiricism, the work on sport of John Hargreaves can be said to err in some respects in the opposite direction. In his foreword to Hargreaves's *Sport, Power and Culture* (1986), Stuart Hall praises the author for offering an 'historical treatment' that 'does not simply provide a chronological and evolutionary framework for the study, but a context in which serious theoretical issues can be posed'. We agree. We also agree with Hall when he writes that, in Hargreaves's work, the concept of hegemony is 'not merely parachuted into place'. In other words, Hargreaves's use of the theory of Gramsci (1971) has considerably advanced our understanding of the development of modern sport. Where we take issue is over Hargreaves's reliance on secondary research, for it seems to us that he has not taken sufficiently to heart the strictures of writers such as Thompson (1978) on 'the poverty of theory'. Hargreaves appears not to have undertaken substantive research of his own. Such a reliance on the empirical work of others is liable to increase the chances of bias in the selection of material, to minimize the chances of unintended discovery—what Merton (1957) called the 'serendipity effect'—and hence to make one's use of theory self-confirming. It is principally through engaging in empirical research rather than relying on illustrations drawn selectively from the work of others that one's theoretical position can be anything other than an unfalsifiable *idée fixe*.

True to his reliance on Mills as well as Gramsci, Gruneau has, in our opinion, achieved a more satisfactory balance between theory and research than either Clarke and Critcher or Hargreaves. Concerned with establishing the options that are open to people in the field of sports, Gruneau contends that

the answer is an historical one, and requires that we situate our study of play, games and sports in the context of understanding the historical struggle over the control of rules and resources in social life and the ways in which this struggle relates to structured limits and possibilities. (Gruneau, 1983, p. 51)

Although we have doubts regarding his partial reliance on the 'structuration theory' of Giddens (Giddens, 1984; Dunning, 1992) and believe that, besides considerable strengths, there are weaknesses inherent in any Marxist position (Dunning, 1992), Gruneau's approach is open-ended and hence testable and falsifiable in the sense that he has conducted his own original research. As such—and within the constraints and limitations that we believe to be inherent in Marxism—it is, in our opinion, an example of sociological 'best practice'.

Let us turn our attention to some recent work by historians of sport. The first thing worthy of note in this connection is that, to a degree, a welcome convergence between sociologists and historians working in the field of sports studies appears to have recently occurred. Some historians (Jones, 1988; Holt, 1989) have sought to make explicit some of the theoretical assumptions that underpin their work. They have moved, in this respect at least, beyond the view that sees the production of a narrative as the historian's principal task. In his study of working-class sport in Britain between the wars, for example, Jones suggested that 'a framework for analysing the historical development of sport must be firmly based on the socio-economic totality'. He added that, 'though writing as a historian rather than a social theorist, it is useful for the narrative to embrace elements of theory and concept, and to blend them in with the historical evidence' (Jones, 1988, p. 3). Holt went even further. Historians and sociologists, he argued, 'need each other' (Holt, 1989, p. 358). Up to a point, we agree. Where we depart from Holt and Jones is over their view of the relationship between research and theory and between history and sociology. Holt writes in this connection that

> history crudely weighted down with the apparatus of theory and couched in specialist language spoils the enjoyment of a subject without enhancing our understanding of it. Clarity must be a precondition of explanation. Yet hacking through the thickets of jargon there are some good things to be found. Of course such interesting ideas remain nothing more than assertions unless proper historical evidence for them can be produced. This is why the theorists and the historians should get together. (Holt, 1989, pp. 357-358)[2]

Holt and Jones, we think, have made valuable contributions to our understanding of the development of sport. We welcome the evidence of convergence that is provided in their writings. Where we begin to have doubts is over Holt's idea of a marriage between a largely unreformed history and a mainly unchanged sociology. A relationship of this kind, of course, is preferable to a situation where sociologists and historians are constantly at war or where sociologists simply study 'the present' and historians simply study 'the past'. What we have in mind is more radical. It is a fusion of the two disciplines into one, a dismantling of the artificial barriers between sociologists and historians that are so deeply entrenched in the division of academic labour. In order to move towards such an ideal, however, a number of things will be necessary. For example, historians like Jones and Holt will have to move beyond their evident belief in the separation of theory and data. They will have to get away from the idea that facts somehow exist independently of concepts and theories, and that historians are privileged as producers of 'proper' historical evidence. They will also have to get away from the idea that concepts and theories are pure mental constructs elaborated by social theorists in a social vacuum independently of experience, that theories are interesting or useful ideas waiting to be plucked arbitrarily from the air because they take the historian's fancy.

It is as if historians like Holt and Jones have never encountered work such as that by Auguste Comte, who coined the term 'sociology'. Comte wrote as early as 1830 that

> since Bacon, intelligent people are agreed that there is no real knowledge save that which rests on observed facts. But . . . it is no less certain that in order to devote itself to observation the mind needs some kind of theory. If in contemplating phenomena we had no principles to which to attach them, not only would we find it impossible to combine isolated observations, and therefore to profit from them, but we would not be able to remember them, and most of the time the facts themselves would pass unperceived before our very eyes. (Comte in Andreski, 1974, pp. 21-22)

According to Comte, then, theories are necessary to perceive and remember facts and to establish explanatory connections. It follows, whatever the historians themselves may believe, that history cannot be an atheoretical subject. It is, rather, a subject in which guiding principles and theories tend to be implicit rather than explicit, and that means they are liable to take the form of myths, prejudices, fantasies, and biases of various kinds. It also follows that facts cannot have an existence independently of theories. Like beauty, they are 'in the eye of the beholder'. That is, what one believes 'the facts' about the history of sport or anything else to be is an artefact of the relationship between observer and observed. It is a relationship in which specific principles adhered to by the observer are crucial in both an empirical and an explanatory sense. What one believes the facts to be is also inherently social and conflictful in the sense of involving struggles between groups over what the facts are and how they are to be discovered and explained.

Combining this argument with our earlier strictures against sociologists who do not engage in empirical research, it would seem that one of the central differences between history and sociology as they exist at present is as follows: History is based for the most part on implicit concepts and theories. As a result, historians find it difficult to get beyond myths, prejudices, and 'common sense' of various kinds. By contrast, sociology is an openly theoretical subject, but some of its practitioners, because they do not engage in direct empirical research, treat the theories they adhere to as untestable *idées fixes*. Such a situation is conducive as much to fruitless boundary wars between historians and sociologists and to sterile controversies among the conflicting sociological factions as it is to the growth of knowledge. We agree with Elias when he wrote in this connection of the need for a 'two-way traffic', a constant cross-fertilisation of ideas and evidence, theory and observation, if knowledge in a field is to advance (Elias, 1987).

Mennell (1990) has recently written of a 'sociology of the past', a kind of research where an historian or sociologist uses sociological concepts and theories to investigate groups of people who lived in a specific society in a specific period in the past. Research of this kind can be fruitful and illuminating. It can, for example, provide a comparative backdrop against which present social structures and behaviour can be judged. Some of the contributions to this volume are, in this sense, contributions to the 'sociology of the past'. But there is another, more radical way forward. It has been proposed in different ways by scholars as diverse in their orientations as Abrams (1982), Anderson (1974), Elias (1978), and Wallerstein (1987). It does not envision a dialogue between sociologists and historians of the kind spoken of by Holt. Nor does it envisage a plundering of ideas from sociologists by historians or of facts from historians by sociologists. On the contrary, as we previously argued, it seeks to achieve a blending or fusion of the two subjects into one; it involves abandoning the crude dichotomy between the past and the present that is implicit in the division of academic labour between historians and sociologists. Its central objective is the tracing and explaining of long-term structured processes of social development (Mennell, 1990), processes that occurred in the past and that are continuing to occur. It sees processes as structured and structures as processual. It was our commitment to such a view that led us to construct the present reader and to call it *The Sports Process*.

It is important to make it clear that we are not arguing for a special branch of sociology called 'historical sociology' that stands alongside various 'sociologies of the present'. Nor are we advocating an historical sociology of sport that studies sports practice in the past for its own sake or because some 'ludic form'[3], say in Ancient Greece or Rome, medieval Europe or Japan, nineteenth-century America or Britain, is held to be interesting or exotic, quaint or amusing, barbaric or strange. We agree with Wright Mills: A comparative and developmental sociology constitutes the very essence of the subject. That is why we have been arguing not for a closer relationship between history and sociology, but for a reconstruction of both subjects that will facilitate what we take to be their overriding common objective: increasing the understanding of the short- and long-term processes involved in the interweaving of human actions. In the study of sport, it is a question, for example, of exploring why ludic practice takes different forms in different sociohistorical and sociogeographical contexts and why the processes involved lead to more or less rapid changes of form.

It is also our view (and that of the majority of contributors to the present reader) that an historical—we prefer the term *process-sociological*—approach, constitutes the best—perhaps the only?—available means for contributing to the resolution of such age-old philosophical and sociological problems as that of the relationship between the individual and society (what is currently fashionable to call the 'agency-structure dilemma'). We agree with Abrams when he wrote that

the most promising move I can envisage . . . so far as the dilemma of human agency is concerned is to insist on the need to conceive of that dilemma historically: to insist on the ways in which and the extent to which the relation-ship of action and structure is to be understood as a matter of process in time. I would almost say that it is a question of trying to build a sociology of process as an alternative to our tried, worn and inadequate sociologies of action and system, and that is where the problematic of structuring comes in. It re-unites sociology with the other human sciences, especially history. And it does so, not by way of a casual marriage of defective theory to an unprincipled empiri-cism, but through the rediscovery of an authentic and fundamental common interest. Whatever the apparent preoccupations of historians and sociologists, whatever excesses of self-indulgent fact-grubbing or zealous theory-construction may have distracted them, it is the common and inescapable problematic of structuring which gives their work its final seriousness. (Abrams, 1982, p. xv)

It is a question of attempting to grapple with the puzzle of human agency in terms of the process of social structuring over time. Sociology, according to this perspective, has to be concerned with actions and events because it is through the interweaving of the actions of pluralities of interdependent individuals that structuring or patterning occurs. History has to be theoretical because that is how actions, events, and structures are apprehended. The adoption of a comparative and developmental perspective of the kind we are envisioning signifies an attempt to understand the relationship between the actions and experiences of persons and what is conventionally called 'social organization' or 'social structure' as processes that are continuously constructed in time and space. Such a perspective involves abandoning the commonsense distinction between the past and the present. It also places central stress on human interdependency. As Goudsblom expressed it,

What happens in the present can only be understood in the context of what has happened in the past. What is happening here can only be understood in the context of interdependencies with human beings elsewhere. (Goudsblom, 1977, p. 109)

While all the contributors to the present volume would, we think, agree with Goudsblom on this issue, not all of them would necessarily agree with everything we have written. As we said earlier, comparative and developmental sociology (and, as part of it, the comparative and developmental sociology of sport), remains in its infancy. It is also contested; it is a subject of intellectual struggle and dispute. We have alerted the reader to aspects of the struggle between historians and sociologists and to some of the disputes between sociologists of different 'schools'. In putting *The Sports Process* together, we have tried to reflect this state of affairs and to include chapters representative of most of the different positions. We have not tried to construct a volume that is representative of the contemporary sociology of sport as a whole. In particular, we have not included material by functionalists, systems theorists, or interactionists, because the 'today-centred' character of most of the work they carry out embodies what Elias (1987) called 'the retreat of sociologists to the present' and, despite the merits of their work, imposes distinct limitations on the explanations they are able to achieve. As we see it, even the small-scale social situations that symbolic interactionists and other 'action theorists' study in sport and elsewhere are best considered as histories or studies of processes in which individuals loom larger than is usually the case with studies on a more 'macro' scale. Similarly, while the today-centred studies of functionalists and systems theorists in the sociology of sport and other areas often successfully illuminate the synchronic connections that exist, for example, between race and sport or gender and sport, because they abstract what they study from the flow of time, they are unable to shed light on the diachronic connections that explain how and why such patterns are socially generated and how and why, under specific conditions and for specific periods of time, they persist or undergo structured processes of change. The essays in *The Sports Process* are concerned with developing diachronic explanations of this kind. At the very least, they are, in Mennell's sense, sociologies of the past concerned with providing an historical backdrop against which the sports practices and problems of today can be fruitfully compared.

One more thing needs to be said. It should be clear, given the importance we place in an historical or process-sociological approach as a means of shedding light on issues such as the relations between agency and structure, that we are not advocating some kind of crude evolutionary sociology or sociology of unilinear and irreversible development. On the contrary. Social processes in sport and elsewhere depend fundamentally on the human capacity for learning; unlike biological evolution, which is genetically based, they are reversible. They are also based on variable, socially determined balances between, for example, freedom and constraint, balances that the type of comparative and developmental sociology we are advocating seeks to illuminate. We think that the essays in *The Sports Process* will give the reader a good introduction to the present state of knowledge in this field and will provide a stimulus to further thought and further research into the complexities of sport in our developing social world.

NOTES

1. In England, the term *public school* refers to a set of boarding schools that charge high fees and are attended mainly by the sons and daughters of members of the upper and upper-middle classes.
2. Holt was referring here to the jargon in Alt's 'Sport and Cultural Reification', *Theory, Culture and Society*, 1983 (3), pp. 93-107. It is perhaps worth recording in this connection that one of C. Wright Mills's main targets in *The Sociological Imagination* was the jargonistic language in particular of Talcott Parsons. In other words, the struggle against jargon is not by any means the sole preserve of historians.
3. 'Ludic' is derived from *ludus*, the Latin word for 'play.' A 'ludic form' is thus a play form.

REFERENCES

Abrams, P. (1982). *Historical sociology*. Somerset: Open Books.

Alt, J. (1983). Sport and cultural reification: From ritual to mass consumption, *Theory, Culture and Society*, (3), pp. 93-107.

Anderson, P. (1974). *Lineages of the absolutist state*. London: New Left Books.

Andreski, S. (1974). *The essential Comte*. London: Croom Helm.

Clarke, J., & Critcher, C. (1985). *The devil makes work: Leisure in capitalist Britain*. London: Macmillan.

Dunning, E. (1992). Figurational sociology and the sociology of sport; some concluding remarks. In Dunning, E., & Rojek, C. (Eds.), *Sport and leisure in the civilizing process: Critique and counter-critique* (pp. 221-284). London: Macmillan.

Dunning, E., & Sheard, K. (1979). *Barbarians, gentlemen and players: A sociological study of the development of rugby football.* Oxford: Martin Robertson.

Elias, N. (1978). *The civilising process* (Vol. 1). Oxford: Blackwell.

Elias, N. (1987). *Involvement and detachment.* Oxford: Blackwell.

Elias, N. (1986). Introduction. In Elias, N., & Dunning, E., *Quest for excitement: Sport and leisure in the civilising process* (pp. 19-62). Oxford: Blackwell.

Fine, G. (1986). Small groups and sport: A symbolic interactionist perspective. In Rees, R., & Miracle, A., (Eds.), *Sport and social theory* (pp. 159-169). Champaign: Human Kinetics.

Gardner, P. (1974). *Nice guys finish last: Sport and American life.* London: Allen Lane.

Giddens, A. (1984). *The constitution of society.* Oxford: Polity Press.

Goudsblom, J. (1977). *Sociology in the balance.* Oxford: Blackwell.

Gramsci, A. (1971). *Selections from the prison notebooks.* New York: International Publishers.

Gruneau, R. (1983). *Class, sports and social development.* Amherst: University of Massachusetts Press.

Hall, S. (1986). 'Foreword' to Hargreaves, J. (1986), *Sport, power and culture,* (pp. xi-xii).

Hargreaves, J. (1986). *Sport, power and culture.* Cambridge: Polity Press.

Holt, R. (1989). *Sport and the British: A modern history.* Oxford: Clarendon Press.

Jones, S. (1988). *Sport, politics and the working class.* Manchester: Manchester University Press.

Loy, J., McPherson, B., & Kenyon, G. (1978). *Sport and social systems.* Reading, MA: Addison-Wesley.

Mennell, S. (1990). The sociological study of history: Institutions and social development. In Bryant, C., & Becker, H. (Eds.), *What has sociology achieved?* (pp. 54-68). London: Macmillan.

Merton, R. (1957). *Social theory and social structure.* Glencoe, IL: Free Press.

Thompson, E.P. (1978). *The poverty of theory and other essays.* London: Merlin Press.

Wright Mills, C. (1959). *The sociological imagination.* Oxford: Oxford University Press.

Wallerstein, I. (1987). World system analysis. In Giddens, A., & Turner, J. (Eds.), *Social theory today* (pp. 309-324). Stanford: Stanford University Press.

PART I

Perspectives on the Making of Modern Sports

In heading this first part 'Perspectives on the Making of Modern Sports', the editors are seeking to achieve a number of objectives. Through our use of the term *perspectives*, for example, we are emphasising the fact that—despite protestations to the contrary from some historians—the past cannot speak for itself. It is an open book that needs to be interpreted, and interpretation means employing some kind of perspective or theory. All the contributors to this section recognise this sociologically self-evident fact. Accordingly, the interpretations that they place on the evidence they have uncovered regarding the making of modern sport are based, more or less explicitly, on a perspective or theoretical framework.

The term *perspectives* also conveys the idea that the past is open to a number of interpretations. In other words, what any historical account of sport or some other aspect of social life looks like is not simply a consequence of the available data, but crucially depends on the framework of assumptions, questions, and concepts—the *overall problematic*—that is used in approaching it. Sociology at the moment is a multiparadigmatic and contested subject. While the writers included in this section represent a number of paradigms or sociological traditions, they by no means exhaust the range of existing approaches[1]. Undoubtedly, each will disagree with much of what the others have written. We suspect, however, that they will all agree with our basic premise, namely that study of the past is both an empirical *and* a theoretical enterprise. We think they will also agree that the past in its various aspects is open to a range of interpretations.

The heading we have given to this section implies that sports have not always existed in their present forms. Rather, they have been 'made'. With one or two exceptions—such as basketball[2], for example—they are social or collective products rather than the inventions of particular individuals. That is, they are play-activities that developed over shorter or longer periods of time out of or as replacements for earlier, very different forms of ludic practice[3]. In his chapter, Dunning attempts to illuminate some aspects of one such process—the development in England of fox hunting and rugby out of their ancestral forms—and McIntosh, in a wide-ranging, scholarly, and incisive survey of sports in the Ancient World, sheds light on the great differences that existed between the play-contests of Ancient Greece and Rome and those of the present day.

Our use of the term *modern sport* is not, of course, meant to convey the idea that present-day sports have reached some kind of 'fixed and final' state and certainly not a 'perfect' one. Just as past forms of sporting practice were often contested and tended to change at different rates, so modern sports are sites of struggle and conflict and are undergoing processes of transformation. We cannot be sure how sports are going to develop in the future, but we hope that historical and comparative studies of the kind exemplified in this section—and in *The Sports Process* as a whole—will contribute to a knowledge base that will enable persons with an involvement in sport to orient themselves in our changing and uncertain world more effectively and less wastefully—in a word, more rationally—than often proved possible in the past.

Let us contextualise the items in this section by briefly summarising the existing state of knowledge in the field. According to Guttmann (1978), modern sports contrast with earlier forms in that they are characterised by higher levels of rational-isation, standardisation, secularisation, specialisation, and quantification. They also involve a stronger orientation towards the establishment and breaking of records. There is a general consensus that forms of sport embodying these characteristics began to emerge first in England in the eighteenth and nineteenth centuries (Dunning, 1971; Malcolmson, 1973; Baker, 1982; Mandell, 1984; Elias, 1986; Hargreaves, 1986). However, when we ask *why* these forms of play began to develop in England first, the consensus breaks down. Guttmann, for example, attributes the process primarily to the growth of science. Malcolmson, by contrast, sees it as a consequence of industrialisation and the industrial rationalisation of time, a fundamentally economy-driven social change. Elias traced it to an overall 'civilising' transformation in which what he called 'the parliamentarisation of political conflict' provided the first decisive momentum. Gruneau (1988) is critical of such views. Similarly, Hargreaves sees them as exemplifications of an 'industrial society' or 'moderniza-tion' thesis that downplays issues of class and class conflict; this, he says, compares unfavourably with a Marxist account that lays stress on economic processes and struggles over hegemonic ideas, including ideas about what constitutes sport.

We agree with much of what Gruneau had to say in his 1988 essay. (It is *not* the same as the one included in this book.) It seems to us, however, that his approach in that context was overly simple. In particular, it is difficult to see how the explanation of the rise of modern sport in relation to the theory of 'civilizing processes' (Elias, 1978, 1982)—as is attempted, for example, by Dunning in chapter 2 of this volume—can be fitted into a classificatory framework that admits the existence of only the industrial society/modernisation thesis and its Marxist alterna-tives. It is also arguably the case that Gruneau pays insufficient attention in that essay to questions of gender in his analysis of the emergence of modern sport. This is an area that has recently been subjected to preliminary exploration by Mangan and Park (1987) and forms the focus for Hargreaves's discussion in chapter 3.

The subsequent development of sport in Britain has also been the subject of recent research and debate. A number of questions have been raised in this connection. For example, were all modern sport forms the creations of the higher social classes? Did they diffuse down the social scale in a relatively orderly, even, and unproblematic way? To what extent and how successfully did 'ordinary' people—the 'working class' or 'working classes'—struggle to retain traditional practices? What part did processes of resistance, contestation, and voluntary adaptation play in their adoption of modern sporting forms? Did working men and women play an active part in the making of any of these forms? To what extent has modern sport been contoured in its development along class, gender, ethnic, and age-group lines, and to what extent, if any, has it served to reinforce or enable people to transcend such social divisions? Was sport adopted simply as an enjoyable leisure pursuit? Was it adopted for its supposed 'character-forming' properties? Or was it primarily an aid to more powerful groups, helping them divert the less powerful from political protest and strengthening the local or national economy? This range of questions has been dealt with extensively in British work on the history and sociology of sport (Bailey, 1978; Dunning & Sheard, 1979; Cunningham, 1980; Clarke & Critcher, 1985; Hargreaves, 1986; Mangan, 1988; Vamplew, 1988; Holt, 1989). Similar questions could usefully provide a focus for historical and sociological research on the making of modern sport in other countries.

The contributors to Part I of *The Sports Process* do not only address these sorts of issues. They also exhibit the hallmarks that, we believe, characterise good developmental and comparative studies. McIntosh, for example, although his chapter cannot be classed as representative of any particular sociological paradigm or theory, uses sociological reasoning to construct an account of sport in the Ancient World. It focuses less on the attributes, activities, and achievements of particular performers than on the structural characteristics of the sports they pursued and the balance of opportunities and constraints within which, in societies at what we now call the ancient levels of social development, they operated. McIntosh concerns himself in this connection with a select number of ancient cultures, aware that those he has chosen are not necessarily representative of the Ancient World as a whole and that the changes and developments that occurred in them may not have been typical in some or all respects. He also acknowledges the limitations of the surviving sources and the difficulties in interpreting them. He nevertheless manages successfully to show how the sports of the Ancient World were deeply embedded in the sociocultural and sociopolitical contexts of the societies where they were enacted and/or played. In Ancient Greece, for example, 'agonistic' or competitive play-forms, which started as the exclusive preserve of a male warrior elite, formed the basis from which developed a series of athletic festivals in which the principal participants were full-time professional performers. Although most athletes continued to be recruited from the higher social strata, payment did not lead to loss of social status, and the demonstration of athletic prowess constituted a major means of attaining political power and office. By the time of the Roman Empire, McIntosh concludes, the promotion of 'sport-like' forms of entertainment had become a device for securing social control in a type of society where the majority of citizens had no chance to take part directly in the exercise of political power.

McIntosh's analysis of sport in the Ancient World, an example of what Mennell (1989, 1990, 1992) describes as sociology of the past, is not engaged in simply for its own sake. On the contrary, it is used, where relevant, to draw instructive parallels with modern sport and to debunk such present-day ideologies and myths as 'amateurism' and 'Olympism'. Last but not least, McIntosh uses his analysis to cast doubt on the adequacy of such recent accounts of the violence of sports in Ancient Greece as that offered by Elias (1971, 1986).

Dunning's contribution to this section, as we suggested previously, involves an attempt to explore some aspects of the making of modern sport using the figurational or process-sociological approach advocated by Elias (Elias, 1978; Elias & Dunning, 1986; Dunning & Rojek, 1992). Central to the work of figurational sociologists is Elias's theory of 'civilizing processes' (Elias, 1978, 1982), and Dunning starts by responding to some of the criticisms recently offered of this theory in the sociology of sport and elsewhere. He also seeks to challenge the widely held belief that modern civilisation and modern sport are getting so violent that both are on the brink of collapse. Compared with the sports of Ancient Greece, for example, and the folk games of the European Middle Ages, Dunning suggests that modern sports seem to be relatively nonviolent, and he traces the civilising processes that fox hunting and rugby football appear to have undergone in the course of their early development as modern sports. Finally, he addresses the subject of football hooliganism. Contrary to the widespread idea that the occurrence of this form of deviance in a football context constitutes an empirical refutation of Elias's theory, Dunning argues that, if properly interpreted (i.e., as a *nonevolutionary* attempt to theorise social developments as long-term processes that can regress as well as progress), the theory of civilising processes provides a valuable means of shedding light on both the social production of male violence as expressed in football (and elsewhere) and on the condemnation of such violence by more powerful members of society at large.

Hargreaves writes from the perspective of feminist cultural studies. However, she also integrates into her chapter aspects of 'hegemony theory', a form of Marxist analysis that developed principally out of the writings of Gramsci (1971). Hargreaves's contribution provides a powerful corrective to the pervasive tendency to think of the making of modern sport and its study as exclusively male preserves. Above all, she clearly shows the importance of distinguishing between sex and gender—the unlearned, biological level of feminity and masculinity versus the learned, sociocultural level—and shows how, in sport and elsewhere, male dominance or patriarchy was based on a kind of hegemony that attributed many aspects of the socially defined and socially constructed gender roles of females to their biological sex. These ideas were buttressed by the ideology of Social Darwinism and were widely accepted by females as well as males, helping to restrict females to the 'private' sphere of procreative and familial roles and to exclude them from such 'public' realms as work and sport. The Victorian cult of the family, Hargreaves argues, was crucial in this regard. In its origins, it was a bourgeois phenomenon, a product of the development of capitalism restricted mainly to the middle classes, and it acted as a dominant constraining force on the early development of women's sport. More particularly, it enabled females to participate only in sports and games that could be played in a domestic context and that did not contradict ideas and ideals of femininity that defined women as the weaker sex. This familial ideology played an important part in the development of Colleges of Education for females and hence in the early stages of physical education as a school subject and career for women. Such nineteenth-century developments and contradictions have had continuing repercussions on the gendered character of sports practice right through to the present day, and Hargreaves has provided here an indispensable starting point for anyone who wants to take the historical/developmental exploration of this important subject further.

Gruneau's scholarly and stimulating chapter criticizes conventional theories of the modernisation of sport, which see it as an 'abstract evolutionary process' rather than as a system that is relatively open-ended and characterised by contradictions, pressures, and struggles. A degree of critical understanding of modern sport was provided, Gruneau suggests, by early Marxists such as Adorno, Horkheimer, and Marcuse, the founders of the Frankfurt school. Systematic critique, however, awaited the work of Rigauer (1981), Vinnai (1973), and Brohm (1978), scholars who saw modern sport both 'as a symbolic representation and physical embodiment of capitalism's insatiable demands for ''performance'' in the service of profit, and the technocratic ideology of science and the machine'. In this, Gruneau maintains, Rigauer, Vinnai, and Brohm anticipated a number of present concerns. However, he argues, there was a tension in their work between a critique of capitalism and a critique of modernity as such. They also tended to see oppression everywhere and to take a nondialectical view. As a result, their work is conducive to cynicism and despair. What is needed, according to Gruneau, is a theory that links understandings of 'agency', 'structure', and 'social reproduction' into a broader theory of social development.

Gruneau suggests that such a theory can be found through a synthesis of modified versions of the theories of Bourdieu (1972, 1978, 1988), Foucault (1977, 1980), the English 'cultural studies' school of Marxism (Clarke, Critcher, & Johnson, 1979; Hall, Hobson, Lowe, & Willis, 1980), Giddens (1976, 1977, 1981, 1984), and Gramsci (1971). A theoretical synthesis of this kind, Gruneau argues, will permit a critique of: (i) the Eurocentrism and the class and gender biases of modern sport; and (ii) the ways in which the emancipatory potential of sport is warped by market capitalism, consumerism, and forms of inequality that are contoured and reinforced by approximations to and deviations from bodily ideals engendered and promoted by advertising. It is also a theory that, because it is dialectical and emphasises agency and the enabling as well as the constraining effects of power, will not be conducive to cynicism and despair but to a concern with realising the emancipatory and socially transformative potential of modern sport.

We sympathise with Gruneau in his concern over class, gender, and racial bias as they are expressed in modern sport. We share his dismay regarding the forms of bodily inequality and appearance that are being engendered and promoted in sport and elsewhere by consumerism, advertising, and market capitalism. We are less sure, however, that Giddens has, through his theory of 'structuration', successfully resolved the so-called 'agency-structure dilemma' rather than having produced simply another variant of it (Dunning, in Dunning & Rojek, 1992). We are also less sure regarding the degree to which the 'pathologies' of modern sport can be simply 'read off' from theories that label modern societies as capitalist and leave it at that. It is not that we take a view so different from Gruneau's regarding the balance between enablement and constraint permitted by the structures of capitalist societies. It is rather that we see capitalist societies as having developed in the past and continuing to develop today in a context of conflicting and developing international interdependencies that cannot be wholly explained simply by reference to economic categories. In our view, this is an area in which much more theorising, research, and constructive debate will be necessary before definitive statements can be made. All we are certain of at the moment is that this theory, research, and debate will be greatly impoverished if it fails to pay serious attention to Gruneau's important contributions.

NOTES

1. As we made clear in the Introduction, perspectives such as functionalism, symbolic interactionism, and ethnomethodology, whose practitioners do not usually carry out historical, developmental, or process-sociological studies, have not been included in this volume.
2. Basketball is said to have been invented by Dr. James Naismith at the YMCA, Springfield, MA, USA, in 1891.
3. The adjective 'ludic', is derived from the Latin noun *ludus*, which means a game or play. The term *ludic practice* thus means *play practice*.

REFERENCES AND
SUGGESTIONS FOR FURTHER READING

Adelman, M. (Ed.) (1986). *A sporting time: New York City and the rise of modern athletics*. Urbana: University of Illinois Press.

Adorno, T. (1978). Culture and administration. *Telos, 37*, 97-111.

Bailey, P. (1978). *Leisure and class in Victorian England: Rational recreation and the contest for control, 1830-1885*, London: Routledge and Kegan Paul.

Baker, W. (1982). *Sports in the western world*. Totowa, NJ: Rowman & Littlefield.

Bale, J. (1989). *Sports geography*. London: Spon.

Bordieu, P. (1972). *Outline of a theory of practice*. Cambridge: Cambridge University Press.

Bourdieu, P. (1978). Sport and social class. *Social Science Information, 17* (6), 819-840.

Bourdieu, P. (1984). *Distinction: A social critique of the judgement of taste*. Cambridge, MA: Harvard University Press.

Bourdieu, P. (1988). Program for a sociology of sport. *Sociology of Sport Journal, 5*, 153-161.

Brohm, J.M. (1978). *Sport: A prison of measured time*. London: Ink Links.

Clarke, J. & Critcher, C. (1985). *The devil makes work: Leisure in capitalist Britain*. London: Macmillan.

Clarke, J., Critcher, C., & Johnson, R. (1979). *Working class cultures: Theory and history*. London: Hutchinson.

Cunningham, H. (1980). *Leisure in the industrial revolution*. London: Croom Helm.

Deem, R. (1986). *All work and no play? The sociology of women and leisure*. Milton Keynes: Open University Press.

Dunning, E. (Ed.) (1971). *The sociology of sport: Selected readings*. London: Cass.

Dunning, E., & Sheard, K. (1979). *Barbarians, gentlemen and players: A sociological study of the development of rugby football*. Oxford: Martin Robertson.

Dunning, E., & Rojek, C. (Eds.) (1992). *Sport and leisure in the civilising process: Critique and counter-critique*. London: Macmillan.

Elias, N. (1971). The genesis of sport as a sociological problem. In Dunning, E. (Ed.), *The sociology of sport: Selected readings* (pp. 88-115). London: Cass.

Elias, N. (1978). *The civilising process. Vol. 1: The history of manners*. Oxford: Blackwell.

Elias, N. (1982). *The civilising process. Vol 2: State formation and civilization*. Oxford: Blackwell.

Elias, N. (1986). Introduction. In Elias, N., & Dunning, E., *Quest for excitement: Sport and leisure in the civilising process* (pp. 19-62). Oxford: Blackwell.

Elias, N., & Dunning, E. (1986). *Quest for excitement: Sport and leisure in the civilising process*. Oxford: Blackwell.

Foucault, M. (1977). *Discipline and punish: The birth of the prison*. New York: Vintage Books.

Foucault, M. (1980). *The history of sexuality*. Vol 1. New York: Random House.

Giddens, A. (1976). *New rules of sociological method*. London: Hutchinson.

Giddens, A. (1977). *Studies in social and political theory*. New York: Basic Books.

Giddens, A. (1981). *A contemporary critique of historical materialism*. London: Macmillan.

Giddens, A. (1986). *The constitution of society: Outline of the theory of structuration*. Cambridge: Polity.

Golby, J.M., & Purdue, A.W. (1986). *The civilization of the crowd*. London: Batsford.

Gramsci, A. (1971). *Selections from the prison notebooks*. New York: International Publishers.

Gruneau, R. (1983). *Class, sports, and social development*. Amherst, MA: University of Massachusetts Press.

Gruneau, R. (1988). Modernization or hegemony: Two views on sport and social development. In Harvey, J., & Cantelon, H. (Eds.), *Not just a game: Essays in Canadian sport sociology* (pp. 9-32). Ottawa: University of Ottawa Press.

Guttmann, A. (1978). *From ritual to record: The nature of modern sports*. New York: Columbia University Press.

Hall, S., Hobson, D., Lowe, A., & Willis, P. (1980). *Culture, media and society*. London, Hutchinson.

Hargreaves, John (1986). *Sport, power and culture*. Cambridge: Polity Press.

Holt, R. (1989). *Sport and the British: A modern history*. Oxford: Clarendon Press.

Horkheimer, M. (1972). *Critical theory: Selected essays*. New York: Seabury Press.

Jones, S. (1988). *Sport, politics and the working class*. Manchester: Manchester University Press.

Malcolmson, R. (1973). *Popular recreations in English society, 1700-1850*. Cambridge: Cambridge University Press.

Mandell, R. (1984). *Sport: A cultural history*. New York: Columbia University Press.

Mangan, T. (1981). *Athleticism in the Victorian and Edwardian public school*. Cambridge: Cambridge University Press.

Mangan, T. (Ed.) (1988). *Pleasure, profit and proselytism: British culture and sport at home and abroad, 1700-1914*. London: Cass.

Mangan, T., & Park, R. (1987). *From fair sex to feminism: Sport and the socialization of women in the industrial and post-industrial eras*. London: Cass.

Marcuse, H. (1964). *One dimensional man*. London: Abacus.

Mason, T. (Ed.) (1989). *Sport in Britain: A social history*. Cambridge: Cambridge University Press.

Mennell, S. (1989). *Norbert Elias, civilization and the human self-image*. Oxford: Blackwell.

Mennell, S. (1990). 'The sociological study of history: Institutions and social development.' In Bryant, C., and Becker, H. (Eds.), *What has sociology achieved?* (pp. 54-68). London: Macmillan.

Mennell, S. (1992). *Norbert Elias: An introduction*. Oxford: Blackwell.

Rigauer, B. (1981). *Sport and work* (A. Guttmann, Trans.). New York: Columbia University Press.

Vamplew, W. (1988). *Pay up and play the game: Professional sport in Britain, 1875-1914*. Cambridge: Cambridge University Press.

Vinnai, G. (1973). *Football mania*. London: Ocean Books.

Walvin, J. (1978). *Leisure and society, 1830-1950*. London: Longham.

The Sociology of Sport in the Ancient World

Peter C. McIntosh

The 'Ancient World' is a term that, by common usage in Europe and America, encompasses a considerable period of time from the neolithic agricultural revolution at about 7,000 B.C. to the fall of the Roman Empire. The Western Empire collapsed in the sixth century A.D. but the Eastern Empire with its capital city at Constantinople continued to exist for nearly another one thousand years. As a geographical entity the ancient world stretched from the river valleys of Mesopotamia (some would say from the Indus valley on the Indian subcontinent) to the Atlantic coast of Portugal and from the upper Nile to the highlands of Scotland. General statements, therefore, about sport in the ancient world, let alone about the sociology of sport in the ancient world, are likely to be vague, misleading, and inaccurate. It seems best to focus upon a few cultures, recognizing that the features that they displayed may not have been characteristic of other cultures in the ancient world. Four have been chosen: the Minoan culture of Crete in the third and second millennium B.C., the Mycenaean culture of the mainland of Greece in the second millennium B.C., the city-states of Greece in the sixth, fifth, and fourth centuries B.C., and the urban societies of the Roman Empire from the first century A.D. until the end of the fourth century when the termination of the Olympic Games marked the end of a sporting era.

The sociologist studying these cultures is at once faced with an historical problem. The data available for study are scanty, sometimes unreliable, and often difficult to interpret. The earliest extant alphabetical writing is upon an Athenian vase of the early geometric period which has been dated at 735 B.C. Alphabet writing was in use long before, even if we have no surviving examples. Hieroglyphic and linear writing and inscription were far earlier and the recent decipherment of 'linear B' from Crete 1450 B.C. has shown that the language being used was Greek. However, the financial accounts and catalogue of contents of the palace of Knossos that comprise the major exemplars of linear B are not the evidence that the sociologist of sport would have chosen for survival from Minoan culture. The same may be said of other literary and epigraphic remains that we have. We do not know what is missing. Archaeological discoveries on building sites and sports arenas are a major source of information; so too are inscriptions and artefacts such as pots, paintings, sculpture, coins, and medals, but again artists were not historians and the correct interpretation of what is depicted is not always obvious. In this situation, we can hardly do better than follow the precept of Aristotle in his introduction to the study of moral philosophy.

We must be content, then, in speaking of such subjects and with such premises to indicate the truth roughly and in outline, and in speaking about things which are only true in a general sense and with premises of the same kind, to teach conclusions that are no better. In the same spirit, therefore, should each type of statement be received; for it is the mark of an educated man to look for precision in each class of things just so far as the nature of the subject admits. (Aristotle, Ethics I.3. 1094b)

MINOAN AND MYCENAEAN CULTURES

Our major sources of literary evidence on life in Minoan and Mycenaean civilizations are the Iliad and the Odyssey, epic poems of some twenty-eight thousand lines of hexameter verse. The age that they portrayed is often referred to as the 'Heroic Age' but they offer a conglomerate account rather than a coherent portrait of a single age. Composition stretched over some two thousand years when the deeds of the heroes and descriptions of their ways of life were handed down by oral tradition. They were finally committed to writing by Homer at about 800 B.C. They thus spanned three archaeological eras. At first sight the poems appear to describe life and death in that part of the bronze age when the mainland city of Mycenae was in the ascendant and conducted a long drawn-out war against the city of Troy on the mainland of what is now Turkey. The siege of Troy occurred in the thirteenth century B.C. The bronze age collapsed and Mycenae was burnt in 1125 B.C. (Kirk, 1964, p. 25). It was succeeded by an early iron age in the eleventh and tenth centuries when the Dorians invaded Greece from the North. This was a 'dark age' of which we know little. The epic poems that emerged in written form some time after 800 B.C. described events and objects from several cultures through which they had passed. The beliefs and customs that were observed by the heroes were derived from a similar number of cultures. A single and simple instance of the confusion is the giving of a lump of iron, not bronze, as a prize in two athletic contests organised by Achilles at the funeral of Patroclus.

A general and persistent feature of Homer's poems is emphasis on physical prowess, whether this be manifested in armed combat, in organised athletic contests, in acrobatic dancing, in erotic adventures or in the sheer capacity for survival displayed by Odysseus on his way home to Ithaca from Troy. Before examining this feature more closely it is worth pointing out that the poems were regarded by the later Greeks as an important element in their culture. Just as in Europe after the Napoleonic Wars, Scandinavia saw in Gothicism a romantic re-creation of an heroic viking past, which in turn supported P.H. Ling's development of Swedish gymnastics, and Germany threw up the Turnbewegung, which also looked back to mythical and real heroes of great physical and military achievement, so the Greeks from the ninth century onwards sought to re-create their own heroic past of which physical prowess was a prime characteristic. The great athletic and religious festivals at Olympia, Delphi, Isthmia, and Nemea were panhellenic festivals uniting those of Greek race throughout the Mediterranean basin. The recital and singing of heroic songs about a greater past and about a physical prowess was a persistent cultural influence in the development of hellenism and panhellenism in the Ancient World.

The kind of sport depicted in the Odyssey is somewhat different from that in the Iliad and it is possible that the Odyssey draws upon the Minoan culture of Crete rather than later Mycenaean culture. Odysseus, after many adventures, is shipwrecked and struggles ashore on the coast of Phaeacia. No one has identified the territory or its people. While Odysseus sleeps, exhausted, in the bushes, the king's daughter Nausicaa comes with her attendant maidens to wash clothes. While they wait for the clothes to dry they play ball. It is clearly a catching and throwing game and after a time there is a misthrow and the ball lands in a pool. The laughter and shrieks awake Odysseus, who emerges, modestly concealing his nakedness. In the ball game the use of the preposition μετά—'at' or 'after'—suggests to Harris that it was a misthrow, not a miscatch, that provided the dramatic incident. The game may thus have been a variant of 'Kingie' or 'Queenie' that, the Opies have shown, has been so ubiquitous in time and place that it is rarely described (Opie in Harris, 1972, p. 18). The object of this game is for one designated player to hit one of the other players with the ball. He or she then takes over the role of thrower. It is far removed from competitive athletics, which were not regarded as the most important physical recreation in Phaeacia; nor were the inhabitants very good at them. When some competitions in boxing, wrestling, running, and throwing a weight were arranged, Odysseus at first refused to take part, but when he was finally goaded into doing so he outthrew and outshone all the local inhabitants. It was in dancing and especially acrobatic dancing that the Phaeacian courtiers excelled. After a demonstration of dancing and leaping combined with throwing a purple ball Odysseus exclaimed, 'My Lord Alcinous, ruler of rulers, you told us that your dancers were the best, and now it is proved true. This sight is wonderful.' (Homer, Od. VIII, l. 284.)

This is akin to the acrobatic bull dancing that was a prominent feature of the Minoan court in Crete and has been so vividly depicted on the 'Taureador Fresco' (Evans, 1930, III, p. 144). It was very dangerous and required a high level of skill for proficiency and even for survival. Both in the legendary Phaeacia and in Crete there was a professional corps of acrobatic dancers who were recruited, maintained, and patronised by the rulers. We have evidence, then, of simple and traditional child's play that was freely shared by a princess with her servants or friends and also of institutionalised and professionalised acrobatic dancing for entertainment. Patronage of this dancing marked out the aristocracy, perhaps even the ruling dynasty itself.

The prominence of athletic contests in the life-style of the leaders both Greek and Trojan is attested by numerous references in the Iliad. Throwing javelins, throwing discoi, archery, and boxing are several times referred to, while athletic similes are used to describe military combat. It is however the funeral games of Patroclus described in Book XXIII that give us the clearest picture of athletics. Achilles organised in honour of his friend a chariot race, a boxing match, a wrestling match, a footrace, a contest in armour, a discus throwing competition, an archery contest, and a spear throwing contest. Both the society and sport within it were hierarchical. Slaves were lowly and were treated as chattels but even others, not of leadership rank, fared little better.

> But whenever he (Achilles) cames upon a commoner shouting out,
> He struck him with his sceptre and spoke sharply:
> 'Good for nothing! Be still and listen to your betters,
> You are weak and cowardly and unwarlike,
> You count for nothing, neither in battle nor in council.'
> (Homer, Iliad in Weil, 1945, p. 11)

It is not surprising to find that the contests were confined to a few named 'heroes'. The chariot race reveals a pecking order within even that select group. Antilochus overtook Menelaos despite the fact that he had slower horses and defeated him by guile. There was a protest and Antilochus gave way having conceded that Menelaos was older, higher, and better, i.e., more heroic than he. A prize was also given to a noncompetitor, Nestor, in virtue of his venerable age and the achievements of his youth. The organisation of the race was not by any means haphazard. Achilles made the drivers draw lots for starting position and he placed an umpire, 'godlike Phoinix', at the turning post in this out and back race. The description of the race reads convincingly, which is more than can be said for descriptions of the use of chariots in combat. The heroes fought on foot after dismounting from their chariots and Kirk has concluded that Homer was writing when chariots as luxury items of the very rich had disappeared. He knew that at one time they had denoted noble rank and he knew that they had been used in war but he misunderstood their use and described an almost laughable 'equine taxi service' to the front line (Kirk, 1964, p. 23).

Every contestant received a prize and they were valuable and useful, not merely symbolic. Furthermore the prizes reveal male domination. For the wrestling match the winner was to receive a tripod valued at twelve oxen, and the loser a woman 'skilled in many arts' who was valued at four oxen. In the chariot race the winner received a woman 'skilled in handicraft' as well as a tripod.

Violence has been a feature of sport in a great many societies, but generalisations about violence in sport reflecting violence in society are apt to be misleading. There is evidence that the society depicted by Homer was violent. Achilles cut the throats of 12 Trojan captive boys and sacrificed them on the funeral pyre of Patroclus. In his fight with Hector, when he had him at his mercy, not only did he show him none but, having killed him, he immolated his corpse by dragging it round the walls of Troy behind his chariot. The athletic contests, by contrast, were constrained not so much by rules as by a code of conduct accepted and well understood by heroes. The boxing match between Epeios and Euryalos ended with a knockout blow to the head of Euryalos, but Epeios immediately picked him up and helped him from the ring. The contest in armour between Aias and Diomedes was never completed but was brought to an end by the spectators to avoid bloodshed. The wrestling match between Aias and Odysseus was similarly stopped by Achilles with the words, 'No longer press each other, nor wear you out with pain. Victory is with both; take equal prizes and depart' (Homer, Iliad XXIII, l. 735). In the chariot race Menelaos accused Antilochus of driving recklessly on a dangerous part of the course and endangering them both. Antilochus took no notice and after the race a protest was lodged against him for dangerous driving. Weiler has pointed out that 'to be always the best' (αἰὲν ἀριστύειν), which is the ideal of Achilles, is not to be equated with always winning. The ideal of winning, an agonal ideal, Weiler maintains, came with the Dorian invasion. It is true that Achilles fell short of the heroic ideal; when he refused to go into battle because of a quarrel with King Agamemnon, Patroclus chided him and asked how his descendants would judge such behaviour. This incident, however, underlines the heroic ideal of the Mycenaean culture, which was only later transformed into a militaristic and then an agonal ideal (Weiler, 1975).

The association of athletic contests with religion in the heroic age has been a subject of some controversy. The anthropomorphism of the gods in Homer is not in dispute. The gods were portrayed as enjoying the same things as the heroes, including their sports, to such an extent that they interfered with the course of events. In the footrace it was the goddess Athene who, in answer to a prayer from Odysseus, caused Aias, who was winning, to slip on some offal that had been left over from a sacrifice of oxen for the funeral, so that Odysseus won. The intervention of the gods in sport and in battle is not uncommon in the Homeric poems but hardly indicates a deep religious significance. Harold Harris is quite scornful of any connection at all between sport and religion. 'The descriptions of athletics in Homer show that no such link existed in the age he was depicting. His games in the Iliad are part of a funeral ceremony with the purpose of distributing the belongings of the dead Patroclus to the heroes most worthy of them' (Harris, 1972, p. 16). Had the funeral games for Patroclus been an isolated instance of association between sport and religion, Harris's view might be accepted, but the names of thirty-three heroes for whom funeral games were held before recorded Greek history are known (Robinson, 1955, p. 30). Such frequent association needs explaining. In 'The Golden Bough' Frazer suggested that athletic competition was at one time viewed as mimetic magic; that the vigour expended in them was thought to transfer to crops, herds, and the race itself. The dead, too, would be assisted in their strenuous journey by the athletic efforts spent by survivors (Frazer, 1951, pp. 89ff). This was his explanation of the origin of the Olympic Games in the Mycenaean age long before the first surviving record of a victor in 776 B.C. Certainly there was a persistent tradition in the ancient world that games at Olympia had been celebrated on and off since the fourteenth century and that their origin and periodic revival were associated with religious sanction and religious ritual.

THE GREEK CITY-STATES

The city-states of the Greek mainland from the seventh century onwards were characterised by a class structure that was reflected in their sport. In Sparta the structure of the state was the result of military conquest and was perpetuated in order to maintain military domination. The citizen body was also a citizen army. Its two kings were leaders in battle as well as in councils of state. In addition to the citizens were resident aliens or perioicoi who engaged in trade and supplied many of the material needs of the citizens. Below them were the Helots, the indigenous and conquered population who were tied to the land in serfdom. It was recorded that the ephors, senior magistrates, declared war upon the Helots each year in order to make quite clear their subservient and perilous state. The citizen body, both boys and girls, men and women, underwent a rigorous military and physical training. Military training and physical training for sport were not to be exactly equated. Pausanias and Philostratus indicated a distinction between the pancration, a form of all-in wrestling practised as a sport at the Olympic Games, and pancration as unarmed combat used by the Spartans. In the former certain practices such as gouging the eyes were forbidden but not in the latter. 'They fight hand to hand, and with running kicks they bite and gouge, man to man' (Pausanias III.14.10). Nevertheless the two forms of training were close enough to have carryover value. Between 776 B.C. and 600 B.C., of sixty-six victories recorded for the Olympic Games, thirty-three were by athletes from the single city of Sparta. According to Aristotle, however, their militarism was their undoing. 'While warfare was their means of self preservation, the hegemony which they achieved, occasioned their decline, because they were ignorant of the use of leisure and had mastered no higher form of training than the art of war' (Aristotle, Politics.1271). Between 596 B.C. and 300 B.C. the number of victories won by Spartans was exceeded by athletes from three other states and after 300 B.C. their eclipse was even more marked.

In Athens the social stratification was in early years by birth but Solon at the beginning of the sixth century formalised it on a basis of wealth. Citizens with an income of 500 measures of corn, 'pentacosiomedimnoi', were the highest class. Below them were the 'hippeis', horse owners, with an income of 300 measures, then the 'zeugitae', owners of a yoke of oxen, with an income of 200 measures, and at the bottom were 'thetes' with an income of less than 200 measures. By the fifth century the total number of citizens in all classes was about 170,000. Athens also accommodated some 35,000 resident aliens and 120,000 slaves. It seems likely that participation in the Olympic Games and other athletic festivals was restricted to the upper classes of citizens. It was a requirement that competitors must train for 10 months, the last month being spent in the neighbourhood of Olympia, and only richer citizens could afford to be absent from their homes or farms. Obviously chariot racing and equestrian events were confined to those who owned horses. Participation in other events stretched farther down the social scale. Alcibiades junior is recorded by Isocrates as saying that his father disdained gymnastic contests because he knew that some of the contestants were of low birth, inhabitants of petty states and of mean education—he therefore took up horse breeding, which was not possible for one of low estate (Isocrates, 33). Finley and Pleket believe this to have been an instance of personal snobbishness rather than of social distinction within sport (Finley & Pleket, 1976, p. 58). Pleket's view that from the sixth century local contests were opened up to the hoplite middle class cannot be substantiated, as he himself admits, for lack of evidence (Pleket, 1975, p. 73). Even if runners, throwers, pentathletes, and fighters were drawn from all social classes of free-born Greeks, equestrian events probably remained socially exclusive if only because of the high cost of horses and equipment. After about 400 B.C. it is plausible to suggest that the system of subsidising athletes and rewarding the successful made all events more generally accessible despite the fact that in surviving records of individual athletes receiving honorary citizenship, there is little to indicate whether he was 'a product of social mobility or belonged to a municipal elite class' (Pleket, 1975, p. 73). Whatever the social origin of athletes may have been in the classical period, the association of success in sports with political leadership is well attested. Perusal of the list of victors at Olympia from 776 onwards (Moretti, 1957) shows a number of men who achieved political power in their own cities. The most specific association of sport with politics is seen in the career of Alcibiades, and it is mentioned by both Thucydides and Isocrates, writing in the fifth and fourth centuries B.C., respectively. In 416 B.C. Alcibiades entered seven chariots at Olympia and took first, second, and fourth places according to Thucydides (first, second, and third according to Isocrates). Alcibiades claimed that these victories supported his claim to military leadership in the expedition that the Athenians were contemplating against Syracuse. 'For by general custom', he told the assembly at Athens, 'such things do indeed mean honour and from what is done men also infer power' (Thucydides VI.16). Alcibiades was appointed general and the expedition was a disaster. There were a number of writers in the fifth and fourth centuries who expressed a highly critical view of the popular acclaim that athletes enjoyed whether or not this led to political power. Xenophanes in the sixth century inveighed against athletes, saying in the course of his diatribe, 'even if he won a victory with race horses . . . yet would he not be as worthy as I. For our wisdom is a better thing than strength of men and horses. But this is a most unreasonable custom, and it is not right to honour strength above excellent wisdom' (Xenophanes, Frag. 2 in Robinson, 1955). The playright Euripides, and in the fourth century philosophers Plato and Aristotle, all decried the popular adulation and the social uselessness of athletes. The criticisms, however, are themselves evidence supporting the claim that Alcibiades made about sport and political power in the fifth century. There was another connection between sport and politics in classical Greece. The Olympic Games were preceded by the declaration of a truce. This did not stop all wars. What it did was invoke the wrath of Zeus and exclusion from the Games of any athlete from a state that did not afford safe conduct to those travelling to Olympia. In 420 B.C. Sparta was fined for a breach of the truce, refused to pay, and was excluded from the religious rites and the athletic contests. Thucydides says that everyone was afraid that the Spartans would force their way in but they did not, whether from religious or political considerations it is impossible to say. The same kind of truce seemed to apply to other panhellenic festivals. Pausanias says that athletes from Elis always refused to take part in the Isthmian Games because two of her citizens had been murdered in Argos on their way to the Games. Elis requested Corinth, the city responsible for the Isthmian Games, to exclude Argos. Corinth refused and Elis withdrew her competitors and continued to do so in subsequent celebrations. In 1980 and 1984 this story had a familiar ring, but no one in classical Greece pretended that sport was free of politics.

After the tragic and disastrous war between Athens and Sparta from 431 B.C. to 404 B.C. the city-states of Greece went into political decline until Philip of Macedon and his son Alexander the Great established their empire over the whole region. There was then an inversion of sport and political power. Alexander was an athlete of ability but gave up competitive events because it was considered inappropriate for a king to be defeated, and he disliked being allowed to win. He still encouraged athletics, probably for its political payoff as well as for other benefits. Indeed, according to Harris, 'when Alexander spread Greek civilization all over the Eastern Mediterranean every city in the newly Hellenized world took steps to provide itself with a stadium to inaugurate athletics meetings' (Harris, 1972, p. 18). Alexander himself took up noncompetitive ball play and built a court, 'sphairisterion', in which to play. Theophrastus, writing at the end of the fourth or beginning of the third century, says that from then onwards a sphairisterion became one sign of a social climber (Harris, 1972, p. 84). Sport was thus still associated both with social mobility and with the exercise of political power and continued to be so for many centuries and long after the empire of Alexander had given way to the empire of Rome. Although the social and political framework of the Greek city-state had gone, Greek athletics persisted and played an important but somewhat different social and political role, as we shall see.

The decision of the upper and middle classes in Britain from about 1860 to deny themselves money or value prizes for successful participation in competitive sport, except in horse racing, and to incorporate this self-denial in the definition of an amateur led to the assumption that remuneration was incompatible with upper class participation. From this a second assumption followed, namely, that those who were remunerated were socially inferior. A social stigma was, then, attached to them. These assumptions cannot be made about athletics in the ancient world, certainly not about athletics in the city-states of classical Greece.

At the beginning of the sixth century at Athens, Solon, as part of his social and economic reforms, decreed that Athenian citizens who were victorious at Olympia should be paid 500 drachmas and victors at the Isthmian Games 100 drachmas. In the fifth century this smaller amount was somewhere near the annual wage of a working man. A victory at Olympia would certainly enable the athlete to devote himself to training for the next contest in four years' time. There is however no reason to think that 500 drachmas was the equivalent of 500 medimnoi thus putting the victor in the highest socioeconomic group for one year (Thompson, 1978). As well as cash, remuneration also took other forms. Socrates, on trial for his life, having been found guilty of subversion and having been required to suggest an appropriate penalty said, 'Nothing is more becoming, men of Athens, than for a man like me to receive public maintenance in the Guildhall—a reward he deserves far more than a citizen who has won a victory at Olympia in horse or chariot race—and whereas he needs no maintenance, I do' (Plato, Apology, 26). In other cities, too, rewards for success were considerable. At Acragas in Sicily in 412 B.C. a returning victor was accompanied into his native city by 300 chariots drawn by white horses. This, of course, had no monetary value but free meals seem to have been a common concomitant of public honour. 'Payment by results' was an accepted procedure for Greek athletics. An interesting question is how did an athlete finance his first success? After victory rewards were plentiful but there is little evidence of athletes in the sixth and fifth centuries being paid to train. Gymnasia and palaestrae, facilities for training, were in many cities provided at public expense. Coaching was cheap and coaches were reputedly underpaid, but how did the up-and-coming athlete support himself? We do not know, but there was certainly no lack of entrants to keep the Olympic Games going for more than 1,000 years, and other panhellenic and local contests, too, for a considerable length of time.

It has been suggested, for instance, by Elias, that the sport of ancient Greece was based upon an ethos of warrior nobility and upon traditions of 'honour' rather than 'fairness' (Elias, 1971, p. 101). The association of success at Olympia with military prowess has already been stressed. However, there is considerable evidence that the Greeks did indeed value 'fairness'. In the first place they had elaborate rules for ensuring equal chances for competitors and for eliminating factors other than strength and skill. In footraces stone sills, grooved for the athletes' toes, still survive in many stadia. As time went on a starting gate, a 'husplex' was devised. The arrangements for starting chariot races were even more elaborate. Because the charioteer nearest the centre turning pole had an advantage, the starting stalls were staggered with the inside charioteer furthest forward but not released from his stall until the others were alongside. He therefore had a standing start while they had a flying start. 'After this', writes Pausanias, 'it is left to the charioteers to display their skill and the horses their speed' (Pausanias VI, 20: 10-13). Other events had their own rules and devices. Enforcement, too, was rigorous. Before the husplex was invented those who started before the signal were flogged. There was an additional sanction. All competitors and their relatives and trainers had to swear an oath to Zeus on slices of boars' flesh to observe the rules. This ritual was based on the recognition that not all offences were detectable but it also evidenced the belief that rule breaking was itself an offence deserving religious sanction. κακούργημα was the offence mentioned by Pausanias, meaning fraud or cheating (Pausanias V.XXIV). The clearest evidence for the value placed upon fairness is the use in sport of the root word δίκη, also used for custom, for law and for legal trial. It is also the root word for justice, δικαιοσύνη. The search for justice and its application to life was not only the theme of Plato's dialogues, The Republic and the Laws, and of Aristotle's books on ethics, politics, and the Athenian Constitution; it was also the concern of the hellanodikai (δίκη again) and of the state of Elis, which administered the Olympic Games. Herodotus writes of a deputation sent from Elis to Egypt in the sixth century B.C. to enquire whether the Egyptians, who had a reputation for wisdom, considered the rules for the organisation of the Olympic Games to be as fair as was possible. The word that Herodotus used was δικαιότατα, meaning most just. The only modification that the Egyptians suggested was that the Eleans who judged the contests should not themselves compete because they were bound to favour their own countrymen. The advice was not taken.

Love of honour, as well as love of victory (φιλοτιμία and φιλονικία) were also characteristic of the Greeks. The behaviour and the words of Alcibiades, which have already been quoted in another context, are evidence of love of honour. Love of victory was not always unbridled but harnessed to social or political purposes. This was succinctly stated by Demosthenes. 'The freedom of a democracy is guarded by the rivalry with which good citizens compete for the rewards offered by the people' (Demosthenes XX: 107). Often love of honour and love of victory were displayed together. Heracles, a traditional hero, the 'author of many benefits to mankind, devoted his life to a laborious quest of victory and honour' (Lysias ii: 16). Both qualities were praised in the lyrical odes that Pindar wrote in honour of victors at Olympia and other festivals.

> Do thou, oh father Zeus, that rulest over the height of Atabyrium, grant honour to the hymn ordained in praise of any Olympic victor and to the hero who hath found fame for his prowess as a boxer; and do thou give him grace and reverence in the eyes of citizens and strangers too. For he goeth in a straight path that hateth insolence. (Pindar, O.O. VII: 84-95)

The demeanour of the victor was important as well as the victory itself. The word insolence here is hubris, ὕ'βρις. In some contexts it could be translated pride, the pride that comes before a fall, νέμεσις. Hubris was abhorred in literature and in legal proceedings as well as in sport. This tempered the value set upon victory which was not overriding. Pleket claimed that ' "To participate is more important than to win"—the slogan of the Coubertinians of 1896 and of their successors at the present day—is probably the most unGreek statement that can be made' (Pleket, 1975). But how, then, can we explain the advice of Pythagoras, which has survived in a literary fragment (Bowra, 1953, Chap. 11) that men should compete at Olympia but not win? Victory would defile them and make them liable to the envy of others, just as in life itself a love of power and leadership and desire to win were marks of a mania for prestige, δοξομανία—a minority view perhaps but not un-Greek. On the other hand there was little praise for the 'good loser'. Pindar certainly rarely mentions a loser and then pictures him slinking home in shame and not even being welcomed back by his mother. Jibes of contempt or obscurity are the lot of the loser (Pindar, Ol. Ode. VIII).

The assessment of violence in Greek athletic contests has been a matter of argument among scholars. There is no doubt that violence was a feature of life and particularly of relations between states. The Spartans declared war annually upon their subservient Helot population. They also gave their young men a public flogging on initiation to manhood and some died from the ritual. Thucydides gives a graphic and dramatic account of events and negotiations that led to a siege of Melos by Athens in 416. The whole of the adult male population was killed and the women and children enslaved. Thucydides did not approve but neither did he suggest that such a practice was unprecedented. Indeed it was not. In such a world the athletic contests were remarkably lacking in violence. Boxing was probably the most violent and bloody. The pancration, too, was violent and occasionally led to accidental deaths but it was nevertheless restricted by some rules. There were accidents, too, in the chariot racing, some of them fatal. The race in armour, which some have claimed gave a military turn to the Games, did nothing of the kind. It was introduced late and came to be regarded as a light-hearted event. The sight of naked men running down the stadium wearing nothing but a helmet and greaves and carrying a shield must have delighted the spectators. The ethos of sport tended to discourage violence as did the ethos in drama. No act of violence was done on stage. When Oedipus blinded himself and Medea killed her children, they committed their atrocities off stage. This ethos was in sharp contrast with later practices when Rome had conquered the Mediterranean world and had established a pax Romana. In a world at peace the most violent and bloody affairs were enacted in the theatre and the amphitheatre. It is to this era that we must now turn our attention.

CITIES OF THE ROMAN EMPIRE

The sack of the city of Corinth by Mummius and his soldiers in 146 B.C. marked the end of the political independence of the Greeks but not the end of their cultural and social institutions. Athletic contests and training for them survived and developed in cities throughout the Eastern Roman Empire. The programme of events in the Olympic Games and other festivals showed little change under the Roman Empire but the substructure of training and organisation took on new forms, and Greek athletics, as an institution, assumed a new social and political importance.

Some of the changes that had taken place by the end of the first century A.D. are revealed in two sets of correspondence between Pliny, who was governor of Bithynia, and the emperor Trajan in 111 A.D. In the first set of letters Pliny informs the emperor that the citizens of Nicaea who are rebuilding a gymnasium destroyed by fire have exhausted their funds before completing improvements to the building. The emperor replies:

> The poor Greeks have a weakness for gymnasia so perhaps the citizens of Nicaea have attacked its construction too enthusiastically. But they will have to be satisfied with a gymnasium which is just big enough for their needs. (Pliny, Epist. IV. 39,40)

The fact that the governor of Bithynia felt it necessary to refer the matter to Rome indicates that athletics were politically important and that the provision of facilities for training as well as for competition from public funds was accepted as normal. From time to time, then as now, the central government found it necessary to curb public expenditure, but Trajan did not deny all financial liability by government.

In the second correspondence Pliny tells the emperor that the athletes thank him for the remuneration that he has fixed for 'Iselastic' games—that is, those in which victory is marked by a triumphal entry into the home town by the athlete on his return—but they make two further requests. First, payment should start from the date of the victory, not from the date of arrival at home. Second, that back payment of maintenance (obsonia) should be made if a festival has been upgraded to 'Iselastic' after the athlete won his event there. Trajan rejected both demands stating with bureaucratic logic, which is familiar today, that when he downgraded a festival he did not demand a refund of what athletes had previously received (Pliny, Epist. X. 118, 119). Even as early as the first century B.C., according to Vitruvius, victors in the four panhellenic festivals of Olympia, Delphi, Nemea, and Isthmia enjoyed a fixed grant from the public treasury for life (Vitruvius X. 1). These four festivals had come to be known as the περίοδος ('the circuit') and at least one of them occurred every year. Under the Roman Empire they were known as crown, sacred, or 'iselastic' games. Other games were added to this category at the Emperor's discretion. This had a higher status than games that were designated merely 'prize games'. At these latter, value prizes were offered and the organisers had to provide the financial incentives to attract competitors. For a long time it was believed that the only reward offered at Crown games was a wreath or garland for the head—στέφανος[1]—and that it was the home city of the competitor that, for the sake of prestige and by decree of the Emperor, provided remuneration. However, Pleket has now produced evidence that a number of crown games did offer value prizes as well as the crown (Pleket, 1975, pp. 54-71). In the Fitzwilliam Museum at Cambridge, England in the Leake Collection is a gold medal struck for the crown games instituted in Macedonia by the emperor Gordian in 242 A.D. This medal had intrinsic as well as symbolic value. Similar gold medals were awarded in other sacred crown contests especially those held to mark the emperor's victory over external enemies. At Olympia, however, no value prizes were ever awarded, so great was the continuing prestige and status of that festival.

The correspondence between Pliny and Trajan also reveals that athletes were organised or 'unionized' and this is supported by other evidence. There were probably local unions or guilds throughout the empire but there were two and later one worldwide association. When there were two associations one was open to all who made a living from touring the festivals, the other was restricted to those who had won a victory in one of the crown or sacred Games. They were given a headquarters in Rome by the emperor Hadrian in 134 A.D. and this was confirmed by Antoninus Pius nine years later. To the 'xystic guild of athletes'—xystos being the name of a facility for training—'the sacred and garlanded victors who keep the cult of Heracles, greetings. I have ordered a site assigned to you where you will put your cult objects and your records, near the baths erected by my deified grandfather just in the spot where you gather for the Capitoline Games' (IG XIV.1055b). At about this time both guilds merged into one xystic association. Those who serviced the athletic festivals, the trainers, the veterinarians for equestrian events, and others also had their organisations. Athletes then were professionalised to a large extent.

It is necessary to distinguish between professionalism and professionalisation. The former term refers to a state of affairs arbitrarily defined by some authority. If we apply the definition of amateur/professional given by the International Olympic Committee or the International Amateur Athletic Federation from the twentieth century to the ancient world then a very large number of competitors in the Olympic and other Games were professionals during most of the time that those festivals were held. Professionalisation, however, is a process with reference to those possessing a body of knowledge and skill, forming themselves into an organisation requiring entry qualifications and laying down codes of conduct and terms and conditions for the performance of their skills. The correspondence of the Emperors Trajan, Hadrian, and Antoninus Pius indicates that the professionalisation of athletes had by then developed a long way from the unorganised individuals who did the circuit of panhellenic and local Games in the fifth century B.C.

In the nineteenth century in Britain the distinction between amateur and professional was at first a social distinction and had nothing to do with making money out of sport by wager or prize. Many upper class competitors did just this. Only late in the century were financial restrictions used to maintain social exclusiveness. In the Roman Empire athletics were not socially exclusive. Furthermore success made for some social mobility. An epigram in honour of T. Domitius Prometheus about 250 A.D. for his victories in the 'circuit' and other Games shows that he was a wealthy man of leisure, deputy director of the Athenian epheboi who was not averse to receiving valued prizes although he did 'wrap them up in a sanctifying ideology' (Pleket, 1975, p. 70). At the other end of the social scale, according to Claudius Galen, were a number of illiterate philistines or 'jocks'. In the middle were those who, like the family of Herminus Moros, were important in the 'gymnasium' set for several generations. This boxer's membership certificate of the athletic guild was signed by two officers who, like Galen himself, surgeon to the emperor Commodus, were popular in court circles (Robinson, 1955, pp. 200-201).

There is some evidence, albeit scanty, that women who were debarred from taking part or being present at the Olympic Games even as late as the first century A.D., nevertheless had then their own athletic competitions at Delphi, Isthmia, Nemea, Sicyon, and Epidaurus as well as at Olympia itself in honour of the goddess Hera.

In 67 A.D. the Emperor Nero himself competed in the Olympic Games, having had them postponed from 65 A.D. so that he might also take part in the Pythian and Isthmian festivals in the same year. This may have raised the already high social status of the Olympic Games but it reduced competition to absurdity. The emperor had to win. Neither he nor his successors repeated this performance, Nero because he died in 68 A.D. and his successors because they were wiser and were preoccupied with other matters of state.

Greek athletics, then, flourished in the East but in the city of Rome itself, after initial introduction by the first emperor, Augustus, in 30 B.C. they had modest popularity and a doubtful social status. The Actian Games initiated to celebrate the final pacification of the empire and elimination of rivals at the battle of Actium in 31 B.C. were celebrated every five years but scarcely survived the Emperor's death. The Augustalia at Naples, which included music and dramatic competitions, lasted until the third century A.D. Nero founded the Neronia in Rome in 60 A.D. and encouraged knights and senators to compete, but the Neronia are not mentioned after 66 A.D. The emperor Domitian established a quinquennial replica of the Olympic Games and built a permanent stadium holding 30,000 spectators to accommodate them. Augustus had also included a Lusus Troiae in the foundation celebration for the temple and cult of the Divine Julius in 29 B.C. To what extent the competitors were Greek athletes imported for entertainment or were indigenous citizens, as Augustus and Nero hoped they would be, must remain in doubt. The Romans tended at first to associate athletics with the pastimes of a conquered race. They also objected to nudity and suspected homosexuality and degeneracy; Cicero quotes

Ennius: 'To strip naked among one's fellow citizens is the beginning of vice' (Cicero iv.10).

The poet, Horace, too, showed a contempt for Greek athletics (Horace, Epistles II, i. 93) but how else were the sons of Rome to satisfy a desire for physical competition? Some emperors, Nero and Commodus for instance, who wished to degrade the upper classes encouraged senators and knights to fight in the arena as gladiators, and the mob would be delighted to see them exhibit themselves 'like slaves or hirelings' (Friedlander 1908-13 in Pearson, 1973, p. 115) but Augustus, Tiberius, and Vitellius tried to stop the practice. Games on the Greek model may therefore have been promoted as an alternative outlet for aspiring young Roman athletes, especially among the families of Senators and Knights. Support is given to this view by the account of Games in the fifth book of Virgil's Aeneid (Virgil, Aen. V), which have a remarkable affinity with Augustus' Lusus Troiae. This affinity has been analysed and documented by Ward Briggs, who claims that the Lusus Troiae 'was Augustus' favorite exercise for the youths of Rome. It was regularly performed only by the very persons to whom Augustus was directing his athletic encouragement, the youths of aristocratic families. Virgil's account is our only source of the details of the manoeuvres' (Briggs, 1975, p. 281).

The gladiatorial shows that had been begun during the Republic and were accommodated in the Flavian Amphitheatre, popularly known as the Colosseum, after it was inaugurated by the emperor Titus in 80 A.D., might well fall outside the definition of sport and therefore outside the scope of this chapter. In them commercialised cruelty for public entertainment and political manipulation was carried to the ultimate. However, as they made use of the skills of combat in genuine competition, often to the death, something must be said about their place in the social and political life of Rome.

Rome in the early empire was a city of about 1-1/4 million inhabitants most of whom lived in appalling conditions in dangerous high rise buildings with no water above ground level. It has been estimated that 170,000 heads of families were supported by a public distribution of food. Thus some 500,000 to 700,000 were state supported. Many were unemployed but even those who were at work, including slaves, had most of each afternoon free from labour. In the reign of Claudius (41-54 A.D.) there were 159 official holidays in the Roman calendar to which were added such special holidays as a capricious emperor might decree. The population under this despotism had no political duties or rights. The combination of poverty, leisure, and political inactivity posed serious problems for the government and above all for the emperor. Two of the political instruments used to keep the mass of the people contented and subservient were 'ludi' in the circus and the amphitheatre. The elaborate organisation of mass pursuit and slaughter of wild beasts, the throwing of condemned criminals and others 'ad bestias'—to starved and thirsty beasts of prey—and the multiple combats of gladiators, many of which amounted to the butchery of prisoners or slaves by experienced and trained killers, was deliberately set up by Augustus as an instrument of government and social control to bring to an end a prolonged period of civil strife and urban turbulence in Rome. Under Augustus the system worked and Rome was controlled. Thereafter it continued inexorably under its own momentum and no emperor until Constantine in 326 A.D. felt able to abandon it. Tiberius, who succeeded Augustus, had no taste for the excesses of the arena and tried to dissociate himself from them. He provided no shows and was unpopular and reviled as a result. His successor Caligula learned his lesson and celebrated his accession with a profusion of shows. Thereafter the emperors of Rome felt either constrained or inclined to continue the policy of control by bloody entertainment. It has often been suggested that gladiatorial and other cruel combats were finally swept away by outraged Christian feeling. Certainly Constantine, who issued the decree abolishing them, had made Christianity the official religion of the empire, but it is probable that economic factors were as powerful as Christian protest (Pearson, 1973, p. 167). The same factors probably led to the decree of Theodosius II who in 393 A.D. put an end to the Olympic Games and other Games on the grounds that they were pagan religious festivals.

Another policy of government, more beneficient than the provision of 'ludi' was the building of 'thermae' or baths. They not only helped to keep the people contented, they also enabled a minimum level of physical fitness to be maintained by an idle populace. The thermae were far more than bathing establishments. The thermae built by Trajan measured 280 metres by 210 metres and embraced three main features. The central complex included a cold room, swimming pool, central hall, warm room, and hot room, together with dressing rooms and small bathrooms. There were also two open palaistrae surrounded by colonnades. Outside this central complex was open ground laid out as gardens with a running track. Beyond this again was the peribolus containing libraries, reading rooms, gymnasia, ball courts, and administrative offices. By the third century A.D. it is probable that 80,000 Romans could be using such facilities at minimal cost or none at any one time. They were available to all and sundry, including slaves, and were used by both sexes. Seneca in his letters vividly described the life of the thermae and the activities of those so concerned to keep fit. He himself merely wanted 'short and simple exercises which tire the body rapidly and so save time' (Seneca, Epistles LVI & XV). Juvenal lets us know that fashionable ladies also went to the baths.

It is at night that she goes to the baths, at night that she gives order for her oil flasks and other impediments to be taken there; she loves to sweat among the noise and bustle. When her arms fall to her sides, worn out by heavy weights, the skilful masseur presses his fingers into her body, and makes her body resound with his loud smack. (Juvenal, Satyre VI:419)

The general need to arrest physical deterioration made the thermae cosmopolitan institutions.

The great authority on keeping fit was Claudius Galen, a doctor and prolific writer, many of whose works have fortunately survived. In his monogram entitled 'Exercise with the Small Ball' he writes:

The best gymnastic is that which not only exercises the body but which delights the spirit. This is especially true of small ball gymnastics. (McIntosh, 1981, p. 58)

The years of the Roman Empire may well have been the first time that hedonistic inducements to keep fit had to be devised. In earlier times the exigencies of earning a living, military service, or just personal survival in a hard world were sufficient incentives. In his massive work on hygiene, usually known as *De Sanitate Tuenda*, as well as in his minor works, Galen developed physiological theories, classifications of exercises, and programmes of work, including routines of weight training, for improving the physical condition of ordinary men and women. He was not interested in athletics. He drew a sharp distinction between normal fitness and athletic fitness and emphasised several times that the latter was dangerous to health and socially useless. Gymnastics devoted to that end was a perversion of true gymnastics and a disreputable occupation (McIntosh, 1981, p. 58).

Galen was not the only writer on physical training. Professionalisation of athletics, whether in the gymnasia, training athletes for the stadium, in the schools of gladiators for the arena, or in the army was not confined to performers. It extended to coaches and advisers. There were a host of training manuals in antiquity, and one of them written by Philostratus in the third century has survived. He gives us an account of many theories and practices. Some of them now appear absurd; others have provided a basis for subsequent development. Quite laughable are some theories on diet: Pigs that have fed on sea garlic or crabs should be avoided, and only those fattened on cornel berries or acorns should be eaten while training. He describes in some detail the 'tetrad system' of training, or four-day cycle, only to condemn it, 'for it is because of this that the whole system of gymnastics has gone to rack and ruin' (Robinson, 1955, p. 229). More sensible is a primitive attempt at somatotyping and psychological typing for particular events. With professionalisation came specialisation: 'If you had been born in Greece,' writes Tacitus, 'where athletics is an honourable profession, and heaven had granted you the sinews of Nicostratus, I should not allow those mighty muscles, simply made for boxing, to be wasted on mere javelin or discus throwing' (Harris, 1972, p. 65).

Military training was another form of specialisation. An account of recruit training by Vegetius written about 390 A.D. describes pace training in marching and weapon training by weight training. The recruit had to learn his art with sword and shield twice the weight of those which he would use on active service and his spear, too, was heavier than his fighting weapon (Gibbon, 1776-88, Vol. 1, Chap. 1). Professionalisation of physical training whether for sport, entertainment, or war and the professionalisation of the performers was a feature of the Roman Empire. It was certainly not confined to physical activities but perhaps was a factor in the persistence and survival of the empire despite the manifest corruption that often occurred in administration and the madness and incompetence of some of its emperors. It is the more flamboyant emperors who have enjoyed the historical limelight but others were activated by a sense of moral purpose. There is a passage in the meditations of Marcus Aurelius advocating a transfer of behaviour from the gymnasium to life outside, a muscular morality, suggesting that the gymnasium was an instrument of socialisation as well as of social control.

In the field (ἐν τοῖς γυμνασίοις) a player may have scratched us with his nails or given us a blow with his head, in a rage, yet we do not label him for that or hit back or suspect him afterwards of designs against us. Still, we do, in fact, keep away from him, not, however as a foe and not with suspicion but with good natured avoidance. Let us take this as an example in other departments of life. Let us overlook much in the case of those who are, so to speak, our opponents in the game (προσγυμναζομένων); for it is possible to avoid them, yet neither to suspect nor to hate them. (ἀπέχφεσφαι) (Marcus Aurelius VI. 20)

A postscript to this sociological study of sport in the ancient world may be written upon spectators and their role. Not all Greek athletics came to an end with the Olympic Games in 393 A.D. Chariot racing and equestrian events persisted in the Eastern Empire long after Alaric the Goth sacked Rome in 410 A.D. Spectators played a vital part, for chariot racing seemed to be more closely bound up with its spectators than any other sport. In the reign of Justinian in Constantinople they brought it temporarily to an end. This is how Gibbon described the Nika riots that were sparked off by the Emperor Justinian's refusal to release two prisoners who had been condemned to death.

Constantinople adopted the follies, though not the virtues, of ancient Rome; and the same factions which had agitated the circus raged with redoubled fury in the hippodrome. Under the reign of Anastasius, this popular frenzy was inflamed by religious zeal; and the greens, who had treacherously concealed stones and daggers under baskets of fruit, massacred, at a solemn festival, three thousand of their blue adversaries. From the capital, this pestilence was diffused into the provinces and cities of the East, and the sportive distinction of two colours produces two strong and irreconcileable factions, which shook the foundations of a feeble government

Insolent with royal favour, the blues affected to strike terror by a peculiar and Barbaric dress, the long hair of the Huns, their close sleeves and ample garments, a lofty step, and a sonorous voice. In the day they concealed their two-edged poniards, but in the night they boldly assembled in arms and in numerous bands, prepared for every act of violence and rapine. Their adversaries of the green faction, or even inoffensive citizens, were stripped and often murdered by these nocturnal robbers, and it became dangerous to wear any gold buttons or girdles, or to appear at a late hour in the streets of a peaceful capital. A daring spirit, rising with impunity, proceeded to violate the safeguard of private houses; and fire was employed to facilitate the attack, or to conceal the crimes, of these factious rioters. No place was safe or sacred from their depredations; to gratify either avarice or revenge, they profusely spilt the blood of the innocent; churches and altars were polluted by atrocious murders; and it was the boast of the assassins that their dexterity could always inflict a mortal wound with a single stroke of their dagger

The hippodrome itself was condemned during several years to a mournful silence; with the restoration of the games, the same disorders revived; and the blue and green factions continued to afflict the reign of Justinian, and to disturb the tranquillity of the Eastern empire. (Gibbon, Vol IV. Ch XL)

These so-called 'factions' existed from the principate of Augustus until the eve of the crusades, about 1,200 years. It became a traditional view that they were quasi-political parties able even to make or unmake emperors. Marxists claimed that their terrorist activities in the great cities of the Eastern Empire in the fifth and sixth centuries A.D. marked the growth of popular sovereignty. This is too simple a view. It has been my contention in this chapter that the promotion of sport and sporting entertainment was a governmental measure of social control in a system where the exercise of political power by ordinary citizens was prevented. In such circumstances popular emotions found what means of expression they could, and circus factions provided one such outlet. It is possible that soccer hooliganism in Britain in the 1970s and 1980s similarly coincided with a decline of opportunity for popular political expression, but hooliganism does not signify a growth of popular sovereignty, nor does it invest the supporters of Manchester United or Liverpool Football Clubs with the panoply of a political party. Cameron has convincingly shown that the Blues, Greens, and in early days the Whites and Reds too, were fan clubs of supporters and so they remained.

'Their sudden leap to prominence in the fifth century is largely illusory, not a new phenomenon at all but the incidental consequence of a reorganisation of public entertainment. . . . Hooliganism at theatre and circus had always been rife in the Roman world. It merely got worse under the Blues and Greens. (Cameron, 1976, p. 310)

NOTES

1. στέφανος is also the word used in the gospels of Mark (XV.17), Matthew (XXVII.29) and John (XIX.2) for the crown of thorns placed by the Roman soldiers in mockery upon the head of Jesus Christ before his crucifixion. It is possible that to contemporaries this symbolised athletic as well as political opprobrium. The normal term for a king's crown was διάδημα, or diadem.

REFERENCES

A. Latin and Greek Authors
The works of all authors are to be found in English translation in the Loeb Classical Library with Latin or Greek and English on opposite pages, published by Heinemann, London. Many portions relevant to sport are included in R.R. Robinson, 'Sources for the History of Greek Athletics', Cincinnati, 1955.

Aristotle   Nichomachean Ethics
Aristotle   Politics
Cicero   Tusculan Disputations

Demosthenes	Orations
Euripides	Plays and Fragment Autolycus
Galen	Exercises with the Small Ball
Galen	Health
Galen	Health, Medicine and Gymnastics
Herodotus	History
Homer	Iliad
Homer	Odyssey
Isocrates	Team of Horses
Juvenal	Satyres
Lucian	Anacharsis
Lysias	Orations
Marcus Aurelius	Meditations
Pausanias	Description of Greece
Philostratus	Gymnastics
Pindar	Olympian Odes
Plato	Apology of Socrates
Pliny	Epistles
Plutarch	Lives
Seneca	Epistles
Strabo	Geography
Suetonius	The Twelve Caesars
Tacitus	Annals
Thucydides	History
Vegetius	Military Affairs
Virgil	Aeneid
Xenophanes	Fragments

B. Modern Authors

Balsdon, J.P.V. (1969). *Life and leisure in Ancient Rome*. New York: McGraw-Hill.

Bowra, C.M. (1953). *Problems in Greek poetry*. Oxford: Oxford University Press.

Bowra, C.M. (1964). *Pindar*. Oxford: Oxford University Press.

Briggs, W.W. (1975). Augustan athletics and games of Aeneid V. *Stadion* 1,2 *Cambridge ancient history*. 1970-75. Cambridge: Eng. University Press.

Cameron, A. (1976). *Circus factions. Blues and greens at Rome and Byzantium*. Oxford: The Clarendon Press.

Daremberg-Saglio, 1877-1919. *Dictionaire des antiquités grecques et romaines*. Paris: Hachette.

Dover, K.J. (1974). *Greek popular morality in the time of Plato and Aristotle*. Oxford: Blackwell.

Dudley, D.R. (1967). *Urbs Roma*. London: Phaidon.

Elias, N. (1971). The genesis of sport as a sociological problem. In Dunning, E. (Ed.), *The sociology of sport*. London: Cass.

Evans, A.J. (1921-1935). *The palace of Minos at Knossos*. London: Macmillan.

Finley, M.I., & Pleket, H.W. (1976). *The Olympic Games: The first thousand years.* New York: Viking.

Frazer, J.G. (1951). *The golden bough.* Part III: 'The Dying God.' London: Macmillan.

Friedlander, L. (1908-28). *Roman life and manners under the early Empire.* London: G. Routledge. New York: E.P. Dutton.

Gardiner, E.N. (1930). *Athletics of the ancient world.* Oxford: The Clarendon Press.

Gibbon, E. *Decline and fall of the Roman Empire.* New York: E.P. Dutton.

Harris, H.A. (1964). *Greek athletes and athletics.* London: Hutchinson.

Harris, H.A. (1972). *Sport in Greece and Rome.* London: Thames and Hudson.

Harris, H.A. (1976). *Trivium: Greek athletics and the Jews.* Cardiff: University of Wales Press.

Howell, M.S., & Howell, R. (1979). Physical activities and sport in early societies. In Zeigler, E. (Ed.), *History of physical education and sport.* Englewood Cliffs: Prentice Hall.

Huizinga, J.H. (1949). *Homo ludens.* London: Routledge & Kegan Paul.

Inscriptiones Graecae 1. Berlin 1924 and Supplementum Epigraphicum Graecum, Leyden, 1923 sqq.

Jaeger, W. (1934). *Paideia.* Berlin und Leipzig: W. de Gruyter.

Kirk, G.S. (1964). *The Homeric poems as history.* Cambridge University Press. Reprint of Cambridge Ancient History Vol II, Chap. XXXIX (b).

Lanciani, R.A. (1967). *Ancient Rome in the light of recent discoveries.* New York: Blom.

Liddell, H., & Scott, R. (1878). *Greek-English lexicon.* Ed. 6. New York.

McIntosh, P.C. (1981). Physical education and recreation in Imperial Rome. In McIntosh, P.C. (Ed.), *Landmarks in the history of physical education.* London: Routledge & Kegan Paul.

McIntosh, P.C. (1963). *Sport in society.* London: Watts.

Moretti, L. (1953). *Inscrizioni agonistiche Greche.* Roma: A. Signorelli.

Moretti, L. (1957). *Olympionikai, i vincitori negli antichi agoni olimpici.* Roma. Academia nazionale dei lincei. Classe di scienze moral, storiche. Ser. 8.

Myres, J.L. (1930). *Who were the Greeks?* Berkeley: University of California Press.

Opie, I., & Opie, P. (1969). *Children's games in street and playground.* Oxford: Clarendon.

Pearson, J. (1973). *Arena: The story of the Colosseum.* New York: McGraw-Hill.

Pleket, H.W. (1975). Games, prizes, athletes and ideology. In *Stadion* I, 1:49-89.

Robinson, R. (Sargent) (1955). *Sources for the history of Greek athletics.* Cincinnati: Author.

Thompson, J.G. (1978). Solon on athletics. *Journal of Sport History,* 5, 1.

Weil, S. (1945). *The Iliad or the poem of force.* Pendle Hill Pamphlet No. 91: Wallingford, Pennsylvania.

Weiler, I. (1975). Αἰέν ἀριστεύειν In *Stadion* I, 2:195.

Zeigler, E.F. (1973). *A history of sport and physical education to 1900.* Part I. Champaign, IL: Stipes.

Sport in the Civilising Process: Aspects of the Development of Modern Sport

Eric Dunning

It is widely believed that we are living today in one of the most violent periods in history. A not insignificant part of this belief consists in the widespread feeling that violence is currently increasing in, and in conjunction with, sports. The Americans Yiannakis, McIntyre, Melnick, and Hart, for example, wrote not too many years ago that

> during the past few years, crowd and player violence in sport has increased to such an extent that it has drawn the attention of the mass media, school officials and academicians and resulted in considerable debate regarding its antecedents and consequences. A specific type of violence, namely player violence has even been taken up by American courts. This burgeoning of violence has also prompted the formation of special commissions at both local and national levels to investigate its causes. (Yiannakis, McIntyre, Melnick, & Hart, 1979, p. 216)

In his book, *Blood and Guts: Violence in Sports*, the Australian-born journalist Don Atyeo, referring to what he takes to be a worldwide trend, concluded that

> the future of violent sports seems assured. Games will grow harder and bloodier to feed the rising appetite of an audience which will grow both increasingly more jaded and satiated with violence, and increasingly more violent itself, until, perhaps, something happens to bring it all crashing down. This time around, though, the likelihood is that it won't be the barbarian hordes banging on the gates outside which will destroy the Colosseum. This time the violence will be of sport's own making and will come from within the walls of the Colosseum itself. (Atyeo, 1979, p. 377)

The beliefs of Atyeo and Yiannakis et al. are representative of a much more widely held belief, namely that modern sport and modern civilisation are getting so violent that both are on the brink of collapse. What light does sociological research throw onto this complex and contentious issue? That, especially the sports side of the equation, is what I shall be concerned with in this essay.

Apart from its intrinsic significance, the issue of violence in sport is interesting and important because one of the central ideologies associated with the rise and spread of modern sport—the so-called 'catharsis theory' (see, e.g., Lorenz, 1966)—holds that human beings are instinctively aggressive and that sport represents the best available means for discharging this instinct in a socially constructive way. However, if writers such as Atyeo and Yiannakis et al. are to be believed and modern sports really are increasingly violent, it follows that the sports movement loses one of its principal ideological props: Sports do not and cannot form an arena for the constructive and cathartic discharge of aggression but are, on the contrary, not only bent on a self-destructive course but are a positive source of danger to the societies where they are played.

I shall return to the subject of catharsis at the end of this paper. However, that will not be the principal focus of what I have to say. I shall, rather, be concerned with the implications of research into this issue for the theory of civilising processes propounded by Elias (1978a, 1982). I shall start by responding to some criticisms of Elias's theory and, after that, I shall present a thumbnail sketch of some of the key elements of what the theory actually entails. Then I shall summarise:

1. Elias's work on the sports of Ancient Greece (Elias, in Elias & Dunning, 1986);
2. my own and Sheard's work on the development of rugby football (Dunning & Sheard, 1979);
3. Elias's study of the development of fox hunting (Elias, in Elias & Dunning, 1986);
4. some of the historical work we have done at Leicester on the subject of violence generally (Dunning, Murphy, Newburn, and Waddington, in Gaskell & Benewick, 1987); and finally,
5. the work on football hooliganism that I have been carrying out in Leicester with Murphy and Williams (Williams, Dunning, & Murphy, 1984; Dunning, Murphy, & Williams, 1988).

SOME CRITICISMS OF THE THEORY OF CIVILISING PROCESSES: A CRITICAL RESPONSE

In a review of Rojek's, *Capitalism and Leisure Theory* (Rojek, 1985), a book in which many aspects of Elias's 'figurational' approach to sociology are recommended, Newman refers to 'Elias's notion of the ever civilizing trend of social life' and then continues: 'in the face of ubiquitous "class warfare," violence on the picket lines, sexual harassment, genocide, terrorism and abortion—what of drug abuse, urban riots, street crime and hooliganism—even Rojek finds such generalizations hard to sustain' (Newman, 1986). In a review of Elias and Dunning's *Quest for Excitement* (Elias & Dunning, 1986), the anthropologist Edmund Leach even refers to what he calls Elias's 'very Germanic, nineteenth century ideas of longterm social progress' and suggests that Elias's theory 'is impervious to test'. Indeed, says Leach, it was formulated 'precisely at the time when Hitler was refuting the argument on the grandest scale' (Leach, 1986).

Not dissimilar criticisms are contained in articles by Hargreaves (1986) and Curtis (1986). Curtis, for example, writes:

As interesting and insightful as Elias's analyses are, his theory has a flaw. His assumption of more or less unilinear evolution is very questionable. For example, he says that ontogeny repeats phylogeny, that societies go through a process of development similar to that of humans, from infants [*sic*] through childhood and adulthood. Surely, we must reject this view. One problem is that the process of civilization is not as irreversible as biological maturation. (Curtis, 1986, p. 59)

A little later, Curtis continues:

While reading *The Civilizing Process*, I could not help thinking of all the contrary evidence . . . from the past few years: the slaughter of Jews in Nazi Germany; the devastation laid on people in Dresden; the destruction of life and property in the bombing of Tokyo; and the massacres at Mai Lai and in other places in Vietnam, to name but a very few. How do we reconcile these events with the notion that people are moving towards a pinnacle in self-restraint of aggression? (Curtis, 1986, pp. 59-60)

Ian Taylor even identifies Elias as an 'evolutionary idealist' and, in an unsubstantiated attack on the developmental work on football hooliganism that Murphy, Williams, and I have been engaged in, writes dismissively that:

The project appears to be to find evidence of violent incidents at soccer games continuously *throughout* the history of the professional game and also to locate examples of violence amongst crowds at soccer games outside England. One can see why this project is helpful to Dunning in his attempt to illustrate the evolutionary and idealist social theory of Norbert Elias—but the evidence *is* stretched . . . and the theory's stress on an ongoing process of civilization *surely* is a very unhelpful framework through which to analyze the current condition of working class youth in Britain. (Taylor, 1985)

As I shall show later, what we have tried to do in the Leicester project is to trace *variations* in the reported incidence of soccer spectator misbehaviour over time, but Taylor confuses this with a nondevelopmental notion of an unchanging historical continuity. Moreover, *pace* Taylor as I also hope to show, Elias's theory provides an *extremely* helpful 'framework through which to analyze the current condition of working class youth in Britain'. However, in order to recognise that one has to pay attention to what Elias actually wrote. Before I provide a thumbnail sketch of some key aspects of Elias's theory of civilising processes, let me first of all respond briefly to these criticisms by Newman, Leach, Hargreaves, Curtis, and Taylor.

The first thing worthy of note is that these five authors, but particularly Newman, Leach, and Curtis, fail to take adequate account of the fact that Elias is a German of Jewish descent; that the two volumes of *Über den Prozess der Zivilisation* (Elias, 1939) were written just after he had been forced to flee Nazi Germany; that Elias lost both his parents in the Nazi terror (his mother died in Auschwitz); and that Elias was forced to flee his native Germany and take up residence in England.

Either Elias at the time was an individual completely detached from and unaware of what was going on around him, or these scholars have fundamentally misunderstood vital aspects of his work. As I hope to show, Elias's approach has been, from the outset, more reality-oriented than many others at present offer in sociology. It is, therefore, reasonable to suppose that Newman, Leach, Hargreaves, Curtis, Taylor, and others who argue like them have taken aspects of Elias's work out of its wider—and developing—context, and, furthermore, that they have simply failed to grasp the range, complexity, and subtlety of the theory he proposes. Let me push this criticism a little further.

The common strand in these attacks is the identification of Elias's theory of civilising processes as a theory of 'unilinear evolution'. Beyond that, the critiques of Taylor and Curtis, the most elaborate of the four, are different. Taylor attacks the theory as 'idealist', while Curtis attacks it for allegedly asserting that 'ontogeny repeats phylogeny'. Taylor is evidently so attached to the idea of Marxist materialism as the *only* form of radical commitment that he is unable to appreciate a theory that strives to transcend the crude dichotomization of 'the material' and 'the ideal' (see, e.g., Elias, 1982, p. 282ff). For his part, Curtis is evidently so attached to the idea that *any* developmental theory must *necessarily* take the form of an eighteenth- or nineteenth-century theory of 'unilinear evolution' or 'progress' that he equates Elias with Auguste Comte.

A modification and elaboration of aspects of Comte's theory is certainly *one* of the bases from which Elias's emergent synthesis has been built (see, e.g., Elias, 1978b, especially Ch. 1). However, while it may be correct to criticise Comte for mistakenly believing that the 'law of the three stages' as a social process replicates the stages through which the thinking of an individual human being passes (Martineau, 1853, p. 3), it is difficult to see how such a flaw can be attributed to Elias. He takes pains to stress, again and again, not only the evolutionary connections between but also the relative autonomy of structures at the physical, biological, and social levels. One of his clearest statements on the relative autonomy of the social came when he wrote this:

> In sociology distinct and specific forms of integration and disintegration, patterns of order and disorder, and types of structure and function are encountered which differ from those on all previous levels of integration and cannot be reduced to them, even though the forms encountered on all levels constitute ontogenetically a single, if subdivided, developmental continuum. (Elias, 1978b, p. 107)

One of the implications of this is that, while the sequence of biological stages through which an individual human being or any other organism passes on its way from birth to death is necessary and irreversible, the compulsions involved in a process of social development do not have the same character of inevitability and irreversibility (see, e.g., Elias, 1978b, pp. 161, 163ff). That is in large part because the processes at work in a human society depend on learning. They may, for example, lead it to become more differentiated and integrated at a higher level, less differentiated and integrated at a lower level, or to remain for a greater or lesser length of time fixed at a given level of differentiation and integration. But these are relatively autonomous *social* processes, and they have to be understood as such. The point, of course, is that, although it is a developmental theory and although Elias focused primarily on West European developments, or what he calls 'civilising spurts', his theory of civilising processes is a twentieth-century synthesis that seeks to avoid eighteenth- and nineteenth-century mistakes (or those that, in the twentieth century, are more or less wrongly attributed to eighteenth- and nineteenth-century theories). It is, therefore, fully attuned to the occurrence of short- and long-term 'regressions', that is, 'counter-civilising' developments or 'de-civilising spurts'. For example, Elias writes:

> This movement of society and civilization certainly does not follow a straight line. Within the overall movement there are repeatedly greater or lesser counter-movements in which the contrasts in society and the fluctuations in the behaviour of individuals, their affective outbreaks, increase again. (Elias, 1982, p. 253)

There is, moreover, according to Elias, no 'zero-point' of civilisation, no 'absolutely uncivilised' human society, group, or individual, either today or in the past[1]. By the same token, societies or groups that today are more 'advanced' in this regard are not 'civilized' in some absolute sense. As Elias puts it:

> We cannot expect of people who live in the midst of (present) tensions, who are thus driven guiltlessly to incur guilt upon guilt against each other, that they should behave to each other in a manner representing—as seems so often to be believed today—an ultimate pinnacle of 'civilized' conduct. The continuous intertwining of human activities again and again acts as a lever which over the centuries produces changes in human conduct in the direction of our standard. The same pressures quite clearly operate in our own society towards changes transcending present standards of conduct and sentiment in the same direction—although today, as in the past, these trends can go at any time into reverse gear. No more than our kind of social structure, is our kind of conduct, level of constraints, prohibitions and anxieties, something definitive, still less a pinnacle. (Elias, 1982, p. 331)

Let me become more concrete and present a thumbnail sketch of some aspects of Elias's emerging synthesis. Before discussing the theory of civilising processes at some length, I shall first look briefly at two of Elias's key concepts, those of 'development' and of what he calls 'the immanent dynamics of figurations'.

'DEVELOPMENT' AND THE 'IMMANENT DYNAMICS OF FIGURATIONS'

The term *figuration*, as Elias uses it, refers to a web of interdependent human beings (Elias, 1978b) and, according to Elias, like all other aspects of known reality human figurations are inherently processual. Life itself is a process and the living human beings who form figurations are not only interdependent with each other but have to act and interact—both with each other and the rest of nature—to secure the production and reproduction of their lives. Over time, the interweaving of their actions unintentionally produces changes and, since the dawn of recorded history, the rate of change has been tending more or less constantly to increase. Since around the eleventh and twelfth centuries, this speeding up of change has occurred at a faster rate in the West than anywhere else.

However, the concept of change is too general in order adequately to capture the complexity of processes of this kind. As a minimum, concepts are needed; first, to convey the fact that social processes can involve changes in different directions, for example towards higher or lower levels of differentiation and integration, or towards higher or lower levels of 'civilisation'; and second, to capture the connections between stages in such processes. The concept of 'development' refers, in a minimum sense, to a change towards higher levels of differentiation and integration; the concept of 'regression' refers to a change in the opposite direction; and the adjective 'developmental' refers to a study that is concerned to trace such changes over time and to explain the connections between prior and subsequent stages[2]. But there is no commitment in the 'Eliasian' approach to the idea that such processes necessarily or inevitably involve changes in a particular direction[3].

As Bauman recognizes, Elias has sought to develop an 'explanatory device better geared to the needs of sociology than naturalistic, causal explanations' (Bauman, 1979). That is, Elias rejects the common *analytical* approach in terms of which social relations are broken down into sets of factors, variables, or spheres (such as the political factor, the education variable, or the economic sphere), and in which the attempt is made to assess the relative causal weights of these factors, variables, or spheres in the social process or some aspect of it. He is concerned, rather, to discover the 'immanent dynamics of figurations'.

What is meant by 'immanent dynamics' is that the dynamics of a social figuration are inherent in its structure and in the makeup and motivations of the people who comprise it. Structure and process, however, are different sides of the same coin, not separate 'things' that affect each other. Nor are figurations separate and apart from the people who comprise them. Human beings always live together, and the pattern of their interdependence, the ways in which their actions interweave as they attempt to secure their shared and conflicting ends, is the structure of the figuration that they form. Struggles within and among groups—for control of the economy or the state, for material goods and services, for income and wealth, for access to occupations and occupational advancement, for control over the production, dissemination, definition, and use of knowledge, for prestige, for love and erotic gratification, for excitement—are crucial in this connection.

Such struggles are chiefly influenced and channelled in seven ways, all of which are developmentally specific:

1. by a society's population size and density;
2. by the length and form of the interdependency chains within it and between it and other societies;

3. by the balance within a society between centripetal and centrifugal pressures, that is, the degree of effectiveness with which stable centralisation and unification have been secured;
4. by the form taken by the state (whether, for example, it is a private or public monopoly, oligarchic or democratic, capitalist or socialist);
5. by whether the society has a 'natural' or a money economy, an agricultural or an industrial one and, whatever its form, by whether and how far its economy is integrated into an intersocietal framework;
6. by the personality pattern of its people, especially the degree to which they have become accustomed to exercising self-control over their affects, that is, the degree and manner in which they have internalized social constraints in this regard; and
7. by the structurally determined balance of power between a society's constituent groups.

This latter balance is held to be fundamentally affected by the degree to which a society's interdependency chains facilitate 'functional democratisation', namely the exercise of reciprocal controls within and among groups (Elias, 1978b, pp. 77ff). It is also held to be affected by the degree to which the position of groups within the overall system of interdependencies and their particular structures facilitate communication, organisation, and solidarity among their members and give them access to key institutions and their resources, including access to strategically significant knowledge.

In the long term, according to Elias, the immanent dynamics of figurations tend to have a 'blind' or unplanned character largely because they are the unintended outcome of the interweaving of the actions of countless interdependent groups and individuals. However, though unplanned, they have a retrospectively determinable structure and direction. That is because the structure of a figuration at any given stage forms a necessary—though not a sufficient—condition for the formation of its structure at a later stage (Elias, 1978b, pp. 160ff). The developmental focus of figurational sociology is concerned with tracing such connections between stages in the longer term 'figurational flow'. It is *not*, however, as I said earlier, committed to the view that this 'flow' has necessarily to change in a particular direction. It is, that is to say, just as attuned to 'regression' as it is to 'progress', and just as concerned with processes that result for a shorter or longer time in persistence rather than change. In the societies of Western Europe between the Middle Ages and the early twentieth century, however, the structure and direction of the long-term figurational flow took, on balance, the form of a 'civilising process'. Since the theory of civilising processes forms the cornerstone of figurational sociology—Elias himself sometimes refers to it as a 'central theory'—it is to that issue that my attention will now be turned.

THE THEORY OF CIVILISING PROCESSES

The central observation on which the theory of civilising processes is based is the fact that, in Western European societies since the Middle Ages, a more or less continuous elaboration and refinement of manners and social standards can be shown to have taken place, together with an increase in the social pressure on people to exercise stricter and more even self-control over their feelings in more and more fields of social relations. (In *The Civilizing Process*, Elias (1978a) demonstrates this principally by means of an investigation of books on manners and etiquette since the Middle Ages.) Correlatively, at the level of personality, there has occurred an increase in the importance of conscience (superego) as a regulator of behaviour. That is to say, social standards and taboos have come to be more deeply internalised. Another way of putting it would be to say that a shift has occurred in the balance between external constraints (*Fremdzwänge*) and self-constraints (*Selbstzwänge*) in favour of the latter.

However, this shift has not involved a simple, unilinear, and continuously progressive increase in self-controls but, rather, a shift towards a dominant type of personality in which, in the normal course of the routines of everyday life, the feelings of individuals fluctuate less violently between extremes than was the case in the Middle Ages. That is the case because people in the more civilised societies of today are taught and expected to exercise more regular, stable, even, and comprehensive control over their behaviour and their feelings; these are based on and oriented towards norms that reflect an attempt to strike a balance between, on the one hand, looseness and laxity and on the other, harshness, strictness, and rigidity. No value-judgment, no statement of 'better' or 'worse' is intended by this diagnosis. It is simply an attempt to come to grips with a process the occurrence of which can be supported by reference to a whole range of evidence—principally time-series of manner books—and by inference to the changes in personality structure that, although they cannot be directly observed in a literal sense, can be reasonably inferred to have correlatively occurred.

A crucial aspect of this process, according to Elias, one that is of central relevance for the developmental study of sport, has consisted of a long-term decline in people's propensity for obtaining pleasure from directly engaging in and witnessing violent acts. He refers in this connection to a 'dampening of *Angriffslust*', literally to a decline in the lust for attacking, that is in people's desire and capacity for obtaining pleasure from attacking others (Elias, 1978a, pp. 191ff). This has entailed, first, an advance in the 'threshold of repugnance' (*Peinlichkeitsschwelle*) regarding bloodshed and other direct manifestations of physical violence; and second, the internalisation of a stricter taboo on violence as part of the superego. A consequence of this is that guilt feelings are liable to be aroused whenever this taboo is violated. At the same time, there has occurred a tendency to push violence increasingly behind the scenes and, as part of it, to describe people who openly derive pleasure from violence in terms of the language of psychopathology, punishing them by means of stigmatisation, hospitalisation, or imprisonment.

Between the Middle Ages and modern times, powerful elites standing at the nodal points of complex networks of interdependence, above all royal courts and large trading and manufacturing establishments, have been the principal standard-setting groups, the initial model-makers in this long-term civilising process from whom standards have subsequently diffused. Their social situation has entailed increasing pressure to exercise self-control and foresight. That is, basically because of the centrality of their role in the interdependency networks in which they occupy a dominant position and because they have found themselves more and more trapped in an unintended 'pincer movement' involving, on the one hand, the growing power of the state and, on the other, the growing power of lower social strata, they have been constrained generally to exercise greater self-restraint over their behaviour and their feelings.

According to Elias, of central importance to this process has been the following complex of interrelated long-term developments: economic growth; the lengthening of interdependency chains (in more conventional sociological language, the growth of the 'division of labour')[4]; the increasing 'monetisation' of social relationships; state-formation, especially the formation of stable monopolies of force and taxation, a process that has involved, as one of its central 'moments', the decreasing privatisation of these monopolies and their subjection to increasing public control; and 'functional democratisation', that is, growing pressure on higher strata from below as increasing interdependence leads to a growth in the power chances of lower social strata[5]. Conflict and violence have, throughout, been central to the unfolding of these processes. For example, 'elimination struggles' between contenders for the 'royal position' were crucial for the formation of the earliest tax and force monopolies, and functional democratisation, to the extent that it has been resisted by dominant groups, has regularly led, at least in the short term, to increasing conflict and violence. Moreover, as is characteristic of social processes generally because of the part played in them by learning, none of these crucial part-developments, to the extent that they are replicated elsewhere, should be mechanistically read as always and everywhere likely to produce identical results. One can speak of probabilities in that connection, but not of cast-iron, lawlike certainties (Elias, 1974, pp. 21-42). One can also add that the theory logically implies a theory of 'de-civilisation'. That is, it leads one, *ceteris paribus*, to anticipate that counter-civilising developments will occur in a society that experiences economic decline, a shortening of interdependency chains, diminishing state monopolies over force and taxation, and growing inequality in the balance of power between classes and other groups. Again, of course, since all social processes depend upon learning, any such regression, however great its duration and extent, is unlikely to replicate in reverse the details and phasing of its progressive counterpart.

Further light on the interpretation of Elias's theory of civilising processes is thrown by a concept that he introduced in *What Is Sociology?* as a means of determining and measuring the level of development that a society has reached, namely the concept of what he calls 'the triad of basic controls' (Elias, 1978b, pp. 156-157). More particularly, the level of development of a society can be determined, Elias suggests, by:

1. The extent of its control over extrahuman nexuses of events, that is, over what are usually referred to as 'natural events' (Elias speaks as he does, of course, because human beings and their societies are part of 'nature')
2. The extent of its control over interhuman connections, that is, over what are usually referred to as 'social nexuses'

3. The extent to and manner in which each of its individual members has learned, from childhood onwards, to exercise self-control.

Scientific and technological developments correspond to the first of these basic controls; the development of social organisation, especially state-formation, to the second; and the civilising process on the level of individual personalities to the third. According to Elias, the three are interdependent both in their development and their functioning at any given stage.

However, he warns against 'the mechanistic idea that the interdependence of the three types of control is to be understood in terms of parallel increases in all three' (Elias, 1978b, pp. 156-157). More particularly, the development of the three types does not occur at the same rate, and developments in one area can contradict, impede, or threaten developments in the others. For example, 'it is highly characteristic of modern societies,' says Elias, 'that the extent of their control-chances over extra-human nexuses is greater and grows more quickly than that over inter-human social nexuses' (1978b, pp. 156-157). Or, to put it another way, the development of knowledge about 'natural' events has grown faster than the development of knowledge about societies, with the result that our ability to control extrahuman nexuses is greater than our ability to control ourselves and the figurations that we form. A corollary of this is the fact that the less amenable a sphere of events is to human control, the more emotional and fantasy-laden people's thinking about it tends to be. And the more emotional and fantasy-laden their thinking about a sphere of events, the less capable they are of constructing more object-adequate models of its connections and hence of controlling it. In short, they become trapped in a negative feedback process, or what Elias calls a 'double-bind figuration' (Elias, 1987, pp. 49ff).

Indeed, the fact that the so-called natural sciences have developed more rapidly than the 'social' sciences has, by contributing to an acceleration in the tempo of social and technological change (hence adding to people's uncertainties and fears), actively contributed to one of the principal double-bind figurations in which we found ourselves trapped until the end of the 1980s: the cold war. It also contributed to the fears and tensions that were thus engendered by permitting the construction of weapons—biological as well as nuclear—that have the potential for destroying civilisation as we know it, and perhaps, via a 'nuclear winter', of completely destroying life on earth. The existence of such weapons intensified the mutual fears and suspicions of the antagonists in the cold war, locking them ever more firmly into a double-bind figuration of reciprocally escalating fears and hostilities. And the greater the hostility and suspicion with which they came to regard each other, the more they armed themselves, hence reciprocally increasing their hostilities and suspicions, and so on in a spiral which escalated up to the point at which the Soviet Union was crippled economically, disengaged from the conflict, and exerienced a process of disintegration the endpoint of which is not yet in sight.

It would be premature for a host of reasons to regard the end of the cold war as signifying that we are about to enter an era of world peace. The disintegration of a nuclear power is without historical precedent and, although the United States and the West "won" the cold war, the United States itself has been economically weakened too much for it to be able to take on the role of "world policeman" unaided and alone. All that can be said with any certainty is that globally, we face an uncertain future.

The point, of course, is that there is no international monopoly of violence comparable to the state monopolies of violence that have had a pacifying, civilising effect within the more advanced nation-states, and this means that international relations continue in many ways to be frozen at a relatively low level of civilisation. That is, in large part, as a result of the lack of a stable and effective international violence monopoly, international relations, compared with domestic social relations within the more advanced nation-states, are characterised to a far higher degree by uncontrolled and, at present, largely uncontrollable, tensions. Indeed, since the end of the cold war there are signs that uncontrollable tensions within and between nations have increased. Think of what is happening in Yugoslavia, for example, or parts of the former Soviet Union. And when, as happens not infrequently, these tensions break out into open warfare, 'de-civilising' effects with wide ramifications are produced, not only on the direct combatants and their immediate victims but, as the American experience in Vietnam showed very clearly, on people at home as well.

I shall return to the theory of civilising processes when I come to discuss football hooliganism. For the moment, this brief and necessarily rather abstract summary must suffice. Let me turn now to Elias's study of the 'sports' of Ancient Greece.

THE 'SPORTS' OF ANCIENT GREECE

It is widely believed—for example, in association with the ideology of the Olympic movement—that modern sports are the revival of an ancient Greek tradition. However, this belief in a simple, straightforward 'renaissance', Elias argues, is a myth. The 'agonistic game-contests' of Ancient Greece—it is not, he says, strictly speaking correct to refer to them as *sports*—were based on the ethos of a warrior nobility and involved traditions of honour rather than of fairness. Their rules were customary and unwritten, and a high level of physical violence was tolerated within them. This corresponds, Elias suggests, to the fact that the Ancient Greek city-states stood at an early stage in a civilising process. Life within them, compared with that in modern nation-states, was generally more violent and insecure. The different city-states went frequently to war. Internally, they lacked that degree of relatively stable and impersonal control of the means of violence which is one of the major structural traits of contemporary nation-states. People were more dependent on themselves and their kinsfolk for obtaining redress for what they regarded as the wrongs done to them than tends to be the case in our type of society. There was no relatively impersonal police force. People could not rely to the same extent on the processes of law. They had, to a much greater extent than tends to be the case in a society such as ours, to be at the ready to defend themselves from physical attack. Vendettas were endemic. Under such circumstances a strong conscience with respect to the exercise of aggression and an advanced threshold of repugnance with regard to engaging in and witnessing violent acts would have proved a disadvantage. The overall social situation and the correlative personality pattern of the people were reflected in their sports. This emerges clearly, Elias argues, if one compares modern freestyle wrestling with its counterpart in Ancient Greece.

Freestyle wrestling is governed by an International Wrestling Federation with headquarters in Switzerland. The written rules of 1967 declare, among other things, that the stranglehold, the half nelson, and the full nelson, whether applied with hands or feet, are 'foul' holds. Punching, kicking, and butting are all forbidden. Each bout lasts nine minutes and is divided into three rounds of three minutes each. There is a one-minute interval between each round. The bout is controlled by a referee, three judges, and a timekeeper. Despite such tight regulation and strict control, freestyle wrestling is still widely regarded as one of the rougher contemporary sports[6]. Compare it, however, says Elias, with the 'pancration', a type of wrestling that formed one of the most popular events in the ancient Olympic Games:

> In the pancration, the competitors fought with every part of their body, with their hands, elbows, their knees, their necks and their heads; in Sparta, they even used their feet. The pancratiasts were allowed to gouge one another's eyes out . . . they were also allowed to trip their opponents, lay hold of their feet, noses and ears, dislocate their fingers and arms, and apply strangle-holds. If one man succeeded in throwing the other, he was entitled to sit on him and beat him about the head, face and ears; he could also kick him and trample on him. It goes without saying that the contestants in this brutal contest sometimes received the most fearful wounds and that not infrequently men were killed! The pancration of the Spartan epheboi was probably the most fearful of all. Pausanius tells us that the contestants quite literally fought tooth and nail and bit and tore one another's eyes out. (Elias & Dunning, 1986, p. 136ff)[7]

There was a judge in these contests but no referee, no timekeeper, and no time limits. The fight simply lasted until one of the contestants gave up or, as happened not infrequently, was killed or so severely wounded that he could no longer continue the struggle.

According to Elias, the warrior ethos on which these ancient Greek contest-games were based emerges even more clearly from the contrast between modern boxing and its ancient Greek equivalent. He writes:

> Representations on Greek vases usually show boxers in a traditional stance so close to each other that each stands with one foot forward, next to, or even behind that of the other. There was little scope for the footwork which enables modern boxers to move quickly, now to the right or left, now backwards, now forwards. To move backwards, according to the code of warriors, was a sign of cowardice. To avoid the enemy's blows by moving out of the way was shameful. Boxers, like warriors at close quarters, were expected to stand fast and not to give way. The defences of skilful boxers might be impenetrable; they might tire their enemies and win without receiving injuries. But if the

fight took too long, a judge could order the two opponents to give and take blow for blow without defending themselves until one of them was no longer able to continue the fight. This agonistic type of boxing, as one can see, accentuated the climax, the moment of decision, of victory or defeat, as the most important and significant part of the contest, more important than the game-contest itself. It was as much a test of physical endurance and of sheer muscular strength as of skill. Serious injuries to the eyes, ears and even to the skull were frequent; so were swollen ears, broken teeth and squashed noses. We hear of two boxers who agreed to exchange blow for blow. The first struck a blow to the head which his opponent survived. When he lowered his guard, the other man struck him under the ribs with his outstretched fingers, burst through his side with his hard nails and killed him. (Elias & Dunning, 1986, pp. 136ff)

Boxing, of course, remains a violent sport. There are no statistics available on injury and death rates in ancient, agonistic boxing to compare with those in its modern counterpart. However, contemporary descriptions such as these, together with what we know about agonistic contests such as the pancration, are consistent with the view that they were representative of a less advanced stage in a civilising process. In Britain—and I suspect this is paralleled in several other countries—the present controversy over boxing and the campaign by groups in the British Medical Association to ban it point in the same direction. There are, moreover, clear parallels between these 'sports' of Ancient Greece and the 'folk-games'—the games of the 'common people'—of preindustrial Britain. They do not represent a line of specific developmental descent but the latter, too, were played according to unwritten, relatively undifferentiated customary rules and reveal a higher social tolerance of physical violence than tends to be the case in modern sports. This corresponds with the fact that British society in the medieval and early modern periods, like the city-states of Ancient Greece, had not reached a level of state-formation, of stable, relatively impersonal, central control of the means of violence comparable with that which is characteristic of the modern nation-state. In order to show how that is so, let me undertake a brief figurational analysis of some crucial aspects in the development of modern rugby.

THE DEVELOPMENT OF MODERN RUGBY

Modern rugby is descended from a type of medieval folk-game in which particular matches were played by variable, formally unrestricted numbers of people, sometimes considerably in excess of 1,000. There was no equalisation of numbers between the contending sides, and the boundaries of the playing area were only loosely defined and limited by custom. Games were played both over open countryside and through the streets of towns. The rules were oral and locally specific rather than written and instituted and enforced by a central controlling body. Despite such local variation, the folk antecedents of modern rugby shared at least one common feature;

they were all play-struggles that involved the customary social toleration of a level of physical violence considerably higher than is normatively permitted in rugby and comparable games today. It must be enough in the present context to substantiate this point by reference to a single example, the Welsh game of 'knappan' as described by Owen in 1603.

According to Owen, the number who took part in knappan matches sometimes exceeded 2,000 and, just as in other folk-games such as Cornish 'hurling', some of the participants played on horseback. The horsemen, said Owen, 'have monstrouse cudgells, of iii foote and halfe longe, as bigge as the partie is well able to wild (wield)'. As one can see from the following extract, knappan was, by present standards, a pretty wild affair:

> At this playe privatt grudges are revendged, see that for every small occasion they fall by the eares, wch beinge but once kindled betweane two, all persons on both sides become parties, soe that sometymes you shall see fyve or vi hundred naked men, beatinge in a clusture together . . . and there parte most be taken everyeman with his companie, so that you shall see two brothers the one beatinge the other, the man the maister, and friende against friende, they . . . take upp stones and there with in their fistes beate their fellowes, the horsemen will intrude and ryde into the footemens troupes, the horseman choseth the greatest cudgell he can gett, and the same of oke, ashe, blackthorne or crab-tree and soe huge as it were able to strike downe an oxe or horse, he will alsoe assault anye for privatt grudge, that hath not the Knappan, or cudgell him after he hath delt the same from him, and when on blowe is geven, all falleth by the eares, eche assaulting other with the unreasonable cudgells sparinge neyther heads, face, nor anye part of the bodie, the footemen fall soe close to it, beinge once kindled with furie as they wholey forgett the playe, and fall to beatinge, till they be out of breathe, and then some number hold theire hands upp over theire heades and crye, . . . peace, peace and often times this parteth them, and to theire playe they goe a newe. Neyther may there be anye looker on at this game, but all must be actours, for soe is the custome and curtesye of the playe, for if one that cometh with a purpose onlye to see the game, . . . beinge in the middest of the troupe is made a player, by givenge him a *Bastonado* or two, if he be on a horse and by lending him halffe dozen cuffs if he be on foote, this much maye a stranger have of curtesye, although he expecte noethinge at their handes. (Owen, 1603, quoted in Dunning & Sheard, 1979, p. 28)

There is ample evidence to show that games of this type were played in various parts of Britain—and, incidentally, in a number of continental countries—from at least the fourteenth to the nineteenth centuries[8]. Moreover, the wildness so vividly depicted by Owen is amply confirmed by other accounts[9]. That is what one would expect in a type of game characterised by the following features: large, unrestricted numbers of players that were not equalised between the contending sides; loosely defined and locally specific oral rules; some participants playing on horseback while others played on foot; the use of sticks to hit other players as well as the ball; control of matches by the players themselves rather than by a referee and touch judges; and the absence of an outside, controlling organisation to establish the rules and act as a court of appeal in cases of dispute.

Not all of these features were present in all cases but most of them were. As one can see, such games were closer than modern sports to 'real' fighting. As Riesman and Denney (1971) have pointed out, modern sports are more 'abstract', more removed from 'serious' combat. The folk antecedents of modern rugby may have been mock battles in the sense that the lives and life chances of the contending groups were not directly at risk and that the infliction of serious injury and death was not their central aim. Nevertheless, their relatively high level of open violence and the opportunity they afforded for inflicting pain probably constituted one of the sources of enjoyment. After all, the people of preindustrial Britain enjoyed all sorts of pastimes—cock-fighting, bull- and bear-baiting, burning cats alive in baskets, prize-fighting, watching public executions—that appear uncivilised in terms of present values. Such pastimes reflected what Huizinga (1924) called 'the violent tenor of life' in Europe during the 'autumn' of the Middle Ages and which continued well into what historians regard as 'modern' times. They also reflected the comparatively non-advanced 'threshold of repugnance' (*Peinlichkeitsschwelle*) with regard to witnessing and engaging in violent acts, which, as Elias (1978a) has shown, is characteristic of people in a society that stands at a less advanced stage in a civilising process than our own.

By contrast with its folk antecedents, modern rugby exemplifies a game-form that is civilised in at least four senses that were lacking in the ancestral forms. It is typical in this respect of modern 'combat sports' more generally. Modern rugby is civilised by:

1. a complex set of formally instituted written rules that demand strict control over the use of physical force and which prohibit it in certain forms; for example, 'stiff-arm' tackling and 'hacking', that is, kicking an opposing player to the ground;
2. clearly defined intra-game sanctions (penalties) that can be brought to bear on offenders and, as the ultimate sanction for serious and persistent rule violation, the possibility of excluding players from the game;
3. the institutionalisation of a specific role that stands, as it were, 'outside' and 'above' the game and whose task it is to control it, that is, the role of 'referee'; and
4. a nationally centralised rule-making and rule-enforcing body, the Rugby Football Union.

This civilising development of rugby occurred as part of a continuous social process. Two significant moments in it were: (a) the institution, at Rugby School in 1845, of the first written rules. These attempted, among other things, to place restrictions on the use of hacking and other forms of physical force, and to prohibit altogether the use of 'navvies' (the iron-tipped boots that formed a socially valued part of the game at Rugby and some other public schools up until the middle of the nineteenth century); and (b) the formation in 1871 of the Rugby Football Union. The Rugby Union was formed partly as a result of a public controversy over what was perceived as the excessive violence of the game (Dunning & Sheard, 1979, pp. 113ff). One of its first acts was to place, for the first time, an absolute taboo on hacking. What happened at each of these moments was that the standards for controlling violence in the game advanced in two senses: First, it was demanded that players should henceforth exercise a stricter and more comprehensive measure of self-control over the use of physical force; and second, an attempt was made to ensure compliance with this demand by means of externally imposed sanctions. It is, perhaps, also significant that the institution of written rules at Rugby School occurred in conjunction with the achievement of greater official control over what had been, up to then, relatively violent and disorderly establishments (Dunning & Sheard, 1979, pp. 46ff). In this respect, this process replicated in miniature the process of state-formation on a societal level and thus provides further confirmation of Elias's theory concerning the relationship between the central control of violence and advancing civilisation.

To speak of rugby as having undergone a limited civilising process is not to deny the fact that, relative to most other sports, it remains a rough game. Features such as the 'ruck' provide the opportunity for kicking and 'raking' players who are lying on the ground, that is, dragging one's studded boots across their faces. The scrum offers opportunities for illegitimate violence such as punching, eye-gouging, and biting. Given the close packing of players that the scrum involves, it is difficult for the referee to control the interaction in it. Nor is the contention that rugby has undergone a limited civilising development inconsistent with the fact that it has probably grown more violent in specific respects in recent years. It has certainly grown more competitive as is shown by the introduction at all levels of cups and leagues. Up until the 1970s in conformity with a strict interpretation of the amateur ethos, even top-level Rugby Union matches were 'friendlies' and not played for points or passage into the next round. Growing competitiveness means that the importance of victory has increased and this has involved even further erosion of the old amateur ethos. It has, for example, diminished considerably the significance of the idea that taking part is more important than winning. It has probably simultaneously increased the tendency of players to play roughly within the rules and to use physical violence illegitimately in pursuit of success. In short, it seems *a priori* likely that the use of *instrumental* violence in the game has recently increased.

To say this is not to claim that, in the past, the violence of the game was entirely nonrational and affective but rather that the balance between instrumental and expressive violence has changed in favour of the former. That is because the structure of modern rugby, together with the relatively civilised personality pattern of the people who play it, means that pleasure is now derived more from the expression of skill with the ball, in evading tackles, in combining with teammates and from more or less strictly controlled and muted forms of physical force, and less from the physical intimidation and infliction of pain on opponents than used to be the case in its folk antecedents and in the public schools up to the middle of the nineteenth century where hacking and the use of navvies remained central and legitimate tactics. But the social and personality structures that have given rise to the modern game have simultaneously contributed to an increase in the incidence of instrumental violence in it. For example, players who are able to gain satisfaction from the *comparatively* mild, 'rough and tumble' forms of physical force that are permitted in the modern game and who do not find pleasure in inflicting pain on others are constrained to use violence, both legitimately and illegitimately, in an instrumental fashion. They do not gain pleasurable satisfaction from such violence per se. It is not engaged in as an end in itself but as a means for achieving a long-term goal, that of winning a league or cup. Furthermore, players who engage in such tactics as 'raking' are publicly condemned and labelled as psychopaths or 'mindless'.

The recent short-term increase in the violence of rugby football is thus explainable in terms of the theory of civilising processes. It does not constitute a refutation of it. The fact that such violence is widely condemned points in the same direction. This is not, though, to deny the possibility that we may, at the moment, be on the brink of a downswing, a 'de-civilising spurt' of greater or lesser duration in rugby and other areas of British social life. The theory of civilising processes is not a theory of necessary and irreversible progress, and such a possibility is something that must always be borne in mind. I shall return to this issue at the end of this paper. Next, it is necessary for me to look briefly at Elias's work on the development of fox hunting.

THE DEVELOPMENT OF FOX HUNTING

Fox hunting is widely considered today to be a marginal form of sport. It is also widely regarded as uncivilised and a campaign exists to ban it. However, in the eighteenth century, it was one of the first activities to which the term 'sport' became attached and, as Elias (Elias & Dunning, 1986, pp. 150-174) has shown, it emerged as an early form of sport in conjunction with what he calls a 'civilising spurt'. In earlier forms of hunting, the excitement of the hunt itself had formed 'a kind of forepleasure experienced in anticipation of the real pleasures, the pleasures of killing and eating' (Elias & Dunning, 1986, p. 161). The pleasure of killing animals, that is to say, was enhanced by its utility, and these forms of hunting imposed in their followers few restraints. They were directly in at the kill, they killed with whatever weapons they could, and, even though they may have set out with a particular quarry in mind, were liable to kill whatever edible prey they came across. Fox hunting as it was developed by the English aristocracy and gentry in the eighteenth century, however, was very different in all of these respects. Foxes were killed 'for sport' and not for any utilitarian reason. Moreover, they were killed 'by proxy', that is, by the hounds and not by the hunting 'gentlemen' themselves. And the hounds were trained specifically to follow the scent of the fox. Other animals were not hunted. How can one explain a development of this type?

According to Elias:

> The direction of the changes in the manner of hunting which one can find by comparing the English fox-hunting ritual with earlier forms of hunting shows very clearly the general direction of a civilizing spurt. Increasing restraints upon the use of physical force and particularly upon killing, and, as an expression of these restraints, a displacement of the pleasure experienced in doing violence to the pleasure experienced in seeing violence done can be observed as symptoms of a civilizing spurt in many other spheres of human activity. As has been shown, they are all connected with moves in the direction of the greater pacification of a country in connection with the growth, or with the growing effectiveness of, the monopolization of physical force by the representatives of a country's central institutions. They are connected, furthermore, with one of the most crucial aspects of a country's internal pacification and civilization— with the exclusion of the use of violence from the recurrent struggles for control of these central institutions, and with the corresponding conscience-formation. (Elias & Dunning, 1986, pp. 162-163)

In the seventeenth century, associated most obviously with the civil war, the execution of King Charles I and the so-called 'glorious revolution' of 1688, England experienced a cycle of violence. Fundamentally underlying this cycle were the struggles between Protestants and Catholics, between the monarchy and sections of the landed upper classes as the former tried to impose absolutist rule and the latter strove to resist it, and between members of the landed upper classes and rising bourgeois groups. In the eighteenth century, however, the cycle of violence gradually calmed down and political conflicts came to be conducted more in terms of a set of nonviolent rules and rituals, the rules and rituals of parliament. As Elias has shown, this 'parliamentarisation' of political conflict went hand in hand with the 'sportisation' of pastimes (Elias & Dunning, 1986, pp. 22, 34ff). That is to say, the ruling groups who devised means for conducting political struggles nonviolently also worked out means for reducing the violence of their pastimes. In both of these regards, their consciences underwent a civilising change. That, in a nutshell, is why the more civilised and restrained English fox-hunting ritual (and with it the earliest forms of cricket and a more civilised form of boxing) developed. However, parliamentarisation did not 'cause' sportisation. Both were aspects of the same overall transformation in social and personality structures.

That this initial process of sportisation should have taken place in England rather than, for example, France was evidently connected with the fact that, in England as opposed to France, parliament and the relatively autonomous 'country house network' of the landed aristocracy and gentry were of equal, even greater, importance than the court as civilising agencies. That, in its turn, reflected the fact that English monarchs failed in their efforts to introduce absolutist rule, hence enabling free associations of 'gentlemen', that is, members of the landed upper classes, to pursue, codify, and civilise their pastimes relatively independently of autocratic interference.

Let me now return to the issue of football hooliganism. On the face of it, that might seem to be an even less auspicious subject than fox hunting for the theory of civilising processes. Indeed, as I suggested earlier, such a sentiment has been voiced explicitly by Taylor. Let me now try to show how, *pace* Taylor, the theory of civilising processes represents a *very helpful* framework through which to analyse football hooliganism. In order to place this subject in wider perspective, it will be useful to begin the analysis with a brief summary of the historical study of violence in Britain generally that we have recently undertaken in Leicester (Dunning, Murphy, Newburn, and Waddington, in Gaskell & Benewick, 1987).

VIOLENCE IN TWENTIETH-CENTURY BRITAIN

Using Leicester's local paper, the *Leicester Mercury*, as our main data source, we have shown that the reported incidence of violence in Britain since the beginning of the twentieth century—our data are for the years 1900-1975—has followed a mainly downward trend. More particularly, the incidence was high before the First World War, fell between the wars, and has increased since the Second World War but still has not, by any stretch of the imagination, come to approximate the levels of the years before 1914.

Thus, as Figure 1 (page 58) shows, there has been a clear, generally downward trend in the reported incidence of political violence in twentieth-century Britain. As Figure 2 (page 59) shows, our findings regarding industrial violence are broadly similar, except that the level of reported violence in the 1920s—in fact right up to the General Strike of 1926—remained high, though not as high as had been the case before the First World War. Figure 3 (page 60), however, shows that, as in the political and industrial spheres, community violence has steadily fallen in the twentieth century. The main form of violence in that category was street fighting, which was common in British working-class districts before the First World War. As one can see from Figure 4 (page 61), according to our research, sport and leisure is the only sphere of British social life in which the reported incidence of violence has more or less steadily risen in the course of the twentieth century. In fact, Figure 4 underestimates the rise of violence in the sport and leisure sphere because it excludes football hooliganism. Had it been included, the graph would have approximated much more closely to a U-shaped curve. The rise indicated by Figure 4 corresponds to the expansion of organised sport and leisure in twentieth-century Britain.

What, in effect, seems to have happened is that, as the tradition of working-class street fighting declined—as a result, for example, of the residential relocation, growing affluence, and increasing 'incorporation' of the bulk of the working class into dominant values—so the comparatively small numbers of people who still cling to the street-fighting tradition, mainly male members of the so-called 'rougher' sections of the working class, have come increasingly to use sport and leisure, and, since the mid-1960s, especially Association football (soccer), as a context for expressing it. This invasion of a national sport by working-class fighting gangs in

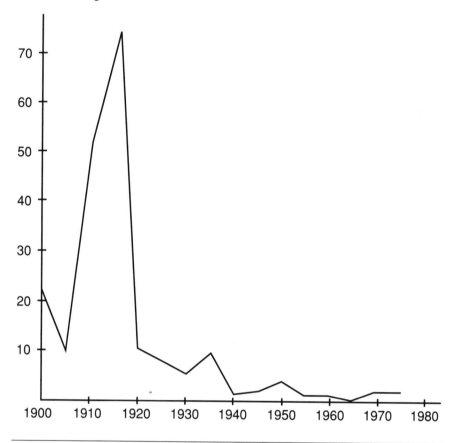

Figure 1.   Violent political disturbances in England, Wales, and Scotland as reported by the *Leicester Mercury*, 1900-1975.

a country that, up until then, had prided itself for some 30 years on having the most peace-loving sports spectators in the world, was exaggerated and amplified by media reports out of proportion to what was actually occurring, contributing to the impression of a society where law and order was on the verge of totally breaking down. However, if one takes the whole picture into account, it is clear that, for most of the twentieth century, the reported—and probably also the factual—incidence of violence in Britain has been falling and that the reported rise in and after the 1960s has been *comparatively* slight. Even the increase in hooliganism at football can be accounted for to a large extent as a kind of transfer of violence from the community sphere where the reported incidence of violence followed the general downward trend.

Let me now turn to the subject of football hooliganism and explore whether and in what degree the theory of civilising processes represents a useful framework for examining it. As I suggested previously, it will be necessary in this connection to draw on aspects of Elias's theory that I have not touched on so far.

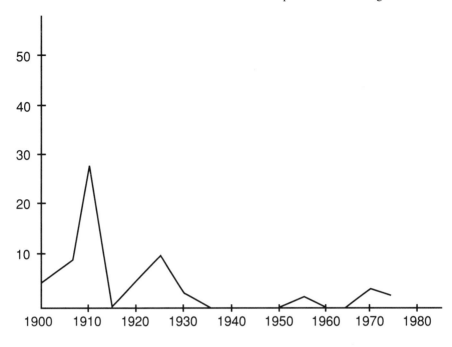

Figure 2.   Violent industrial disturbances in England, Wales, and Scotland as reported by the *Leicester Mercury*, 1900-1975.

THE SOCIOGENESIS OF FOOTBALL HOOLIGANISM IN BRITAIN

It is commonly believed that football hooliganism first became a 'social problem' in Britain in the 1960s (Taylor in Dunning, 1971). Research, however, shows that no decade in the history of the professional game—professional clubs began to emerge in the late 1870s and the Football League was formed in 1888—has gone by without the occurrence of disorderliness on a substantial scale (Dunning, Murphy, & Williams, 1988). In fact, its incidence has tended to follow a U-shaped curve, being relatively high before the First World War, falling between the wars, and remaining relatively low until the mid-1950s. Then, in the 1960s, it increased, escalating fairly rapidly from the mid-1960s onward, coming to form an almost 'normal' accompaniment of the professional game. Despite such variations in its incidence over time, a recurrent feature of football hooliganism is physical violence. This can take the form of assaults on players and referees or of clashes between rival groups of fans. It is clashes between rival fan groups, often with the police involved as well, that are the dominant form of football hooligan violence in Britain in its present phase. In fact, a significant proportion of the fans who attract the 'football hooligan' label appear to be at least as interested in fighting as they are in watching football. For them, the match is principally about expressing their machismo, either factually by inflicting defeat on the rival fans and making them run away, or

Figure 3.   Violent community disturbances in England, Wales, and Scotland as reported by the *Leicester Mercury*, 1900-1975.

symbolically via the medium of aggressive and de-masculinising songs and chants. How is one to explain that?

The currently available evidence suggests that the majority of hard-core football hooligans come from the socioeconomically lowest sections of the working class (see Table 1, page 62). What is it about membership of the lowest levels of the working class that leads to the recurrent generation of an intense 'macho' form of masculine identity, what one might call a 'violent' or 'aggressive masculine style', a form of masculine identity that is in large part determined by willingness and ability to fight and in terms of which physical confrontations form a central source of pleasure and meaning in life? How is one to explain the persistence of this form of masculinity in the face of the civilising pressures that, Elias has hypothesised, have been built into the process of state-formation in Britain and the lengthening of interdependency chains and consequent functional democratisation that have occurred correlatively with industrialisation and urbanisation?

The first thing worthy of note in this connection is the fact that, according to Elias, powerful elites standing at the hub of complex interdependency networks

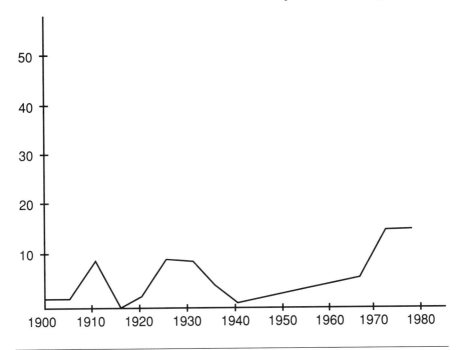

Figure 4.   Violent disturbances at sports and leisure events in Great Britain as reported by the *Leicester Mercury*, 1900-1975. (This graph does not include football crowd disorders.)

have, so far, been the main 'model makers' in the European civilising process. By contrast, members of the lower working class, to the extent that they are able to find employment, do not work in occupations that demand, to anything like the same extent, a permanent effort of foresight and a steady control of conduct[10]. They live in a world of 'dense and extensive bonds of interdependence' (Elias, 1982, p. 248) but, in that context, they have fewer power resources than other groups. Far more than groups higher up the social scale, they are relatively 'passive objects of these interdependencies', being 'affected by distant events without being easily able to influence or even perceive them' (Elias, 1982, pp. 248-249). They are not, in short, subjected to the same civilising pressures as are groups higher in the social hierarchy. Added to this, their life circumstances keep the overwhelming majority of them trapped in relative poverty, and they are more subject than other groups to the regular experience of violence in various forms. Let me elaborate on this by returning to Elias's own exposition.

According to Elias, in a society with a relatively stable monopoly of physical force, most people (not just the members of elites) are largely protected from sudden attack, from the irruption of physical violence into their lives. At the same time, they are forced to suppress their own impulses to attack others physically (Elias, 1982, p. 236). Increasingly, parents demand this suppression of aggression in their children from an early age. As a result, fear, both of one's own aggressiveness and

**Table 1   Social Class Membership of Football Hooligans
(Registrar General's Classification)**

	Numbers	Percentage
1. Professional etc.	2	0.38
2. Intermediate	13	2.50
3. Skilled nonmanual	29	5.58
Skilled manual	98	18.88
4. Partly skilled	132	25.43
5. Unskilled	245	47.20
Total	519	

Source: Dunning, Murphy, and Williams, *The Roots of Football Hooliganism*, 1988.
(reprinted with permission.)

of a punitive response to it from powerful others, becomes internalised, a deep-rooted feature of the personality. As Elias puts it:

In such a society, physical violence is confined to barracks; and from this store-house it breaks out only in extreme cases, in times of war or social upheaval, into individual life. As a monopoly of certain specialist groups it is normally excluded from the life of others; and these specialists, the whole monopoly organization of force, now stand guard only in the margin of social life as a control on individual conduct. (Elias, 1982, p. 238)

Under such conditions, social life becomes more secure, more regular, and more calculable. People learn from an early age to exercise greater rationality and foresight in steering their conduct through the complex networks of interdependency in which they find themselves enmeshed. Fear of social degradation, expressed through feelings of embarrassment or shame, comes increasingly to the fore in place of the fear of physical attack or of a sudden reversal of fortunes that is more common in a society without a stable monopoly of force. In a more civilised society, people become more sensitive, among other things, towards committing and, at a later stage, even towards witnessing violent acts. At the same time, official and many other forms of violence are pushed increasingly behind the scenes, and violent acts lead to the arousal of the anxieties and guilt-feelings that are typically deeply instilled in people in societies of this sort.

In a synthesising statement, Elias outlines a fundamental precondition for the occurrence of a civilising process. It is, he suggests:

A rise in the standard of living and security, or, in other words, increased protection from physical attack or destruction and thus from the uncontrollable fears which erupt far more powerfully and frequently in societies with less stable monopolies of force and lower division of functions. At present we are so accustomed to the existence of these more stable monopolies of force and the greater predictability of violence resulting from them, that we scarcely see their importance for the structure of our conduct and our personality. We scarcely realize how quickly what we call our 'reason', this relatively far-sighted and differentiated steering of our conduct, with its high degree of affect-control, would crumble or collapse if the anxiety-inducing tensions in and around us changed, if the fears affecting our lives suddenly became much stronger. (Elias, 1982, p. 326)

Over the past century, a dominant tendency in British society has been towards the growing affluence and increasing 'incorporation' into dominant values of more and more sections of the working class[11]. The diminishing numbers[12] who have remained relatively unincorporated, however, have had to contend with the regular irruption of specific forms of physical violence into their lives. Their economic circumstances, too, have been generally less secure. Growing affluence and increasing incorporation may have had civilising effects on the majority of working-class men and women but what is today the relatively unincorporated and relatively impoverished 'rougher' working-class minority, the social segment from which the football hooligans are principally recruited, is faced, from early in life, not only with economic insecurity but also with the regular irruption of violence from a variety of sources: when they are children, from their parents; as they grow up, from their peers in the street and at school; as adolescents, from gangs within their own and from neighbouring communities; as young adults, from prowling gangs on their nights 'down town'; and on Saturdays, from invading 'fighting crews' who support a visiting football team. And, of course, in all these settings, because they tend to deviate in public from dominant social standards, they are liable to experience violence at the hands of the police. That is to say, for them, the civil branch of society's 'monopoly of force' is not normally 'confined to barracks' to anything like the extent that is usually the case for members of the higher, more 'respectable' social strata. On the contrary, it is a regular and, as far as its specific manifestations are often concerned, in many ways an unpredictable feature of their lives.

The fact that members of the 'rougher' sections of the working class grow up in a situation of severely limited power chances (consistent with Elias's usage, I am using the term *power* here in its widest sense to include the economic aspects), that they live with a level of violence in excess of that which is usually experienced by groups higher up the social scale and that many of them experience rough treatment at the hands of the police, has manifold consequences for their personality, their social standards, and the structure of the communities that they form[13]. Their male members tend to be constrained from early on to learn how to 'handle themselves', that is, to fight. In the circumstances in which they live, a highly developed sensitivity towards the commission and witnessing of violent acts, a strict and prohibiting conscience or superego in that regard, would be liable in many contexts to be a disadvantage. They have to be ready to respond to attack with counterattack. That is, they are constrained to adjust to the fact that the public expression of violence is a regular feature of their lives. This is reflected in their personalities. Moreover, their standards and values accord prestige to males who display loyalty and bravery in physical confrontations, and their involvement in and enjoyment of fighting are reinforced by the poverty of opportunities available to them in other spheres.

That, in a nutshell, is why football hooligans fight. They develop relatively aggressive personalities, first because their involvement in the interdependency networks of modern society does not lead to pressure to exercise foresight and restraint to the same extent or in the same ways as other groups, and second because their communities receive less protection from the monopoly of violence than other groups. Indeed, because of their structurally generated deviance from dominant social standards, they regularly experience violence at the hands of the agents of the state. Moreover, for lower working-class males, fighting provides one of the few opportunities for obtaining status, meaning, and excitement. They have chosen football as one of the arenas for acting out their masculinity rituals because it, too, is an arena in which working-class masculine identities are at stake. Football also provides a context where there is relative immunity from arrest and where an 'enemy' is regularly provided, the fans of the opposing team.

Thus, even though it has not been possible for me to give a complete account here, I think I have shown that, far from constituting a refutation of the theory of civilising processes or being a form of behaviour that cannot be fruitfully explored from such a standpoint, a complete understanding of football hooliganism is only possible in its terms. Football hooliganism is indicative of the structurally generated unevenness with which the British civilising process has taken and is taking place[14]. The public reaction to football hooligan violence is understandable as the reaction of the dominant, 'respectable' majority to the behaviour of people whose standards deviate for structurally identifiable reasons from their own. They experience it as repugnant because it is indicative of the fact that the people who engage in it are, in Elias's technical sense, less civilised than they. However, the frequency with which such more civilised people demand draconian punishments in order to combat football hooliganism shows clearly the insecure foundations on which their more civilised behaviour is based and how far they have to go before they can claim to have reached a 'pinnacle' in this regard.

CONCLUSION

In a recent review of *Quest for Excitement*, Jary asserts that Elias and I merely 'illustrate' the theory of civilising processes by means of our various studies but that nowhere do we 'test' it (Jary, 1987, pp. 563ff). This is a rather strange claim to make since, prior to embarking on each of our particular researches, we did not know and could not have known that our findings would be largely confirmatory and enable us to elaborate and develop the theory in specific ways. In other words, what may look like simple illustration when written up is, in fact, the end result of what started out as a process of testing. As I suggested earlier, a major difficulty here is that critics such as Jary misconstrue the theory of civilising processes as one concerned with unilinear and irreversible progress. That is, they fail to see that, while empirically based on the observation that, by and large and with many ups and downs, civilising changes have tended to outweigh changes in the reverse direction in the societies of Western Europe since the Middle Ages, what the theory *qua* theory is fundamentally about is the relationships between state-formation, the lengthening of interdependency chains, functional democratisation, the civilisation of social standards, and the changes in personality structure that occur correlatively with all of this. In short, they confuse the theory's empirical base with the theory itself. To put it in a different way, Elias's empirical conclusion that European history since the Middle Ages has been broadly in the direction of a civilising process leads them to misconstrue the theory as a twentieth-century variant of an eighteenth- or nineteenth-century theory of lawlike progress. But it is nothing of the sort. Besides the fact that its empirical base is, itself, potentially open to testing, it stands or falls on the relationships I have specified and is equally open to the empirical possibility of 'regressive' as well as 'progressive' changes.

Having said this, it remains necessary to account for the fact that, at least in Britain over the last couple of decades, the reported and probably also the factual incidence of violence appears to have increased both in sport and elsewhere. I shall concern myself here solely with the increase of violence in sport. As far as players are concerned, I argued that the recent increase of violence in rugby football and probably in other sports as well is largely attributable to the intensification of competition and that it takes a largely instrumental form. That is to say, because it involves a large element of rational calculation, even of preplanning, it is a kind of violence that one would expect people at the present level of civilisation to engage in. Moreover, to the extent that they occur, incidents of more expressive violence are quickly and widely condemned, and their perpetrators, where it is possible to identify them, are punished. (This is not, of course, to suggest that acts of instrumental violence are necessarily less serious in their consequences or that present-day observers, commentators, and judges distinguish between violence in its different forms.) In a society civilisationally more advanced than ours, even instrumental violence might well be totally eliminated from sport or at least very considerably curtailed. However, only if present violence took a largely expressive form, that is, if it were engaged in as a pleasurable 'end in itself', would it contradict the observation that our society is civilisationally more advanced than it was in the Middle Ages. This is not to deny the fact that instrumental violence tends to produce retaliatory attacks with a strong affective component but they are motivated by a desire for revenge rather than by pleasure in violence per se. Nor is it to deny the very real dangers that increasing instrumental violence brings in its wake, though it has to be recognised in this connection that, in present-day society, institutional means for dealing with the problem are available that were lacking in the Middle Ages.

It is perhaps also necessary to add that some people find it difficult to understand that it is possible to talk about an increase in specific forms of violence occurring in a society that, by presently observable standards, stands at a relatively advanced stage in a civilising process. What they fail to appreciate is the fact that Elias's theory attempts to show how an unplanned, violent, and conflictful process led unintentionally to the establishment of a force monopoly by the state, hence increasing its capacity to use violence instrumentally in order to achieve its domestic and external aims. In other words, the theory is fundamentally posited on the observation that civilisational advances crucially depend, among other things, on an increase in the state's potential for instrumental violence. It is not a simple theory about the disappearance of violence but, on the contrary, about changes in its forms and in the ways in which it is socially stored and used.

The theory also helps one to understand why there is a tendency for the rate of violence to be perceptually magnified in a society that stands at a relatively advanced stage in a civilising process. In a society at an earlier stage, violence tends to be accepted fatalistically as an unavoidable fact of life; but in a society where the regular occurrence of serious violence has been removed from large areas of social life, even relatively minor acts of violence (which in earlier periods would probably have been dismissed as excusable 'horseplay') tend to be perceptually magnified and viewed as evidence of a serious civilisational decline.

To say this is not to deny that the world we live in remains a seriously violent place. There may have been no *world* war since 1945 but there have been more than 100 major wars in the last 40 years and it is estimated that they have led to the deaths of more than 30 million people. Most of them, of course, have occurred in Third World countries. Then there is the spectre of nuclear annihilation, to say nothing of the destructive capacity of present-day biological and so-called 'conventional' weapons. They are symptoms of the international tension and the corresponding arms race which, although at the moment we have entered a period of uneasy détente, have been escalating since the end of World War II. As such, they are a source both of insecurity and of the fact that present-day society is perceived to be more seriously violent than is, in fact, the case. The point, of course, is that no counterpart to the civilising processes that have taken place *within* the more advanced industrial societies has yet occurred internationally. Nor is there an *international* monopoly of force and, as a result, the various nation-states continue to compete with and to view each other in terms of their relative positions in a status hierarchy that is fundamentally determined by their military potential (Elias, 1987, pp. 74ff). This situation is not only fundamentally unstable but it also places a brake on the domestic civilising processes of particular countries by forcing them to keep large armies of trained killers. And when, as happens not infrequently, international tensions break out into open warfare, de-civilising effects with wide ramifications are produced.

These few clarifying remarks on the theory of civilising processes must suffice for present purposes. Let me conclude by offering, as I promised at the beginning, a few remarks on the catharsis theory of sport. One of the conclusions that the Leicester research points to in this connection is the fact that sport, like science, is socially neutral, neither intrinsically good nor intrinsically bad. On the one hand, it offers people opportunities for pleasurable and exciting competition and physical combat under controlled conditions. On the other, because it is an inherently zero-sum affair, it is inevitably a source of aggression-engendering frustration. Whether it is engaged in peacefully in a spirit of friendly rivalry or becomes seriously violent appears to depend fundamentally on the values, socialisation, and personality patterns of the participants. If they deplore serious and uncontrolled violence and have a deeply internalised taboo against openly expressing it, they will exercise self-control over their aggressive tendencies, however severe the frustration to which they are exposed in a sporting context. It is probably true to say that sport is a useful vehicle for inculcating self-control. However, it is less important in this regard than the social circumstances of the participants and the cultures in which they are brought up. Where, as with the British football hooligans, these are conducive to violence and aggression, this will be transported into the sphere of sport, whether on the playing or the spectating side. In short, our research strongly suggests that the level of violence in sport depends fundamentally on the level of violence in society at large. In a violent society, the general level of violence will be reflected in its sports. Only in a relatively pacified and civilised society will it be possible for the sports movement to achieve its highest ideals. The regular occurrence of violence in sport today, internationally as well as domestically, shows how far we still have to go before reaching that ideal level.

NOTES

1. Newborn babies are, of course, uncivilised at first and, as a result, a problem for the civilising process is posed by each new generation. This is only a different way of pointing to the centrality of learning in such processes and of reinforcing the fact that they cannot be conceived of as totally subject to necessary and lawlike determination.
2. Although it goes against current linguistic usage, there is no intrinsic reason why the concept of development should not be used to refer to 'regressive' as well as 'progressive' changes. Its basic meaning, in other words, is that a later stage is developmentally connected to a prior stage and that reference to the latter is needed in order to explain the former. That is equally the case whether one is dealing with a process of increasing or decreasing differentiation and integration, or of increasing or decreasing civilisation. It goes without saying, too, that processes of relative figurational persistence over time form part of the overall 'problematic' of figurational sociology.
3. Elias does pose the question: 'How can we explain . . . the fact that, despite all regressions, societies always regain their course, leading to greater functional differentiation, multi-level integration and the formation of larger attack-and-defence organization?' (*What Is Sociology?*, p. 155). However, he is referring here to an observable process since historical records began and not in some crude, lawlike sense to a 'necessary' and 'inevitable' process. In fact, his discussion of 'inevitability' is a complex and highly sophisticated one. See 'The Development of the Concept of Development', *What Is Sociology?*, pp. 145ff; and chapter 6, 'The Problem of the "Inevitability" of Social Development', *ibid.*, pp. 158ff.

4. The concept of interdependency chains refers to the bonds that exist between human beings linked through a system of functional differentiation. Such bonds can exist between, as well as within, societies. The concept is similar to the more usual concepts of 'division of labour' and 'role differentiation' but lacks the economistic connotations of the former and the formalistic emphasis of the latter. It is also used in a nonharmonistic sense and without a connotation of equality; that is, interdependencies tend to involve a conflictual element and they can vary along a symmetry-asymmetry continuum. Finally, the term *chains* carries a connotation of the constraining character of social bonds.

5. There is, of course, an apparent paradox here in that the same overall long-term social process involves simultaneously the centralisation and concentration of power in the hands of those who control the state apparatus and the dispersion of power via functional democratisation.

6. Professional wrestling, of course, *appears* to be very violent but it consists, for the most part, of a highly skilled mimicking of violence (see Stone in Dunning, 1971).

7. Interestingly, in the light of the arguments of Curtis and others, in his essay, 'The Genesis of Sport as a Sociological Problem' (Elias, 1986, pp. 143ff), Elias explicitly compares the Nazi 'holocaust' with the problem of 'genocide' in the Ancient World. He reaches the conclusion that, then, 'the level of ''moral'' repugnance against what we now call ''genocide'' and, more generally, the level of internalised inhibitions against physical violence, were decidedly lower, the feelings of guilt or shame associated with such inhibitions decidedly weaker than they are in the relatively developed nation-states of the twentieth century'.

8. In France, for example, they played a game called 'la Soule'. In England, variants of these folk-antecedents of modern football continue to be played today, for example, at Ashbourne, Derbyshire, every Shrove Tuesday and between the villages of Hallaton and Medbourne in Leicestershire each Easter Monday.

9. See, for example, the discussion in Dunning and Sheard (1979).

10. As one can see from Table 1, the majority of the football hooligans on whom we have data were employed at the time of the research. Although there are complex linkages between football hooliganism and unemployment, one cannot say that the latter 'causes' the former. Its 'causal role' is more indirect, operating principally by means of the way in which unemployment is one factor in the perpetuation of a 'rough' subculture.

11. See Dunning, Murphy, and Williams (1988) for an analysis of this process.

12. Current trends, especially the continuing high rates of unemployment and the increase of relative poverty, may be contributing to an increase in the size of the 'unincorporated' working class.

13. There is insufficient space here to go into all the details, but, in *The Roots of Football Hooliganism*, we use a revision of Suttles's concept of 'ordered segmentation' (Suttles, 1968) in order to explain the sociogenesis of gangs and, correlatively, of aggressive masculinity.

14. It goes without saying that reference to the British civilising process as a currently ongoing process does not imply that current changes are moving in

a 'progressive' direction. It is simply a reference to the changes that are occurring independently of the balance between 'progressive' and 'regressive' elements that is involved.

REFERENCES

Atyeo, D. (1979). *Blood and guts: Violence in sports*. New York and London: Paddington.

Bauman, Z. (1979). The phenomenon of Norbert Elias. *Sociology, 13, 1*, 117-125.

Curtis, J. (1986). 'Isn't it difficult to support some notions of 'The Civilizing Process': A response to Dunning. In Rees, C.R., & Miracle, A.W. (Eds.), *Sport and social theory* (pp. 51-65). Champaign, IL: Human Kinetics.

Dunning, E. (Ed). (1971). *The sociology of sport: A selection of readings*. London: Cass.

Dunning, E., Murphy, P., & Williams, J. (1988). *The roots of football hooliganism*. London: Routledge and Kegan Paul.

Dunning, E., & Sheard, K. (1979). *Barbarians, gentlemen and players*. Oxford: Martin Robertson.

Dunning, E., Murphy, P., Newburn, W.H.T., & Waddington, G. (1987). Violent disorders in twentieth century Britain. In Gaskell, G., & Benewick, R. (Eds.), *The crowd in contemporary Britain*. London: Sage.

Elias, N. (1939). *Über den Prozess der Zivilisation* (2 vols.). Basle: zum Falken.

Elias, N. (1974). The sciences: Towards a theory. In Whitley, R. (Ed.), *Social processes of scientific development*. London: Routledge and Kegan Paul.

Elias, N. (1978a). *The civilizing process*. Oxford: Blackwell.

Elias, N. (1978b). *What is sociology?* London: Hutchinson.

Elias, N. (1982). *State formation and civilization*. Oxford: Blackwell.

Elias, N. (1987). *Involvement and detachment*. Oxford: Blackwell.

Elias, N., & Dunning, E. (1986). *Quest for excitement: Sport and leisure in the civilizing process*. Oxford: Blackwell.

Gaskell, G., & Benewick, R. (Eds.) (1987). *The crowd in contemporary Britain*. London: Sage.

Hargreaves, J. (1986). Where's the virtue? Where's the grace? A discussion of the social production of gender relations in and through sport. *Theory, Culture and Society, 3, 1*.

Huizinga, J. (1924). *Herbst des Mittelalters*. Munich. (Translated into English in 1955 as *The Waning of the Middle Ages*.) Harmondsworth: Penguin.

Jary, D. (1987). Sport and leisure in the 'Civilizing process'. *Theory, Culture and Society, 4*, 2-3.

Leach, E. (1986). Violence. *London Review of Books, 8*, 18.

Lorenz, K. (1966). *On aggression*. London: Methuen.

Martineau, H. (1853). *The positive philosophy of Auguste Comte*. London: Chapman.

Newman, O. (1986). Review of Chris Rojek. *Capitalism and leisure theory* (London: Tavistock, 1985). *Sociology, 20*, 2.

Riesman, D., & Denney, R. (1971). Football in America. In Dunning, E. (Ed.), *The sociology of sport: A selection of readings*. London: Cass.

Rojeck, C. (1985). *Capitalizm and Leizure theory*. London: Tavistock.

Suttles, G. (1968). *The social order of the slum*. Chicago: University of Chicago Press.

Taylor, I. (1985). *Putting the boot into working class sport, British soccer after Bradford and Brussels*. Paper delivered to the Annual Conference of the North American Society for the Sociology of Sport. Boston, MA.

Williams, J., Dunning, E., & Murphy, P. (1984). *Hooligans abroad: The behaviour and control of English fans at continental matches*. London: Routledge and Kegan Paul.

Yiannakis, A., McIntyre, T., Melnick, M., & Hart, D. (1979). *Sport sociology: Contemporary themes*. Dubuque, IA: Kendall/Hunt.

The Victorian Cult of the Family and the Early Years of Female Sport

Jennifer Hargreaves

In this chapter it is argued that during the formative years of female sport—that is, from the middle of the nineteenth century to the early twentieth century—the legitimate use of the female body was redefined to symbolise a more active (yet when compared with men nevertheless still subordinate) role. This development is extremely complex and difficult to analyse because it touches on many different domains, for example, the biological, psychological, medical, moral, and military domains. Importantly, it also incorporates elements of Social Darwinism[1]. However, because of the limited space available here, I have chosen to focus on the Victorian cult of the family because it was a unifying feature of nineteenth-century bourgeois ideology and acted as a dominant constraining force on the early development of women's sport. Furthermore, Victorian familism highlights the specific nature of some of the contradictions facing the nineteenth-century sportswoman that have had repercussions for the development of women's sport until the present day.

It has been argued that the association of women with the domestic sphere and their role in the nuclear family was a modern invention dating approximately from the eighteenth century[2]. However, it became a popular idea that defined what a woman was and that directly related to her being female. The solidification, most notably of the bourgeois family, developed concomitantly with the consolidation of industrial capitalism, and by the turn of the century it was a key institution in the 'social mythology that helped to keep women relatively powerless'[3]. The underlying assumption about the family as the 'natural unit' existing in separation from the total social formation was an intrinsic part of a system of patriarchy with which many women colluded, bound up as it was with ideas about family arrangements, gender identities, sexual mores, and women's biological, psychological, and moral characteristics.

The idealised model of the respectable family centred on the man as the 'head of the household', operating mainly in the economic sphere, the provider of the material requirements of his family and its dominant authority figure. The relationship between the man and the woman was viewed as a reciprocal one in that the woman's dependent role as wife, housekeeper, and childbearer, which confined her to 'the inferior world of the family . . . left the bourgeois man "free" to accumulate capital' in order to maintain her adequately[4]. Additionally, the woman was viewed as the family member whose moral influence should be impeccable. It was from the 'saintly mother' in the home that children first learned about the sexual division of labour and associated attitudes of obedience, hard work, honesty, and loyalty. Thus the family was effectively cemented and its continuity ensured.

This model of the Victorian family may have been a reality for the affluent middle classes, but it was an impossibility for the majority of working-class families, who depended not only on the wife's wage labour to finance the home, but also, in many cases, on the labour of children as well[5]. Nevertheless, in the public image, the woman's work role was always secondary to her role within the family, which constituted the Victorian ideal of the sexual division of labour.

The assumption that this was the 'natural order of things' was underpinned by an implicit belief that the differences between men and women were biologically determined and hence immutable. Women, it was argued, were eminently suited, because of their innate physical and emotional characteristics, to staying at home and being good wives and mothers, and, by the same argument, were poorly equipped for the productive sphere. This was an integral element of the rhetoric of Social Darwinism. It incorporated the medical case for women's physical inferiority, which was employed to justify 'maternity as the "highest function" of womanhood— essential to the healthy progress of the nation'[6].

The extent to which this vision of family life was a reality is less important than the way in which it was elevated as a concept that permeated social consciousness. Its development to a form of institutionalized sexism dominated social relations, thus giving them a material base in the work and family domains and also in the educational and leisure contexts. I suggest that the early years of women's sport gave ideological legitimation to the confinement of women to their separate, private sphere of the home, and to the existing pattern of biological and social reproduction in the home. 'Behaving like a lady' meant adopting the bourgeois values associated with being female, and it appears to have been a prerequisite for the nineteenth-century sportswoman. I have characterised early forms of female sport and physical activity to show how they incorporated the ideology of the family and I shall deal first with conspicuous recreation. Such activities as croquet, early tennis, and spectating at the races were all parts of a process of consumption linked to the technological developments that revolutionized industrial methods of production. The increasing specialisation of labour created a multitude of new jobs for working-class women. At the same time, however, it narrowed the lives of middle-class women and robbed them of their economic usefulness[7]. The idleness of the bourgeois lady became symbolic of her husband's or her father's material success; her finery reflected his affluence, and the way she organised her leisure defined his social standing.

The life-styles of the middle classes, in particular, reflected the increased opportunity for acquisitiveness associated with the garden suburbs that flourished from the middle of the century onward as swelling numbers moved into detached, semi-detached, and terraced houses in the newly developed areas[8]. The insular, self-contained nature of these modern homes made the family a spatially segregated recreation unit, with the woman as its focal object who publicised the spending power of her husband or her father. Middle-class homes became more 'palatial' and gardens became part of the improved amenities of domestic life for the middle classes. By the mid-Victorian period, the bourgeois family had reached a plateau of prosperity sufficient for domestic duties to be taken care of by a growing army of servants. Even when growth and prosperity seemed to suffer a more general contraction from the mid-1870s, the Victorian bourgeoisie were able to resist any serious curtailment of expenditure and consumption and this was reflected in all forms of women's leisure. A whole 'consumer-amusement market' for the family developed[9], and the resultant conspicuous display of affluence was symbolic of the increasing economic dependence of middle-class women on men. It was, also, a reflection of the middle classes increasingly divorcing themselves from their inheritance of thrift and frugality and indulging more openly in social pleasure[10].

Lavish, extravagant clothes and accoutrements were worn to afford evidence of a life of leisure, but they restrained women from performing any but the smallest and meanest of movements. The bourgeois lady remained, even on the tennis court, the wifely ornament of beauty, a physically incapacitated player, inhibited and subdued by convention and, as Veblen put it, 'bound by the code of behaviour as tight as the stays she was compelled to wear'[11]. At competitive events such as horse racing, regattas, or cricket matches, women reinforced the superiority of men by adopting a spectator role as members of an admiring female audience watching the physical antics of men. And women were also absorbed into the leisure sphere by the provision for them of 'gentle, respectable games', eminently suited to the 'weaker sex', and exemplified by croquet and its indoor derivatives like 'Parlour Croquet', 'Carpet Croquet', or 'Table Croquet'[12].

Prints and photographs provide some of the scant evidence available that this model of the conspicuous sporting lady prevailed throughout the nineteenth century, and even beyond 1900. For example, in his *Edwardians at Play*, Brian Dobbs includes 50 engravings, prints, and photographs, many of which feature women spectators: sitting in the stands in flamboyant, wasp-waisted dresses, or walking in a leisurely and self-conscious fashion through the grounds. The one illustration of a woman participant shows her to be a most decorative lady partnering the sporting Prince of Wales at lawn tennis. She is undoubtedly wearing corsets, has a most fashionable pair of shoes, a pretty hat perched on her head, and even with a racquet in her hand looks for all the world unable to move an inch or two in any direction[13].

'Tight croquet', as it was originally called, featured all the most pronounced manifestations of bourgeois 'conspicuous recreation'.

Nobody could have called it a good game played, as it was, with only one hand in order that the womenfolk might be able to guard their complexions from the sun . . . a game of frills and fancies, of petticoats, giggles and maidenly blushes[14].

Croquet was a highly sociable and fashionable pastime and became something of a craze so that 'hardly a house with a lawn was without its croquet set'[15]. Tennis also became a mania for the affluent; it 'swept like a wind of change through the quiet countryside and brought the sexes together on the courts in a wave of exciting activity'[16]. For example, tennis parties 'were the highlight of Cambridge society in the 80s and 90s', although by this time the game had become a good deal more active for women and tennis attire was less restricted—the ladies sometimes tying their long dresses back with an apron.

*NOrMS
in
Society led to present-day*

Generally speaking, women's participatory role in conspicuous recreation embodied the characteristics of passivity rather than activity, subordination rather than ascendancy. The female croquet and tennis player represented an embellishment of men; such games had no natural, organic connection to physical action of the sort that epitomizes the essence of sport as we know it today. Women were obliged to show restraint, be refined and respectable, and confirm at all times the 'ladylike' modes of behaviour prescribed for them. In the home context, the 'playing of games' became an important, fashionable accomplishment for middle-class women, in the same category as those much admired genteel activities like playing the piano, singing, drawing and painting, reciting poetry, and doing needlework. It was a new, comparatively enjoyable way for the middle-class wife to display her talents as a 'cultured' lady of whom her husband could be truly proud, and since the daughter's chief objective was to find herself a husband[17], it gave her scope to disport herself in appealing fashion to the opposite sex, in a seemingly innocent and acceptable form. Furthermore, playing games in the family context was viewed as positively desirable, as well as respectable, because it reflected the close-knit nature of family relationships and promoted the image of family life. The range of family sports increased to include various forms of hockey, badminton, cricket, bowls, and skittles.

The schooling of middle-class girls provided an ideal preparation for all the features of 'conspicuous living' in the ambit of the family. The 'accomplishments' were given primacy in the majority of private girls' schools until 1850, and remained a feature of the curriculum, in a decreasing number of schools, for around 50 more years. Insofar as it is possible to describe the crocodile walks and calisthenics and social dance as forms of physical education, done as they were in a self-conscious manner and in the restricting and fashionable clothes of the time[18], then it is possible to observe that they invoked an attitude—a way of thinking and feeling—about what it was to be feminine, which became internalised and hence 'real'. This image of femininity can be recognised as the same one that applied to 'conspicuous recreation' in the sphere of the home and the family and so they mutually reinforced one another.

Another feature of bourgeois conspicuous living for middle-class women was the development of therapeutic forms of exercise. Middle-class women fulfilled their own stereotype of the 'delicate female' who took to her bed with consistent regularity and thus provided confirmation of the dominant medical account that this should be so. Women 'were' manifestly physically and biologically inferior because they actually 'did' swoon, 'were' unable to eat, suffered continual maladies, and consistently expressed passivity and submissiveness in various forms. The acceptance by women of their own incapacitation gave both a humane and moral weighting to the established scientific so-called 'facts'. One way to avoid constitutional degeneration—a benefit to women as well as to the nation as a whole—was by way of medically prescribed exercise, and middle-class women with affluent husbands made ideal patients who, in addition, supported the economic status of doctors. Gentle exercises, remedial gymnastics, and massage were the prescribed treatments for a whole range of female complaints and became integrated into a new 'medical-business-complex'. There was a boom in the number of clinics, health spas, and seaside holidays and a proliferation in the number and type of personnel employed. A new range of semispecialists such as dieticians, masseuses, and remedial gymnasts emerged[19], and students trained at the new specialist colleges of physical education were incorporated into this movement to service the bodies of middle-class ladies. The prescribed treatments promoted the identification of these women patients as a group who had similar delicate natures and built-in frailties. Rude health in this context was considered quite vulgar—gentle exercise on the other hand was intended to enable women to return to the ambit of their families in order to service their husbands and children and to be able to procreate successfully. Throughout the 1880s, the stereotype of the middle-class lady with her associated limitations remained intact, in one form or another, in the family setting, and she supplied the predominantly institutionalised female image of the late nineteenth century that provided a backward-looking scenario for the 'new woman' to enter.

Gradually, a qualitatively different image connected with the notion of 'positive health' evolved, but it coexisted with a body of medical opinion opposing exercise for women because it was claimed to be damaging to health—a position that was in evidence for a long time. For example, in 1837, riding was condemned because it was believed to produce an 'unnatural consolidation of the bones of the lower part of the body, ensuring a frightful impediment to future functions . . .'[20] and not so differently, in 1910-11, it was claimed that emphasis on games and athletics was likely to do irreparable damage to the adolescent girl and that hockey, specifically, could disable women from breastfeeding[21].

These positions for and against exercise for women were not really in opposition in that they were both related to women's procreative functions and were underpinned by a belief in Social Darwinism and its concern for the future of the human race and the national good by transposing the 'laws' of nature to social phenomena. Only exercise of a suitable kind, in moderation, without overindulgence or risk of strain, was considered to enhance the health of women and their potential to conceive healthy children. In other words, there was a unity of the medical and moral opinions concerning female sport and exercise. This trend can also be viewed as part of the discourse of sexual constraints embodied in Victorian familism. As Foucault says:

> There was scarcely a malady or physical disturbance to which the 19th century did not impute at least some degree of sexual aetiology and which were susceptible to pathological processes and requiring therapeutic interventions[22].

The prudishness associated with sport was also a way of censoring sex. In all forms of exercise for women, a 'proper' demeanour, decency, and modesty were required: The avoidance of overexertion, bodily display, and sensual pleasure was essential. The growing dominance of this position as the century progressed explains how the eroticism of the false contours of the flamboyant dresses worn for 'conspicuous recreation' were replaced by the blouses and skirts of the hockey era, which, though more natural and flowing, covered all possible parts of the body from sight. As activities took on a more vigorous form, the sporting attire for ladies became distinctly shapeless and 'sexless'. The blue serge box-pleated gymslip, with tights sewn into knickers, and black and brown woollen stockings and laced shoes were the attire worn increasingly by numbers of lady gymnasts and games players right into the 1920s[23]. A *Daily News* report of 1890 describes how 'Their costume consists of a dark blue tunic and knickerbockers with a red sash with falling ends tied at the side. A knot of blue ribbon ties the bodice in front, and the stockings are dark blue with red ribbons'[24]. The splashes of colour added a 'feminine' touch to the proceedings but in no way affected the strict uniformity and depersonalising nature of their clothing.

The implication that sport could detract attention from sexuality was made quite explicit in the 1912 *Handbook for Girl Guides*:

> All secret habits are evil and dangerous, lead to hysteria and lunatic asylums, and serious illness is the result. Evil practices dare not face an honest person; they lead you on to blindness, paralysis and loss of memory[25].

The precise nature of the practices was not specified but we may guess what they were because cold baths and healthy exercise were the preferred antidote to sexual desire.

An important feature of late Victorian mores was the de-emphasis of the sensuous nature of women and the predominance given to their actions, missions, qualities of character, and home life[26]. Their conscience or soul, duty or reason, were expressions of the highest part of their nature, whereas the body or appetite, or animalism— in reality the sexual instinct or desire—represented the lowest part of female nature[27].

Moral purity continued to be embraced by better-off middle-class families whose reputations rested upon the chastity of their daughters. Opposition to sports that were viewed as a threat to this convention was commonplace. Cycling for women was described as an indolent and indecent practice that could even transport girls to prostitution; it was said to be an activity far beyond a girl's strength and one that made women incapable of bearing children. Cycling, it was said, 'tends to destroy the sweet simplicity of her girlish nature; besides, how dreadful it would be if, by some accident, she were to fall into the arms of a strange man'[28].

In the context of swimming, the closeness of near-naked bodies smacked of depravity. Separate swimming was rigidly adhered to until the 1920s, and even then, in some areas, mixed participation was only possible in the guise of family bathing. There were separate entrances for men and women, and strict rules of procedure disallowed men from getting out of the water on the 'women's side' of the pool, and vice versa[29]. Even as a feature of the seaside family holiday, bathing was organised with great propriety to avoid embarrassment and to ensure absolute modesty and morality[30].

It is clear from the account so far that changes in women's sport were not abrupt or dramatic but rather a process of adjustment and accommodation, new forms of activity being formulated concomitantly with established conservative attitudes. Patriarchal ideology was the most consistent and sustaining set of values that women learnt to accommodate to, although there was no reason to suspect that the new sportswomen did not believe its basic premises anyway. In order to achieve social approval for their involvement in sport, women had to demonstrate that femininity and more active participation in physical activity were not incompatible. If the activity could be shown to have a utilitarian function, if there was no associated immodesty or impropriety, and if women remained cautious regarding other levels of exertion, then they could extend their physical horizons without threatening their existing social relationships with men—in fact, they could actually show that they positively supported their men in their ventures into sport. In all the different forms of sport, this process of accommodation can be seen and those from the most wealthy sections of society were no exception.

The following examples from pre-1900 publications concerned exclusively with women in sport had distinctly aristocratic overtones, but interestingly rested upon similar justifications to those of the sports of other social groups. I have characterised these as *elite sports* and they exemplify the moral imperatives of women's sport. An unusually diverse assortment of activities—riding, hunting, team and tandem riding, tiger shooting, deer stalking and driving, covert shooting, kangaroo hunting, cycling, and punting—were all deemed highly suitable and desirable pastimes for rich women with a potential to enrich their lives in respect, most particularly, to their essential femininity, to the state of their moral welfare, and to their general health. For example:

> Women . . . who were afraid neither of a little fatigue nor of a little exertion are the better, the truer, and the healthier and can yet remain essentially feminine in their thoughts and manners[31].

This account by Lady Grenville rests upon the implicit assumption that there are innate psychological differences between the sexes and that women 'characteristically' possess an improving nature, an ethical disposition that can 'refine the coarser ways of men . . . contribute to the disuse of bad language', and lead the way to 'habits of courtesy and kindness' in the world of sport. We read that riding tends greatly to moral and physical well-being and improves the temper, the spirits, and the appetite[32]. It is stated that hunting in the shires provides a healthy way of making a man active and training his character, while the woman's most significant contribution as she rides by his side through the countryside is 'tact, kindness . . . courtesy and politeness . . . part of our ideal lady's nature . . . which go a long way towards what is called "Keeping the country together" '[33]. It was recognized that the woman's innate potential to employ her moral influence to improve the condition of the nation was as possible in the realm of sport as in her family role. The influence of the patrician elements, especially, set the cultural tone of women's sport and complemented the restrictions imposed by Social Darwinist beliefs.

The equating of moral rectitude with physical well-being was a fundamental feature of sport in the physical education colleges for women and in the more advanced schools for middle-class girls. Like the mother to her children, the college principals and the physical education mistresses were the moral exemplars for their students and pupils. The first principal of Bedford College (founded in 1903) was described by an old student as 'a sort of moral yardstick', and one who firmly believed that 'the discipline of the school emanates from the gymnasium'[34]. This idea was an element of the ethos of the physical education profession that made an indelible mark on its future development in the twentieth century. Madam Bergman-Österberg, the first principal of Dartford College, was herself an uncompromising disciplinarian who demanded from her students the highest standards of behaviour. She was an autocrat who controlled her students' activities in every practical detail, forbidding them to visit each other's rooms, enforcing an early lights out, imposing cold baths, and refusing weekend leave except in special circumstances[35]. In this way, Madame Bergman-Österberg intended to raise the level of health, intellect, and morality of her students. Her support of female emancipation was effectively a nationalist sentiment, confirming the contemporary Social Darwinist position about the vital importance of motherhood in evolution, and encompassing a belief that the educational arrangements should be geared to the role of women as mothers[36]. Familism was, therefore, incorporated into the rhetoric, ideology, and practical arrangements of college life at Dartford, and later in the other specialist colleges. It was argued that the complete course of training was, in itself, an education for a future life as a wife and mother. 'The outdoor exercise and the training here [at Dartford]', Madame Bergman-Österberg said, would fit a girl 'to become the organiser of the perfect home, or the trainer of a vigorous and beautiful new generation'[37].

Previous medical accounts of the female constitution had directed attention to the physiological vulnerability of the woman's procreative capacity. In a way, they were now turned around by the notion that Swedish gymnastics, with its systematised attention to every part of the human anatomy, could promote healthy procreative functions. The woman's body and her ability to bear healthy children were idealised by Madame Bergman-Österberg:

> [Gymnastics] is the best training for motherhood. Remember it is not 'hips firm' or 'arms upward stretch', it is not 'drill', but it is moulding and reshaping and reforming the most beautiful and plastic material in the world, the human body itself[38].

The physical education of women gained considerable ground by widening the definition of how they could legitimately use their bodies, but although the freedom gained had some reality in relation to what went on before, it was a very limited version of being free and natural. Women's freedom to move rested upon the assumption about the different, innate characteristics and needs of men and women. 'Gymnastics', Madame Bergman-Österberg claimed, 'develop body, mind and morals simultaneously' and are a 'vital factor in making manly men and womanly women'[39].

Encapsulating the physical notion of motherhood was the belief that national efficiency inevitably depended upon a strong tradition of home life. The college, in loco parentis, reproduced the structure and ideologies of the 'perfect' Victorian home with the college principal as both father and mother figure rolled into one—the 'head of the house', the ultimate authority and the inculcator of high moral standards. 'If you want to see something of the home life of my girls, you have come at the right moment' was Madame Bergman-Österberg's greeting to a visitor[40]. 'A small college admits also of home life', she said, 'always essential to woman's happiness, and never more so than during the period of youth'[41]. The students represented the children in their relationship to the principal, and the teaching staff were also, symbolically, part of the same family—their authority over the students was analogous to the authority of an older over a younger sibling. At Dartford, the staff as well as the students were all referred to as 'Madame's girls'.

These familistic authority relations were also reproduced in the student body; the 'college mother' had a responsibility for her 'college daughter' to see that she was integrated into the family community. In a very practical and taken-for-granted way, the general living arrangements of the college household consolidated the ideas about what middle-class family life should be like—meal times especially were formal occasions, with everyone in evening dress, and the principal sitting at the 'head of the table'. A student from Anstey College said, 'At meal times, in keeping with Rhoda Anstey's idea that we were one family, the whole company sat at one vast Victorian dining table'[42]. An old student at Bedford College observed, 'The first refresher course was like a family gathering'[43]. The idealisation of the family was both a central feature of patriarchal ideology and of the version of feminism in the physical education colleges; it was an integral part of everyone's living and thinking. The theory and practice of familism in the colleges reproduced the structure and morality of the patriarchal Victorian bourgeois home and reinforced conventional sexual divisions in society.

Many of the students trained in the colleges became involved in voluntary philanthrophic activities as well as teaching, which seems to reflect a shift from their stereotypical and static wifely roles to a less insular social position that involved an increasing participation in public life. However, their widening sphere of action posed no threat to the traditional family structure—their benevolence was confirmation of a deeply moralistic attitude extending from the home into the community. The absence of any pecuniary profit established the impeccable nature of the enterprise. Feminists themselves often adopted a contradictory position: on the one hand subuscribing to a lessening of inequalities between men and women, on the other implicitly accepting the notion of innate differences that predisposed women to certain occupations—'best suited to work in the fields of Education and Pauperism'[44]. The National Association of Girls' Clubs was instituted in the 1880s, and its associate members included clubs organised by the Church of England, the Girls' Friendly Society, and Mothers' Unions. These clubs offered hockey, swimming, and gymnastics for their 'improving' qualities[45]. Youth work of this sort provided an opportunity for enlightened women to escape from the confines of domesticity without contradicting prior duty to home and family. Middle-class women were the main carriers of ideology within their family context, and their work teaching sport in clubs and elementary schools was an extension of this role where they became carriers of bourgeois ideology into the lives of the working class.

Early rationalised forms of sport were shared between sports clubs, girls schools, universities, and the colleges of physical education and began to unfold during the last third of the nineteenth century. They represented organised forms of sport and included competitive team games with codified rules and bureaucratic procedures. In all forms of rationalised sport, women had to accommodate to public hostility—the freer the activity in terms of bodily and spatial mobility, the more powerful was the opposition, always based on moral and biological criteria. In 1884, when women were first allowed at Wimbledon, it was declared that 'tournament play was all too tiring for the weaker sex'[46], but athletics was viewed more seriously as synonymous with indecency—a corrupting influence for a 'properly brought up girl'. In addition, it was considered to be a form of exercise unsuited to women's physiques that would produce an unnatural race of Amazons, thus destroying the prospect of motherhood and hence affecting the deterioration of the human race[47].

The proliferation of twentieth-century women's sports such as golf, tennis, badminton, skating, hockey, netball, lacrosse, rounders, cricket, gymnastics, swimming, and athletics only became possible because they occurred in separate spheres from the sports of men. By being insular, sportswomen did not constitute a challenge in their relationship to men. If men and women never opposed one another in open competition, the newly learned female 'aggressiveness' and 'competitiveness' could be defined as qualitatively different from men's. Although sportswomen opened a new 'social space' in which they exerted power, it was thought that the power they wielded was not always progressive. The division of social space between men and women was characteristic of the nineteenth century—part of the dominant worldview of that century. Separate male and female sport did nothing to minimise the polarisation between masculine and feminine that was manifest in the separate spheres of private (or family) life and public life.

Sport was still overwhelmingly a symbol of masculinity—the core manly virtues of courage, aggression, and the competitive 'instinct' were intimately associated with it. The cult of athleticism was in essence a cult of manliness, and so, if women joined in on equal footing, they could hardly be simultaneously projected as sexual objects by men, whose position was clear.

> Beauty of face and form is one of the chief essentials (for women) but unlimited indulgence in violent, outdoor sports, cricket, bicycling, beagling, otter-hunting, paper-chasing, and—most odious of all games for women—hockey, cannot but have an unwomanly effect on a young girl's mind, no less on her appearance. . . . Let young girls ride, skate, dance and play lawn tennis and other games in moderation, but let them leave field sports to those for whom they were intended—men[48].

Nevertheless, women's participation in the traditionally all-male competitive sports was symbolic of their competition with men, and they faced harsh ridicule about their de-sexing characteristics. It was imperative, therefore, for women games players to be in every way 'ladylike' in their behaviour both on and off the pitch. It is difficult to conceive of hockey being played by Victorian women in contemporary ladylike fashion since it is a potentially vigorous, aggressive, and dirty game—but that was what was achieved. The ball was frequently lost under the long skirts of the players, who wore hats, and usually gloves as well, and who tackled each other at all times 'gently and fairly'. In 1897 there was a complaint in a game at Frances Holland School that hockey players 'keep the ball too much under their petticoats'[49]. I suggest that even after the turn of the century, as women's games-playing skills increased with the increased freedom of movement afforded by tunics and divided skirts, they nonetheless created and reproduced traditional gender divisions. The ambivalence of, and irony in, the way women accommodated to their role in sport is unwittingly, but perfectly, encapsulated in the compliment paid to a headmistress about the behaviour of her cricket team: 'Your girls play like gentlemen, and behave like ladies'[50].

NOTES

1. For a full discussion of the formative years of female sport see J.A. Hargreaves, 'Playing Like Gentlemen While Behaving Like Ladies: The Social Significance of Physical Activity for Females in Late Nineteenth and Early Twentieth Century Britain' (unpublished M.A. dissertation, University of London Institute of Education, 1979).
2. E. Janeway, in H. Eisenstein, *Contemporary Feminist Thought* (London, 1984), p. 9.
3. Eisenstein, ibid.
4. S. Rowbotham, *Hidden from History* (London, 1973), p. 3.
5. R. Baxandall, E. Ewen, and L. Gordon, 'The Working Class Has Two Sexes', *Monthly Review*, 28 (July-August 1976).
6. C. Dyhouse, 'Social Darwinist Ideas and the Development of Women's Education in England, 1880-1920', *History of Education*, 5 (1976), 41-42.
7. V. Klein, *The Feminine Character: History of an Ideology* (London: 2nd ed., 1971), p. 14.
8. G. Best, *Mid-Victorian Britain* (London, 1971), p. 18.
9. P. Bailey, *Leisure and Class in Victorian England* (London, 1978), p. 18.
10. S. Margetson, *Leisure and Pleasure in the Nineteenth Century* (New York, 1969). The principles of duty, self-sacrifice, and discipline were no longer so emphasised with a resultant tendency for the opulent leisure patterns of the upper classes to be imitated.
11. T. Veblen, *The Theory of the Leisure Class* (London, 1934), p. 181.
12. B. Jewell, *Sports and Games: Heritage of the Past* (Tunbridge Wells, 1977), pp. 96-98. A whole range of commercialised indoor versions of games was produced including billiards, snooker, German billiards, bagatelle, versions of shove halfpenny, quoits, skittles and table skittles, and Aunt Sally.
13. B. Dobbs, *Edwardians at Play* (London, 1973), p. 8.
14. N. Wymer, *Sport in England* (London, 1949), p. 226.
15. Jewell, op. cit., p. 96.
16. Margetson, op. cit., p. 211.
17. Ibid., p. 100.

18. M.C. Borer, *Willingly to School: A History of Women's Education* (Guildford, 1976), pp. 240-243.

19. L. Duffin, 'Conspicuous Consumptive', in S. Delamont and L. Duffin (Eds.), *The Nineteenth Century Woman: Her Cultural World* (London, 1978), pp. 31-32, 41.

20. D. Walker, *Exercises for Women* (London, 2nd Ed., 1937), quoted by R.A. Smith, *American Women's Sports in the Victorian Era* (Pennsylvania State University, 1972), p. 8.

21. L. Murray, 'Womens Progress in Relation to Eugenics', *Eugenics Review II* (1910-1911), quoted in C. Dyhouse, 'Social Darwinist Ideas about the Development of Women's Education in England, 1880-1920, *History of Education*, 5 (1976).

22. M. Foucault, *The History of Sexuality* (Harmondsworth, reprinted 1981), p. 65.

23. L. Desmond, 'Gymnastics in the Roaring Twenties', *B.A.G.A. Journal* (Autumn 1973), 6.

24. Cited by A. Winter, *They Made Today: A History of the Hundred Years of the Polytechnic Sports Clubs and Societies* (London, 1979).

25. K. Middlemass, *High Society in the 1900s* (London, 1977), p. 146. From the Handbook for Girl Guides (London, 1912).

26. H.E. Roberts, 'Marriage, Redundancy or Sin', in M. Vicinus (Ed.), *Suffer and Be Still: Women in the Victorian Age* (Indiana, 1973).

27. P. Cominus, 'Innocent Femina Sensualis in Unconscious Conflict', ibid., p. 156.

28. C. Willett Cunnington, *Feminine Attitudes in the Nineteenth Century* (London, 1935), quoted in M.A. Hall, 'The Role of the Safety Bicycle in the Emancipation of Women', Proceedings of the Second World Symposium of the History of Sport and Physical Education (London, 1971), p. 245.

29. A. Rawlinson, personal interview (2 July 1979). When training for the 100-yard and 200-yard backstroke events he had to take his mother with him in order to gain entry during family bathing sessions.

30. B. Levitt Whitelaw & E. Adair Impey, *Letters of Remembrance* (1965), p. 8. Dartford College Archives.

31. Lady Grenville (Ed.), *Ladies in the Field: Sketches of Sport* (Ward and Downey, 1984), p. iv.

32. Ibid., p. 3.

33. Ibid., pp. 31, 76-77.

34. M. Squire, 'Margret Stansfield 1860-1951. Teaching a Way of Life', in E. & W. Clarke, *Nine Pioneers of Physical Education* (London, 1964).

35. Kingsfield Book of Remembrance, Dartford College Archives.

36. Madame Osterberg, 'Madame Bergman-Österberg's Physical Training College', *Educational Review, XIII* (1896), 7.

37. Ibid.

38. L.D. Swinerdon, Madame Bergman-Österberg's Physical Training College Report 1895, Dartford Archives.

39. Ibid.

40. S. Mitford, 'A Physical Culture College in Kent', *The Girl's Realm* (April 1899) 555.
41. Madame Osterberg, 'The Principal's Report, Madame Bergman-Österberg's Physical Training College Report 1898', Dartford College Archives.
42. C. Crunden, *A History of Anstey College of Physical Education 1897-1972* (Anstey College of Physical Education, 1974).
43. Quoted by I.M. Webb, 'Women's Place in Physical Education in Great Britain, 1800-1966, with special reference to teacher training' (unpublished thesis, University of Leicester, 1967).
44. J. Wedgewood, 'Female Suffrage, Considered Chiefly with Regard to Its Indirect Results', in J. Butler (Ed.), *Women's Work and Woman's Culture* (London, 1869).
45. H. Meller, *Leisure and the Changing City 1870-1914* (London, 1976), p. 177.
46. Wymer, op. cit., p. 250.
47. Winter, op. cit., p. 12.
48. Dobbs, op. cit. Quote from *Badminton* magazine (1900).
49. Borer, op. cit., p. 292.
50. J.F. Dove, 'Cultivation of the Body', in D. Beale et al., *Work and Play in Girls' Schools* (London, 1891), p. 407.

The Critique of Sport in Modernity: Theorising Power, Culture, and the Politics of the Body

Richard Gruneau

In a recent paper Pierre Bourdieu discusses links between sport, the body, and what he calls *l'esprit de corps*. The centrality of discipline, and of the 'methodological manipulation of the body', in sport forces us to consider that sport provides a means of 'obtaining from the body' (*le corps*) a form of 'consent that the mind (*l'esprit*) could refuse' (Bourdieu, 1988, p. 161). Bourdieu acknowledges that this is hardly a new insight. 'It has been known since Pascal', he notes, that to take certain positions or postures is to induce or reinforce the feelings they express. For that reason the analysis of such positions, postures, and feelings leads one inescapably to consider broader issues of power and domination. In this regard, Bourdieu recalls the 'old popular tradition' that to make people dance is to possess them. Totalitarian regimes provide the most graphic example of this tendency, promoting collective corporeal practices that 'help to somatize the social by symbolizing it, and aim at reinforcing social orchestration through its bodily and collective mimesis' (p. 161).

But totalitarian regimes are only the most extreme case. Bourdieu's perspective requires us to consider the link between bodily disciplines, beliefs, rituals, and power in every society. Even in contemporary liberal democracies this link is fundamental to the processes wherein the past is reconstructed and social memory is pressed into the service of social reproduction. Arguing along similar lines, Paul Connerton (1989) has suggested that if there is such a thing as 'social memory', the obvious place to look for it is in commemorative ceremonies such as the opening and closing rituals of sporting events, flag-raisings, ceremonial dinners, and so forth. But when we observe such ceremonies we notice that 'commemorative ceremonies prove to be commemorative only in so far as they are performative: performativity cannot be thought without a concept of habit; and habit cannot be thought without a notion of bodily automatisms' (Connerton, 1989, pp. 4-5).

Of course, the precise relations between bodily disciplines and habits, ceremonies, and power and their numerous manifestations in both pleasurable social forms and oppressive forms vary between societies. Such variations are found within societies as well. Bodily disciplines, habits, and ceremonies both constitute and express the relative powers of classes, regions, racial and ethnic groups, and genders. They also constitute and express differences in power between organizational client groups and their supervisory or administrative superiors. However, there are important differences between organizations that rely primarily upon ceremonial rituals as agencies of social memory and reproduction and those whose routine practices centre on bodily discipline more directly. Direct corporal discipline is most obviously central in those organizations that Erving Goffman (1961) refers to as 'total institutions'—the prison, the convent, or the asylum. But we can also find a deep concern for bodily discipline in fitness studios; school, community, and professional sport teams; and state-supported sport systems.

I do not want to imply that sport organizations are necessarily similar to total institutions the way Goffman means them. But Bourdieu's comments prompt me to consider how closely the analogy might hold in certain instances and how best to theorize it. I wonder too about the extent to which sporting practices actually do 'somatize' the dominant cultural elements of our age in various kinds of bodily and collective mimesis of social orchestration, to use Bourdieu's metaphor. But is orchestration even the right metaphor? Should one talk instead about mimesis of social struggles? Do Bourdieu's suggestions allow sufficiently for contradiction or tension, for example, between unconscious forces of embodiment on the one hand and oppositional consciousness on the other?

I discuss these questions at various places throughout this chapter, although they are not my primary focus. Rather, I raise them as a useful point of entry to a broader consideration of theories of power, culture, and the politics of the body as part of the critique of modern sport. I begin by considering how sport in the late nineteenth century became part of a modernist cultural project that promoted civilizing amateurism and the 'healthy' body as positive social forces. Next I consider some early- and mid-twentieth century challenges to these claims—challenges that took issue with the legacy of modernist 'rationality' in Western sport and its accompanying influences on bodily practices. Finally, I assess more recent critical perspectives on modern sport, with particular emphasis on differing ways to theorize power, culture, and the politics of the body. In these final sections I address Gramscian and Foucauldian perspectives on sport and the body before returning to consider issues raised by Bourdieu.

SPORT AND
THE MEANINGS AND PROBLEMS OF MODERNITY

Thorstein Veblen's (1899/1953) turn-of-the century indictment of sport as a lingering manifestation of the human predatory temperament was an assault on the vitalistic impulses long celebrated within the ruling classes of Western societies. John Hoberman (1984) has also noted how these impulses, and the cult of romantic physicality that accompanied them, had a deeply reactionary side that was readily appropriated by Fascist political movements in the 1920s and '30s. Yet throughout Europe and North America in the nineteenth and early twentieth centuries, the conservative intellectual tradition that emerged among the bourgeois classes and their allies was usually far more hostile to sport than supportive. Sport was widely viewed as valueless diversionary spectacle closely connected to idleness, gambling, drink, and violence—at best crude folk culture, at worst a manifestation of cultural decline and barbarism (Brantlinger, 1983). The growing popularity of sport as mass entertainment seemed to lend support to this view by conjuring up the dark spectre of the Roman Coliseum. Just as in Rome, it was said, the public taste for spectacle was a harbinger of the end of civilization.

Patrick Brantlinger (1983) refers to this view as an example of 'negative classicism'—'the idea that the present is a recreation or repetition of the past in a disastrous way: the modern world is said to have entered a stage of its history like that of the decline and fall of the Roman Empire' (p. 17). Negative classicism implies a critique of the emergence of the modern condition by juxtaposing it against a romanticized past. According to Brantlinger, negative classicism is a discourse loosely connected with the broader critique of the Enlightenment-inspired belief in human reason, the values underpinning both liberal and socialist political philosophies, and accompanying struggles for democracy, freedom, equality, and universal education.

However, negative classicism in the nineteenth century was rivalled by other, more powerful discourses. The expansion of capitalism and liberal democracy was predicated on a belief in progress and a defence of the power and value of unfettered human reason. These beliefs were incorporated into the conception of modernity itself. Self-consciously modern societies could distinguish themselves from the traditional societies they were replacing by applying human reason to the 'problems' of personal and social development. The social world could be remade and the level of civilization upgraded through dispassionate science, new technologies, the rational exercise of legal regulation, and new principles of social and cultural education and reform based on the ideals of equality and self-improvement.

It has been argued (e.g., Guttmann, 1978; Adelman, 1986) that the 'modernization' of sport was closely tied to these tendencies and discourses. Guttmann even goes so far as to identify the emergence of the scientific worldview as the primary causal variable in the social development of modern sport. The more popular position is to locate this development more directly in the technological and cultural forces characteristic of the development of urban industrial societies. There is great merit to these arguments, although, as I have noted elsewhere, they tend to lack sensitivity to their own philosophical and ideological underpinnings and leave far too much out of account (Gruneau, 1988a).

Among the more notable limitations of these theories is the tendency to see the modernization of sport as an abstract evolutionary process rather than a more open-ended set of limits, pressures, and struggles. Ironically, one of the things most neglected in such theories is the constitutive role that the idea of modernity itself plays in negotiating these limits, pressures, and struggles. The work of Elias and Dunning and of others committed to the application of Elias's figurational sociology stands as an exception to this tendency (e.g., Dunning, 1972; Dunning & Sheard, 1979; Elias & Dunning, 1986). Critics of Elias and Dunning (e.g., Giddens, 1984; Lasch, 1985; Horne & Jary, 1987) argue that figurational sociology tends to treat the 'civilizing process' in a functionalist and evolutionary way. Nonetheless, the figurational approach goes much further than other modernization perspectives in viewing the emergence of new forms of regulation and control as a complex series of responses to the perceived condition of modernity, including its apparent problems and changing relations of power. One additional virtue of Elias's (1939/1978) work is the attention given to the control over the appearance, treatment, and functioning of the body and of the problems created by 'uncontrolled' bodies as key features of the development of self-consciously modern societies.

However, one thing that figurational sociology deals with inadequately is the specific set of limits, pressures, and forms of control associated with the advent of capitalism, either as a distinct social formation or as an element in emerging perceptions of the meaning of the modern condition. When capitalism is taken into account, one is immediately forced to consider other versions of the meaning, promise, and central tendencies of modernity. For example, Berman (1983) argues that the emergence of the idea of modernity was tied closely to a Promethean vision of human possibilities based on the necessity for constant growth and continual revolutionizing of production. Marx and Engels recognized this as a fundamental dynamic of the emerging culture and forms of social organization of capitalist societies and noted it in *The Communist Manifesto*:

> Constant revolutionizing of production, uninterrupted disturbance of all social relations, everlasting uncertainty and agitation distinguish the bourgeois epoch from all earlier times. All fixed-fast frozen relationships, with their train of venerable ideas and opinions are swept away, all new-formed ones become obsolete before they can ossify (cited in Berman, 1983, p. 95).

Marx and Engels go on to the memorable statement that 'all that is solid melts into air'—a statement that Berman takes as the fundamental defining condition of modernity. To be modern suddenly meant living in a dynamic world of capitalist social relations where all that is solid melts into air.

The impulse to rational organization in such circumstances was surely tied to the desire to control contingencies. The expansion of free markets and the constitution of the modern liberal state required constant revolutionizing of production on the one hand and a continual push to regulate and control uncertainty on the other. But such attempts at control through regulation or reform were always threatened by being obsolete before they could 'ossify', reaffirming an even greater sense of uncertainty and agitation. The social development of 'modern' sport, with its preferred bodily practices, was necessarily caught up in these multiple pressures and influences.

In this context it hardly seems surprising that regulative and reform impulses initially dominated the making of self-consciously modern forms of sporting practice. For middle-class reformers, the creation of a new, higher, seemingly more civilized form of sporting practice than that of traditional folk games and sports required the rational organization of spectacle, human physical contests, and masculine physicality. But this could only win legitimacy as a cultural project if it could be harmonized with new class needs for labour discipline, education, and the control of public order.

The challenge to those who wanted to make sport into something new in the nineteenth century, something modern, can thus be summarized as a series of daunting questions and problems: How could traditional folk games and sports be remade and given both moral and economic utility as orderly, healthy, and socially improving practices? How could sport be organized to make a claim to 'culture' versus barbarism? If people wanted sporting spectacle, was it not better to give it to them in a nonthreatening, socially positive way, controlling contingencies, than to allow sport to develop completely unregulated? The pursuit of answers to these questions was never undertaken as any kind of coherent master cultural strategy. Rather, it unfolded in an uneven and fragmented way, mediated by subtle shifts in class- and gender-based cultural preferences and perceived needs.

POSITIVE CLASSICISM AND OTHER LEGITIMATING DISCOURSES IN THE MAKING OF MODERN SPORT

Gradually, the initial scattered responses to the problems and questions I've noted became integrated into a more totalizing vision of 'modern' sport—a vision that gained great international legitimacy. Consider Pierre de Coubertin's efforts to 'revive' the Olympic Games at the end of the nineteenth century. Bruce Kidd (1984) has reminded us to view this attempted revival with caution. De Coubertin's proposal for a modern Olympic Games was never simply an attempt to recover the past. Rather, he intended to advance a new vision of sport and the healthy body as a means to solve some of the apparent problems of modernity. Numerous commentators (Weber, 1971; MacAloon, 1981; Hoberman, 1984, 1986) have pointed out how de Coubertin's perception of these problems was highly idiosyncratic, steeped in French nationalism and obsessed with maintaining conditions of social and psychological 'equilibrium'. Nonetheless, out of a complex mixture of motives and impulses, de Coubertin sought to define the shape of sport as a modern social enterprise.

De Coubertin's concerns about social and psychological equilibrium attracted him to the discourses of manly discipline and social improvement characteristic of the British tradition of Victorian athleticism. The rhetoric of 'muscular Christianity' suggested that sport could play a socially integrating and culturally positive role in a frenzied modern world (Mangan, 1981; Hargreaves, 1987). But to do so, sport's association with uncontrolled spectacle and vice had to be eliminated in favour of a view of sport as 'higher' culture. Draping the Olympics in positive symbols from the past proved a convenient way to differentiate modern socially improving sport from other popular physical recreations. In this version of positive classicism the most important signifiers of socially improving sport had to be Greek, not Roman. Modern sport, at least in its ideal form, was to be constituted as the legacy of Pericles rather than Nero, of Olympia rather than the Roman Coliseum.

The fusion of the imagery of positive classicism with the Victorian conception of gentlemanly 'amateurism' lent a transhistorical aura to a set of historically and culturally specific practices. The appeal to positive classicism was the foundation from which the proponents of amateurism and Olympic sport could make their claims to (high) culture. Amateur sport, the argument ran, could provide a new world forum for a culture of modernity that reconciled robust 'manly' physicality with respectability and restraint; passion with discipline and order; individualism with social solidarity. The Olympic project, in particular, was a testament to the view that human reason, in combination with the energy generated from healthy bodies, could recreate a higher form of cultural expression in a world where the pace of social development seemed to be sweeping away the solidarities of the past.

The ideas of rationality, discipline, health, bodily prowess, and masculine loyalty were fundamental to this allegedly higher cultural expression. The institutional groundwork was provided by the necessary rationalization of sporting structures: the creation of written technical and moral rules and of bureaucratic organizations (Gruneau, 1983). But the dominant cultural features of this self-consciously 'modern' form of sporting practice centred on two distinct concepts of discipline: the notion of self-discipline through the exercise of a person's supposedly higher faculties of reason and the disciplinary bodily mastery achieved through technique. Disciplinary mastery in game contests is clearly an old idea, but in the amateur code, these two conceptions of discipline were synthesized into a new cultural form. They coalesced around the growing cultural obsession with cleanliness, health, and social improvement in nineteenth-century middle-class life. They also tended to be defined within an abstract social contract model of personal and social development, a model that blended the ideas of discipline and health with the masculine ideals of mateship and team loyalty. In this model the pathway to individual advancement, honour, and pleasure in sport was seen to lie with voluntary submission to higher rules of authority. Submission to 'the rule' tied the ideal of individual cultural and physical development to the social necessity for orderly conduct and regulation (Gruneau, 1983).

The objective in all this was not just the pursuit of better sporting performances, it was to participate in a certain kind of culture and live life in a certain way. In this way of life, the classical Greek notion that nothing should be done in excess corresponded almost perfectly with the cultural impulses of men in the 'improving' classes in Europe and North America. The exercise of reason meant aspiring to a sense of both stature and proportion. By the end of the nineteenth century, amateur sport had become a key organizational and cultural expression of this aspiration. The 'perfectly' proportioned bodies of Greek male athletes, revealed in the paintings and sculptures being recovered from classical antiquity at the end of the nineteenth century, became the idealized bodily aesthetic (Kidd, 1984).

There is an obvious sense in which the new forms of modern sport were designed to teach young 'gentlemen' a way of competing and of carrying themselves that provided clear ideal definitions of how a male body should look and work. Sport became one of the most important means to promote a conception of masculinity that emphasized the demonstration of controlled force and competence rather than more disruptive and dangerous forms of physicality. Nonetheless, sport still tended to dramatize and embody the prevailing logic of social hierarchy. The definitions of men as holders of power and responsibility and women as dependents or subordinates were literally embedded, as Connell (1983) notes, in the very texture and feel of the male body, its attitudes, muscular tensions, and surfaces (cf. Hargreaves, 1987). At the same time, the intense concerns for healthy male bodies tapped into a wellspring of late nineteenth-century ethnic and racial insecurity. Indolence, poor health, and bad diets among privileged white European and North American males were matters of concern in the face of threats posed by restless colonial subjects, immigrants, and anarchist or socialist 'subversives' (Lears, 1989; Park, 1989).

The emerging emphasis on carriage and bodily competence was also understood in more directly socioeconomic terms. It corresponded with the parallel sense of having stature—that is, prestige and influence—in the community. Such stature might be expected of young men of privilege in any case, but sport came to be viewed as a primary forum for its rehearsal. For young men from underclass families, amateur sport also intimated that such stature could be earned (or, more correctly, learned). Class division was therefore supposedly dissolved on the playing field in favour of a meritocracy of ability materialized in the new sporting structures, beliefs, and bodily practices.

However, the modernist cultural project of socially improving sport was always contradictory, highly contested, and compromised. There were deep tensions, for example, between the pursuit of disciplinary mastery on the one hand and a sense of balance and proportion on the other; between the ideals of controlled masculine competence and competence demonstrated through physical intimidation; between a professed internationalism and the fuelling of nationalist and colonial rivalries; between the alleged purity of amateurism and the economic necessities of holding major competitions. We also know that the cultural and organizational successes of modern amateur sport occurred only by pushing more traditional and alternative forms of folk games, sports, and bodily practices to the cultural periphery.

On this last point, considerable literature documents the struggle to define the female body, or to specify 'legitimate' female physicality in sport in ways that excluded women (e.g., Lenskyj, 1986; Mangan & Park, 1987; Hargreaves, 1991). Similarly, many of the commercial gaming practices and related popular sporting activities of underclass groups were under continual siege throughout the nineteenth and early twentieth centuries (Bailey, 1978; Cunningham, 1980; Hall, 1981). In addition, the growing cult of health and the popularity of an athleticized model of physical perfectability greatly narrowed the social definition of ideal or desirable male physiques and bodily practices (Hargreaves, 1987; Lears, 1989).

I will say more about the role of 'early' modern sport in narrowing the definition of desirable bodies shortly. But first a word about the importance of the frequent tensions between economic entrepreneurship and what might be called *moral entrepreneurship* in the development of modern sporting practice. A lot of evidence suggests that the stubbornly commercial nature of so much of the 'popular cultures' of Western societies consistently offered entertainment-oriented alternatives to the cultural project of socially improving sport (e.g., Cunningham, 1980). For example, when conducting my own research into sport and social development in Canada several years ago (Gruneau, 1983), I was struck by the way in which commercial sport—often anchored in older folk or community cultural practices—flourished alongside the development of amateur sporting organizations in the late nineteenth and twentieth centuries. I was also struck by the depth of tension in Canadian sport between the desire for control through regulation and moral education on the one hand and the ideological commitment to a dynamic form of capitalist entrepreneurship on the other. Moral entrepreneurship in and through sport had to be reconciled continually with the de facto existence of a capitalist marketplace threatening to commodify sport at every turn.

In this context, many amateur organizations were pushed into an uneasy accommodation with more commercially oriented and spectacle-driven sporting practices and disciplines. And in a remarkable cultural appropriation, many promoters of openly commercial sports borrowed the rhetoric of self-improvement and classicist bodily imagery of the amateurs as a way of selling their games. The rhetoric and imagery were useful in securing the orderly audiences and respectability necessary to win public support for commercial sport as an everyday part of family life and entertainment in a growing consumer society. In an effort to shed the negative image of spectacle—the spectre of the Coliseum—promoters insisted that their games differed from amateur sport only with respect to the superior skills of 'professionals'. Whether professional or amateur, the argument ran, modern sport had virtue on its own terms.

Jackson Lears (1989) notes how, in the United States, this idea quickly entered the emerging iconography of early twentieth-century advertising and further marginalized older popular conceptions of sport and the body. Youthful male exuberance, health, and bodily competence were celebrated through advertising codes that equated athleticized body imagery with happiness and success in a market-driven society. These portrayals correlated with a growing popular revulsion toward body odour, stained teeth, halitosis, and other alleged manifestations of ill health. Such views were popularized partly through discourses created by affluent white male advertising executives, whose cultural preferences they dramatized. Early twentieth-century marketers did not necessarily adopt the ideals of amateurism as the defining characteristics of modern sport, but they quickly picked up on the emerging cult of health and bodily perfectability.

The growing celebration of athleticism in American advertising reinforced emergent forms of social distinction. Lears (1989) notes how an emerging American consumer culture based on mass marketing reinforced a growing concern with the need to 'fit in'. The articulation of rigid athleticized codes for bodily propriety and perfection not only made the prospect of belonging more likely for some Americans than others, it also fed a widespread uneasiness about certain natural body features. This uneasiness helped create greater markets for a legion of health, beauty, fitness, and self-improvement products. A good deal of early-twentieth-century marketing promised popularity and success—but only if one mediated the natural body with the right consumer choices. The alternative was the threat of rejection and marginalization.

However, these pressures towards bodily 'normalization' did not develop without resistance. The dominant structures and culture of modern socially improving sport were never able fully to extinguish opposition and alternatives. Indeed, in many instances—as my research on the Canadian case suggests—it became necessary to compromise the more puritanical edges of the totalizing vision to win consent among those groups whose commitment to amateur sport did not extend to imbibing the morality, the preferred cultural vision, or the classicist male bodily aesthetic. These groups brought a sense of cultural form and legitimate practice from other places in the social formation—places represented by other classes, by women, and by differing regions and ethnic groups—and adapted these to the preferred meanings, structures, and disciplines of the culture of moral entrepreneurship.

In other words, the emergence of 'socially improving' amateur sport as the initial dominant structuring element in the making of modern sport was made possible only by compromise. Nonetheless, in its compromised and negotiated form, the ideology of modern amateur sport proved remarkably successful. The Olympic movement illustrates this graphically. By the 1930s the movement had managed to elevate a Eurocentric, class-biased, gender-biased culture of modern socially improving sport to a level where it was widely regarded as a valued framework for the pursuit of international understanding and social improvement worldwide.

SPORT, THE RATIONALIZED BODY, AND THE CRITIQUE OF MODERNITY

Despite such obvious 'success', the claim that sport could be a positive force in modernity was subjected to growing criticism by the early years of the twentieth century. Longstanding conservative arguments about sport as little more than 'bread and circuses'—despite any pretensions to the contrary—never died out and were often taken up in modified form by radicals of all types. Socialist intellectuals, in particular, were quick to view modern 'bourgeois' sport as a waste of time that embodied capitalist values and distracted workers from politics (Hoberman, 1984).

These criticisms gained momentum in the wake of the 1936 Olympics in Berlin and the cold war climate following World War II. But one line of critique is of particular interest because of its immense impact on comparatively recent analyses of sporting practices and bodily disciplines. In Germany, a small group of self-consciously Marxist writers developed a new theory of society that polemicized against the seemingly inexorable forces of rationalization sweeping through the modern world. Most notably, Theodor Adorno, Max Horkheimer, and Herbert Marcuse all argued that the Enlightenment promise of reason and freedom, a hallmark of modernity, had been transformed into unreason and domination in modern mass societies, whether capitalist or socialist. By contrast, the social analysis of contemporary times demanded recognition of what Adorno and Horkheimer (1944/1977) called the 'dialectic of enlightenment'.

Many references to sport are scattered throughout the work of these influential writers. However, most people in sport studies are far more familiar with the elaboration and extension of their ideas made in the critical writings on sport that emerged during the late 1960s and early 1970s. I think Alan Ingham's (1975, 1978) groundbreaking critique of the 'rationalization' of sport, which synthesizes ideas from Marcuse and Max Weber, is notable in this regard for its intelligence and scholarly rigour. But throughout the 1970s, arguments drawn from German 'critical theory' (although sometimes in caricature ways) became staple weapons in the arsenal of nearly every self-professed 'radical' Western sport critic. Among these critics, Bero Rigauer (1969/1981) and Gerhard Vinnai (1970/1973) in Germany and

Jean Marie Brohm (1976/1978) in France emphasized the subordination of the human body to the logic of efficiency characteristic of the capitalist labour process and of socialist bureaucratic management. Sport was seen as both a symbolic representation and the physical embodiment of capitalism's insatiable demands for 'performance' in the service of profit and the technocratic ideology of science and the machine.

The 'countercultural' criticisms posed by such writers as Brohm, Vinnai, and Rigauer now seem old hat, and they have been so widely criticized that one might wonder why I even mention them. My reason is that many of the concerns voiced by these critics have become more pressing than ever and continue to surface in other guises and intellectual traditions. Most notably, the emphasis of these critics on consumer culture, the politics of spectacle, and the politics of the body anticipates in fragmentary ways arguments that have recently come back into intellectual fashion in current criticisms of the ideologies of modernism and in debates about the existence of a 'postmodern' condition (Conner, 1989; Harvey, 1989).

Let me risk a digression here to elaborate on the antimodernist slant of the countercultural sport criticism I have noted. The critical theory of Adorno, Horkheimer, Marcuse, and their colleagues in the so-called Frankfurt School of German Marxism was a hybrid of diverse philosophical and theoretical influences. But despite this melange of influences, the Frankfurt School theorists always saw themselves as extending Marx's critical legacy (Held, 1980). Despite their recognition of the 'dialectic' of Enlightenment, their rejection of Stalinism, and their pessimism about the forces of contemporary pacification and oppression, they remained largely committed to an Enlightenment vision of universal emancipation. Only reason itself could interrogate the irrationality of 'unreason' in modern mass societies.

But these writers did not see reason as Marx did—something that could be concretized in the historical ascendency of the proletariat. They argued that the classical Marxian vision of class struggle resulting in the triumph of socialism had been preempted by the power of the modern culture industry to create mindless diversion and false consciousness. Modern times required a new critical theory of society as a foundation for human emancipation. Adorno, in particular, also suggested the possibility that modern culture might yet maintain a basis for a radical emancipatory aesthetic. The 'negative' power of 'autonomous art'—for example, certain modernist artistic genres such as surrealism or the atonal music of Schoenberg—kept the promise of liberation alive (Adorno, 1938/1980, 1975; Held, 1980).

Most self-professed radical critics of sport in the late 1960s and early '70s essentially adopted the critique of false consciousness and pacification from the mainstream of German critical theory, and accepted the related idea that classical Marxism required updating and revising. For one thing, Marxian categories simply could not readily be stretched to accommodate all of the objects of modern oppression. Sexual oppression, technocratic rationality, bureaucratic domination, scientism, and their manifestations in the seemingly expansive practices of bodily discipline so fundamental to the modern high-performance sporting experience could only be seen within Marxism as expressions of alienation. The problem was that modern sport seemed to involve aspects of domination that existed independently of capital and class.

Marcuse's enthusiasm for Freud was quickly taken up as one possible way to solve these problems (Hoch, 1972; Vinnai, 1970/1973). By contrast, there was very little support among radical sport critics for the inherent elitism of Adorno's views on the emancipatory potential of a modernist avant-garde. The dominant preference was to shift the emphasis to other potential sources of liberation sometimes noted in German critical theory, again, especially in Marcuse's (1955/1962) work. The later radical criticism of sport was drawn to ideas central to the broader wave of countercultural criticism breaking across Western societies. Primary among these ideas was the notion that play, or the erotic, was the only real basis for a truly emancipatory aesthetic.

All of this contained residues of the Enlightenment promise of the possibility of universal emancipation, but it also featured a retreat from the values of reason and of the possibilities of modernity that, in my view, went much further than that demonstrated in the mainstream of German critical theory. Communist, trade union, and party politics were all seen to be outmoded, but there was considerable confusion about goals and strategies for effective political opposition. Part of the problem was that most 'countercultural' critics of the time inevitably found themselves in a theoretical and political halfway house. The source of their anger was never really capitalism, or even the authoritarian technocratic establishment—it was modernity itself.

We can discern this tension between the critiques of capitalism and of modernity in the many contradictory tendencies in radical critiques of sport published during the late 1960s and early '70s. Traditional Marxist language was mixed with an ironically anti-Marxist nostalgia for a utopian individual autonomy; the critique of bureaucratic rationality was expressed in ways that appeared to reject any form of complex social organization altogether; and self-righteous statements of principle typically appeared side by side with an unconsciously Nietzschean vision of the all-enveloping character of power in modern life. The fact that sport in Communist countries had developed to become even more rationalized and oppressive than in capitalist ones merely suggested the hopelessness of any Enlightenment-inspired faith in the power of human reason for social emancipation. The implicit conclusion was inevitable: Modern sport, like modern societies themselves, was inherently totalitarian.

This conclusion always struck me as silly, even though I had sympathy for many of the criticisms raised. Under various guises of educative and civilizing cultural practice, forum for international understanding, or socially valued commercial or noncommercial entertainment, the dominant forms of modern sport had indeed come to embody a new totalizing vision of bureaucratic organization and instrumental rationality. But was this necessarily totalitarian in any political sense? Did it invade the consciousness and bodies of individuals so totally that sport participants and fans ceased to act as agents, only as mindless carriers of the dehumanizing manifestations of reason gone mad?

I think not. It was possible to believe the arguments of countercultural critics only if one accepted that the millions of people who so passionately craved sports either as fans or athletes had been completely duped by the capitalist culture industry or by socialist technocrats. There was simply no way to explore the popularity or the positive possibilities of modern sports from this perspective, only their socially produced limits. And there was no way to argue that, even in its most commodified and administered form, sport might prove to be a contested area of social life or that certain practices in sport might take on an oppositional or emancipatory character for certain groups in certain times.

Countercultural sport critics may have intuitively grasped the dialectic of Enlightenment suggested earlier by Adorno and Horkheimer, but they forgot about dialectics and contradiction in social life and culture as lived in contemporary societies. Instead, they tended to see oppression everywhere—an oppression 'totalized' in the relentless processes of rationalization and instrumentalization literally embodied in the ceremonies, disciplines, and bodily practices of modern sport. This view was popularized through a series of powerful stereotypes: the coach as fascist, the athlete as one-dimensional automaton, the fan as narcotized seeker of diversion. The inevitable result of this decidedly nondialectical view was a slide into cynicism and despair. The tacit critique of modern rationalized sport was linked to a self-consciously antimodernist solution, the return to simple play. Only through such a return could the mechanized and alienated sporting body become liberated and the cycle of ideological indoctrination and social reproduction through sport be broken.

SPORT CRITICISM AND THE TURN TO GRAMSCI

Through the 1970s and '80s much of the critical work on sport in Western societies struggled to free itself from radical pessimism and the romantic antimodernism implicit in the initial wave of countercultural sport criticism. Important in this struggle was restoration of the sense of contradiction and conflict that had always been a hallmark of the Marxian tradition. Also necessary was recovery of Marx's faith in the possibility of human reason's moving analysis beyond despair—the part of Marxism that, in Raymond Williams's words, has always promised to 'make hope practical rather than despair convincing' (cited in Corrigan, 1988, p. 44).

To achieve these ends it was necessary to develop a more adequate understanding of human agency, to reject a totalizing conception of power as constraint and of ideology as a kind of all-enveloping—and literally embodied—false consciousness. In part, that meant coming to terms with the limitations of German 'critical theory', but it did not allow a simple return to classical Marxism. It seemed especially necessary to break from Marxism's logocentric vision of the inevitability of capitalist collapse and its representation of the interests of the proletariat as automatically equivalent to overall human emancipation. What seemed required was a new critical theory of power, social practice, and cultural struggle.

There was a great deal of groping about for such a theory throughout the late 1970s, and many sources of inspiration. My own groping (Gruneau, 1983) was rooted in an early attraction to C. Wright Mills's sociology (e.g., Mills, 1959/1970). But I soon became heavily influenced by the theory of 'structuration' championed by Anthony Giddens (1976, 1977, 1981) and by the immensely innovative theoretical ideas and debates about social determination, 'relative autonomy', and social reproduction being worked out both in British 'cultural studies' (e.g., Williams, 1977; Willis, 1977; Clarke et al., 1979; Hall et al., 1980; Hall, 1981) and in Bourdieu's sociology (e.g., Bourdieu, 1972/1977; 1978). The problem was how to link up all this abstract theorizing about agency, structure, and social reproduction with a broader theory of social development. Like many others, I turned to Antonio Gramsci and Raymond Williams for a possible solution. Gramsci's discussion of 'hegemony' in *The Prison Notebooks* (1971) and Williams's (1977) discussion of hegemony, language, and ideology in the analysis of 'cultural production' provided what I believed to be the best framework for bringing things together.

My argument in *Class, Sports and Social Development* (Gruneau, 1983) was that the act of structuring sport in a certain way—creating an organization, specifying a rule, defining a legitimate or valued practice or the conditions for habitual practice—is an exercise of power that both defines and draws upon different societal capacities, competencies, and values. In this formulation I adopted Giddens's (1977) suggestion that power can be viewed as a differential capacity to use resources of different types to secure outcomes. The obvious problem in unequal societies is that the structures that constitute sports as social possibilities are not negotiated equally. Furthermore, once constituted, different structures open up quite different possibilities—social, political, and psychological—for various individuals and groups while limiting other possibilities (Gruneau, 1983).

The creation of modern sport as a coherent and institutionally distinct field of cultural practice in the nineteenth century is a powerful example of these varying limits and possibilities. The struggle to define sport as a civilizing and healthy set of cultural and bodily practices conducted by gentleman 'amateurs' allowed for standardized orderly sporting competition in and between nations, and it created a powerful new forum for health, bodily expression, recreation, personal achievement, and spectator enjoyment. But this occurred only in ways that privileged the material resources, cultural competencies, and preferred beliefs of European and North American males from a particular class. The fragile public consensus that briefly emerged around amateur organizations in the late nineteenth and early twentieth centuries and around the philosophy of socially improving sport and its ceremonies, disciplines, and bodily aesthetic was never the result of some abstract inevitable process of modernization. Rather, it was something that was *won* through a complex history of negotiations, struggles, and compromises.

Throughout the twentieth century, this earlier dominant 'moment' in the institutional structuring of sport and the dominant social definition of sport that accompanied it have become increasingly residual in the face of the relentless expansion of capitalism's universal market and challenges from various new social movements. Older, more romantic images of amateurism still linger in popular memory—indeed, they now provide much of the basis for popular criticism of commercialism in sport—but they are no longer embedded in the structures and meanings of sporting practice as they once were, nor do they have quite the same degrees of embodiment in sporting ceremonies, bodily practices, and disciplines. Today's dominant structures and meanings of sport, and the bodily practices they animate, now take virtually all of their cues from capital, advertising, commercial media, the entertainment industries, and the development strategies of modern nations.

Yet today's dominant tendencies in sport coexist with a multiplicity of residual, emergent, and alternative structures, activities, bodily practices, and aesthetics (Gruneau, 1983, 1988a). Examples include such new (and old) sporting structures as independently organized community leagues, women's teams, Masters' competitions, beer leagues, and so on; 'new' sporting practices ranging from bungee-jumping to snowboarding; and a range of new bodily aesthetics, both for men and women, tied variously to function, performance, or just plain marketing. Bodily prohibitions and ideals based on the popularity of athleticized imagery still prevail but in a more fragmentary way than in the immediate past. The idealized aesthetics of male athletic proportion appropriated from classical Greece stand in contrast to a new array of available bodily aesthetics for both men and women—for example, the functional height of basketball players; the overblown, neckless bodies of football players; the gauntness of marathon runners; the muscle development of the pioneers of women's bodybuilding; and the more mainstream sexualization of women's emergent sporting physicality.

We are just beginning to explore how each of the structures, practices, representations, and aesthetics I have noted has a place in contemporary systems of power, how each fits into what Bourdieu (1979/1984) has called prevailing 'logics of social distinction', and how each offers various degrees of opposition to or accommodation with dominant interests. It is tempting to consider these differences in sporting practice as a powerful affirmation of cultural pluralism—a manifestation of the vast range of sites for identity construction, counterideological practice, and alternative conceptions of the body available in contemporary consumer capitalism. But difference alone does not necessarily translate into equality or opposition. Few of the differences I have noted are taken up and popularized in media or through state or commercial sponsorship in ways that offer much threat to capital, masculine hegemony, or Eurocentrism.

I am not suggesting that every sporting practice—every contest and every representation of a contest—necessarily has, or ought to have, an overtly political character. John MacAloon (1984) is fundamentally correct to remind us of the often open-ended metaphoric character of cultural performances of all types. But we are condemned to discuss politics whenever we seek to understand how particular fields of social and cultural practice are constituted, reproduced, and transformed. That is why it is so important to explore how the dominant structures and representational practices in sport are constituent elements in the ongoing negotiation of cultural and ideological hegemony in capitalist consumer cultures.

Hegemony works best when it concedes to opposition on the margins in order to retain the core principles upon which particular forms of dominance are sustained. And even in the face of contemporary diversity, my research convinces me that certain class, gender, and Western cultural and bodily practices continue to be represented in modern sport as if they were universal and natural, thereby marginalizing many alternative conceptions of sport and the body (Gruneau, 1988b, 1989). There may well be ongoing struggles on the margins to redefine the dominant structuring principles of the field. But in struggles over 'common sense' and public consent, dominant interests often are able to delegitimize alternatives by labelling them as frivolous, unnatural, or archaic. In the meantime, other sources of difference frequently get incorporated in a compromised and nonthreatening manner.

None of this should be taken to suggest that sport today is any more stable or less contradictory than in the past. No hegemonic settlement of forces and interests is forever, and now more than ever we appear to be living through a time when 'all that is solid melts into air'. Indeed, there is a notable tension between all totalizing visions of 'modern' life and the sweeping forces of social and cultural differentiation characteristic of contemporary—some people say 'postmodern'—consumer societies. But is this tension the result of a breakdown of the old 'master narratives' of the past (Lyotard, 1984)? Does it reflect a new emphasis on and respect for cultural, stylistic, and aesthetic differences on their own terms? Or is it simply an expression of the inherent dynamism of the capitalist marketplace—the result of market segmentation and the transition to what neo-Gramscian political economists call new 'post-Fordist' regimes of capital accumulation (Hall & Jacques, 1989)?

The issue is by no means clear. However, if the post-Fordist case is generally true—and I suspect it is—then we can expect the wide range of structures, beliefs, styles, and bodily practices emergent in sport to continue to be incorporated into marketing and commerce in the manner that poses little threat to the new bloc of interests that will define global capitalism in the twenty-first century. I have no way of knowing what the field of sporting practice will look like in the times that lie ahead. But I suspect that the commodification of sport will continue apace. One thing is sure: In an increasingly international consumer culture, the sphere of 'the popular'—which centrally includes sport and the body—will be more important than ever before in the formation of social and political identities.

This emphasis on the popular as a central site for the struggle over hegemony—indeed, over common sense itself—is a central insight of a neo-Gramscian conception of social development (Bennett, 1986; Gruneau, 1988c). But the insights one gets from Gramsci come at a price. First, Gramsci's emphasis on the struggle over common sense in the negotiation of hegemony virtually leaves the body out of account as an object domain. Gramsci's primary concern is with consciousness and language as central points of struggle in the formation of active political subjects. Even the unconscious and habitual features of common sense are given a markedly cognitive tilt. A neo-Gramscian perspective can certainly accommodate discussion of the representation of the body as a bearer of social and political meanings, but it has much greater difficulty discussing how bodies are variously constituted or how the body might provide, in Bourdieu's words, 'an adherence that the spirit might refuse' (1988, p. 161). For Gramsci, all people are intellectuals, and their capacity to act as conscious agents interests him far more than any unconscious choreography of authority that might be sedimented in the body.

With this the case, it is not surprising that neo-Gramscian perspectives like my own have not really followed up on earlier countercultural criticisms of the regulated manipulation of the body in high-performance sport—a system of manipulation that can be viewed as a form of domination in itself. Nor have neo-Gramscians been sufficiently concerned—in the way that Bourdieu has, for example—with the precise ways in which particular sporting structures and beliefs materialize a logic of social distinction in various sport styles and practices and in their accompanying constitution of the body.

Another limiting feature implicit in neo-Gramscian perspectives is worth noting. Gramsci did not believe that social identity or political awareness flowed from group membership in any natural or automatic way. For example, he argued that classes do not magically 'know' their interests; rather they have to form conceptions of them. They do this through ideas and values found in the language and outlook of their time and culture. This is why he believed struggles over the sphere of 'the popular'—over common sense—were decisively implicated in the formation of active political agents and any alliance of 'collective wills' that could be forged into a hegemonic historical bloc.

In analyzing the struggle over the popular, Gramsci paid considerable attention to the importance of nationalism in the construction of social consent to particular forms of rule, and there is no reason why a Gramscian-inspired framework could not be extended to include struggles over gender, race, ethnicity, or a host of other issues as they surface in diverse areas of cultural life. Nonetheless, Gramsci himself consistently emphasized the role of class agents in hegemonic struggles and the formation of historical blocs. Attendant to this, his concern for the importance of civil society often smacks of Leninist opportunism. One struggles to win consent in the sphere of the popular only to advance the interests of the party. This lingering vanguardism has been rejected by most contemporary neo-Gramscians—some of whom even define themselves as 'post-Marxists' (Laclau & Mouffe, 1985). Nonetheless, the overriding concern with class continues to dominate Gramsci's legacy, and I am not sure it can be so easily wished away simply by piggybacking a consideration of nonclass struggles onto the analysis of hegemony.

FROM GRAMSCI TO FOUCAULT?

Despite these caveats, I still do not believe that Gramsci's limitations sufficiently offset the immense usefulness of some of his ideas, particularly as a link between an abstract theory of practice and the more concrete study of social development. However, the limitations cannot be ignored. Is there a more adequate general framework that might acknowledge the constitution and politics of the body in sport while simultaneously accommodating the analysis of interests other than those of capital or the state in its view of power?

Some suggest that one way of solving such problems is completely to reorient the conception of power away from readily identifiable historical agents in order to concentrate on power's abstract and unconscious character. Such a move away from issues of conscious agency decentres the subject better to allow the body to be fully understood as an independent object domain. Similarly, it is argued that a more abstract analysis allows one to see how power operates at all levels of social interaction, with no one source of power necessarily privileged over others. This supposedly frees the debate about power from an overly close association with the traditional universal subjects of earlier modernist discourse—notably, man, the proletariat, the party, or the state. Instead attention is directed to the micropolitics of power implicit in everyday interaction and the 'normalized' practices demanded in various institutional settings.

The theorist most closely associated with these ideas is Michel Foucault. Power for Foucault has little to do with class or gender or any recognizable social group. It is not something wielded by an agent but a relation of force. As Foucault notes, 'Power is everywhere; not because it embraces everything but because it comes from everywhere' (1980, p. 93). Giddens (1982) has emphasized how this view is declaredly opposite to Marx. Marx understood power as the noxious expression of class domination capable of being transcended by some progressive moment in history. But for Foucault power is not inherently repressive (a view Giddens shares and I support). It is more, Giddens suggests, than just the capability to say no: 'If this is all power were', Foucault asks, 'would we really consistently obey it? Power has its hold because it does not simply act like an oppressive weight, a burden to be resisted' (1982, p. 219). On the contrary, Foucault argues, power is actually the means by which things happen. It is productive; 'it produces reality; it produces domains of objects and rituals of truth' (1977, p. 194). The individual and an individual's knowledge belong to this production.

So for Foucault the production of things, of knowledge and forms of discourse, even of pleasure, are all instances of power (cf. Hargreaves, 1987). His classic example is sexuality. Sexuality is often understood in the West as something repressed by external powers—this is a fundamental notion in the Freudian paradigm, for example. But Foucault argues that sex is a product of power—an historical product produced in discourse through the interplay of power and desire (1980). Furthermore, the case of sexuality demonstrates aptly how power has a 'capillary form of existence'. Power seeps into the very grain of individuals and the body is the key site where this seepage occurs.

Giddens (1982) notes how the concern for bodily discipline in Foucault's discussion of sexuality has evident connections with Foucault's account of the origins of the modern prison. Foucault sees the characteristic forms of power in the modern prison as discipline and surveillance, essentially new 'technologies of power' that arose in the nineteenth century. For example, Foucault notes how discipline dissociates power from the body, contrary to older traditions of direct corporal punishment in which the body was marked. Disciplinary power has a much less visible character than punishment; its power is 'interiorized'. Those who experience it acquiesce, and this acquiescence becomes essential in the new technology of power (Giddens, 1982, p. 220).

The most visible counterpart to discipline for Foucault is surveillance. He points out that the idea that individuals should be under constant observation is 'the natural correlate of discipline, once the latter is manifested externally in the regularity of conduct by ''docile bodies'' ' (Giddens, 1982, p. 221). For example, Bentham proposed in the panopticon a model for prison design to allow for all inmates' activities to be observed from a single central tower. But, as Giddens notes, this is only an 'ideal' physical layout for the 'discipline/surveillance relationship'. Discipline involves the 'specified enclosure of space, the partitioning of space according to specialized criteria' (Giddens, 1982, p. 221). And, Foucault suggests such spatial sequestration is not limited to the prison—it is a key feature of factories, schools, offices, and other organizations.

Giddens goes on to argue, persuasively in my view, that if Marx saw the factory, or the site of economic production, as exemplifying our Western conception of modernity, for Foucault it is the prison and the asylum (1982, p. 221). Discipline and surveillance have become such central features of human life that we now take the modern technologies of normalization for granted—indeed, our pleasures are often intimately connected to them. Foucault notes that resistance to the forces of normalization clearly exists in contemporary institutional life, but he seems to make resistance into little more than a functionally necessary counterpoint to the omnipresence of power (e.g., 1980, p. 95). In my view all of this leaves a rather pessimistic vision of the docility of the body as a 'normalized' condition of modernity.

Despite some notable exceptions (e.g., Rojek, 1985; Hargreaves, 1986, 1987), I have long been struck by the comparative absence of Foucauldian analyses in English-language writing on sport and physical recreation. It does not take much imagination to suggest what such an analysis might look like. The emergence of modern sport forms governed by a push for rational organization, discipline, and self-improvement could be analyzed as part of the technologies of power that developed in the nineteenth century. The values of discipline, health, and self-improvement as sources of pleasure could be seen as interiorized in the body in ways that supported powerful new forms of docility and normalization. It would then be possible to study the discourses of sport promoters and health and physical education professionals as essential to the emerging technology of normalization. One could also study with respect to the strengthening discipline/surveillance relationship the changing nature of training regimes, of relationships of athletes to coaches and administrators, and of spatial arrangements of training locales. And, more broadly, one would want to consider the forms of normalization associated with the increased incorporation of sport into capitalist consumer cultures.

John Hargreaves's book *Sport, Power and Culture* (1986) is the closest to a sustained discussion of such issues available in English (see also Hargreaves, 1987). Hargreaves's analysis, however, is by no means purely Foucauldian. On the contrary, he attempts to weave arguments and ideas derived from Foucault with a Gramscian conception of hegemony and social development. Foucault's presence makes itself known in Hargreaves's definition of power, his attention to the body, and his analysis of the discourses of normalization employed by physical education 'professionals'.

Sport, Power and Culture is a remarkably insightful and extremely ambitious work, perhaps the 1980s' best book-length piece of sport and social criticism. But

I have reservations about the compatibility of Gramsci with a Foucauldian theory of power, and I am not convinced that Hargreaves's ambitious synthesis is ever quite successful. A large part of the problem lies in the difficulty of synthesizing Gramsci's inherently modernist belief in the possibility of emancipatory social transformation with Foucault's Nietzchean vision of the omnipresence and inevitability of power.

For Gramsci, power is grounded in real historical practice—in agency—and its most noxious forms are potentially transformable. But for Foucault, discipline and power are characteristically spoken of as if they were agents in themselves—the real agents of history (Giddens, 1982). I do not think you can have it both ways. For example, in some instances Hargreaves speaks of the changing place of sport in a hegemony contested by class and gender agents with a readily demonstrable historical presence, and there is recognition of the possibility of emancipatory oppositional practice. But in other instances, Hargreaves treats power as omnipresent, a Foucauldian technology linking the physical body to the social body in an unmediated manner. However, Hargreaves does not provide (I suspect cannot provide) any consistent principles to determine when one view of power ought to be employed over the other, or when and in what circumstances the two might be combined.

The virtue of Foucault for the study of sport is that he demands consideration of administrative power in the broadest possible range of practices and discourses that impinge on the human body. This encourages a sensitivity to pressures and limits on human practice beyond those that can be linked directly to class, race, ethnicity, or gender. In addition, Foucault virtually forces one to consider the body by making it the primary site for the deployment of various technologies of power in modernity. He does this without vague promises of 'human' or 'social' emancipation. On the contrary, he would argue that such totalizing conceptions inevitably contain their own technologies of normalization.

There are some terribly important insights in all this. But there are also grave dangers in swallowing Foucault whole. For one thing, there are immense conceptual problems with the idea of a history 'without subjects'. As Giddens (1982, p. 222) points out, there is nothing wrong with the argument that history has no subject if that phrase means a rejection of the view of one 'transcendental subject' as either the source or goal of 'progressive' social transformation. Similarly, there is nothing wrong with the idea of decentring the subject if that means one cannot take an originating subjectivity or social identity as given. But any theory that denies the possibility of conscious agency—the possibility that men and women have to make history even if it is under conditions that are not of their own choosing—leads to problematic conclusions.

It also seems important to raise questions about the limitations inherent in the Foucauldian emphases on discipline and surveillance and in the analogy of the prison as something reflected throughout the institutions of modernity. This point has implications for the kind of musing at the outset of this chapter about comparisons between sport and 'total institutions'. If we take the Foucauldian perspective, we are drawn to see how technologies of normalization produce docile bodies and how some forms of sport and fitness pedagogy, or discipline/surveillance relationships, appear to operate like those of total institutions in certain instances. But the focus on discipline, surveillance, and discourses of normalization can too easily deflect attention from analyzing the creative possibilities, freedoms, ambiguities, and contradictions also found in the sport forms under study.

Important distinctions exist in this regard between differing types of organizational setting in sport. For example, the closer sport becomes to the workplace, the more pressing the problem of exploring the limits and possibilities of wage labour weighed against other constituting powers. A Foucauldian perspective can help identify the powers at play in the complex regimes of discipline and surveillance that govern athletes who work for a living. But little in this perspective theorizes the difficulties of 'managing' athletes who are formally free to withdraw their labour or to respond collectively (e.g., through player associations or unions) to attempts to expand discipline or surveillance (e.g., mandatory drug testing). School sports, 'voluntary' sports clubs, and higher level state-sponsored teams all present different situations, and in each case one can find differing dialectics of choice and of constraint, of pressures to conform and to resist. It does not seem very useful to conceive of power here as an abstract, disinterested agent operating behind the backs of owners, administrators, coaches, fans, and athletes. It is far better, in my view, to link the issues of choice and constraint, conformity and resistance to the historically shifting powers and interests of really existing individuals and groups.

It is undoubtedly correct to emphasize that power is chronically and inevitably involved in all social processes. To recognize this, as Giddens (1982) points out, is to say that power and freedom are not inimical and that power is more than outright constraint or coercion. Indeed, this recognition has been key in my own work on the limits and possibilities of modern sport (Gruneau, 1983). But the elevation of power on its own terms to a privileged place in action and discourse is something else again. There can be no truth, no meanings outside of technologies of power, no values outside of power, and very little sense that some meanings and values are more or less oppressive than others. All we are left with as a guard against radical pessimism is some vague notion of the value of individual and local struggles against the abstract forces of 'normalization'. The value of local struggle has been aptly noted by a number of feminist theorists and by many recent proponents of 'postmodernism' (e.g., Martin, 1982; Chambers, 1986; Fraser & Nicholson, 1988), but I am not convinced that a politics centred on locality is enough. Furthermore, I wonder if the abstract radicalization of power implicit in such perspectives does not have the unintended consequence of actually displacing criticism away from analysis of the unequal powers of collective agents who can actually be named (e.g., the class, gender, or racial groups assembled into a hegemonic historical bloc).

CONCLUDING COMMENTS

Let me return to some of the observations made by Bourdieu that I noted at the outset of my discussion. Bourdieu's language sounds Foucauldian at times, especially with respect to its emphasis on bodily discipline, 'domestication', and the tendency to concede belief even when the mind (*l'esprit*) says no. But despite these Foucauldian overtones, Bourdieu has something different in mind. He argues that sport, like dance, is an area where teaching bodily discipline, as well as 'learning with one's body' (1988, p. 161) is much more evident than in many other areas of cultural practice. But even in sport, it is important to study *l'esprit* and *le corps* as a 'dialectical relation'. Bourdieu goes on to suggest that through a better understanding of the body in sport or dance 'one could possibly contribute to a theory of belief' (1988, p. 161). And a theory of belief is absolutely essential in the world of politics because of the 'problem of seizing awareness' (1988, p. 161).

Bourdieu's recognition of the 'problem' of the struggle over awareness—over common sense—in contemporary politics is vastly more Gramscian than Foucauldian, and I favour it for that reason. Indeed, if one wants to study the politics of the body as part of the critique of sport in modernity, there may well be more scope for imaginative and useful analysis in Bourdieu than in Foucault. There is much to recommend in Bourdieu's emphasis on the relational nature of sports as a field of practice, his attempts to link its constitution to broader logics of distinction, and his discussion of the complexity of relationships between the social production of sport and the different contexts in which sport is consumed—a complexity that he likens to 'a piece of music' (1988, p. 158).

Nonetheless, even Bourdieu's immensely complex analyses of meanings, logics, and practices are sometimes less sensitive than they ought to be about the centrality of the ambiguities and contradictions of contemporary cultural life. In the article 'Program for a Sociology of Sport' (1988) Bourdieu recognizes that 'dominant meanings' in sport are rarely interpreted uniformly and can change historically. But when viewed in the context of his overall work, Bourdieu's discussion of reversals—instances where the 'logic of distinction' seems to collapse—suggests that ambiguity and contradiction are exceptional conditions rather than the norm.

Arguing along similar lines, John Frow (1987) has noted how Bourdieu's work tends to view cultural forms and practices as noncontradictory expressive unities rather than ongoing sites of political tension. Commenting on Bourdieu's analysis in *Distinction* (1984), Frow notes how for Bourdieu

> it thus becomes impossible to read, for example, a painting by Goya in terms of contradictions between its functions of cognition and exclusion, or indeed its changing relation to the art market-place; and, conversely, the kind of political analysis that informs the work of, say, Stedman Jones on the music hall, or Willis on working-class counter-school culture, or Sennet and Cobb on the ethos of self-sacrifice in the American working class—work which stresses the ideological and political ambiguity of popular cultural forms. (pp. 66-67)

In other words, to turn around Bourdieu's comment about dance that I cited earlier, we might say that to make people dance may not be to possess them in every instance! Bourdieu is surely correct to say that in most instances of domination in modern societies the possessor and the dispossessed seem locked into a relationship of endless asymmetry, a relationship where even the criticisms raised by the dispossessed are formed in terms encouraged or defined by dominant discourses (a point Bourdieu makes throughout his work and one reminiscent of Foucault). But so often the power of this dominant discourse is lost in ambiguity or contradiction, differentially interpreted and transformed in different contexts of use. The point is to attempt to understand how some measure of social reproduction occurs in this dynamic context rather than postulate an existing logic of distinction and social reproduction against which one seeks to account for and to examine 'reversals'.

The idea that such reversals are atypical is implicit throughout Bourdieu's various discussions of the ways corporeal practices often work to 'somatize' social elements through bodily and collective mimesis of social orchestration. The idea that social reproduction occurs through embodiment outside of the reach of consciousness is one of his key analytical basepoints. Undoubtedly, there is a great deal to this, and Bourdieu's comments about the significance of such orchestration in totalitarian societies seem apt. But even here one wonders about the effectiveness of this mimesis of social orchestration. Recent events in Eastern Europe suggest a degree of caution in overstating its successes even in totalitarian regimes.

Contemporary liberal democracies provide even greater complications. This does not mean that sporting practices and beliefs in capitalist liberal democracies necessarily provide for bodily and collective mimesis of social struggles, the opposite of the totalitarian case. Rather, these practices and beliefs have a far more open-ended character. Their various meanings and links to forces of incorporation and struggle change with historical circumstances. However, to maintain a proper sensitivity to this dynamic, it still seems useful to link sport and the body to a theory of power, structure, and social development that operates with Gramsci in mind.

REFERENCES

Adelman, M. (1986). *A sporting time: New York City and the rise of modern athletics.* Urbana, IL: University of Illinois Press.

Adorno, T. (1975). The culture industry reconsidered. *New German Critique,* **6**.

Adorno, T. (1980). On the fetish character of music and the regression of listening. In A. Arato & E. Gebhardt (Eds.), *The Essential Frankfurt School Reader.* New York: Continuum. (Originally published in 1938.)

Adorno, T., & Horkheimer, M. (1977). *Dialectic of enlightenment.* New York: Seabury Press. (Originally published in 1944.)

Bailey, P. (1978). *Leisure and class in Victorian England.* London: Routledge.

Bennett, T. (1986). Introduction: The turn to Gramsci. In T. Bennett, C. Mercer, & J. Woolacott (Eds.), *Popular culture and social relations.* Milton Keynes: Open University Press.

Berman, M. (1983). *All that is solid melts into air: The experience of modernity.* London: Verso.

Bourdieu, P. (1977). *Outline of a theory of practice.* Cambridge: Cambridge University Press. (Originally published in 1972.)

Bourdieu, P. (1978). Sport and social class. *Social Science Information*, **17**(6).

Bourdieu, P. (1984). *Distinction: A social critique of the judgement of taste*. Cambridge, MA: Harvard University Press. (Originally published in 1979.)

Bourdieu, P. (1988). Program for a sociology of sport. *Sociology of Sport Journal*, **5**.

Brantlinger, P. (1983). *Bread and circuses: Theories of mass culture as social decay*. Ithaca: Cornell University Press.

Brohm, J. (1978). *Sport: A prison of measured time*. London: Ink Links. (Originally published in 1976.)

Chambers, I. (1986). *Popular culture: The metropolitan experience*. London: Methuen.

Clarke, J., Critcher, C., & Johnson, R. (1979). *Working class culture: History and theory*. London: Hutchinson.

Connell, R. (1983). Men's bodies. In *Which way is up? Essays on sex, class, and culture*. Sydney: Allen and Unwin.

Conner, S. (1989). *Postmodernist culture: An introduction to theories of the contemporary*. Oxford: Basil Blackwell.

Connerton, P. (1989). *How societies remember*. London: Cambridge University Press.

Corrigan, P. (1988). The politics of feeling good: Reflections on Marxism and cultural production. In R. Gruneau (Ed.) *Popular Cultures and Political Practices*. Toronto: Garamond.

Cunningham, H. (1980). *Leisure in the industrial revolution, 1780-1880*. New York: Saint Martin's Press.

Dunning, E. (1972). *Sport: Readings from a sociological perspective*. Toronto: University of Toronto Press.

Dunning, E., & Sheard, K. (1979). *Barbarians, gentlemen and players: A sociological study of the development of rugby football*. Oxford: Martin Robertson.

Elias, N. (1978). *The civilizing process: Vol. 1. The history of manners*. Oxford: Basil Blackwell. (Originally published in 1939.)

Elias, N., & Dunning, E. (1986). *Quest for excitement: Sport and leisure in the civilizing process*. Oxford: Basil Blackwell.

Foucault, M. (1977). *Discipline and punish*. New York: Vintage Books.

Foucault, M. (1980). *The history of sexuality: Vol. 1*. New York: Random House.

Fraser, N., & Nicholson, L. (1988). Social criticism without philosophy: An encounter between feminism and postmodernism. *Theory, Culture, and Society*, **5**.

Frow, J. (1987). Accounting for tastes: Some problems in Pierre Bourdieu's sociology of culture. *Cultural Studies*, **1**(1).

Giddens, A. (1976). *New rules of sociological method*. London: Hutchinson.

Giddens, A. (1977). *Studies in social and political theory*. New York: Basic Books.

Giddens, A. (1981). *A contemporary critique of historical materialism*. London: Macmillan.

Giddens, A. (1982). From Marx to Nietzsche? Neo-conservatism, Foucault and problems in contemporary political theory. In *Profiles and Critiques in Social Theory*. London: Macmillan.

Giddens, A. (1984). *The constitution of society.* Berkeley, University of California Press.

Goffman, E. (1961). *Asylums.* Harmondsworth, England: Penguin.

Gramsci, A. (1971). *Selections from the prison notebooks.* Q. Hoare and G. Nowell-Smith (Eds. and Trans.). New York: International Publishers.

Gruneau, R. (1983). *Class, sports and social development.* Amherst: University of Massachusetts Press.

Gruneau, R. (1988a). Modernization or hegemony? Two views on sport and social development. In J. Harvey and H. Cantelon (Eds.) *Not just a game: Essays in Canadian sport sociology.* Ottawa: University of Ottawa Press.

Gruneau, R. (1988b). Television, the Olympics and the question of ideology. In *Proceedings of the international symposium on the Olympic movement and the mass media.* Calgary: Hurford Publishing.

Gruneau, R. (1988c). Notes on popular culture and political practice. In R. Gruneau (Ed.) *Popular cultures and political practices.* Toronto: Garamond.

Gruneau, R. (1989). Making spectacle: A case study in television sports production. In L. Wenner (Ed.) *Media, Sports, and Society.* Beverly Hills: Sage.

Guttmann, A. (1978). *From ritual to record: The making of modern sports.* New York: Columbia University Press.

Hall, S. (1981). Notes on deconstructing the popular. In R. Samuel (Ed.) *People's history and socialist theory.* London: Routledge and Kegan Paul.

Hall, S., Hobson, D., Lowe, A., & Willis, P. (1980). *Culture, media, language.* London: Hutchinson.

Hall, S., & Jacques, M. (1989). *New times: The shape of politics in the 1990s.* London: Lawrence and Wishart.

Hargreaves, J. (1986). *Sport, power and culture.* New York: St. Martin's Press.

Hargreaves, J. (1987). The body, sport and power relations. In J. Horne, D. Jary, & A. Tomlinson (Eds.) *Sport leisure and social relations.* London: Routledge and Kegan Paul.

Hargreaves, J. (1991). Sex, gender and the body in sport and leisure: Has there been a civilizing process? In E. Dunning and C. Rojek (Eds.) *Sport and leisure in the civilizing process.* London: Macmillan.

Harvey, D. (1989). *The condition of postmodernity: An enquiry into the origins of cultural change.* Oxford: Basil Blackwell.

Held, D. (1980). *Introduction to critical theory.* Berkeley: University of California Press.

Hoberman, J. (1984). *Sport and political ideology.* Austin: University of Texas Press.

Hoberman, J. (1986). *The Olympic crisis.* New Rochelle: Caratzaz Publishing.

Horne, J., & Jary, D. (1987). The figurational sociology of sport and leisure of Elias and Dunning: An exposition and critique. In J. Horne, D. Jary, & A. Tomlinson (Eds.) *Sport, Leisure and Social Relations.* London: Routledge and Kegan Paul.

Ingham, A. (1975). Occupational subcultures in the work world of sport. In D. Ball and J. Loy (Eds.) *Sport and Social Order.* Reading: Addison-Wesley.

Ingham, A. (1978). *American sport in transition: The maturation of industrial capitalism and its impact on sport.* Unpublished doctoral dissertation, University of Massachusetts.

Kidd, B. (1984). The myth of the ancient games. In A. Tomlinson and G. Whannel (Eds.) *Five Ring Circus: Money, Power and Politics at the Olympic Games.* London: Pluto.

Laclau, E., & Mouffe, C. (1985). *Hegemony and socialist strategy: Towards a radical democratic politics.* London: Verso.

Lasch, C. (1985). Historical sociology and the myth of maturity—Norbert Elias's ''very simple formula.'' *Theory and Society*, **14**.

Lears, J. (1989). American advertising and the reconstruction of the body, 1880-1930. In K. Grover (Ed.) *Fitness in American Culture.* Amherst: University of Massachusetts Press.

Lenskyj, H. (1986). *Out of bounds: Women, sport and sexuality.* Toronto: Women's Press.

Lyotard, J. (1984). *The post-modern conditions: A report on knowledge.* Minneapolis: University of Minnesota Press.

MacAloon, J. (1981). *This great symbol: Pierre de Coubertin and the origins of the modern Olympic games.* Chicago: University of Chicago Press.

MacAloon, J. (1984). Olympic games and the theory of spectacle in modern societies. In *Rite, drama, festival, spectacle: Rehearsal toward a theory of cultural performance.* Philadelphia: Institute for the Study of Human Issues Press.

Mangan, A. (1981). *Athleticism in the Victorian and Edwardian public school.* Cambridge: Cambridge University Press.

Mangan, A., & Park, R. (1987). *From fair sex to feminism.* London: Frank Cass.

Marcuse, H. (1962). *Eros and civilization.* New York: Vintage. (Originally published in 1955.)

Martin, B. (1982). Feminism, criticism and Foucault. *New German Critique*, **27**.

Mills, C.W. (1970). *The sociological imagination.* Harmondsworth/Middlesex: Penguin Books. (Originally published in 1959.)

Park, R. (1989). Educational views of exercise and athletics in nineteenth century America. In Kathryn Grover (Ed.) *Fitness in American culture.* Amherst: University of Massachusetts Press.

Rigauer, B. (1981). *Sport and work.* New York: Columbia University Press. (Originally published in 1969.)

Rojek, C. (1985). *Capitalism and leisure theory.* London: Tavistock.

Veblen, T. (1953). *The Theory of the leisure class.* New York: Mentor. (Originally published in 1899.)

Vinnai, G. (1973). *Football mania.* London: Ocean Books. (Originally published in 1970).

Weber, E. (1971). Gymnastics and sports in fin-de-siecle France: Opium of the classes. *American Historical Review*, **76**(1).

Williams, R. (1977). *Marxism and literature.* Oxford: Oxford University Press.

Williams, R. (1982). *Towards 2000.* London: Chatto and Windus.

Willis, P. (1977). *Learning to labour: How working class kids get working class jobs.* Westmead: Saxon House.

Conclusion to Part I

SUGGESTIONS FOR ESSAYS AND CLASS DISCUSSION

To make the best use of the material in this section, it might be helpful if teachers and students were to orientate their essay writing and discussion around questions and issues such as the following.

1. The chapters by McIntosh, Dunning, Hargreaves, and Gruneau involve the presentation of arguments and data that reflect or have been influenced by the problematics—the conceptual and theoretical orientations—to which they adhere. McIntosh does not express a preference for any particular paradigm or theory. Is it nevertheless possible that some such construct can be detected —as a kind of 'hidden agenda'—in the analysis that he offers? Alternatively, can his position be described as 'empiricist' or perhaps even as 'eclectic'? Is it stronger or weaker by virtue of not involving explicit commitment to a particular theory?

2. Are the chapters by Gruneau, Hargreaves, and Dunning strengthened or weakened by their strong commitment to a particular paradigm? What, in general, is the relationship between theory and research?

3. What form might be taken by an empiricist or an eclectic critique of the chapters by Dunning, Hargreaves, and Gruneau; a figurational critique of those by McIntosh, Hargreaves, and Gruneau; a feminist critique of those by McIntosh, Dunning, and Gruneau; by a Marxist/hegemony theory critique of those by McIntosh and Dunning?

4. What were the principal structural characteristics of sports and games in various societies of the past? What functions did they perform? Were they dysfunctional in any way or were they perceived to be dysfunctional by specific groups?

5. What social ideologies and values were articulated in relation to or expressed in the sports and games of various historical societies? What patterns of opposition, struggle, conflict, and resistance can be discerned in this connection?

6. Is there a direct line of descent that can be traced from modern sports back to their forerunners in the Ancient World? Has the development been less continuous in the sense that modern sports are traceable only to the Middle Ages, say, or to the eighteenth or nineteenth centuries?

7. Do the modern Olympics constitute the revival of an ancient tradition, or is this merely a legitimating ideology for a form of athletic contests that is entirely new?

8. Are modern sports in general specifically modern creations with no links at all with the past? In other words, can one construct what Giddens might call a 'discontinuist view' of the history of modern sports[1]?

9. What forms of sports and games are or were played in tribal societies around the world? What are or were the sports and games of nonwestern societies such as India, China, or the Middle East?

10. Why did modern sport develop in England first rather than developing from the indigenous sporting forms of European countries other than England or from sport forms from other non-European cultures (Japan and the martial arts, for example)? Was there something connected with the structural characteristics of the non-English sports that inhibited their development in a modernising direction?

11. To what extent (if any) are sports and games autonomous in relation to the societies where they are watched and played? Are all sports equally autonomous or do some enjoy greater autonomy than others?

12. To what extent is the relative autonomy of sports bound up with such structural aspects as: the power of the groups who play and watch them; their popularity; whether they are amateur or professional; whether they are solely or mainly participant affairs or are organised and played for spectators as well as direct participants; the degree to which commercial, media, and political interests are involved in their staging and organisation?

13. What light is shed by sports and games on the societies where they are watched and played? Conversely, what light is shed by the structural and cultural characteristics of societies on their patterns of sporting activity?

SOME POSSIBLE RESEARCH TASKS

Project One: An Investigation of Folk (Tribal) Games

Using source material such as local newspapers and public records, document the folk recreations reported in particular years, for example, 1700, 1750, 1800, 1850, 1900. American, Australian, and Canadian students might do this either for European settlers or indigenous peoples or both. Investigation and comparison of the folk games of settlers from the different European countries might be especially fascinating and rewarding. Your project should

1. describe and account for any changes you detect;
2. record the functions these activities appear to have performed for the groups most centrally involved;
3. review the direct reports and less direct indications of conflicts, struggles, and resistance in relation to these activities; and
4. spell out any methodological problems and difficulties encountered.

Project Two: A Film-Related Study

Watch and evaluate the film *Chariots of Fire* in the light of evidence regarding the sociocultural history of athletics in Britain. To what extent does the film accurately portray British athletes and athletics in the 1920s? What light does it throw onto questions of class, class attitudes, and class ideologies at that time? Were such patterns found in countries other than Britain?

Project Three: Has There Been a 'Civilising Process' in the Development of American or Australian Sports?

Examine the history of American football or Australian rules football and attempt to assess whether a 'civilising process' can be held to have occurred in the course of their development. Other sports could, of course, be examined in this light as well. Boxing, wrestling, and hockey (field as well as ice) might prove particularly revealing in this regard, as might also the various forms of hunting, bull fighting, and the American rodeo sports. Noncontact sports could be studied in this connection, too.

Project Four: An Historical Study of Crowd Behaviour

Using newspaper and official records, enquire into whether the sort of pattern reported by Dunning in chapter 2 in relation to football (soccer) hooliganism is repeated in different countries and different sports.

Project Five: The History of the Martial Arts

Using secondary sources, explore the history and development of the martial arts. To what extent is a 'civilising process' exemplified in their development?

Project Six: The Ancient and the Present-Day Olympic Games

Using secondary sources, compare and contrast the ancient Olympics with their counterpart today. What are the principal similarities and differences between them?

NOTES

1. The editors and contributors to this section, of course, believe that there *are* traceable historical links as well as discontinuities. We think, nevertheless, that it might be a fruitful pedagogic exercise to consider matters from such a radically different point of view. See Anthony Giddens (1984), *The Constitution of Society*, Oxford Polity Press. See also his (1985) *The Nation-State and Violence*, Oxford: Polity.

PART II

Aspects of the Diffusion and Development of Modern Sports

Kitchin (1966) described soccer as the only 'global idiom' apart from science[1]. Such a description is not wrong. It is, however, an oversimplification, because modern sports generally and not just soccer have become activities that are played and watched all over the world. The essays in Part II of *The Sports Process* seek to shed light on this developing 'globalisation'. Let us briefly summarise the existing state of knowledge in the field.

As we noted earlier, there is general agreement that modern forms of sport first began to emerge in England in the eighteenth and nineteenth centuries. The subsequent diffusion of these forms has not yet been extensively researched, but it has become clear that what started out as English sport forms began to spread around the globe in the last three decades of the nineteenth century in a structured rather than haphazard way. Mangan (1986), Stoddart (1986, 1988), and Metcalfe (1988), for example, have shown the importance of British trade links and imperial dominance as structuring influences in this connection; Perkin (1989) and Arbena (1988) have pointed to the significance of what they call the 'informal' British Empire.

Further insights have been furnished by the sports geographer John Bale (1989). According to Bale, twin processes of outward radiation and downward diffusion have been involved in the spread of modern sports. That is, sports have tended to spread spatially both within and between countries. They have also tended to spread hierarchically, that is, within countries from higher to lower levels of the social scale. Such processes of geographical and social—or stratificational diffusion—have often been interwoven. Another way of putting it would be to say that elite groups have tended to be the principal actors in both the initial creation and the initial spread of modern sports, but these activities—within limits that vary from country to country according to their social structures, cultures, and levels of development—have tended subsequently to undergo processes of popularisation and democratisation. A similar pattern appears to have recurred as sports have spread intranationally, intracontinentally, and intercontinentally.

Research has also been undertaken recently on the spread of sport within Europe and its diffusion to the rest of the world. Holt (1981), for example, has studied the spread of sport to France, and Riordan (1977, 1978) has traced its spread to the Soviet Union. Similarly, Wagner (1989) has examined the spread of sport to Africa and Asia, while the authors in Arbena (1988) have investigated its diffusion to the countries of Latin America. Great gaps, however, remain in our knowledge of the processes involved. That is the case regarding the spread of sport to particular countries and regarding the causes and consequences of such diffusions. For example, little has been written so far on the spread of sport within Europe to Germany and Italy, or to the Scandinavian countries and those of the Iberian peninsula[2]. Similarly, the study of the spread of sport to the so-called 'developing countries'—conceived of sociologically and not just as geographical entities—remains in its infancy. The same is true regarding the organisation and functioning of sport in such contexts and regarding the later spread of American and Japanese/Asian sport forms around the world.

A plethora of issues needs to be explored in this connection. For example, what happened to indigenous forms of sport in the course of such diffusions? Did they die out completely, or did they survive but become marginalised? What sorts of conflicts and struggles were involved? Can some sports cultures be described as 'dominant' and others as 'emergent' or 'residual' (Gruneau, 1988; Donnelly, 1993)? Why did some originally English sports—soccer, for example—spread almost universally, while others (e.g., rugby and cricket) remained confined almost wholly to the countries of the former British Empire? How and why, given such a pattern, did rugby also spread to such countries as France, Argentina, and Japan? Why, when rugby spread from England to the United States, was it transformed into the very different 'gridiron' game? Why did other originally English sports diffuse without undergoing such fundamental changes? Why has professional soccer failed to catch on in the United States? Will it do so now that the World Cup Finals are to be staged there in 1994? And what about the spread outside the United States of such American sports as gridiron football and baseball? Even though the Americans do not have a formal empire, is the diffusion of these sports in any way connected with America's industrial and military dominance of the contemporary world? How and in what ways is the spread of martial arts connected with Japan's emergence as a major industrial and trading power? Is this process of diffusion connected with the growing commercial and industrial power of the countries of Southeast Asia more generally? Are we at present witnessing the early stages of a worldwide competitive struggle between what started out as English, American, and Japanese forms of sport, or will it be possible for these different forms to coexist and prosper in some kind of *modus vivendi*? What is the connection between these processes and, for example, changes in the world political order, the emergence of the new international division of labour, and the globalisation of the media of mass communication? As we have said, sociologists, historians, and geographers are only beginning to tackle questions such as these. The essays in this section of *The Sports Process* will assist considerably in the performance of this task.

The section starts with Guttmann's scholarly contribution. The spread of sports beyond their loci of origin, he suggests, is a complex matter, a question of interaction among several factors: the 'ludic properties' of the sports involved per se (i.e., of their intrinsic qualities as forms of play); such power differentials as there may be between the 'originating' and the 'receiving' societies or groups; and what Guttmann calls 'extrinsic cultural associations'. It is his contention that cultural factors are of greater significance in this connection than the majority of fans believe. He also attempts to discuss problems of 'ludic diffusion' and 'cultural imperialism' in a nonmoralistic way. Ludic diffusion refers to the sociogeographic spread of sports and games; cultural imperialism refers to the cultural adaptations that are forced on subjugated peoples by their colonial and imperial masters. Cultural imperialism, of course, has often been adduced in attempts to explain the spread of Western sports.

As one would expect of a scholar who is wedded to a comparative and historical approach, Guttmann's focus is not confined simply to the contemporary world. He starts with an analysis of the diffusion of Greek and Roman sports in the Ancient World, paying attention in this connection both to processes of hellenisation (the adoption by non-Greeks of Greek cultural forms) and romanisation (the adoption by non-Romans of Roman cultural forms). One of his more interesting conclusions—based on the research of Robert (1940)—is that, contrary to an old belief, gladiatorial games *did* spread to the hellenic and hellenised parts of the Roman Empire. *Munera* (gladiatorial combats) were even held in Athens.

Turning his attention to the modern world, Guttmann shows how sports and games sometimes change structurally in the course of a process of diffusion and how sometimes they do not. The spread of rugby to the United States and its transformation into the gridiron game provides his principal example of a process of the former type; that of soccer around the world, his principal example of the latter. He also discusses the diffusion of judo from Japan and shows how, while the structure of soccer has remained the same wherever in the world it is played, the rituals associated with the game vary considerably according to cultural context.

The history of the Olympics serves as Guttmann's principal vehicle for illustrating the occurrence of cultural imperialism in a sports context. However, while not seeking to deny that Western colonisers suppressed many indigenous forms of sport, he argues persuasively that proponents of the cultural imperialism thesis often fail to take sufficient account of the frequency with which non-Western peoples have adapted Western sports to their own needs, including that of gaining superiority in a variety of sporting fields over their former colonial masters. Finally, Guttmann discusses a number of nationalist-inspired attempts to revive and promote traditional/ indigenous sports. His prediction is that modern Western sports are likely to continue to dominate the world stage into the foreseeable future. Only time will tell, but all the present indications are that he is right. However, whatever the future holds in this regard, it is indisputably the case that Guttmann's elegantly written chapter is a model of how to carry out comparative and developmental research.

Guttmann's contribution is followed by Heinemann's chapter on 'Sport in Developing Countries', an essay that touches on several of the issues that Guttmann discusses. Before commenting on it, let us first attempt to clarify one or two conceptual issues.

Although, as Heinemann notes, there are numerous differences within each category, the societies of the world today can be broadly divided into three types: 'first world', 'second world', and 'third world' countries. Third world countries are those that stand at or near the bottom of the international hierarchy of social stratification, what Elias (1987) calls the 'international rank order of states'. They are poor, hardly industrialised if at all, and usually heavily dependent in various ways on countries in the first and second worlds. They are sometimes called 'developing societies'; such a usage is acceptable, though it could be misleading if it were taken to imply that the so-called 'developed societies' of the first and second worlds are not themselves continuing to change and develop in specific ways. But let us turn to Heinemann's contribution.

Little research has so far been carried out on sport in developing or third world countries. Heinemann is one of the pioneers, and he has provided in his chapter a masterly summary of current knowledge in the field. He uses three theories of development to throw light on the situation: industrialisation or economic growth theory; modernisation theory; and imperialism or dependency theory. Sport, he shows, is a Western cultural product and reflects the social structures and values of the advanced industrial (first world and second world) countries. It is exportable to the third world but, in these contexts, it tends to replace indigenous forms and to undergo changes of meaning if not, perhaps, of form. In some developing societies, sport is seen as a status symbol implying 'modernity' and in others, as a means of coping with the strains engendered by industrialisation. In others still, it is rejected as a product of the 'imperialist West'. In fact, all three responses are sometimes characteristic of different groups in the same society. By and large, however, modern forms of sport have not yet taken firm root in most developing countries. On average, only between 2% and 5% of a developing country's population take part in sport, mainly the Western-oriented upper and middle classes. Only with successful industrialisation and the attendant economic growth, Heinemann concludes, will third world countries be able to develop the forms of 'mass' sport characteristic of the first and second worlds, and only then will they be able to emerge as more or less equal participants in competitions involving elite performers such as the Olympic Games or the World Cup. This is a conclusion that is at least partly contradicted by some of the issues discussed by Arbena in the third contribution to this section. In fact, Heinemann's analysis is in some ways highly generalised. The reader may note, for example, that mass participation rates in many first and second world countries are not so very different from those proposed by Heinemann for the developing societies. Conversely, while the reader may wish to accept the evidence that links achievements in high-performance sport to levels of political and economic development, there are a number of contemporary developing countries that, relative to their levels of development as measured in these terms, overachieve in high-performance sport. The growing commercialisation and politicisation of top-level sport and particularly the trend towards the adoption of elitist sports policies by central governments in countries at all levels of development have considerably distorted the structural relationship between mass sport and high-performance sport. It is clear that the width of the base is but one determinant among others of the height of the apex of the 'sporting pyramid'.

Most people—at least most aficionados of the game—will agree that the greatest soccer player that the world has so far seen was the Brazilian, Pele. The first soccer World Cup Finals were held in Uruguay in 1930, and South and Central American teams have been a powerful force in that competition ever since its inception. Given the preeminence of Latin Americans in at least this one sporting field, it may be difficult to accept Heinemann's conclusion *in toto* or at least to think of Latin American countries as underdeveloped. However, that is what they are. They were formed as a result of the colonial expansion of Spain and Portugal, and, to this day, they remain for the most part poor, relatively unindustrialised, and in many ways dependent on the United States, the 'colossus to the North'.

In a whole variety of ways, the sports and games of Latin America reflect these historical and social facts. This is an area, however, in which little sociological and historical research has been carried out, and Arbena's chapter on 'International Aspects of Sport in Latin America: Perceptions, Prospects, and Proposals' represents a pioneering attempt to advance knowledge in an interesting, important, but hitherto sadly neglected field. In an erudite and wide-ranging survey, Arbena addresses such issues as: sport as a vehicle for nationalism and the forging of national sentiments in the multicultural contexts of Latin America; sport as a means for promoting development; the use of sport in the achievement of foreign policy goals; and sport as a source of cooperation and conflict in international relations. He finishes by articulating a series of proposals for research on the coverage of sport in the Latin American media, the international migration of professional players, and the role of foreign manufacturers in selling sports equipment in Latin American countries.

The sorts of problems that Arbena addresses are, of course, by no means restricted solely to a Latin American context. That this is the case is perhaps revealed most graphically by the trend in recent years for soccer players from northern European countries to migrate southward, particularly to Italy and Spain. Such a pattern in some ways mirrors and in others is connected with the pattern identified by Arbena. As he clearly shows, it raises important questions regarding the continuing viability of sports in the 'producer-exporter' countries and, as such, is deserving of much more research attention than it has received up to now. It is also indicative of the sorts of insights that are potentially obtainable from carrying out comparative and historical/developmental studies in this and other fields.

The fourth contribution to this section, 'The Industrialisation of the United States and the Bourgeoisification of American Sport', written by Ingham and Beamish in the early 1980s, involves a change of focus. More particularly, while Guttmann, Heinemann, and Arbena were all concerned in their different ways with tracing the causes and consequences of the spread of modern sports from their Western home-lands to other parts of the world, Ingham and Beamish concern themselves with the development of a specific nexus in the West itself: namely, the development in the United States of sport as a 'product' to be 'consumed'. To shed light on this process, they utilise a combination of concepts drawn from Marx and Weber: the Marxist concept of 'valorisation', the transformation of goods or services from products that can be directly used into commodities that can be bought and sold on the market; and Weber's concept of 'instrumental rationality', the calculation of means and ends to determine the most advantageous course of action. They then seek to show how, at a specific stage in the emergence of industrial capitalism in the United States, material conditions began to be provided that made it possible for new forms of sport to emerge that could be instrumentally developed for profit. Ingham and Beamish focus principally in this connection on the creation of a consumer market for 'valorised' sport—the term 'commodified', which has recently gained greater currency, captures their meaning more exactly and is also closer to the original meaning of Marx—and they explain this process partly by reference to the existence of cultural and economic barriers that militated against direct working-class participation in sport, and partly by reference to the impact on working-class life of the activities of middle-class social and educational reformers. These reformers shared with growing numbers of members of the employing class a belief in the value of sport as a vehicle for the achievement of desirable social ends, but a principal unintended consequence of their actions was, as Ingham and Beamish show, that they contributed to the creation in American schools and colleges (and society in general) of forms of sport oriented towards profit, the marketplace, and the interests of the corporate elite.

Ingham and Beamish finish with a pessimistic conclusion regarding the possibilities for more democratic forms of sports participation in the United States, what they call a 'popular reclamation of sport in American life'. Whether they are right to be so pessimistic, only time will tell. It is important, though, to emphasise in this connection that Ingham and Beamish say they see history as an open-ended process and not as subject to cast-iron and immutable laws. The reader might want to question in this connection whether, despite this avowal, Ingham and Beamish have adequately captured the balance between determination and freedom regarding the ways in which the development of industrial capitalism has affected the development of sport in the United States. But whether the reader agrees with them or not, what is certain is that they have produced a scholarly and insightful account that fruitfully applies high-level conceptual analysis to the study of a concrete sociohistorical process. They also make substantial cross-cultural references to the history of sport in Britain, bringing out contrasting as well as parallel developments in the two countries. As such, their study can serve as a model for further comparative and historical/developmental research on sport not only in the United States and Britain, but in other capitalist-industrial societies as well.

The final contribution to this section is Maguire's study of the spread of American football to Britain, a process that he seeks to understand by locating his analysis in the context of the more general debates on globalisation and the 'Americanisation' of Britain and other European societies. After noting that, probably as an adjunct of its more general marginalisation as a subject for academic discussion and research, sport has not so far featured centrally in the debate, Maguire goes on to provide a critical discussion of the literature on Americanisation. Mass society theorists, he suggests, tend to be cultural elitists with a conservative view of popular culture. Marxists who have contributed to the debate, especially writers from the Frankfurt School and authors influenced by them, tend to treat 'ordinary' people as 'cultural dopes', that is, as totally at the mercy of American cultural products and lacking in the power to redefine these products for their own ends. According to Maguire, scholars working in the cultural studies tradition have usually managed to avoid such weaknesses but even they, he argues, lack an adequate theory of power. They also tend to take for granted the pleasure that can be obtained from consuming

American cultural products rather than seeing it as something that has to be theorised and explained.

It is Maguire's contention that a figurational approach offers a chance of shedding further light on Americanisation without falling foul of the limitations that he claims to have identified in other positions. That is particularly the case, he suggests, if such an approach places recent developments in a longer-term context and combines figurational insights with insights drawn from Marxian political economy. He goes on to analyse what he calls 'the making' of American football in Britain, particularly England, a process that took place in the 1980s. Above all, he seeks in this connection to identify the network of interdependencies within which this development took place. The principal actors in it, he suggests, were Channel 4 TV, the (American) National Football League, and the brewing combine, Anheuser-Busch. However, although great, their power and control were far from total. The appeal of American football in Britain, Maguire argues, was uneven. Avid devotees were drawn mainly from groups whose values were already cognate with those inherent in the American game. Others were hardly touched by the marketing campaign. Moreover, the limited spread of American football in Britain took place in a context where the government, through its concept of an 'enterprise culture', was trying without conspicuous success to transform British society in an 'American' direction.

Maguire next goes on to suggest that the whole problem of the Americanisation of British culture only makes full sense sociologically when account is taken of the fact that America was originally a British colony and that—although Maguire does not use this term—processes of what one might call 'Anglicisation' were conspicuous in its early development. However, he notes, the Americans had sufficient power in that context to reinterpret cultural imports from what had originally been the 'mother country' as is shown by the transformation of rugby into gridiron football.

Finally, Maguire discusses the spread of soccer to the United States in an attempt to show that diffusion can be a two-way process involving cultural exchange. This suggests that the international diffusion of sports and other cultural products can only be fully understood when the shifting balance of power between the countries involved is taken centrally into account. When, as with the spread of sports from a first world to a third world country, the power discrepancy between them is very great, the diffusion is likely to be a one-way affair. When, however, diffusion takes place from one first world country to another, a two-way process is more probable. That is likely even when, as in the case of Britain and America, the former imperial power declines and the former colony develops into a superpower. Is it possible to detect parallels here with Guttmann's analysis of the diffusion of sports between Greece and Rome and the twin processes of hellenisation and romanisation in the Ancient World that he discusses? Whether such parallels exist or not, it is certainly the case that the United States is, far and away, the most powerful country in the world today. Nevertheless, as Maguire shows very clearly, its power, including that of its capitalist or entrepreneurial class, is far from absolute or total. We hope that his study will serve as a stimulus to others to carry out research along similar lines on other sports and on sports in other countries. We hope, too, that his chapter will contribute to a refocusing of what has been up to now, despite the intrinsic importance both of Americanisation and of sport, a disappointingly narrow and restricted area of sociological debate.

NOTES

1. Kitchin, L. (1966). 'The Contenders'. *The Listener*, 27 October pp. 694-695.
2. We realise, of course, that this statement may reflect our ignorance of material in the native languages of such countries more than an absence of such material per se. That this may well be the case is suggested, for example, by the excellent doctoral thesis on sport in Catalonia written by Francisco ('Paco') Lagardera i Otero. See his *Una Interpretacion de la Cultura Deportiva en Torno a los Origens del Deporte Contemporaneo en Catalunya*, PhD, University of Barcelona, 1991. See also Zaragoza, A., and Puig, N. (1990). *Oci, Esport, Societat*, PPU; and Puig, N., and Garcia, M. (1986). *L'Esport en Edat Escolar a la Ciutat de Barcelona*, Barcelona, Ajuntament de Barcelona.

REFERENCES AND SUGGESTIONS FOR FURTHER READING

Arbena, J.L. (Ed.) (1988). *Sport and society in Latin America: Diffusion, dependency and the rise of mass culture*. Westport: Greenwood Press.

Arbena, J.L. (Ed.) (1989). *An annotated bibliography of Latin American sport: Preconquest to the present*. Westport: Greenwood Press.

Baker, W. (1982). *Sports in the western world*. Totawa, NJ: Rowman & Littlefield.

Baker, W., & Mangan, J.A. (Eds.) (1987). *Sport in Africa: Essays in social history*. New York: Africana.

Bale, J. (1989). *Sports geography*. London: Spon.

Blanchard, K., & Cheska, A. (1985). *The anthropology of sport*. Massachusetts: Bergin and Garvey.

Cashman, R., & McKernan, M. (Eds.) (1981). *Sport: Money, morality and the media*. Sydney: New South Wales University Press.

Donnelly, P. (1993, in press). Subcultures in sport: Resilience and transformation. In Ingham, A.G., & Loy, J.W. (Eds.), *Sport in social development: Traditions, transitions and transformations*. Champaign: Human Kinetics.

Elias, N. (1987). *Involvement and detachment*. Oxford: Blackwell.

Gruneau, R. (1988). Modernization or hegemony: Two views on sport and social development. In Harvey, J., and Cantelon, H. (Eds.), *Not just a game: Essays in Canadian sport sociology* (pp. 9-32). Ottawa: University of Ottawa Press.

Guttmann, A. (1986). *Sport spectators*. New York: Columbia University Press.

Holt, R. (1981). *Sport and society in modern France*. London: Macmillan.

Holt, R. (1989). *Sport and the British: A modern history*. Oxford: Clarendon Press.

Holt, R. (Ed.) (1989). *Sport and the working class*. Oxford: Oxford University Press.

James, C.L.R. (1963). *Beyond a boundary*. London: Stanley Paul.

Kirsch, G.R. (1989). *The creation of American team sports: Baseball and cricket 1838-1872*. Champaign, IL: University of Illinois Press.

Kitchen, L. (1966). The contenders. *The Listener*, 27 October.

Knuttgen, H., Qiwei, M., & Zhongyuan, W. (Eds.) (1990). *Sport in China*. Champaign: Human Kinetics.

Lawrence, G., & Rowe, D. (1986). *Power play: The commercialization of Australian sport*. Sydney: Hale & Iremonger.

Lever, J. (1983). *Soccer madness*. Chicago: University of Chicago Press.

Mandell, R. (1984). *Sport: A cultural history*. New York: Columbia University Press.

Mangan, J.A. (1986). *The games ethic and imperialism*. Harmondsworth: Viking Press.

Mangan, T. (Ed.) (1988). *Pleasure, profit and prosleytism. British culture and sport at home and abroad 1700-1914*. London: Cass.

Metcalfe, A. (1982). *The emergence of modern sport in Canada, 1867-1914*. Toronto: McLelland & Stewart.

Metcalfe, A. (1988). Leisure, sport and working class culture: Some insights from Montreal and the north east coalfield of England. In Cantelon, H., & Hollands, R. (Eds.), *Leisure, sport and working class cultures* (pp. 43-54). Toronto: Garamond Press.

Parratt, C. (1989). Athletic womanhood: Exploring sources for female sport in Victorian and Edwardian England. *Journal of Sport History*, *16*, 2, 140-157.

Perkin, H. (1989). Teaching the nations how to play: Sport and society in Britain. *International Journal of the History of Sport*, *6*, 2, 145-155.

Riordan, J. (1977). *Sport in Soviet society*. Cambridge: Cambridge University Press.

Riordan, J. (Ed.) (1978). *Sport under communism*. London: Hurst.

Riordan, J. (1991). *Sport, politics, and communism*. Manchester: Manchester University Press.

Robert, L. (1971). *Les gladiateurs dans l'orient grec* (rev. ed.). Philadelphia: Coronet Books.

Schneidman, N.N. (1979). *The Soviet road to Olympus*. London: Routledge and Kegan Paul.

Stoddard, B. (1986). *Saturday afternoon fever: Sport in Australian culture*. Sydney: Angus and Robertson.

Stoddard, B. (1988). Cricket and colonialism in the English-speaking Caribbean to 1914: Towards a cultural analysis. In Mangan, T. (Ed.), *Pleasure, profit and proselytism: British culture and sport at home and abroad 1700-1914* (pp. 231-257). London: Cass.

Wagner, E. (Ed.) (1989). *Sport in Asia and Africa: A comparative handbook*. Westport: Greenwood Press.

The Diffusion of Sports and the Problem of Cultural Imperialism

Allen Guttmann

Men and women play as animals do, instinctively, but sports, which are by definition *regulated* physical contests, are the product of culture[1]. Some sports, like running, jumping, throwing, and wrestling, are so close to the activities of primitive hunting and warfare that one can credit the Marxist claim that they derive more or less directly from 'the processes of production' (at least as those processes existed in prehistorical times)[2]. Such sports are apparently cultural universals; they are found everywhere. It is difficult to believe that even those cultures that avoid contests and competitions, like that of Sumatra, have children completely without the desire to test their strength and speed against that of their peers[3]. Other sports, like cricket, are obviously the result of cultural processes that are distantly if at all related to the economic sphere. Such sports are not explicable in terms of capitalism or industrialism, but they do bear the unmistakable stamp of the culture that invented them. Without going as far as Blunden and others who have written ecstatically of cricket as the expression of the English soul, one can acknowledge a close relationship between the game and the people who play it. If the sun never sets on the game of cricket, the reason is clearly that Englishmen carried it with them to the ends of the earth. From the remnants of wickets and bats, future archaeologists of material culture can reconstruct the political boundaries of the British Empire.

The prevalence of French words in military terminology (*lieutenant, reconnaissance*) and of Italian terms in music (*aria, allegro*) are the linguistic record of bygone political and artistic hegemony, and the language of sports provides a similar clue to social history. Throughout the world, the language of modern sports is English. Germans admire *einen guten Kicker* and the French sprinter waits nervously in *le starting-block,* while Russian readers admire the heroes portrayed in *Sovetskii Sport* and Japanese fans go wild over *Besuboru* and the players wear English team-names on their uniforms (*Yomiuri Giants*). Everyone speaks of 'fair play' (in English) and some attempt, like the gentlemanly amateurs of nineteenth-century Oxford and Cambridge, to practice it. (Indeed, the great Spanish historian Salvador de Madariaga maintained that fair play characterised the English as *le droit* did the French and *el honor* the Spanish[4].) Given the sad facts of ethnocentrism and xenophobia, one must expect that the diffusion of sports, like that of any other aspect of culture, will be accompanied by nationalistic resistance to what some will feel to be cultural imperialism. The failure of cricket in the United States can be explained by the ardent desire of Americans to establish a national identity that was not English; the common evolutionary origins of cricket and baseball were consciously, intentionally disguised in the chauvinistic fog of the Abner Doubleday myth, and Americans *still* express shock at the thought that the 'national game' was not invented in a Cooperstown cowpasture.

To talk as I have done about ludic diffusion and cultural imperialism is to insist that the adoption by one group of a game popular among another is only partly the result of recognising the intrinsic properties of the game. In the long run, a modern sport like soccer may become so thoroughly naturalised that the borrowers feel that it is *their* game, an expression of their unique national character, but the transmission of a sport is certainly a complicated matter in which intrinsic ludic properties are jumbled together with extrinsic cultural associations in ways not easy to untangle. The history of sports suggests that the cultural factors are far more important than most fans believe.

The ancient Olympics are an instructive case study. The games began as part of a local religious festival; the earliest victors were from Elis, Pisa, and other cities in the immediate vicinity of the sacred site. Not until the XV Olympiad, celebrated in 720 B.C., do the Spartans appear in the list of victors, which they then dominate for the next century and a half[5]. Gradually, the spread of Greek culture throughout the eastern Mediterranean was manifested in the athletic triumphs of Theagenes of Thasos, Milo of Krotona, and Diagoras of Rhodes. The local games became 'national'. For Herodotus, the Olympic Games symbolised the cultural superiority of the Greeks over the Persian invaders. When King Xerxes learns, shortly before the battle of Salamis in 480 B.C., that the Greeks are engaged in the games at Olympia, he asks, 'And what is the prize for which they contend?' When informed that the Greeks struggle for a mere olive branch, Xerxes cries out to his general, 'Good God, Mardonius, what manner of men are these against whom you have brought us to fight—men who contend with one another not for money but for honour!'[6] The disheartened Persians were defeated.

A century and a half later, Alexander the Great, whose Hellenism was demonstrated by his athleticism as well as by his love of the *Iliad* and the *Odyssey*, defeated the heirs of King Xerxes and carried Hellenistic culture, including Greek sports, across Asia Minor to India. In a remark that echoes the lament of Xerxes to Mardonius, Alexander looked upon the statues of athletes in the city of Miletus, which he had freed from Persian rule, and asked, 'Where were these fighters when you accepted the Persian yoke?'[7]

It was not long before the Greeks of Alexandria and Antioch built their gymnasia and sent their contestants to Olympia. And it was inevitable that Greek contests became the focus of cultural conflict in Jerusalem, where King Herod built a theatre and an amphitheatre and introduced the typically Greek festival of Panegyris, with running, jumping, wrestling, boxing, and even chariot races. 'With these contests in Jerusalem itself', comments a German scholar, 'the king signalled his determination, in agreement with Roman interests, to hellenise Judea and to incorporate it into the Greco-Roman world'[8]. In their various responses to the festival of Panegyris, the Jews demonstrated their readiness to adopt Hellenistic customs or to adhere to their own traditions. (Saint Paul's familiarity with athletic terms suggests that he was a very Hellenised Jew before his conversion to the gospels of Jesus[9].)

The Greeks were able to impose their civilisation upon the people of Asia Minor, but the cultural relations between Greece and Rome—a topic that has fascinated historians for generations—were complicated by the fact that the politically and militarily superior Romans acknowledged their literary and artistic inferiority to the Greeks. While the attraction of the Olympic Games was powerful enough to motivate Nero to interfere in them and to have himself declared a victor, the Romans generally resisted the Greek tradition of athletics (to use the British term for what Americans refer to as track and field sports). 'The only athletic events which interested them at all', wrote Gardiner of the Romans, 'were the fighting events, wrestling, boxing, and the pankration'[10]. It was not that the Romans were indifferent to Greek athletics. As Ludwig Friedländer made clear in his classic study of Roman morals and customs, the issue was one of cultural identity: 'The Greek *agones* met with a very hostile reception at Rome from true-spirited Romans'[11]. When Scipio Africanus appeared at the gymnasium in Greek clothing, he was hooted at by his xenophobic friends[12]. The prejudice against 'alien' athletics never disappeared.

What ludic diffusion took place was generally in the opposite direction. If athletic festivals like those at Olympia and Delphi are forever associated with Greek culture, gladiatorial games (which may have had a Campanian origin) are perhaps even more closely identified with the Romans. Although it was once thought that the Hellenized eastern half of the *Imperium* resisted the encroachments of this most brutal of sports (if gladiatorial games *were* a sport), Robert's *Les Gladiateurs dans l'Orient grec* (1940) has documented the appearance of Roman *munera* throughout the Hellenized cities of Asia Minor and Africa and even at Athens. 'Greek society was gangrened by this sickness contracted from Rome. It was one of the successes in Romanizing the Greek world'[13].

The history of sports is full of other examples of ludic diffusion. The classical Japanese ritual game of *kemari* was introduced into eighth-century Japan by the Chinese, from whom the Japanese borrowed numerous elements of culture with an apparent minimum of ethnocentric resistance[14]. The game of polo, described by the Persian poet Firdusi in the eleventh century, was brought to Europe by the Crusaders, only to be more or less forgotten until its rediscovery by nineteenth-century British colonisers of conquered India[15].

Baseball's stunted diffusion is particularly interesting because it demonstrated clearly that extrinsic factors can be more important than intrinsic ones. Where the United States was perceived as *the* modern society, baseball was seen as a splendidly exciting game; where Americans did not serve as role models, baseball seemed the embodiment of tedium. The Japanese, for instance, were introduced to the game in the 1870s by American educators who seemed convinced that 'baseball could effectively break down cultural barriers'[16]. It has been suggested by a recent authority that baseball 'caught on' in Japan because it 'seemed to emphasize precisely those values that were celebrated in the civic rituals of state: order, harmony, perseverence, and self-restraint'[17]. While this is possible, I incline to the opinion that the popularity of the game depended at least as much on the Japanese perception of the United States as the most modern of nations. Enthusiasm for the game seemed to accompany the growth of American economic and political influence in the Far East.

Inevitably, the Japanese began to chafe at the Americans' arrogant assumption of cultural superiority. Their national pride became identified with their ability to beat the Americans at their own game (an extremely suggestive phrase). As Japanese students became increasingly proficient at bat and in the field, an 'international confrontation on the diamond [became] unavoidable'[18]. The Americans of the Yokohama Athletic Club refused to take the Japanese seriously enough to accept their challenge and 'a simple game of baseball . . . began to assume the dimensions of a righteous struggle for national honor'[19]. When the students of the Ichiko School, an elite preparatory institution in Tokyo, were finally admitted into competition with the Yokohama Athletic Club at the latter's field on May 23, 1896, the 'borrowers' humiliated the game's 'owners' by the lopsided score of 29-4. In the history of Japanese sports it was a moment of sweet satisfaction comparable to the Australian 'coming of age' against English cricket on August 29, 1882, or the Hungarian football triumph over England at Wembley on November 25, 1953. (Since England was justifiably seen as the 'mother' of sports, it has been inevitable that almost every country in the world has longed for and eventually celebrated the *rite de passage* of trouncing the English.)

Ludic diffusion is quite obviously a complex social process. As Riesman and Denney have shown, the British game of rugby, itself the product of centuries of evolution, underwent so many changes once it arrived in the United States that the final product seems to represent American rather than British culture[20]. Informal consensus on the rules, quite appropriate for a sport confined to a small public-school or university elite, gave way in America to increasingly complicated written regulations that made the sport accessible to millions. A 'feel' for the game was replaced by new rules formalizing what was previously customary[21]:

Consider the fact that the development of Rugby rules in England was accomplished by admitting into the rules something that we would call a legal fiction. While an offensive runner was permitted to carry the ball, the condition of his doing so was that he should *happen* to be standing behind the swaying 'scrum' (the tangled players) at the moment the ball popped back out to him. An intentional 'heel out' of the ball was not permitted; and the British rules of the mid-nineteenth century appear to take it for granted that the difference between an intentional and an unintentional heel-out would be clear to everyone.

The American solution was to allow the centre, commanded by the quarterback, to begin each play by passing the ball to the backfield. The rule transformed the game. A process of 'procedural rationalisation' changed the game to the point where many American colleges now field both football and rugby teams (in addition to soccer teams)[22].

A similar process of modernisation has taken place in the course of the diffusion of judo. Originally a martial art, judo was transformed by Dr. Jigoro Kano, founder of the Kodokan Judo School in 1882. His approach to the activity was moral and aesthetic rather than competitive. Brought to England by Gunji Koizumi in 1918, judo remained Japanese in its cultural orientation until after World War II. A study of postwar British judo compares seventeen British black-belt judokos from the years 1948 to 1960 with fourteen from the post-1960 period. While eight of the first group had made a serious study of Zen Buddhism, none of the second group had; while none of the first group daydreamed of winning matches, six of the second group admitted to such fantasies[23]. The acceptance of judo into the Olympic programme in 1964 ubdoubtedly accelerated the modernisation of the sport. The authors of the cited study conclude that judo 'has become increasingly Westernized and oriented towards international competition. The strong competitive ethos, individualism, instrumental views of practice and rational, scientific approaches to training are typical of the wider culture within which judo now flourishes'[24].

The example of sumo wrestling proves that a highly ritualised sport with religious significance need not be exported in order to surrender elements of its tradition to the ethos of modern sports, but transplanted activities are the ones most likely to leave their cultural roots behind. The sport adopted from another country may be perceived as foreign and may be prized for its cultural rather than for its intrinsically ludic characteristics, but the borrowers are quite liable to interpret the sport in their own way. Coming from Britain to America in the 1970s, soccer was seen in the United States not as a working-class sport but as the perfect game for suburban children too small for basketball and too light for American football.

The diffusion of soccer is an excellent case for careful study because the game is complex enough not to have been invented independently by many preliterate cultures and yet simple enough to have become the world's most popular team sport. Although the antecedents of the game are ancient, one can take the formation of the Football Association in 1863 as a starting point for the study of diffusion. Despite enthusiasm for the 'national game' of baseball, Americans were among the first to follow the British lead. The first American soccer game is usually credited to Princeton and Rutgers, which met on November 6, 1869[25]. The Australians claim to have begun even earlier; indeed, Mandle asserts that Victoria had its own football cup competitions in the 1860s, 'almost a decade before England', with league tables in the 1880s (while England's Football League was not founded until 1888)[26]. Playing their first game in 1884, the Canadians seem almost backward[27].

Prior political colonisation was, however, certainly not a prerequisite for early adoption of soccer. The aura of Thomas Arnold and the English public school inspired eighteen-year-old Konrad Koch to introduce football at Braunschweig's Gymnasium Martino-Katharineum in 1874[28]. Pim Mulier, a Dutch schoolboy who had studied at an English boarding school, founded the Haarlemsche Football Club in 1879 and another student, August Wagner, brought the game from Czechoslovakia, where it was played as early as 1892, to Austria, where students in Graz seem to have been the first players[29]. World Cup victories by Brazil and Hungary can be traced back to other schoolboy beginnings; Charles Miller, whose English parents lived in São Paolo, brought home a soccer ball in 1894 when he returned from study and play in England and Charles Löwenrosen, whose parents had emigrated to England, introduced the game to his Hungarian relatives when he visited them in 1896[30].

When Edoardo Bosio, a businessman from Turin, returned home in 1887 from a trip to London afire with enthusiasm for soccer, he founded an Italian club; but it was the English in Turin who began the famed Juventus Football Club in 1897[31]. Similarly, British diplomats, military personnel, and businessmen, especially those connected with railroad construction or the textile industry, were responsible for the spread of the game to France (1872), Denmark (1874), Belgium (1880), Russia (1887), Uruguay (1891), Spain (1893), and Mexico (1900)[32]. The origins of the first football club in Russia were quite typical. Among the many English textile workers in the Slavic nations of eastern Europe were Clement and Harry Charnock, employed at the Vicoul Morozov factory near Moscow. They began a football club in 1887 and advertised in the *Times* of London for workers who might double as players.

Knowing of the Japanese determination to modernise their country, we are not surprised that Englishmen interested them in soccer as early as 1875[33]. Considering the entire pattern of ludic diffusion in football, one suspects that *some* kind of British influence stirred the Poles of Lvov to begin to play soccer in 1894[34]. If we but had the information, it is more than probable that we would discover a schoolboy back from Rugby or a construction engineer homesick for a Liverpudlian pastime.

Although YMCA workers seem to have played a major role in the diffusion of basketball, which was invented in 1891 at their college in Springfield, Massachusetts, missionaries seem not to have done a great deal for football, but they did carry the sport to Kampala in 1910. In the words of the secretary-treasurer of the Uganda Olympic Committee, 'Soccer was introduced here by missionaries from the United Kingdom, our former colonial masters'[35].

Although the British have undisputed right to the title of inventors and propagators of the modern game of soccer, a kind of insularity or arrogance prevented them from controlling the growth and development of the sport in quite the way that the Marylebone Cricket Club controlled cricket. When Belgium, France, Germany, Holland, and Spain met to form an international football association in 1903, they sent Robert Guérin of France to see Frederick Wall, secretary of the Football Association, who showed no interest whatsoever in the project. Some months later, Guérin managed to speak with A.F. Kinnaird, president of the F.A., but it was, reported Guérin, 'like beating the air'[36]. The continental nations went ahead and the Fédération Internationale de Football Association was formed in 1904. The British joined within two years and were allowed four votes (for England, Ireland, Scotland, and Wales), but refusal to play against Austria and Germany led to British withdrawal from FIFA in 1920. Back in 1924, the British dropped out again in 1928 (this time over the reimbursement of amateurs for time lost from their regular jobs). In the absence of the British, it was the French, led by Henri Delaunay and FIFA president Jules Rimet, who persuaded their colleagues to launch a quadrennial championship, the World Cup, in 1930. The British were not represented until the World Cup of 1950, at which time their team failed to survive to the semifinal round[37].

Despite its British origins, soccer has been adopted around the world. The rules of the game are international, but the associated rituals are often the product of native culture. The folklore of Brazilian soccer is unlike that of the German game; watching Santos of São Paolo is not the same as a visit to the terraces of Schalke

O4. Among the Zulus of South Africa, pregame ceremonies include incantations, dances, and ritual incisions performed on the players by witch-doctors[38]. The room allowed for national and ethnic variation has undoubtedly done a great deal to allay resentments aroused by cultural imperialism. The intense ritualism associated with the Olympic Games, however, has done the opposite. It has emphasised the European origins of the games and has made it necessary for non-Western nations to participate in the Olympic movement on Western terms. In Parsonian language, there has been a conflict between the universalistic ideals of the movement and its particularistic forms.

The modern games were founded by Pierre de Coubertin and an International Olympic Committee that was composed almost exclusively of Europeans. At the first session of the IOC, the ancient 'Hymn to Apollo' was interpreted by Jeanne Remacle and sung by the chorus of the Opéra. In his *Memoires Olympiques*, Coubertin described the effects of this philhellenism: 'Hearing the sacred harmony plunged the numerous participants into the proper mood. A subtle emotion spread as if the ancient rhythm had arrived from the distant past. Hellenism filled the vast hall'[39]. That Coubertin's impulse had its origins in the classical tradition as well as in the games culture of the English public school was obvious in the very name, 'Olympic', and in the decision to revive the games in the land from which they had originally sprung. Consciously hellenising, the IOC revived the discus throw and invented the marathon race. Coubertin was not an antiquarian and the games included numerous events unknown to the ancients—weight lifting, fencing, rowing, and cycling—but the modern additions to the classic contests were clearly European in form.

The most obvious instance of classical symbolism is probably the relaying of the torch from ancient Olympia to the site of the games. This particular ritual was inaugurated in 1936 by the German sports administrator and scholar Carl Diem. The message is plain; from the pure Hellenic source at Olympia, the flame is carried forth to the world. Leni Riefenstahl's monumental documentary film, *Olympia*, made to commemorate the 1936 Olympics, begins with a Hellenism so intense that it borders on the absurd. After film credits that appear to be carved in stone, the camera moves from classical landscape to ancient ruins and to Greek statuary until Myron's discus thrower turns and melts into the discus thrower of today. Naked maidens dance and a loin-clothed youth lights the torch at the Olympic altar. The flame is carried from Olympia to Berlin while Wagnerian music swells and the alleged kinship between the ancient Greeks and the modern athlete is triumphantly asserted.

Although the Greeks themselves, initially somewhat reluctant to sponsor the games, became enthusiastically proprietary and wanted to keep the quadrennial celebrations in Greece, Coubertin and his colleagues were adamant about Olympic internationalism. The next Olympiads were to be celebrated in Paris, in St. Louis, and in London (after Rome found itself unable to follow through on its original offer). Nonetheless, it was an internationalism on European terms. The reason that the Olympiads were to be celebrated in various places was the desire to propagate the Olympic ideal, to spread the light. *Terras irradient.* Avery Brundage, president of the IOC from 1952 to 1972, was especially concerned that the games be hosted by an Asian nation (Japan in 1964) and by a developing nation (Mexico in 1968). Although the newly independent African nations were judged unready to stage the games themselves, which had become logistically enormous affairs by the time of Brundage's tenure, the IOC did schedule one of its sessions in Nairobi (only to have to move it to Baden-Baden when the Kenyan government declared itself unready to issue visas to the South African members of the IOC).

Originally a coterie of Europeans and Americans, mostly titled or wealthy or both, the IOC intentionally sought to enlarge itself by electing members to serve as delegates *to* (not *from*) nations that had not yet joined the Olympic movement. Brundage was especially eager to discover Latin American sportsmen who might proselytise an area not yet imbued with Olympism. Writing to R. C. Aldao of Argentina in 1945, Brundage noted that the IOC had not yet elected members from Bolivia, Chile, Columbia, Ecuador, Paraguay, Venezuela, and Central America; could Aldao suggest qualified people[40]? Brundage's ecumenicism was strong enough to overcome his personal hostility to Communism, and eastern European bureaucrats joined the nobility of western Europe in worrying about amateur sports. The IOC, however, remained under Western control. The first member from North Africa was Angelo Bolanaki, an ethnic Greek resident in Egypt, and the first members from sub-Saharan Africa were white men like Reginald Honey of South Africa (elected in 1946) and Sir Reginald Alexander of Kenya (elected in 1960). Not until 1963 was a black African elected, Sir Adetoklunbo Ademola of Nigeria. Despite a conscious effort to make the IOC truly international, all but one of its six presidents has been a European, and the sixth was an American. In 1954, 56% of the members were Europeans; in 1977, Europe still had 48% of the membership. The somewhat diminished hegemony of Europe and America can be seen in Table 1, showing IOC membership in 1954, 1977, and 1990[41].

Since the delegates to Oceania are from Australia and New Zealand, the Western preponderance is unmistakable. Repeated efforts on the part of the Soviet Union to 'democratise' the IOC by allowing representation from *all* of the recognised National Olympic Committees have been routinely rejected by the non-Communist majority from Western Europe and the Americas.

Control of the IOC has meant that the sports included in the Olympic programme have their origin in the West, or, if they are as international as archery, that they

Table 1   IOC Membership

	1954	1977	1990
Africa	2	13	14
America	16	18	19
Asia	10	13	18
Europe	39	38	38
Oceania	3	3	4

are represented in their distinctively modern form (i.e., the targets are made up of regularly spaced concentric circles, the bows are those developed by modern technology)[42]. With its power to determine the athletic programme of the games, the IOC can withhold or confer a kind of ludic legitimacy. Accordingly, IOC sessions have frequently included wrangles over the inclusion or exclusion of particular sports. As early as 1930, the prestige of the Olympic Games was so great that representatives of the international federations for baseball, billiards, canoeing, lacrosse, pelota, and roller skating vainly requested recognition of their sports[43]. Baseball became an Olympic sport in 1992—to the delight of the Cubans and Japanese eager to demonstrate prowess in their national pastimes. By the late 1960s, the knocking at the gate was almost incessant; the bowlers and the roller skaters seemed never to weary of campaigning[44]. Although softball's partisans could claim millions more participants than bobsledding, the Executive Board of the IOC turned them down on June 2, 1969, and May 9, 1970, and the full IOC rejected them in 1971[45]. The tireless advocates of billiards, bowling, and roller skating tried and failed at the same IOC session in Luxembourg[46].

The IOC *has* offered its imprimatur to new sports and the programme *has* grown considerably. During the 1950s, Armand Massard and Vladimir Stoytchev, influential IOC members from France and Bulgaria, campaigned for volleyball in letters to Brundage and in repeated appeals to their assembled colleagues[47]. After a heated debate in Melbourne in 1956, Massard and his Communist allies lost once again, by a vote of 19-13, but Stoytchev kept the cause alive by promising to stage a convincing exhibition of the sport when the IOC met in Sofia in September 1957[48]. The campaign achieved success with the inclusion of volleyball for both men and women in Tokyo in 1964.

Although volleyball is widely played in the third world, especially in Asia, it too was invented in the West (at the YMCA's college in Springfield, Massachusetts). The *only* sport in the Olympic programme that has distinctly non-Western origins and associations is judo, which appeared for the first time in 1964 when the games of the XVIII Olympiad were celebrated in Tokyo. Judo's inclusion, which Brundage opposed, was clearly a favour done for the Japanese hosts[49]. Although the vote at the 57th IOC session in Rome had been an overwhelming 39-2 in favour of volleyball, judo was removed from the programme of the 1968 games in Mexico City by a vote of 37-16 (at Baden-Baden in 1963)[50]. Brundage's friend Ayotoro Azuma, member from Japan, had to use his considerable influence to bring the sport back into the programme for 1972[51]. The Olympic programme remains essentially Western. African and Asian athletes compete on Western terms, in sports that either originated in or have taken their modern form in the West.

This is not the result of a conspiracy on the part of the IOC. The entire structure of international athletic competition is Western. The federations that control international competition were created in Europe and have simply assumed the norms shared by Europeans and Americans. The industrialised nations of the West have been the most eager supporters of these international federations and are characterised by the number of their memberships. In 1974, the French were members of 73 international sports associations and the Belgians and the West Germans belonged to 71; indeed, of the 25 most actively involved nations, 20 were European[52]. When the Fédération Internationale du Sport Universitaire, founded in Luxembourg in 1948, began to hold its own World University Games, seven of the first eight summer games were held in the West and the eighth took place in Tokyo[53]. When African nations stage their own regional games, like the Jeux Africains celebrated at Brazzaville in July of 1965, the events of the programme are almost identical with those of the Olympic Games[54]. At the second All-African Games held in Lagos in 1973, Western sports dominated the actual competition while traditional African dances preceded the athletic contests[55]. One reason for the weak commitment to traditional sports is that they are ethnically specific and too local for political elites who see modern sports as an instrument to unify a multinational state.

While a modern nation like Japan can preserve its traditional sumo and kendo along with the more popular sport of baseball, the international dominance of Western sports continues and resistance to this form of cultural imperialism remains weak. The spread of the Japanese martial arts to the West has been accompanied, as we have seen, by their modernisation, by their transformation in accordance with Western assumptions about the nature of sports. Philosophers like Eugen Herrigel, fascinated by Zen in the art of archery, are few compared to the modern missionaries of physical education who venture forth from Europe and North America to convert the world to the gospel of modern sports. Even more numerous are the athletes from Asia, Africa, and Latin America who study at American or European universities and compete as 'student athletes'. For better or for worse, foreign athletes studying in Moscow, Leipzig, Cologne, Loughborough, and Berkeley learn more from their hosts than they teach them—at least as far as sports are concerned. We shall see whether or not the reemergence of repressed national groups, like the Basques of Spain and the French of Quebec, and the more militant assertion of traditional nationalism, like that of Iran, lead to a kind of ludic apostasy from Olympism. The most likely outcome is that traditional games and dances will survive as a kind of *entr'acte* while modern sports, Western style, continue to dominate the international stage.

NOTES

1. Definitions of sport differ. Mine are given in *From Ritual to Record: The Nature of Modern Sports* (New York, 1978), pp. 1-14.
2. For a brief account of the Marxist view, see my *From Ritual to Record*, pp. 57-64; for an extended statement, see Gerhard Lukas, *Die Körperkultur in Deutschland von den Anfängen bis zur Neuzeit* (Berlin (East), 1969) and Andrzej Wohl, *Die gesellschaftlich-historischen Grundlagen des bürgerlichen Sports* (Köln, 1973).
3. For Sumatra, see Henning Eichberg, 'Spielverhalten und Relationsgesellschaft in West Sumatra', *Stadion*, I (1976), 1-48.
4. *Englishmen, Frenchmen, Spaniards* (London, 1928).

5. See the 'List of Ancient Olympic Victors' in Nicolaos Yalouris (Ed.), *The Eternal Olympics* (New Rochelle, 1979), pp. 289-296.
6. *The Persian Wars*, VIII, 26.
7. Quoted in Carl Diem, *Alexander der Grosse als Sportsmann* (Frankfurt, 1957), p. 10.
8. Manfred Lämmer, 'Griechische Wettkämpfe in Jerusalem und ihre politischen Hintergründe', *Kölner Beiträge zur Sportwissenschaft* II (1974), 197.
9. On this and related matters, see H.A. Harris, *Greek Athletics and the Jews* (Cardiff, 1976).
10. *Athletics of the Ancient World* (Oxford, 1930), p. 49.
11. *Roman Life and Manners under the Early Empire*, trans. J.H. Feese, A.B. Gough, and L.A. Magnus (London, 1908-1913), II, 122.
12. Peter L. Lindsay, 'Attitudes toward Physical Exercise Reflected in the Literature of Ancient Rome', *History of Sport and Physical Education*, edited by Earle F. Zeigler (Champaign, Illinois, 1973), pp. 177-186.
13. *Les Gladiateurs dans l'Orient grec* (rev. ed., Amsterdam, 1971), p. 263.
14. F.M. Trautz, 'Kemari, das klassische altjapanische Fussballspiel', *Fussball: Soziologie und Sozialgeschichte einer populären Sportart*, edited by Wilhelm Hopf (Bensheim, 1979), pp. 37-40.
15. Carl Diem, *Asiatische Reiterspiele* (Berlin, 1941).
16. Donald Roden, 'Baseball and the Quest for National Dignity in Meiji Japan', *American Historical Review*, LXXXV (June 1980), 519.
17. *Ibid.*
18. *Ibid.*, 520.
19. *Ibid.*, 521.
20. 'Football in America: A Study in Culture Diffusion', in David Riesman, *Individualism Reconsidered* (Glencoe, Illinois, 1954), pp. 242-257.
21. *Ibid.*, p. 246.
22. On this process, see Eric Dunning and Kenneth Sheard, *Barbarians, Gentlemen and Players: A Sociological Study of the Development of Rugby Football* (Oxford, 1979).
23. B.C. and J.M. Goodger, 'Organization and Cultural Change in Post-War British Judo', *International Review of Sport Sociology*, XV, No. 1 (1980), 21-48.
24. *Ibid.*, p. 43.
25. John A. Lucas and Ronald A. Smith, *Saga of American Sport* (Philadelphia, 1978), p. 197.
26. 'Games People Played: Cricket and Football in England and Victoria in the Late Nineteenth Century', *Historical Studies*, XV (April 1973), 511-512.
27. Kevan Pipe, Program Director, Canadian Soccer Association, to author, 14 November 1980.
28. Wilhelm Hopf, 'Wie konnte Fussball ein Deutsches Spiel werden?' In Hopf (Ed.), *Fussball*, pp. 54-80.
29. Dutch information supplied from pamphlet by Koninklijke Nederlandsche Voetbalbond; Czech from V. Hubicka, Chairman, Czech Olympic Committee,

to author, 20 October 1980; Austrian from Dr. Peter Pilsl, Secretary-General, Austrian Olympic Committee, to author, 29 October 1980.

30. Brian Glanville, *Soccer: A Panorama* (London, 1969), p. 57; Jozsef Veto, *Sports in Hungary* (Budapest, 1965), p. 45.

31. Paul Gardner, *The Simplest Game* (Boston, 1976), pp. 36-37.

32. *Ibid.*, pp. 36-39; James Walvin, *The People's Game* (London, 1975), pp. 92-112.

33. Arthur E. Grix, *Japan's Sport* (Berlin, 1938), p. 64.

34. Janusz Piewcewicz, Deputy Secretary General, Polish Olympic Committee, to author, 14 October 1980.

35. Sev A. Obura, General Secretary-Treasurer, Uganda Olympic Committee, to author, 29 October 1980.

36. Glanville, *Soccer*, p. 52.

37. Gardner, *The Simplest Game*, pp. 39-41; Walvin, *The People's Game*, pp. 121-122, 152.

38. N.A. Scotch, 'Magic, Sorcery, and Football among Urban Zulu', *Journal of Conflict Resolution*, V (1961), 70-74.

39. *Mémoires Olympiques* (Lausanne, 1931), p. 18. See also Otto Mayer, *A Travers les Anneaux Olympiques* (Geneva, 1960), pp. 41-42.

40. Brundage to Aldoa, 29 October 1945, Brundage Collection, University of Illinois Archives, Box 50.

41. Drawn partly from *Bulletin du Comité Internationale Olympique* No. 47 (15 August 1954) and Gregor Mlodzikowski, 'Das olympische Ideal und die friedliche Koexistenz', *Zeitschrift für Kulturaustausch*, XXVII (1977), 27-29.

42. On modernisation in sports, see my *From Ritual to Record*, pp. 15-55.

43. *Bulletin Officiel du C.I.O.*, V, Nr. 16 (July 1930), 19.

44. *IOC Newsletter* No.15 (December 1968).

45. *Minutes of the Executive Board Meetings*, Lausanne, 2-3 June 1969, and Amsterdam, 8-16 May 1970; *Minutes of the 71st Session of the International Olympic Committee*, Luxembourg, 15-17 September 1971 (Brundage Collection, Boxes 94-95).

46. *Ibid.*

47. Massard to Brundage, 14 September 1955; Stoytchev to Brundage, 2 February 1957 (Brundage Collection, Boxes 60, 63).

48. Brundage's notes on meeting, 21 November 1956 (Brundage Collection, Box 78).

49. Brundage to Otto Mayer, IOC Chancellor, 4 February 1961 (Brundage Collection, Box 48).

50. *Minutes of the 60th Session*, Baden-Baden, 16-20 October 1963 (Brundage Collection, Box 92).

51. Azuma to IOC, 28 January 1966 (Brundage Collection, Box 74).

52. James E. Harf, Roger A. Coate, and Henry S. Marsh, 'Trans-Societal Sport Associations: A Descriptive Analysis of Structures and Linkages', *Quest Monograph* #22 (Spring-June 1974), 52-62.

53. C. Lynn Vendien, 'FISU and the World University Games,' *Quest Monograph* No. 22 (Spring-June 1974), 74-81.
54. Achot Melik-Chakhnazarov, *Le Sport en Afrique* (Paris, 1970).
55. Ralph C. Uwechue, 'Nation Building and Sport in Africa', *Sport and International Relations*, edited by Benjamin Lowe, David B. Kanin, and Andrew Strenk (Champaign, Illinois, 1978), pp. 538-550.
56. See John Bale, The Brawn Drain (Urbana, 1991).

Sport in Developing Countries

Klaus Heinemann

Although there are numerous greater and lesser differences within each category, the world today can be broadly divided into three kinds of societies that vary in terms of: (i) their levels of development, above all their degrees of industrialisation and urbanisation, (ii) the historical periods in which they embarked on industrialisation; and (iii) the degree to which their industrialisation involved elements of deliberate planning and the kinds of ideologies that were involved. It has now become standard, not just in academic circles, to call these three types of societies 'first world countries', 'second world countries', and 'third world countries'. First world countries are those (such as Britain, Germany, and the United States) that industrialised first, that are now industrially the most mature, and where the process of industrialisation took place in terms of liberal-capitalist ideologies and was not state planned. Second world countries are those (such as the former Soviet Union and its satellites) where, by contrast, industrialisation did not involve state planning and where a communist/socialist rhetoric provided much of the momentum. Third world countries are those that stand at the bottom of the international hierarchy of social stratification. They are poor, hardly industrialised if at all, and heavily dependent on countries in the first and second worlds. Sometimes, as in the present chapter, they are also called 'developing countries', a usage that could be misleading if it were taken to imply that the so-called 'developed societies' of the first and second worlds are not, themselves, continuing to change and develop in specific ways.

There is no such thing as 'the' developing country or 'the' sport. On the contrary, there are more than 100 developing countries that differ greatly in their social and economic orders, in their per capita incomes, in their traditions and histories, and in their strategies of development. Sport, too, has a whole variety of manifestations, such as traditional sport, mass sport, and high-performance sport. Then there are the different characteristics of particular sports disciplines, with their respective organisational features, their historical development, their public ranking, and their degrees of professionalisation. Sport is also structured differently in particular developing countries. Such variety cannot be fully discussed in this chapter. Furthermore, the limited amount of data currently available on the functions of sport in the development process of nations has to be taken into consideration. Consequently, it is necessary to rely more on suppositions than on substantive knowledge. This is also the case with sport politics and the promotion of sport in these countries. Are the functions of sport in developing countries similar to those in modern societies? Is it possible for developing countries to have the same sports as we have, or will they or must they be completely different? How is sport integrated into the peculiar culture and traditions of a country? What challenges are made to sport in those countries where leisure is frequently the result of unemployment and where a large part of the population is made up of marginal social groups? Very little is known about such issues. In order to give a general idea of the situation of sport in developing countries in the face of these uncertainties, I intend:

1. to deal with particular problems of development and modernisation in the context of a general characterisation of the developing countries;
2. to elucidate the differences that exist between sport in modern societies and sport in developing countries; and
3. to examine the manifestations and rank of sport in third world countries and to allude to the function and meaning of sport in these countries, especially in connection with the various strategies for the development, modernisation, and building of a nation.

CONCEPTS OF DEVELOPMENT

There is a multitude of rival theories both on how to explain the situation of underdevelopment and on the features and strategies of development that should consequently be pursued. It is necessary to deal with these theories to a certain extent since they are not merely statements from the standpoint of a sociology of development. On the contrary, such developmental strategies are very often interpretations, especially of the political elites of these countries, that explain their respective situations and emphasise the importance of particular developmental aims in an overall developmental strategy (Diegel, 1976, p. 3). Thus, they are both reality constructions and models of political action. We must, therefore, be aware of these models and the explanatory patterns behind them, not only because they describe social circumstances and problems of social change, but also because the sport politics of particular countries can constitute a part of these development strategies.

One can distinguish three concepts of development:

1. Underdevelopment is understood as economic retardation, development as economic growth. Development aims are aspired to that are oriented toward European and North American examples, such as industrialisation, improvement of industry, specific furtherance of scientific progress, and adoption of technical innovations. Fundamental indicators of development are the per capita national income and its average annual growth rate, which reflect the standard of living, the ratio of population in urban and rural areas, the numbers employed in agriculture as opposed to those employed in industry, the number of scientists and technicians, and expenditure on science and technology. These factors also determine the position occupied by particular nations in the rank order of international social stratification (which is structured according to economic development) and are at the same time the preeminent components of their own development policies.
2. Developing countries are traditional societies; development means the transition to a modern society, that is, first an amalgam of both forms and then a

gradual decrease in traditional structuring in favour of modern features. Development therefore results in:

a) the dissolution of the fundamental meaning of kinship and of deep-rooted primary bonds that are determined by language, religion, race, values, customs, social orientation, and obligations of loyalty, and that are geographically limited to neighbourhoods, villages, and regions;

b) an increase in social differentiation, that is, the relation of fundamental social functions—such as management of the economy, religion, the military, social security, and other autonomous organisations—to the overall social system (Eisenstadt, 1966).

c) the formation of institutions and forms of control that secure the coordination and collaboration of the various autonomous fields of existence, such as the utilisation of money, the increase in the power of the central political authority, the development of mass parties, the emergence of nationalist movements or movements for religious freedom;

d) the appearance (in a society in the process of modernisation) of a new personality structure, because only intellectually, geographically, and socially mobile persons will remain capable of action, that is, be able to cope with completely unknown fields of existence and be able to identify themselves with the position, situation, and experience of unknown persons, political rulers, and foreign and new ideologies and be able to experience society as a field of possibilities—an orientation pattern Lerner calls 'empathy';

e) finally, the overcoming of critical situations that initially result from an identity crisis, that is, the lack of a binding national feeling in societies that have developed out of a multitude of tribes and culturally and politically divided population groups. In many cases, no formal organisation of the state existed until the colonial powers established one. In conjunction with this, a political system undergoes a legitimation crisis if bureaucrats, local officials, ethnic groups, and representatives of economic interests all contend for a greater share of power without having a common ideological conception. The gravity of the crisis will increase if the controlling groups are not able to penetrate every region of their country and effectively enforce their policies and aims everywhere (a 'penetration crisis') (Pye, 1966, pp. 62ff).

3. Theories of imperialism bring the developing countries into complete correlation with the inherent laws of the capitalist economic structures prevalent in western industrial nations. Underdevelopment is construed as resulting from extraneous imperialist rule, which develops out of immanent contradictions of the capitalist economic and social systems. Colonialism means economic and political suppression; it leads to an expansion of the markets for capitalist countries, not only securing the supply of raw materials for industrial nations, but also creating new sales prospects. Thus, the dangers of overproduction and the falling rate of profit characteristic of advanced capitalist countries

are decreased, thereby concealing the internal contradictions of the capitalist system. Above all, development means liberation from this extraneous dependency and rule by means of an internal revolution and the mobilisation of the cultural, political, and economic resources of a nation—this being the initial stage of a worldwide process of mobilisation and revolution. Economic development and modernisation thus gain a new importance; the adoption and development of modern technology and the increase in industrial production have to be detached from the social, cultural, and political processes of structural differentiation; revolutions, conflicts, and national ideas and ideologies are ascribed with the function of developing a unique cultural identity.

An amalgam of these conceptions is frequently found in the development strategies of particular countries; industrialisation and modernisation go hand in hand. Liberation from dependency on capitalist societies is combined with an individual path to a modern society. A country frequently follows various strategies in the course of its development—as for example Iran, which initially concentrated on rapid industrialisation and then sought its own cultural identity and independence borne by a religious freedom movement.

Both the development and the phenomenon of sport are closely related to modern societies. In the following paragraphs this will be illustrated by referring to a society's social constitution, its determining values, and its underlying understanding of the human body (Heinemann, 1980, pp. 142ff).

Principles that are dominant in industrial societies as a whole are reflected in sport: the performance-achievement principle with its tenets of freedom, equality, and competition; the institutional autonomy of sport, that is, its differentiation as an independent sphere of existence with the separation of the individual and the organisation, of internal and external roles, and, thus, its independent organisation according to its own inherent laws and factual necessities and its own specific formalised system of rules. Simultaneously, the institutional autonomy of sport enables it to be a contrasting world to work and to everyday reality, that is, to contribute to relaxation and to provide spheres of tension, risk, and drama in a society that lacks excitement due to its being mainly regulated by norms and being divided into spheres of existence with functionally specific organisation.

Value-orientations that form some of the most dominant and determining value-patterns of modern societies are also prevalent in sport. These include, among others, the readiness and capability of resisting the immediate satisfaction of needs and wishes and of suppressing them in the interest of long-term objectives; the control of physical energy, aggression, and emotion; a readiness to plan objectively; the ethics of personal responsibility, self-reliance, and personal initiative; a high valuation of marked achievements that are considered as being proof of personal capabilities and efforts.

These values have already been imparted and internalized before the actual commencement of sports activities, particularly by socialisation in the family. They are the precondition for a capability and readiness to go in for sports or one particular kind of sport because, in modern societies, sport is organized in such a manner that the dominant values of a modern society take effect and are rewarded. Characteristics for sport are discipline, long-term training programmes, regularity of effort, the necessity for individual effort and responsibility, stress on performance-achievement and an orientation to competition, and partnership attributes such as comradeship, fairness, etc.

In modern societies, sport is related to a particular understanding of the human body. The body is, to a great extent, an object for commanding the environment and an instrument for increasing efficiency and production. Thus, it is becoming more and more difficult to develop an attitude toward one's body that is free from these object- and function-related constraints. In conjunction with this, a decline in the functions of body language can be observed. After all, in modern societies physical prowess and capabilities are of very little importance either for the acquisition of personal and social identity or for the functioning of social systems. The adoption of modern sport means change, for instance change in the understanding of time and the body, an increase in rationality and performance orientation, and a pronounced stress on competitive thinking and calculation of tactics.

The following consequences for sport in developing countries would seem to follow from the above reflections. If sport is the expression of a specific social structure and is formed and altered by its relationship to the society where it takes place, there will be no sport in developing countries similar in its organization, value orientation, body understanding, functions, etc., to that of modern societies. On the contrary, one must proceed from the fact that three different forms of sport can be ascertained in developing countries:

1. folk-games handed down from traditional modes of games and sport;
2. mass sport, as it developed in modern societies and was exported to developing countries and practised there;
3. high-performance sport.

FOLK-GAMES

Characteristic of games, sport, and physical culture in preindustrial societies is their realisation in a whole variety of different forms. This is already extensively documented in the ethnological literature and it is impossible in this chapter even to attempt to give a complete description. Only a few features will be mentioned. In preindustrial societies, games and sport are related to the respective contexts of family, village, tribe, and affiliation to social positions and classes, etc. Sports and games can, therefore, only be understood in their respective social contexts. Sports and games are interwoven with military, political, religious, and domestic functions, thus forming various combinations. They are often organisationally linked with celebrations, ritual actions, political decisions, and military confrontations. They are dependent on religious and moral orientations and are thus connected to the respective social and political order and its functioning and stability (Dunning, 1973, pp. 215ff).

The functional and institutional nexus of sport and its close dependency on other spheres of social existence is also reflected in the regulation structure of sport in these societies. It is impossible to organize sport according to its inherent principles. On the contrary, sport must correspond to the social conditions and functions of the specific spheres of existence to which it is affiliated. Thus, in preindustrial societies, sports and games seldom exhibit an actual, formal institutionalisation, but only an informal organisation that is mainly on a regional level. Likewise, there are often only simple unwritten rules, partly traditional, which are, however, relatively flexible and variable, and on which consensus has to be reached again and again.

Similar differences generally exist in the value-orientations of these societies, although it is hardly possible to make assertions that are valid for all preindustrial societies. However, in these societies, it is highly likely that one will find a subordination to obligations of loyalty and bonds of solidarity rather than an orientation to individual performance. Interactions as a result of norms of reciprocity are more likely than competition and rivalry, just as past-orientation and cyclical conceptions of time are more probable than future-orientation and rational planning as factors that determine the character of sports and games.

Finally, a different kind of body consciousness is predominant in these societies. In preindustrial societies, physical proficiency and capability have a much greater meaning for the attainment of personal and social identity, as well as for the functioning of social systems. They have an important function in all spheres of social life and social institutions. Physical strength, dexterity, and agility are not only necessary traits for sports competition. They are also virtues that are important for the attainment of military and political office. The meaning of physical proficiency and capability, their uses and values, are so apparent that sports and games do not necessarily have to be constituted as a separate social system and legitimised, for example, by health ideals. Physical features such as size, skin colour, growth, and dexterity are of extreme importance both for social rank and stigmatisation.

In developing countries, the traditional culture of games and sports is becoming increasingly less significant. It was the first missionaries who frequently exercised a destructive effect. They regarded popular sport, especially dancing, as immoral, and felt it was too closely associated with the myths and cults of the traditional society. They were also afraid that such pursuits could prevent people from attending church services (Dunlap, 1951, p. 305; Stumpf, 1948, p. 5).

The sport of western industrial societies is frequently initiated in those countries that have adopted the western model of social and political development and industrialisation according to the first development strategy. On the one hand, it is regarded as being modern and, on the other, since it was originally practised by the colonial masters, as exclusive. It is also understood to be exemplary for the western way of life. The import of European sport often entails the destruction or supercession of a traditional games culture. This is only artificially retained within the framework of a government's cultural politics as a tourist attraction or as television entertainment (e.g., professional dance groups). If a traditional culture is preserved in this manner, it becomes depleted of such basic functions as its cults and myths. Ignorance of the cultural tradition, of its contribution and meaning, leads very rapidly to the destruction of traditional ties. Traditional sport falls into oblivion and is seldom found to synthesise with modern sport. A decrease in the varieties of physical expression and the destruction of the traditional body culture become apparent.

When the modernisation of developing countries is oriented towards the second development strategy, the traditional social structure is often considered as being a component of this development. Development is not meant to lead to the destruction of the elements of the traditional structure but rather to facilitate their selective preservation and to give them a new definition. It is most important, however, to retain traditional local communities that convey a common culture and identity to their members. Communalism and national integration represent both development strategies and problem areas that result from this form of modernisation. In this respect, sport assumes an autonomous importance. Traditional modes of sport—especially dancing in the third world countries—are cultivated in order to sustain and convey a common culture and identity. This can be understood as a possibility for attaining both the collectivism contained in the functionally diffuse ties of language and culture and the individualisation necessary for performance in a modern commercial and industrial milieu. However, even in these cases, popular sport remains largely artificial and is deprived of its original basic functions. This loss in the meaning of popular sport is inevitable. The increase in social differentiation, the adoption of western-oriented value-patterns, and the changed attitude towards the body must lead to the downfall of games and sports that are structurally and functionally embedded in other spheres of social existence and closely linked with traditional values. As a result of social changes, they lose the basis of their existence.

MASS SPORT

Developing countries are faced with various problems such as population surplus, inadequate nutritional resources, low economic growth, lack of jobs, and low educational levels. These problems certainly have greater priority than the attempt to furnish the whole population with the means for developing sport and attaining the sorts of performance levels prevalent in industrial countries. However, many developing countries do not consider sport as being superfluous, as is proved by their efforts in this field.

Nevertheless, one has to proceed fundamentally on the assumption that sport as mass sport and high-performance sport, as it has developed in western societies, is of only minor importance in developing countries. Factors such as financial possibilities, provision of facilities, the availability of managers and trainers, and the culturally determined way of life, action-orientations, and limited socialisation into sport lead to limited possibilities, capabilities, and readiness to participate in sport as it is exported from western industrial societies. The characteristics of modern sport on the one hand, and the social structures and ways of life of a traditional society in the process of change on the other, impede the popularisation of sport in these societies. Orientation towards achievement and competition are very seldom evident because physical consciousness, time awareness, readiness to plan, and cultural patterns and value-orientations very seldom correspond to the conditions and demands of modern sport. Thus it is estimated that, at most, 2% to 5% of a country's population actively participate in sport. Besides, mass sport seldom corresponds in its contents, functions, and meanings to what it is understood to be in the modern societies from which it has been exported.

It is to be expected that modern sport will generally develop with the degree of industrialisation, that is, it will initially follow industrialisation in large and small towns. It can be demonstrated, for example, that the propagation of sport corresponds to the development of the educational system. On the one hand, sport is an important school subject in many developing countries because it is expected to contribute to the formation of the individual's personality and to his or her adaptation to the living and working conditions of a modern society. On the other hand, the educational system is above all open to the upper classes who have, as a result, the closest contact to western culture and adopt sport as an example of the western way of life (Clignet & Stark, 1974, pp. 81ff).

Very often in leisure sport a culturally specific selective reception of modern sport takes place. With the adoption of sport, the specific cultural characteristics intermingle and—although they do not determine the formal aspect, which is bound by rules—they do determine contents and realisation in specific situations. Allison and Lüschen (1979) demonstrate, for example, that the adoption of basketball by the Navaho Indians on the one hand, and by members of the 'Anglo' culture in the southwestern United States on the other, took place in different ways. These dissimilarities are evident in the development of different game strategies, in the frequency of physical contact, in the different attitudes to competition and aggressiveness, and in the fact that the game is played according to different rules. In the same manner Eichberg (1975) shows the culturally specific selective reception of sport, using sporting behaviour in West Sumatra as an example. The sporting behaviour characteristic of this culture is sustained by the (selective) adoption of modern western sport: More specifically, only those modes of sport that correspond to this pattern of sporting behaviour are adopted. Thus, 'the selection from among modern sports begins with those sports where achievement (performance) as such cannot be objectified but can only be expressed in relation to the performance of other players, that is, goal differences or point differences. Achievement-orientation is only evident with regard to relative performance' (Eichberg, 1975, p. 37).

Thus traditional behaviour has a certain stability, which permits the adoption of other forms of sport and the redefinition and realisation of their contents and outer forms. As a result, they are adopted in a culturally specific manner. This selective adoption increases the attractiveness of sport because, on the one hand, such sports are considered as being modern and, in addition, often as paradigmatic and exemplary. On the other hand, traditional, culturally specific elements are retained, thus permitting a differentiation from the sport of the industrial countries and simultaneously unfolding the possibility of personal, local, and national identification.

The attractiveness of modern sport can be increased by organising it in sports clubs, that is, by offering the possibility of participation in voluntary organisations—as is the case in many developing countries (Heinemann & Horch, 1981, pp. 133ff). Even in modern societies, voluntary organisations have developed in conjunction with the problems that occur in the processes of social differentiation and industrialisation. These organisations are to be explained by the functions they perform in these societies. Voluntary organisations remain durable social groups that transmit a feeling of solidarity, facilitate conviviality, engender a conformity of social aims, and solve identity problems. These functions are of particular importance in the transition from preindustrial to modern societies with the social and geographical mobility attached to this, the differentiation of organisations it entails, and the loss in meaning of environing social groups and the dispersion of values and ideas. One can therefore assume that clubs absorb some of the problems attendant on industrialisation, especially those that result from social and regional uprooting and the loss of importance of environing social groups. These achievements are derived from the capability of voluntary organisations to combine various, sometimes even contradictory, structural principles: They facilitate the transition to modern society not only because they replace premodern solidarity units and, as a result, help to alleviate the internal and external behavioural uncertainties found in individuals during the transitional period, but also because they evidently do this in a manner that combines the maintenance of traditional standards and values with the gradual introduction of new social structures. Thus it is no coincidence that sports clubs in developing countries are very often directly government controlled and of political significance (cf. Rittner, 1978, p. 37). Even the colonial administration realised the special function of voluntary sports organisations. On the one hand, they expected them to channel political and emotional energies as well as to interweave modern and traditional features. On the other hand, these organisations were suspected of supporting political and military upheavals. Subsequently, the problems of political independence and national integration within a political order arose for third world countries whose regional borders had originally been determined by the colonial powers. It is very often characteristic of these societies to be split up into a multitude of ethnic groups, tribes, and regionally bound political loyalties that lack a common and unifying national feeling. To be more exact, the strong identification with their own culture and society in the respective regional communities leads simultaneously to a definition of other societies as being 'not us', as 'not belonging', and other analogous evaluations that are often negative. Thus, these segmental cultures remain mutually unfamiliar in their respective peculiarities and particularities, as well as in their forms of language and values. A national feeling, a self-identification of the whole society (Frohlich, 1970, p. 29) does not exist. It is, therefore, an important development strategy to propagate national ideologies that ensure a national identity, redefine cultural traditions, and determine the relationship to other countries, especially the colonial powers.

The maintenance and furtherance of traditional games and modes of sport and the development of leisure and mass sport based on the sport of western industrial societies not only assume the function of developing cultural identity and creating an awareness of tradition but also involve the attempt, by means of sport, to provide a solution for certain problems that occur as a result of rapid social change and industrialisation. Thus, sports clubs and teams are expected to create new identification spheres as a substitute for those that have disappeared after the dissolution of the environing social groups. Sport is also meant to convey values of achievement-orientation and competition, of cooperation and individualism, thus forming the personality and, at the same time, helping to overcome the negative influences that result from industrialisation. Above all, sport is meant to further a common, unifying national feeling.

Sport has an important function in this process of nation-building. It is supposed to contribute to the consolidation of a nation, especially when the nation has originated out of various tribes, traditions, and cultures, and to foster the development of a national identity. However, it is doubtful whether sport actually has these desired integrating powers. The splitting up of local segmental cultures is reflected in the national organisation of sport as well as in sports competition. Existing antagonisms and conflicts among these segmental cultures are projected into these competitions.

Frequently, the process of development is urged on by religious freedom movements—as for example in Iran—which are meant to offer these countries an identification-sphere prior to nationalism that will enable the population to express their religious and anticolonial emotions as well as to find a crystallisation-point for their diffuse and often latent feelings of insecurity and discontent. In addition, since religions such as Islam often consider the body as an object of aversion, there is a great gulf between these religions and popular sport, especially of the modern kind. In such countries, sport assumes hardly any importance because it is understood as being an expression of (rejected) western culture. In addition, an apprehension prevails that sport could detract attention and energies from the revolutionary mission.

Particularly in those countries where revolutionary techniques are rationalised and become a deliberate development policy—according to the third development strategy—sport can also be adopted as an instrument of revolutionary development. Thus, sport is seen to symbolise the viability and efficiency of the new social system. It is simultaneously a means for delineating the political and social system and for furthering the development of integrating forces both within the nation and with other third world countries that have common grounds concerning culture, history, and language. Modern sport is adopted but assumes a new significance and is defined by its functional meaning for the development of a particular social order and a particular cultural self-assurance.

HIGH-PERFORMANCE SPORT

A high price must be paid for success in high-performance sport. It necessitates an increasing amount of financial and personal support. Its successful furtherance, therefore, depends first on a country's specific resources such as size of population and per capita income, and second on the country's readiness to apply these resources to the furtherance of high-performance sport. Thus, a country's economic power determines, to a great extent, its participation and success in the Olympic Games. National income is a particularly useful indicator. This is valid to a lesser extent for the degree of industrialisation, for labour productivity, and for the proportion of the population employed in agriculture (Ibrahim, 1969; Ball, 1972; Pooley, 1975; Colwell, 1981). In addition, factors such as protein consumption, degree of urbanisation, and numbers employed in industry have been ascertained as being important for Olympic success (Ibrahim, 1969; Nowikov & Maximenko, 1973).

Above all, the political system and how development strategies are pursued determine how existing resources are used for and applied to sport. Research results show that the stability and maturity of a political system are more likely to lead to success in Olympic competition (Ball, 1972; Colwell, 1981), that power and international influence are closely connected to success in international sport (Pooley, 1975), and that political constitution is an influencing factor inasmuch as totalitarian systems are more successful than democratic and authoritarian systems (Colwell, 1981). Simultaneously, a country's social organisation, especially the extent of social inequality, affects sports success. Success at international level is more probable if there are only slight differences within and between the various social layers, that is, if the structure of the society is homogeneous (Ball, 1972), if there are only minor social differences between the sexes (Seppanen, 1981), and if there are only slight differences in income (Ibrahim, 1969).

Finally, to estimate the chances of success for third world countries in international competition, it is necessary to bear in mind that these countries almost exclusively had to adopt sports disciplines that originated in industrial countries. This also constitutes a disadvantage and limits their chances of being successful at an international level. 'How about rock garden polo which is played by the Pathans and other mountain tribes in the border regions of Pakistan and Afghanistan . . . and which is the most popular sport there? It is easy to imagine the indignation which would arise if this form of polo became an Olympic discipline, for example, as a substitute for show jumping in which the Germans have very often been successful' (Eppler, 1978, p. 102). Even if developing countries concentrated the means at their disposal for sports advancement on high-performance sport, their chances of success would still be very limited. Thus, high-performance sport remains almost exclusively limited to industrial countries. Financial reasons as well as other factors lead to a lack of equal opportunities. Equality of opportunity is a fundamental feature of modern sport and is crucial for its legitimation. For these reasons a marked success of third world countries in international competition is most improbable.

REFERENCES

Allison, M.T., & Lüschen, G. (1979). A comparative analysis of Navaho and Anglo basketball sport systems. *International Review of Sport Sociology*, **14**(3-4), 75-86.

Ball, D.W. (1972). Olympic games competition: Structural correlates of national success. *International Journal of Comparative Sociology*, 13.

Clignet, R., & Stark, M.(1974). Modernization and the game of soccer in Cameroun. *International Review of Sport Sociology*, 9.

Colwell, B.J. (1981). *Sociocultural determinants of international sporting success: The 1976 summer Olympic Games*, PhD Thesis, Waterloo, Ontario.

Dunlap, H. (1951). Games, sports dancing and other rigorous recreational activities and their function in Samoan culture. *Research Quarterly*, 22.

Dunning, E. (1973). The structural-functional properties of folk-games and modern sports. *Sportwissenschaft*, 3.

Eichberg, H. (1975). Spielverhalten und relationsgesellschaft in West Sumatra. *Stadion*, 1.

Eisenstadt, S.N. (1966). *Modernisation: Protest and change*. Englewood Cliffs, NJ: Prentice Hall.

Eppler, E. (1978). Entwicklungshilfe durch Sport. In Tetsch, E. (Ed.), *Sport und Kulturwandel*. Stuttgart.

Fröhlich, D. (1970). *Nationalismus und Nationalstaat in Entwicklungsländern*. Meisenheim.

Heinemann, K., & Horch, H.D. (1981). Soziologie der Sportorganisation. *Sportwissenschaft*, 11.

Heinemann, K. (1980). *Einführung in die Soziologie des Sports*. Schorndorf: Karl Hofmann.

Ibrahim, H. (1969). *Olympic achievement and social differentiation*. Lagos.

Novikov, A., & Maximenko, A. (1972). The influence of selected socio-economic factors on the level of sports achievement in various countries. *International Review of Sport Sociology*, 7.

Pooley, J. (1975). *Winning at the Olympics: A quantitative analysis*. Paper presented at the APHPERs Conference, Charlotte Town.

Pye, L.W. (1966). *Aspects of political development*, 8th Ed. Boston: Little, Brown.

Riegel, K.G. (1976). *Politische Soziologie Unterindustrialisierter Länder*. Wiesbaden.

Rittner, V. (1978). Sport als kulturexport. In Tetsch, E. (Ed.), *Sport und kulturwandel*. Stuttgart.

Seppanen, P. (1981). Olympic success: A cross-national perspective. In Lüschen G., & Sage G. (Eds.), *Handbook of social science of sport* (93-116). Champaign, IL: Stipes.

Stumpf, F. (1948). Some aspects of the role of games, sports and recreational activities in the culture of primitive people. *Research Quarterly*, 20.

Sutphen, R. (1973.) *National power and Olympic success*. Memphis.

International Aspects of Sport in Latin America: Perceptions, Prospects, and Proposals

Joseph L. Arbena

The structure and practice of sport in twentieth-century Latin America are fundamentally an expression of international forces, tempered by national and local environments. Put another way, we cannot understand the evolution of Latin American sport over the last hundred years or so apart from an international—both regional and global—context. Even those institutions and activities that are nominally domestic are significantly shaped in both form and function by international (or extranational) forces[1].

Working from that assumption, I propose first to set out examples of some of the more obvious areas of international sporting relationships in the recent Latin American experience, noting particularly where research has already been done or can be most easily advanced[2]. Second, I propose to raise some other international questions that have thus far not received much attention but which offer exciting possibilities both for study and for application to policies and programmes.

SPORT AS VEHICLE FOR COLONIALISM AND ANTICOLONIALISM/NATIONALISM

With little debate, it seems fair to follow Bale, Guttmann, and others in concluding that the history (and language) of 'modern', organised sport in Latin America is the history of the diffusion, adoption, and manipulation of sports invented and/or codified and institutionalised by Europeans, mainly the British and Anglo-Americans[3]. One need spend only a weekend in (say) Buenos Aires (or perhaps Montevideo or Santiago) to appreciate the pervasiveness today of such sports as soccer, rugby, polo, cycling, boxing, horse racing, rowing, tennis, golf, auto racing, even—though less important than a few decades ago—fencing, and track and field. In a few places, several Iberian sports (such as bullfighting[4] and derivatives of the Basque family of ball games,[5]) persist on a lower level, while indigenous survivals are mainly anthropological or recreational curiosities[6]. Basketball[7] and volleyball are now widely played from north to south. Regionally, in Anglo-Caribbean areas cricket fills the top sporting spot, while among many circum-Caribbean hispanophones, both Indo and Afro, baseball is 'el rey de los deportes' ('the king of sports')[8].

Elsewhere, I have speculated on why it was that these changes, which were already visible long before the end of the last century, occurred so rapidly in Latin

America and with what consequences. No doubt, it was a combination of both the 'intrinsic ludic properties' and the 'extrinsic cultural associations' that led Latin Americans increasingly to play European games[9]. Likewise, I do not doubt that those imported sports had a partly imperialistic impact in that they helped to shape local elites and their values in ways at least initially beneficial to the Europeans and that those sports made the Latin Americans just a bit more 'dependent' on the dominant European world[10]. The irony, then, is that while Latin American societies were gradually trying to strengthen nationalistic feelings, they were often doing so along with, and at times by means of, the increasing presence of imported European culture[11]. The resultant paradox is that, if sport was a mechanism for reinforcing formal or informal colonial relationships, it would eventually become one of various means by which the subjects turned the tables on their masters[12].

This is most directly seen in areas held into the present century as part of formal colonial empires, the best example being that of the British West Indies. Virtually everyone who writes on the subject concedes that learning the game and the ethic of cricket may have initially made West Indian blacks better colonial subjects. Eventually, however, their enthusiasm for and skill at the sport made it easier for those blacks to challenge the foundations of racism, to prove their social and mental worth, and to pursue more confidently the road to national independence and self-government[13].

Less overt, but detectable nonetheless, is the place of sport in promoting a sense of national identity and importance, which can also contribute to weakening the hold of informal empires and the constraints of cultural dependency in the Latin American world[14]. For example, Argentine historian José Speroni would later classify the bout between Luis Angel Firpo and Jack Dempsey at the Polo grounds in 1923 as an important event in the development of Argentine sport, national identity, and international image. Despite his controversial loss, Firpo's mere participation at that level made him 'the first Argentine athlete to attract world attention', represented Argentina's 'first great sporting triumph', and affirmed that 'we were more than a pasture populated by cows'. Also, public interest in the event, aided by new communications technology, helped build national unity and provide a myth in the formation of a sense of nationhood[15]. Forty years after the fact, a Venezuelan president and a sportswriter would look back to their country's victory over a powerful Cuban team to win the amateur baseball World Series played in Havana. The 20 members of the 1941 squad that accomplished this magnificent feat, Venezuela's first great triumph in international sport, were all heroes. The memory of those 'generals in peacetime battle' was revived to stimulate a renewed Venezuelan national pride and a commitment to building a sporting spirit[16].

With a bit less hyperbole and perhaps also a bit less accuracy, a Costa Rican writer would pronounce soccer 'our most popular sport which across the years has brought recognition and prestige to the country'[17]. And, more recently, when they had little else to cheer about, Peruvians could proudly point to the continued international achievements of their women's volleyball team. This success was gained, some writers suggest, because the players do not behave like typical Peruvians, or at least not like typical Peruvian males, in that they have learned to sacrifice in preparation and to cooperate in play[18].

In her oft-cited work, Lever argues strongly that soccer has aided the process of Brazilian national unity by making citizens aware of other regions of their country through the regular competition with other teams, through the lottery that accompanies league and championship play, and through the symbolism of the national team, composed of players from all regions and for whom all Brazilians can cheer. Over the long haul, it is unclear if such feelings run deep—if Brazilians in the south, for example, really do identify with those in the northeast or the Amazon basin. But in the short run there is no denying that Brazilians become very passionate about the fortunes of their representatives in the World Cup[19].

To the extent that these examples and claims are accurate, we may conclude that, in selected cases, sport has contributed to a sense of identity within colonial or neocolonial communities; and this in turn may have facilitated certain political or cultural reactions against outside domination[20]. Still, after reviewing the larger pattern of Latin American history, it seems to me questionable that sport has contributed significantly or uniquely to the construction of cohesive national identity—to the building of 'nations' in the old-fashioned sense of the word—a position consistent with the view of Frey that, in terms of development and nation-building, the impact of sports policy and sporting activities is likely to be 'short-term, superficial . . . superfluous'[21].

In fact, it seems fair to conclude that in some instances sport has provided the site or the circumstances in which internal regional, ethnic, gender, or class conflicts have been not merely expressed but intensified[22]. Certainly, the recent events in Eastern Europe, particularly in the case of East Germany, suggest that success in the international sporting arena is no guarantee of national vitality or state stability[23]. Obviously, whether sport serves to unify or divide at any given level of community identity depends on a multiplicity of contextual factors.

SPORT AS MEANS TO PROMOTE DEVELOPMENT

Related to the achievement of national independence and a degree of national identity in the international community has been the pursuit of 'development' as measured by standards generally set by the Western or Westernised international community. In general, those sports imported after the middle of the nineteenth century came to be inextricably intertwined with other European (or North American) institutions, such as schools, athletic and social clubs, and commercial enterprises[24]. To the extent that sport, as many Victorian proponents hoped, also conveyed values and models, they likewise offered a potential means to modify traditional Latin American society, be it some remnant of an indigenous culture or more likely some creole or mixed variety[25]. Following the oft-cited teachings of the Argentine politician and educator Domingo F. Sarmiento, that the only way for any country of Latin America to progress was through a major acceptance of European behaviour, leaders in different parts of the hemisphere began to embrace European sports and physical education, along with other cultural forms, as a viable means to develop their own national societies[26]. Even José Vasconcelos, Mexico's renowned nationalist and progressive educator, would propound the utility of play, exercise, and sport as part of the total education process because of what these would teach students: (Yanqui-style) teamwork, loyalty, and sacrifice useful in the workplace, as well as an appreciation for beauty and Christian virtue[27].

Later efforts to promote greater nationalism and development were not accompanied by serious efforts to discard the sports, games, and physical education programmes of the Western colonists/imperialists, though in some cases questions were raised about the efficacy of the structures and, especially, commercial values often attached to those practices[28], and a few commentators did propose the revival or maintenance of selected traditional folk games and recreational activities[29]. Despite the latter, most of the familiar arguments have been heard from the 1880s to the present in support of expanding opportunities and resources for the practice of those 'modern', imported sports: Sport encourages hygiene and health; sport teaches cooperation and discipline; sport moulds better workers; sport reduces vice and crime; sport makes people happier[30]; and, it is hoped, a successful sports programme or a positive sports image can attract foreign investment and tourism[31].

SPORT AS FOREIGN POLICY

Parallel to and often in support of programmes of anticolonialism/nationalism and of domestic development has been the use of sports as a part of the foreign policy of different Latin American countries. This has taken various forms, such as the hosting of international sporting competitions, the preparation of athletes capable of winning on the international playing field, or the sending of athletic advisors to less blessed countries. In general, the objectives of these efforts have been to raise a country's international prestige, to legitimise an incumbent regime, and to attract such beneficial rewards as foreign aid, foreign investment, and tourism[32].

Examples of these over the last 60 years are numerous, especially in reference to the hosting of international sporting events on any of several levels. As early as 1930, for example, Uruguayans gained great satisfaction from both hosting and winning the inaugural soccer World Cup[33]. In later years Brazil (1950), Chile (1962), Mexico (1970 and 1986), and Argentina (1978) would pride themselves on their ability to organise this increasingly complicated affair; Mexico, of course, would also sponsor the 1968 Olympiad. Still, the hosting of these events was never without major critics, and, by contrast, few Colombians were seriously upset when their government opted not to sponsor the 1986 festival[34]. Examples of more modest attempts at using such events to stimulate national pride and the legitimacy of regimes include Mexico's inauguration of the Central American and Caribbean Games in 1926 (at a time when Mexico was seeking reacceptance in the international community following its destructive Revolution of 1910-1920 and was attempting to become a 'subregional' power in Central America)[35]; the convening of the first Bolivarian Games in August 1938 in conjunction with the four hundredth anniversary of the founding of Bogotá, Colombia; Peronista Argentina's invitation to launch the Pan American Games in 1951[36]; and Guatemala's hosting, in 1950, of the sixth edition of the games begun in Mexico in 1926. The last is instructive because it permitted a self-styled revolutionary regime to present itself at home and abroad as competent, democratic, peace-loving, and worthy of popular support. 'Doing sport, we build the Fatherland' became a motto of the Games, and Guatemalans were encouraged to take national pride in what they had accomplished, while remembering their ties to other brown-skinned and dark-eyed peoples of America[37].

Surely one of the most extreme, even disgusting, examples of sports as foreign (and domestic) policy in the context of hosting an international competition involved the Argentine military and the soccer World Cup of 1978. Here a brutally repressive regime sought to strengthen legitimacy at home and to expand approval abroad by effectively organising the event, by investing in conspicuous infrastructure (e.g., colour television capabilities, improved stadiums and airports, new hotels, etc.), and by putting a competitive team on the field. This they did, and the short-run payoff was favourable to the generals and admirals. But later revelations—most of which were suspected all along—of corruption, assassinations, media control, and basic ineptitude led to ever greater repudiation of the military junta and its collaborators, though most Argentines remained cautiously content with the Cup victory[38].

In short, the most common form of direct government involvement in sports as foreign policy has been in hosting international competitions, perhaps because this has a more obvious domestic physical payoff and offers the chance for somebody to make money.

No doubt the most comprehensive use of sports as an element in the conduct of foreign policy is found in Castroite Cuba. The Cubans have been particularly effective in using their successes in sport to support and publicise their version of socialism both at home and abroad. They have likewise used sports continually to highlight their conflicts with the United States, while strengthening their friendship with the former Soviet Union and (until 1989-90) the Eastern Bloc. And they have manipulated their sporting image, the personal appeal of their athletes, and their technical assistance as tools in reinforcing a claim to be a leader among third world countries[39].

Despite these examples, I conclude that, with the exception of Cuba since the early 1960s, Latin American governments have not made sports a consistent and meaningful component of their official foreign policy. This is mainly due to a lack of resources and hence of influence in international sports arenas. In theory they might wish to do more, but those who control the allocation of necessary funds just have not desired to make a long-term commitment in that area; in some cases, critics contend, they have used their positions for personal profit and pleasure rather than the enhancement of national sports performance[40].

SPORT AS SOURCE
OF INTERNATIONAL COOPERATION AND CONFLICT

Clearly the creation (and maintenance) of organisations that promote regular international athletic competition and, in some instances, physical education as well, represents a move towards regional cooperation, at least a modicum of friendship, and a step away from overt political conflict. The Central American and Caribbean Games, the Bolivarian Games, the Pan American Games, the Copa Libertadores, various South American championships, and the Latin American and Caribbean Intergovernmental Organisation (ODILAC)[41] all demand a willingness to contribute and work together, all require visits to neighbouring countries, all promote a feeling of shared problems and of a common destiny[42].

If sporting competition has helped build friendly bridges across national boundaries, we should also ask if sport in Latin America has contributed to promoting friction among peoples and their governments across those same frontiers. There is, of course, the oft-cited case of the 'Soccer War', the rather short (100 hours) armed conflict between El Salvador and Honduras that broke out in 1969 after a series of regional matches in the elimination round prior to the 1970 Mundial. The truth is that, even here, the name is a misnomer, in that events on the pitch were at best a catalyst, at worst an excuse, the causes of the conflict residing in much deeper socioeconomic and political factors that were likely to have provoked some confrontation whatever the final goal tally[43].

Beyond that, except for occasional complaints about the comportment of a player on the field or the decisions of certain officials, I find little evidence that the emotions associated with sporting competitions have exacerbated international tensions or deepened negative feelings towards outsiders, though the Cuban factor has provoked a few unpleasant incidents at the sites of international competition[44]. While United States athletes did compete in the August 1991 Pan American Games in Cuba, U.S. spectators and U.S. cash were excluded to the extent that American officials could control them, and U.S. media coverage often reflected U.S. political biases[45].

Sporting events, in sum, may be modified or suspended because of political considerations, but sporting problems in Latin America do not alter normal political activities or policy guidelines. This conclusion seems compatible with the view of Günther Lüschen that there is evidence to support both the argument that sport may serve to defuse and reduce social tensions and the argument that sport may create conditions or stimulate emotions that provoke social tensions: 'Conflict resolution or conflict instigation through sport is a functional not a causal question'[46].

RESEARCH PROPOSALS

While there is surely more material available on Latin American sports than most of us would have realised a mere five years ago, much of this, whether quantitative or qualitative, is neither highly sophisticated nor analytical. And the overwhelming bulk of it is still in either Spanish or Portuguese. So, as I have been suggesting, we know many questions to ask and perhaps even possess the basis for offering some tentative answers, but we need an exceptional amount of field work if we hope to understand how these processes have worked themselves out at various social and geographical levels in different cultural and historical contexts; for historical questions we still even need to identify potential sources[47].

Before ending, I would like to go beyond the four broad historical themes I have already articulated and pose three more questions that are of immediate significance on the Latin American sporting scene and that have major implications for the evolution of Latin American sport and culture.

Foreign Sports in the Latin American Media

On my trips to Latin America during the last decade—that is, since I entered the field of sports studies—I have been most impressed (along with the sheer quantity of material on sports) by the increasing visibility of foreign sports in the Latin American media. One aspect of this is the reporting in the print media of news, especially game results, from foreign countries both within and, more striking, outside Latin America. This includes Europe and, increasingly, the United States. For sports like soccer, cycling, boxing, baseball, and even Formula I and Indy car racing, in which Latin Americans compete, this may be reasonable, but such is hardly the case with American football and basketball[48].

A second feature, which may partly explain the first, is the growing availability of cable television from the United States: ESPN, CNN, the major networks, and more. And, where cable goes, so go sports! I've watched NCAA basketball tournament games in Guatemala City and NFL playoffs in the Key Largo bar in downtown San José, Costa Rica. I've seen late-night scores in a hotel on Copacabana Beach in Rio de Janeiro and cheered for Clemson against Penn State in the Citrus Bowl while visiting a small town in rural Mexico.

It may be some years before we fully appreciate the meaning of these phenomena, but as the Mandles have been doing in the Anglophone Caribbean, it is not too soon to start investigating[49]. Who programmes and sponsors these events (or chooses to write these articles) and why? Who watches (reads) and why? And how do these images—written or visual—affect cultural forms and values, racial attitudes, commercial and consumption drives, and the nature of language, itself such a powerful force in moulding social attitudes and behaviour[50]?

International Migration of Players

Before 1959, many Cubans took pride in the number of their countrymen who became successful professional athletes, mainly boxers and baseball players and mainly in the United States. Since 1959, the anti-Castro community still cites those heroes of their youth as evidence that the old Cuba was a source of champions[51]. Not surprisingly, since 1959, the backers of the Revolution cite that same evidence to support their contention that capitalist/neocolonial Cuba had an elitist sports system that gave opportunities to few people and then exploited, through export, those few (usually black) athletes from the lower classes who did reach the top[52]. Whatever the merits of the debate, it is clear that before 1959, for Cuban athletes to succeed as professionals, they had to leave their island republic[53].

Following the Cuban Revolution, the supply of Cuban athletes for North American markets dried up. In the case of baseball, at least, new sources were found in other areas of the circum-Caribbean. The most prominent of these has been the Dominican Republic, though baseball players in smaller numbers have also reached the Major Leagues from Mexico, Panama, Nicaragua, Colombia, Venezuela, and Puerto Rico. Those same countries have also provided many of the boxers of the last two decades, and even a few jockeys and American football players. Despite periodic sketches offered in *Sports Illustrated* and occasional popular biographies—most in Spanish unless dealing with Roberto Clemente—we really know very little about these 'migrant workers', their backgrounds, their experiences, and the impact of their careers on their homelands and their host societies[54].

Much to the dismay of soccer fans in the far south, a similar relationship has developed between various South American countries and wealthy European professional clubs[55]. In the words of Argentine journalist Osvaldo Bayer: 'The central countries, in the same manner as they carry away the riches of the Third World, likewise carry off their best soccer players'[56]. The result for Uruguay, laments long-time player and coach 'Pepe' Sasía, is that 'now the best Uruguayan players play here as little boys, when they are just beginning, and as veterans when they are finishing. Their [full] youth and their peak athletic years are spent abroad'. It is a problem, argues Sasía, rooted in the region's social and economic conditions[56]. Those clubs with players to sell make money up front, and the families of those who play in Europe may gain from the inflated salaries. But the quality of play on the field drops markedly, as do attendance and gate receipts. The geographical dispersal of the best players from the Southern Cone countries also allegedly makes it more difficult for the coaches of their national teams to put together an experienced, winning combination for international competition.

This is not exactly a new phenomenon even in South America. For a variety of reasons, athletes, especially professional and semiprofessional soccer players, have been crossing international borders, even oceans, for several generations. In particular, there has long been easy movement among the neighbouring countries of Argentina, Paraguay, and Uruguay, while a few Latin stars were testing the European fields of Italy and Spain. Following the Argentine soccer players' strike of 1948, there was an even greater exodus from the pampas, both to Europe and to other South American countries such as Chile and Colombia that were struggling to catch up athletically with their more powerful continental competitors. Vacant positions in Buenos Aires were filled in turn by players imported from weaker South American economies (e.g., Peru, Bolivia, and, as before, Paraguay), intensifying a process that continues to the present[57].

In a sense, what we are asking here is whether certain international sporting relationships actually produce underdevelopment or if these patterns of 'muscle drain' are merely reflections of deeper, more pervasive structural problems that affect sports but are not caused by them. Or, by bringing income into the exporting country via player sales or the return flow of salary earnings, are they really benefiting the country economically, even though they may be damaging the quality of play and the psyche of frustrated fans? Klein, in his work on American baseball recruitment in the Dominican Republic, has suggested how the penetration of a 'foreign' sport and its institutions can be, for the recipient country (whose athletes then emigrate), at one and the same time a source of exploitation and development, of cultural colonialism and nationalism, of domination and creativity, of humiliation and pride, of hegemony and resistance[58].

Foreign Role in Manufacture and Sale of Sports Equipment

Another economic dimension of Latin America's international sports environment is alluded to by Maurice St. Pierre, who notes that the ex-colonial power benefits financially from the continued practice of European sports in the third world: With respect to cricket, 'most of the game's paraphernalia continues to be made in the UK' and exported to the former West Indian colonies[59]. It is suggested that one reason A.J. Spalding wished to introduce baseball into Mexico was because of a desire to sell bats, balls, and gloves in a new and expandable market. And much has been made of the fact that in the early years of the Cuban Revolution, sports programmes were severely handicapped by the lack of access to equipment for sports and physical education due to the embargo spearheaded by the United States. To produce athletes, Cubans also had to learn to produce athletic gear[60]. Following the Sandanista victory in July 1979, Nicaraguan sports administrators faced a similar shortage of domestically manufactured sports equipment and likewise made the decision to create a national sports industry[61].

I admit that I have little hard data on this subject. But I have seen enough posters of Michael Jordan, Spud Webb, Dominique Wilkins and most recently, the 'Dream Team', around Latin America to be convinced that, either through direct exports or licensing arrangements, someone in the United States is making a good deal of money selling footwear and outerwear down south. It is certainly an area that merits study, for as Hardy observed, whether nationally or internationally, 'the social history of sport does not constitute the totality of sports history'[62]. We need to look equally, among other things, at the goods and services that surround the sports industry, ultimately asking 'to what extent the rise of an integrated industry of sport, encompassing both production and distribution, has limited our choices of consumption, both in terms of the range of sports we play and in terms of the *way* we play that limited range'. And here 'we' applies to everybody, everywhere[62].

CONCLUSION

My advice (plea?) to historians and sociologists who in the future look at sport in Latin America—might I apply this to all areas of the world?—is that they consider always the international context. Looking both at institutional structures and operations and at individual human experiences, we need to understand sport as a carrier and modifier of culture, as an expression of national differences and international homogenisation, as a promoter of social stability and social change, as a mechanism for development and underdevelopment, and as a tool of governments and other political agents in pursuing their special agendas.

But I would also, as a humanist (secular or otherwise), beg them not to be excessively utilitarian, deterministic, or pessimistic, not to ignore the basic human qualities that make sport a global source of pleasure, excitement, creativity, and artistic expression[63], whatever the domestic and international contexts. Understand the limitations set by those contexts, but appreciate the latitude and potential that exists for the human will to bend, modify, even break those restraints on both body and mind. As Wagner observes, within certain historical and institutional limits 'it is the people themselves who generally determine what they do and do not want, and it is the people who modify and adapt the cultural imports, the sports, to fit their own needs and values'[64].

NOTES

1. Brian Stoddart, 'Sport in the Social Construction of the Lesser Developed World: A Commentary', *Sociology of Sport Journal*, 6:2 (June 1989), 125-135. See also the essays in Joseph L. Arbena, ed., *Sport and Society in Latin America: Diffusion, Dependency, and the Rise of Mass Culture* (Westport, CT: Greenwood Press, 1988).

2. Research on sport, recreation, and leisure as part of the Iberian conquest and colonisation of Latin American is disappointingly sparse. A few examples of the role of sport in that more distant international experience are found in Eugenio Pereira Salas, *Juegos y alegrías coloniales en Chile* (Santiago: Editora Zig-Zag, 1947) and Nicolás Rangel, *Historia del toreo en México: Epoca colonial (1529-1821)* (México, D.F.: Editorial Cosmos, 1980).

3. John Bale, 'International Sports History as Innovation Diffusion', *Canadian Journal of History of Sport*, XV:1 (May 1984), 38-63; Allen Guttmann, 'Our Former Colonial Masters: The Diffusion of Sports and the Question of Cultural Imperialism', *Stadion*, XIV:1 (1988), 49-63; Part II, chapter 1, pp. 125-137 of the present volume.

4. Historical literature in English on the bullfight across Latin America is limited compared to that on Spain. For an introduction to the Mexican scene, see Linda Cahill, 'Horns, Capes & Courage', *Américas*, 40:6 (November-December 1988), 38-41. The best overall analysis of the bullfight, at least in its Spanish context, may be Garry Marvin, *Bullfight* (Oxford: Basil Blackwell, 1988).

5. Jai-alai, handball, and related games/sports were often associated with French and Spanish immigrant communities from Mexico to Argentina; see Ricardo M. Llanes, *Canchas de pelotas y reñideros de antaño* (Buenos Aires: Municipalidad de la Ciudad de Buenos Aires, 1981).

6. Ted J.J. Leyenaar, *Ulama: The Perpetuation in Mexico of the Pre-Spanish Ball Game Ullamalitzli* (Leiden: E.J. Brill, 1978); Luis Perdomo Orellana, 'The Prehispanic Ballgame Tradition', *Voices of Mexico*, 2 (December 1986-February 1987), 64; Agustín Selza Lozano, 'Apuntes sobre la historia del hockey', *Revista de Derecho Deportivo*, II:6 (1962), 399-416.

7. For information on the role of the Y.M.C.A. in introducing basketball to southern South America, see Enrique A. Birba, *El basket-ball en el Río de la Plata* (Buenos Aires: Imp. Ferrari Hnos., 1930).

8. One view of baseball around the Caribbean is offered in John Krich, *El Béisbol: Travels Through the Pan-American Pastime* (New York: Atlantic Monthly Press, 1989). For a more historical perspective on baseball in Mexico's Yucatán region, see Gilbert M. Joseph, 'Documenting a Regional Pastime: Baseball in Yucatán', in *Windows on Latin America: Understanding Society Through Photographs*, ed. Robert M. Levine (Coral Gables, FL: North-South Center, University of Miami, 1987), pp. 76-89.

9. See Guttmann, 'Our Former Colonial Masters'.

10. Joseph L. Arbena, 'The Diffusion of Modern European Sport in Latin America: A Case Study of Cultural Imperialism?' *South Eastern Latin Americanist*, XXXIII:4 (March 1990), 1-8.

11. Some aspects of the tensions created by the contradictions between the modern and traditional forms of popular culture are analysed in William H. Beezley, *Judas at the Jockey Club and Other Episodes of Porfirian Mexico* (Lincoln: University of Nebraska Press, 1987).

12. Colonial games as a simultaneous source of both proselytism and resistance/ subversion are discussed by Richard Cashman, 'Cricket and Colonialism: Colonial Hegemony and Indigenous Subversion?' in *Pleasure, Profit, Proselytism: British Culture and Sport at Home and Abroad, 1700-1914*, ed. J.A. Mangan (London: Frank Cass, 1988), pp. 258-272. Harold Perkin also observes that in the British Empire of the last hundred years 'sport played a part in holding the Empire together and also, paradoxically, in emancipating the subject nations from tutelage'; see his 'Teaching the Nations How to Play: Sport and Society in the British Empire and Commonwealth', *The International Journal of the History of Sport*, 6:2 (September 1989), 145-155 (quote from p. 145).

13. I cite only a few of the more recent sources: Christine Cummings, 'The Ideology of West Indian Cricket', *Arena Review*, 14:1 (May 1990), pp. 25-32; Brian Stoddart, 'Gary Sobers and Cultural Identity in the Caribbean', *Sporting Traditions*, 5:1 (November 1988), 131-146; Keith A.P. Sandiford, 'Cricket and the Barbadian Society', *Canadian Journal of History*, XXI (December 1986), pp. 353-370.

14. Perkin comments on the place of sport in the operation of Britain's 'informal' empire, including the South American colonies of Argentina and Chile in 'Teaching the Nations How to Play'.

15. José Speroni, 'Firpo-Dempsey; el combate del siglo', *Todo Es Historia*, I:6 (October 1967), 26-32. Earlier Argentine glorifications of Firpo are found in Carlos Berdier Uriburu, *Hacia el campeonato mundial; las grandes peleas del 'Toro Salvaje de las Pampas'* (Buenos Aires: Agencia General de Librería y Publicaciones, 1923) and Horacio Estol, *Vida y combates de Luis Angel Firpo* (Buenos Aires: Editorial Bell, 1946).

16. Alí Ramos, *Todos fueron héroes* (Caracas: Ministerio de Información y Turismo, 1982), with a Prologue by President Luis Herrera Campíns.

17. Fernando Naranjo Madrigal, *Epoca de oro del fútbol en Costa Rica* (San José: Editorial Costa Rica, 1988), p. 11.

18. Abelardo Sánchez León, 'Laboratorio', *Debate*, IX:51 (July-August 1988), 67; José María Salcedo and Abelardo Sánchez León, 'Voleibol peruano: matar por amor al arte', *Quehacer*, 18 (August 1982), 67-83; *Sobre la net: itinerario de victorias* (Lima: Edición Copé, 1983); José Pezet Miró-Quesada et al., 'El fenómeno del vóley', *Debate*, X:53 (November 1988), 30-35.

19. Janet Lever, *Soccer Madness* (Chicago: University of Chicago Press, 1983). Alan Klein refutes Lever's contention that soccer promotes Brazilian national unity, but suggests that it could serve as a 'social bonding mechanism on a regional level'; see his review of *Soccer Madness* in *Sociology of Sport Journal*, 1:2 (1984), 195-197. On the painful reaction to Brazil's loss in the World Cup final of 1950, see Paulo Perdigão, *Antonomia de uma derrota* (Porto Alegre: L&PM Editores, 1986).

20. Geoffrey Caldwell argues strongly that sport has helped strengthen nationalism in such states as Australia, Canada, and the former Soviet Union; see 'International Sport and National Identity', *International Social Science Journal*, XXXIV:2 (1982), 173-183.

21. Joseph L. Arbena, 'Sport and Nationalism in Latin America, 1880-1970: The Paradox of Promoting and Performing "European" Sports' (Paper presented at the second conference of the International Society for the Study of European Ideas, Leuven, Belgium, September 1990); James H. Frey, 'The Internal and External Role of Sport in National Development', *Journal of National Development*, I:2 (Winter 1988), 65-82 (quote from p. 79).

22. Kevin A. Yelvington, 'Ethnicity "Not Out": The Indian Cricket Tour of the West Indies and the 1976 Elections in Trinidad and Tobago', *Arena Review*, 14:1 (May 1990), 1-12; Gilberto Mantilla Garzón et al., *Los Terceros Juegos Deportivos Nacionales y la prensa* (Quito: Secretaría Nacional de Información Pública, 1975); 'FBC Melgar: Una selección nacional', *Debate*, 17 (November 1982), 73-75. For a broader theoretical view of the issue, see Peter Donnelly, 'Sport as a Site for "Popular" Resistance', in *Popular Cultures and Political Practices*, ed., Richard B. Gruneau (Toronto: Garamond Press, 1988), pp. 69-82.

23. John M. Hoberman, 'The Transformation of East German Sport', *Journal of Sport History*, 17:1 (Spring 1990), 62-68.

24. The connections between modern sports and the values and attitudes associated with urban, industrial, and technological society are analysed by Lincoln Allison, 'Association Football and the Urban Ethos', in *Manchester and São Paulo: Problems of Rapid Urban Growth*, eds. John D. Wirth and Robert L. Jones (Stanford: Stanford University Press, 1978), pp. 203-228.

25. Richard W. Slatta, 'The Demise of the Gaucho and the Rise of Equestrian Sport in Argentina', *Journal of Sport History*, 13:2 (Summer 1986), 97-110.

26. E. Bradford Burns, *Poverty of Progress. Latin America in the Nineteenth Century* (Berkeley: University of California Press, 1980); Carlos Vera Guardia, 'La educación fisica en América Latina', in *Geschichte der Leibesübungen*,

Vol. 6: *Perspektiven des Weltsports*, ed. Horst Ueberhorst (Berlin: Bartels & Wernitz, 1989), pp. 830-842.

27. José Vasconcelos, *Antología de textos sobre educación*, ed. Alicia Molina (México, D.F.: Fonda de Cultura Económica, 1981), pp. 93-101, 127-134.

28. See, for example, Alejandro Cadavel, *El deporte visto por los universitarios* (México, D.F.: UNAM, 1979).

29. Sergio Elías Ortiz, 'Tres modos de jugar a la pelota en Colombia', *Revista Colombiana de Folclor*, 2nd phase; III:8 (1963), 79-88; Daniel Aeta Astorga, *Juegos y deportes con un diccionario de equivalencias* (Santiago: Editorial Nascimento, 1930 [1929]); Marta Lydia Lemus de Storek et al., *Juegos educativos y tradicionales de Guatemala* (Guatemala City: Editorial del Ministerio de Educación Pública, 1961).

30. For some other of the many Latin American statements that link sports and physical education to various standards of progress, see the following: Fernando Coto Martén, 'Recreación y prevención del delito', *Ciencias Sociales*, 34 (1986), 89-96; Numael Hernández, *Educación física escolar* (Bogotá: Imprenta Nacional, 1964); Carlos Ermel de la Cruz, *El Ecuador y sus deportes*, Vol. I (Quito: Imprenta de Suministros, 1957); Enrique Romero Brest et al., *El deporte y la vida* (Buenos Aires: Ministerio de Justicia e Instrucción Pública, 1935); Carlos Felice Castillo, *El deporte institucional* (Caracas: Tipografía Remar, 1973); César Viale, *La educación física obligatoria impulsaría la grandeza nacional* (Buenos Aires: Talleres Gráficos de la Penitenciaría Nacional, 1924). In particular, I have summarised the developmentalist argument as a justification for promoting physical education and sports in twentieth-century Mexico in 'Sport, Development, and Mexican Nationalism, 1920-1970', *Journal of Sport History*, **18**(3), (Winter 1991), 350-364.

31. On the eve of Mexico's hosting of the 1986 soccer Mundial, Adriana de la Mora predicted cautiously that 'Mexico will once again host an international event that will put us in the global limelight and will attract millions of European and American fans whose affluence and goodwill toward our country is more welcome today than ever before'; 'The World Soccer Cup Is Here!' *Voices of Mexico*, No. 10 (June-August 1986), 8-10 (quote from p. 10).

32. For a general summary and analysis of the options available to governments that wish to use sport as an element in the conduct of foreign policy, see James A.R. Nafziger, 'Foreign Policy in the Sports Arena,' in *Government and Sport: The Public Policy Issues*, eds. Arthur T. Johnson and James H. Frey (Totowa, NJ: Rowman & Allanheld, 1985), pp. 248-260.

33. Enrique E. Buero, *Negociaciones internacionales* (Brussels: Imp. Puvrez, 1932); Arturo Carbonell Debali, *Primer campeonato mundial de football* (Montevideo: Impresora Uruguaya, 1930).

34. 'Contra el reloj', *Semana* (Bogotá), No. 421 (May 29-June 5, 1990), 124-126, expresses relief that Colombia rejected the 1986 Mundial. More critical of President Belisario Betancur's decision to let someone else be the host is Cristina de la Torre, '¿Qué pasó con el Mundial?' in Cristina de la Torre et al., *Las cinco maravillas millonarias de Colombia* (Bogotá: Editorial Oveja Negra,

1982), pp. 11-64; she blames the shift on an international plot engineered by Henry Kissinger, probably in hopes of winning the prize for the United States.

35. Mexico also sent small squads to the Olympic Games of 1924 and 1928 as part of this campaign. For sport in Mexican foreign policy in the 1920s and beyond, see my article 'Sport, Development, and Mexican Nationalism, 1920-1970' cited in 31.

36. A brief survey of the history of the Pan American Games is found in Rob Ruck, 'Swifter, Higher, Stronger Around the Hemisphere', *Américas*, 39:4 (July-August 1987), 2-7, 62-63. For comments on sport and Peronismo, see Alberto Ciria, *Política y cultura popular: la Argentina peronista, 1946-1955* (Buenos Aires: Ediciones de la Flor, 1983) and [Juan Domingo Perón], *Delegados del deporte argentino escuchan a Perón* (Buenos Aires: Presidencia de la Nación, 1950).

37. Among many sources on the Guatemalan case are Carlos A. Paz Tejada, *Discurso pronunciado . . . en al acto de inauguración de los VI Juegos Deportivos Centroamericanos y del Caribe* (Guatemala City: Tipografia Nacional, 1950) and Benjamín Paniagua S. et al., *Guatemala* (Guatemala City: Tipografia Nacional, 1950).

38. Joseph L. Arbena, 'Generals and *Goles*: Assessing the Connection Between the Military and Soccer in Argentina', *The International Journal of the History of Sport*, 7:1 (May 1990), 120-130. To some degree the Argentines were merely copying earlier Brazilian military efforts to gain political benefit from the successes of their national soccer team; see Lever, *Soccer Madness*, and Peter Flynn, 'Sambas, Soccer and Nationalism', *New Society*, 18:464 (August 19, 1971), 327-330.

39. John Sugden, Alan Tomlinson, and Eamon McCartan, 'The Making and Remaking of White Lightning in Cuba: Politics, Sport and Physical Education 30 Years After the Revolution', *Arena Review*, 14:1 (May 1990), 101-109; Paula J. Pettavino, Novel Revolutionary Forms: The Use of Unconventional Diplomacy in *Cuba: The International Dimensions*, eds. George Fauriol and Eva Loser (New Brunswick, NJ: Transaction Books, 1990), pp. 373-403.

40. Typical comments on chronic underfunding and mismanagement of international athletic programmes are found in Rafael Matallana Rivera, 'The COC, el avestruz y el deporte', *Cronómetro*, No. 451 (August 6, 1988), 3-5; Augusto Antonio Cornejo, 'Historia de la educación física y el deporte en El Salvador', in *Geschichte der Leibesübungen*, Vol. 6: *Perspektiven des Weltsports*, ed. Horst Ueberhorst (Berlin: Bartels & Wernitz, 1989), pp. 1070-1078.

41. *¿Qué es ODILAC?* (Caracas: Instituto Nacional de Deportes, 1981).

42. Roman Czula contends, without much empirical evidence, that given the pressure to win games and medals, thus intensifying serious competition and nationalism, more harm than good results from international contacts among athletes; see 'Sport as an Agent of Social Change', *Quest*, 31:1 (1979), 45-49. As discussed, I doubt the validity of this view at least as it applies to Latin America, perhaps because historically the latter has been an area already relatively free of major international hostilities, even if it has not always enjoyed cooperation sufficient to produce meaningful integration.

43. William H. Durham, *Scarcity and Survival in Central America. Ecological Origins of the Soccer War* (Stanford: Stanford University Press, 1979).

44. Cubans themselves comment on both the problems and successes they experienced, athletically and politically, during the Tenth Central American and Caribbean Games held in Puerto Rico (June 1966), in Juan Marrero, *Nos vimos en Puerto Rico (crónicas)* (La Habana: Ediciones Granma, 1966).

45. Sandra Levinson, 'The Pan American Games: Millions Do the Wave,' *Cuba Update*, XII:4 (November 1991), 5-7.

46. Günther Lüschen, 'Sport, Conflict and Conflict Resolution', *International Social Science Journal*, XXXIV:2 (1982), 185-196 (quote from p. 190).

47. Eric A. Wagner, 'Sport', in *Handbook of Latin American Popular Culture*, eds. Harold E. Hinds, Jr. and Charles M. Tatum (Westport, CT: Greenwood Press, 1985), pp. 135-150; Joseph L. Arbena, comp., *An Annotated Bibliography of Latin American Sport: Pre-Conquest to the Present* (Westport, CT: Greenwood Press, 1989); Joseph L. Arbena, 'Winners Without Losers: Perspectives on Latin American Sport', *Studies in Latin American Popular Culture*, 7 (1988), 303-308. Several examples of the use of old photographs to reveal the history of sport are found in Robert M. Levine, ed., *Windows on Latin America: Understanding Society Through Photographs* (Coral Gables, FL: North-South Center, University of Miami, 1987).

48. Examples of Latin American sports periodicals that offer extensive coverage of foreign sports include *Ovaciones* (Mexico City), *Encestando* (Bahía Blanca, Argentina), *Meridiano* (Caracas) and *Play Ball* (Panama). An interesting source from the late 1940s is *Deporte Gráfico* (Mexico City).

49. Jay R. Mandle and Joan D. Mandle, *Grass Roots Commitment: Basketball and Society in Trinidad and Tobago* (Parkersburg, IA: Caribbean Books, 1988) contains observations on the impact of televised NBA games among Caribbean islanders.

50. I considered this final point in 'Sports Language, Cultural Imperialism, and the Anti-Imperialist Critique in Latin America' (Paper presented at the annual meeting of the Southeastern Council of Latin American Studies, Jacksonville, FL, March 1991). For an introduction to the theme, see Américo Barabino, 'English Influence on the Common Speech of the River Plate', *Hispania*, 33:2 (May 1950), 163-165, who observes that among selected examples of English influence on the language of both sides of the Río de La Plata 'sports have been the richest source of foreign words'; and Héctor Balsas, 'El fútbol y su injerencia en el habla de los uruguayos', *Foro Literario*, X:17 (1987), 57-62. For a larger critical framework for the analysis of foreign popular culture's penetration of Latin America, see Ariel Dorfman, *The Empire's Old Clothes* (New York: Pantheon Books, 1983).

51. On boxing see Julio Ferreiro Mora, *Historia del boxeo cubano* (Miami: Selecta Enterprises [1978]); on baseball see Angel Torres, *La historia del beisbol cubano, 1878-1976* (Los Angeles, CA: [p.p.], 1976).

52. For example, compare Ferreiro Mora's depiction of Kid Chocolate with that presented by Urbano Fernández in 'La leyenda viviente de Chocolate', *Cuba Internacional*, XIII:139 (June 1981), 48-51.

53. Joseph L. Arbena, 'Sport and Revolution: The Continuing Cuban Experience', *Studies in Latin American Popular Culture*, 9 (1990), 319-328. For the extensive travels of one great Cuban athlete of the 1930s and 1940s, see Evelio Mustelier, *Kid Tunero; veinte años de ring . . . y fuera* (Madrid: Editorial Playor, 1985).

54. Some of the problems confronting the Latin players and the lands they leave behind are discussed in Alan M. Klein, 'Headcase, Headstrong, and Head-of-the-Class: Resocialization and Labelling in Dominican Baseball', *Arena Review*, 14:1 (May 1990), 33-46, and David G. La France, 'A Mexican Popular Image of the United States Through the Baseball Hero, Fernando Valenzuela', *Studies in Latin American Popular Culture*, 4 (1985), 14-23.

55. On the issue of international transfers of professional soccer players, see Jean-François Bourg, *Football Business* (Paris: Olivier Orban, 1986), pp. 27-52.

56. Osvaldo Bayer, *Fútbol argentino* (Buenos Aires: Editorial Sudamericana, 1990), p. 118; José F. Sasía, *Al fonda de la red* (Montevideo: Signos, 1989), pp. 101-102.

57. Pablo A. Ramírez, 'Alzas y bajas en el fervor por el fútbol', *Todo Es Historia*, XXIII:272 (February 1990), 88-96; Armando Ramos Ruiz, *Nuestro fútbol, grandeza y decadencia* (Buenos Aires: LV Producciones, 1973). On the life of a Paraguayan who starred in Argentina, see Roque Meza Vera, *Arsenio Erico, el paraguayo de oro* (Asunción: Talleres Gráficos de Imprenta Comuneros, 1978). On the career of an Argentine who played and coached in Colombia, see Julio Tocker, *Mi fútbol* (Cali: Editora Londir Ltda., 1984). Also see the two works cited in the preceding note. One recent estimate suggests that almost 400 soccer players from Argentina alone are currently performing in Europe; Miguel Hernández, '¿Nuevas brisas en Acapulco?' *Cuba Internacional*, XXX:267 (March 1992), 50-52.

58. Alan M. Klein, 'American Hegemony, Dominican Resistance, and Baseball', *Dialectical Anthropology*, 13 (1988), 301-312, and his *Sugarball: The American Game, The Dominican Dream* (New Haven: Yale University Press, 1991). Another study of baseball in the Dominican Republic and its interaction with the United States is Rob Ruck, *The Tropic of Baseball: Baseball in the Dominican Republic* (Westport, CT: Meckler, 1991).

59. Maurice St. Pierre, 'West Indian Cricket: A Cultural Contradiction?' *Arena Review*, 14:1 (May 1990), 23.

60. Geralyn Pye, 'Physical Culture and the Cuban Revolution: Elitism, Egalitarianism and Socialisation in Cuban Physical Culture' (Unpublished Ph.D. thesis, The Flinders University of South Australia, 1990).

61. Wolf Kramer-Mandeau, 'Ocupación, dominación y liberación—La historia del deporte en Nicaragua', in *Geschichte der Leibesübungen*, Vol. 6: *Perspektiven des Weltsports*, ed. Horst Ueberhorst (Berlin: Bartels & Wernitz, 1989), p. 1053.

62. Stephen Hardy, 'Entrepreneurs, Organizations, and the Sport Marketplace: Subjects in Search of Historians', *Journal of Sport History*, 13:1 (Spring 1986), 14-33 (quotes from pp. 15, 33). The highly provocative Argentine sociologist Juan José Sebreli asks a few of the same questions in *Fútbol y masas* (Buenos Aires: Editorial Galerna, 1981).

63. Latin American comments on 'sport as art' are common; see, for example, Mario De la Cueva, 'El deporte como una de las bellas artes', *Excélsior* (October 27, 1970); Orlando García Valverde, *Poesía al deporte* (San José, Costa Rica: Imprenta Nacional, 1980); and Julio Folle Larreto, *Por esos caminos de Dios: Deporte, arte, religión* (Montevideo: Barreiro y Ramos, 1976).

64. Eric A. Wagner, 'Sport in Asia and Africa: Americanization or Mundialization?' *Sociology of Sport Journal*, 7:4 (December 1990), 402. Peter Donnelly also concludes that 'popular culture is *made*, not merely *imposed* from above'; 'Sport as a Site for "Popular" Resistance', p. 80. John Krich, speculating on the spread of 'Anglo' baseball through the 'Latin' Caribbean, remarks that 'baseball wasn't shoved down anyone's throat; the candy was seized even before it was dangled', surviving today 'as tradition, not submission'; Krich, *El Béisbol*, pp. 191, 264.

The Industrialisation of the United States and the 'Bourgeoisification' of American Sport[1]

Alan Ingham
Robert Beamish

A discussion of the maturation of industrial capitalism and the 'bourgeoisification' of game-contests is not a novel undertaking. One of the best known descriptions of this process is Dunning's 'The Development of Modern Football' (Dunning, 1972), which has been incorporated into a more expanded treatment titled *Barbarians, Gentlemen and Players* (Dunning & Sheard, 1979). And there have been others (see Adelman, 1986; Gruneau, 1981; Ingham, 1978; Metcalfe, 1982). Because these earlier studies have brought together considerable historical data to document the rise of organised, consumer-oriented sports, it is not our intent merely to present that material one more time.

INSTRUMENTAL RATIONALITY AND VALORISATION

In this essay, we will employ two key concepts—instrumental rationality and valorisation—drawn respectively from the works of Max Weber and Karl Marx to organize theoretically an analysis of the forces and dynamics that underlay the emergence of consumer sport within capitalist society. This effort to establish a general framework to explain a process that occurred in different places and at different times is an imperative of sociological study. Sociology is not the recounting of isolated events; its goal is to use contemporary and/or historical events as the basis for developing general schemas that provide a comparative framework to enrich our understanding of other particular events and/or social formations (see Ingham, 1979; Ingham & Hardy, 1984, 1993). Our essay uses the conceptions of instrumental rationality and valorisation—which were originally developed to explain certain general features of capitalist society—to analyse the development of sport in the United States from the middle of the nineteenth century on. While details and dates in other countries may differ, we are confident that our framework will explain the same changes in Canada, Britain, France, Germany, and other western European capitalist societies. However, before discussing the rise of commercial sport in America, we will clarify exactly what each of our key concepts stands for.

Instrumental Rationality (*Zweckrationalitat*)

While it is really impossible to separate instrumental rationality from valorisation—the former's emergence was entailed in the growth of the market economy—for explanatory purposes we will treat it separately in this section. At about the same time the market economy began to emerge there was the development of what sociologists term a new 'worldview' (*Weltanschauung*). Alongside the church-dominated, traditional explanations for the social structure and events in nature grew what is now identified as the scientific worldview[2]. Characteristic of the scientific worldview is the use of human reason to determine experimentally, and thereby predict, events in nature (or society) so that people could profitably employ this knowledge in numerous activities. The scientific worldview represents a specific case of what is more broadly termed an instrumentally rational form of viewing the social and natural worlds—calculation and prediction being central components of the worldview. One of the earliest analysts of various worldviews in general, and of the instrumental rationality of western Europe in particular, was Max Weber; his investigations in this area are still highly influential. We have relied heavily on his work for this discussion.

To understand the concept of rationality one must begin with the basic observation that unlike wolf packs, beehives, or ant colonies, human societies are not organised by instinctive 'programmes'. Humans creatively and intentionally (or purposively) organise their social relations to accomplish a wide variety of objectives. We do this on the basis of reason, but reason, it turns out, is a complex analytical category. Initially it may be divided into two areas.

At a fundamental level, we can note that humans act almost always on the basis of (socially determined) typical processes of action. Thus, behaviour and agency are regular and almost always predictable within certain limits. This regularity is due to what Weber (1974, pp. 23-31) termed practical rules of conduct (*Erfahrungs-regeln*). The behaviour of most people, he argued, is not erratic or irrational—those are characteristics of the insane. Human behaviour is usually rational and conforms to patterns (see also Durkheim, 1938, pp. 1-13). This is a constant of human behaviour that underlies the second broad category of reason (see also Berger & Luckmann, 1969).

Reason in the second sense is more significant to our discussion at hand. Within the society as a whole the individual's practical rules of conduct are shaped by a larger framework. Weber (1978, pp. 212-245) identified three basic types of rationality that structure social conduct as a whole. He noted that *tradition* stood as the basis for what would be considered 'reasonable' in some societies—the influence of religious beliefs and feudal traditions on human conduct in Medieval Europe is a good example of a social framework based on traditional authority. Weber also observed that at various times in history powerful *charismatic figures* had emerged, and, on the basis of their own personal strength and appeal, were able to dictate a code of rational behaviour that might diverge considerably in some respects from earlier rules of conduct. Finally, in some societies, a *legal-rational* framework shaped behaviour. In a legal-rational framework, conduct is governed by a public bureau-cracy. We need only think of the United States, Britain, or Canada at the present time to understand this form of social structuring.

Along with these three frameworks of social structure, Weber (1978, pp. 24-26) examined four underlying types of *individual social action*—affectual, traditional, value-rational, and instrumentally rational action. Very briefly, traditional action is determined by 'ingrained habituation'; affectual action is determined by one's emotional state; and value-rational action is action that derives its reasonableness from some strongly held value (usually ethical, religious, or aesthetic). Finally, instrumentally rational action is behaviour in which one calculates various means and ends to determine the most advantageous course of action. In most cases, advantageous is related to the interests of the dominant class.

It is self-evident in some cases, and becomes apparent in others, that the type of social action employed as a rule of conduct corresponds more with one particular form of social authority than the others. Traditional action will occur most often in traditional societies, value-rational action will predominate under conditions of charismatic authority, and while affective action may occur in any social formation it is more likely to be found in traditionally and charismatically based societies than legal-rational ones since emotional attachment to values and goals is stronger in the former types than the latter. Finally, instrumental rationality can only really exist within a legal-rational social structure and a legal-rational social structure can only arise as more and more decisions at the level of individual social action are subjected to rational calculation and removed from the spheres of tradition or value-rationality.

Once broken down into these categories, it is possible to analyse the motives behind social action within a dominant form of authority structure and see not only how the action of individuals and groups conforms to dominant authority patterns, but also supports and reproduces them. In part two of this essay we will show how the overall rational-legal framework of the United States in the post-1850 period, along with the firmly established instrumentally rational forces of individual social action, significantly structured not only the types of leisure activity available to urban dwellers but also how those activities were consumed. Particularly important was the rational calculation of means and ends in the realm of the marketplace (see Clarke, 1993; Hardy, 1990).

Valorisation (*Verwertung*)[3]

One of the Karl Marx's central concerns throughout his intellectual career was to lay out the economic relations peculiar to capitalist society. In doing so, Marx made numerous comparisons concerning how the goods of a society were produced and distributed. In his studies of the economy, Marx (1973, pp. 88-100) distinguished two 'phases' (or *moments*, technically) that were examined separately at first—although this separation was an artificial one—and then as a unity. The two phases dealt with were production and consumption.

Production refers basically to the labour process—the making of saleable goods (technically termed *commodities*). On the basis of extensive comparative research into primitive societies, Greece and Rome in Antiquity, feudal societies, and capitalist societies in the eighteenth and nineteenth centuries, Marx made some significant observations that are still useful today. Marx found, generally speaking, that labour in capitalist society was quite different from work in other social formations because workers did not have *direct* control over, or access to, the materials necessary for maintaining life (like land to produce food or raw materials for clothing and shelter). This contrasted to feudal conditions where serfs could directly produce most goods they needed because they possessed land over which they enjoyed traditional rights of use in exchange for traditionally established obligations relating to military service and/or work on the feudal lord's land. Nevertheless, while landless workers were disadvantaged in one way there was some compensation; they were not tied to the land by traditional rights and obligations as serfs were and could freely seek out employment wherever it could be found. These workers, looking for jobs on capitalistically run agricultural enterprises, in the cottage industries, or in the cities' emerging factories (or ateliers), are technically called *free wageworkers* because of their freedom to find wage-paying work. They would agree, for a specified wage, to work for a day, a week, a fortnight, etcetera, and then rent shelter and buy food and clothing so that they could live and perhaps support a family.

This is all straightforward enough and familiar to us today but our familiarity should not lead us to overlook three key points. First, the existence of a market society based on the employment of free wageworkers as the dominant means of producing goods for sale to consumers is, historically speaking, a relatively recent phenomenon. Although European trade began to revive as early as the eleventh century, it was severely limited in scope and opposed vigorously by tradition and the church. Throughout the Middle Ages, economic activity remained a subordinate aspect of social life. It was not until the sixteenth and seventeenth centuries that commerce really began to blossom and mercantilism was advanced as an economic theory in the middle of the seventeenth century. The use of large machine tools, like Newcomen's atmospheric engine (1717), Hargreaves's spinning jenny (1764), or Cartwright's power loom (1785), was associated with the so-called first industrial revolution (1750-1850). Thompson (1961) argues that a self-defined, conscious working class in England—Europe's most advanced industrial nation—did not exist until 1830. Furthermore, as we will show with the case of sport, not every aspect of social life fell immediately into the market network even though the market continually expanded its influence (the fast-food industry representing a modern example of market movement into an area of previously domestic responsibility). Consequently, we would emphasise that the social relations of production currently existing are the result of fairly recent human history and, as historical construction, they are susceptible to subsequent change.

The second point we want to establish is that as capitalist relations emerged, they subtly but significantly changed the focus of work. Until the sixteenth century the major purpose behind agricultural and handicraft production was either direct consumption or limited trade of the surplus products. Serfs and handicraft workers were concerned chiefly with producing objects of utility (that is, usefulness—or technically, *use-value*). As market relations grew and as production became increasingly oriented to the market, another aspect of the product became important—its *exchangeability*.

The exchange of two dissimilar products—like boots and coats—could only be equitably calculated on the basis of the time and material costs involved in the production of each. As production time increases for a given item, fewer of the items will be produced, increasing each item's value. Thus, economists noted that work not only produced a useful article but also an article that contained a certain measure of *value*.

As the market became the main vehicle for distributing goods and extracting a profit, producers became increasingly interested in the *value-creating capacity of labour* and less in its purely use-creating capacity. Because a worker could be hired for a definite period of time in which she or he could produce goods that, when sold, would return more money than the employer paid out in wages, employers began to focus exclusively on their own enrichment through value creation rather than the stockpiling and/or consumption of material articles for use and/or ornamentation. Through these changes, the focus of work shifted from the utility of the goods produced to the value-creating capacity of labour, which is a key part of the valorisation process.

The third point to keep in mind concerns the second phase of the unity studied by Marx; that is, consumption. In order for any product to realise its value—indeed, in order for capitalist production to succeed—there must be consumers purchasing the products put into the marketplace. Just as there can be no consumption without production, there cannot be capitalist production without a marketplace inhabited by consumers who have money and feel the need for particular goods and services. With respect to the 'bourgeoisification' of sport from 1840 on in the United States, it was the creation of sport consumers that required the longest time to build, and this was necessary before athletes could become full-time wageworkers in the sport industry. Due to this fact, the bulk of our discussion on sport concerns the development of the consumer market.

To put forth the valorisation process in concise terms we note the following points:

1. In capitalist society valorisation depends on conditions where workers can freely seek out wagework to produce saleable goods that return more money upon sale than the employer spent in wages.
2. It represents a labour process that will be refined and developed primarily to return greater profits to the employer, with the use-value component or production having only secondary importance.
3. Finally, valorisation requires consumers who have money to purchase products for which needs or wants have been (objectively and subjectively) created (see Heller, 1976).

We will show in the next section of this essay how the drive to commercialise components of workers' nonwork time had a profound impact upon the leisure time

es available to, and developed for, the newly created urban populations of
ca and how sport became a sphere of valorised activity (see Betts, 1974;
Hardy, 1982; Ingham, 1978).

THE EMERGENCE OF VALORISED SPORT IN AMERICA[4]

America did not become an *industrial* capitalist society until after parts of Europe
(particularly Britain) had already made the transition[5]. There were several reasons
for the delay. First, land had been inexpensive and the products derived from
the land had constituted the nation's primary resources. Here, the opportunity for
independent household production and simple commodity production may have
slowed not only the transition from 'manufacture' to 'machinofacture' but also the
development of a full-blown capitalist mode of production (see Mutch, 1980).
Second, given the fact that land had been plentiful and America had been, for the
most part, an agrarian, artisan, and trader society, workers for the manufacturing
sector had been in short supply (and therefore expensive). Third, colonial rule and
British mercantile policy had fostered, in the main, agricultural and trade as against
manufacturing concerns within America. Hence an urban, industrial, capitalist class
was, when compared with Britain, slow to develop. Fourth, the American domestic
market for manufactured products was underdeveloped—unlike Britain, farmers and
artisans had not become someone else's creatures and their access to the material
means of labour had prevented them from having to buy most of the goods they
needed and desired. Fifth, communications and transport were inadequate, ineffi-
cient, and expensive. Hence, it had been difficult to expand and exploit the domestic
market that did exist. Finally, the financial community was, even up to the time of
the Civil War, fragmented and disjointed. A national banking and currency system
did not exist, so it was difficult to transfer funds across economic and geographic
boundaries (see Conzen, 1977, p. 90).

Nevertheless, American society did begin slowly to move towards industrial
capitalist production by the end of the eighteenth century. The period between the
War of Independence (1776) and the end of the 1837-1843 depression may be
viewed as a phase of incipient industrialisation. During this period family firms
engaged in manufacturing (see Baltzell, 1958, p. 12) and labour was organised in
factories (especially in the New England and middle Atlantic states). In terms of
sport, this phase was associated with growing urbanisation, which increased the
number of potential sport nodules, but few segments of society had the spare time
or income for actual or vicarious participation in sport. Indeed, for most, harsh labour
discipline and powerful religious restrictions produced conditions that *prevented* the
growth of sport rather than encouraging it.

By the 1840s, however, the American industrial revolution began to emerge from
depression as the domestic market grew in size and in affluence (see North, 1966,
pp. 166-167). Increased immigration, rural-urban migration (caused by the commercialisation and subsequent specialisation of agricultural production and by the rural
population's fecund growth), and the transformation of craftsmen and self-sufficient

commodity producers to wageworkers increased the number of con...
growth spiralled as factories began producing more (and less expensive,
boots, shoes, and other furnished commodities, and could incorporate more o..
urban population into the growing division of labour in the manufacturing sector.

It was during the period of industrialisation that evidence emerges of an initially
incipient but later comprehensive movement toward the creation of instrumentally
rational game-contests—that is, sport in its earliest form. Lucas (1968) correctly
identifies the 1850-1860 decade as the 'prelude' to the rise of organized sport, for
it was in this decade that the industrial transformation of American society began
to get underway—a transformation that widely diffused urban-industrial culture, a
component of which was organised sport (see Ingham, 1978; Ingham et al., 1987).

Having established the approximate point at which industrialisation began to
create the sociocultural conditions favourable to commercial sport, we can show
exactly how the relationship between industrialisation and the instrumental rationalisation of sport fit together. The emergence of sport involved basically two sets of
relations—objective ones related to the impact of industrialisation on all social
relations and subjective relations that became part of broadly based sociopolitical
movements. Since these latter movements were rooted in industrial life (and its
conflicts), we will begin by examining the more objective moment first. Then we
will turn to the subjective side and examine it under five subheadings dealing with
class, social reform movements, the playground movement, its relation to the school
system, and the so-called 'inevitability thesis'. In Figure 1 we have diagrammed
the major categories of relations involved in the creation of modern sport.

THE CONTRIBUTION OF INDUSTRIALISATION
TO SPORT DEVELOPMENT

Turner, among others, argues that the industrial city was at the centre of cultural
change:

> [I]t is well to note that no one meant to create the industrial city. . . . It arose
> as entrepreneurs pursued their interests—profits—and engineers served that
> interest by technological ingenuity. But once created, it became something
> other than a center of business and machine industry, that is, it became a milieu
> having the power to organize socially a structure of behavior and thought for
> those coming under its influence. (Turner, 1940, p. 232)

Thus, it was in response to the burgeoning industrial city that a reorientation in
the conception of culture in general and sport in particular began to be evidenced—
culture and sport were slowly yet progressively shaped by the industrial environment
of the city and the urban market.

The reciprocal acceleration of industrialisation and urbanisation reinforced impersonal relations among people located in clustered populations. This population
pattern deprived many urban residents of the opportunity to enjoy traditional physical
games (see Betts, 1953b, p. 231). Rural-type games were not suited to the regimented,

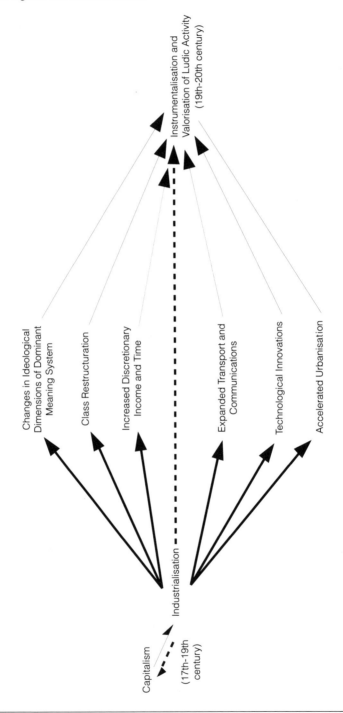

Figure 1.   The long revolution—from tradition to modernity as currently represented by bourgeois hegemony. (Adapted from Ingham, 1978, see also Ingham, 1979).

depersonalised, and cramped urban-industrial existence. Somers makes the point very clearly:

> As thousands of people, both native and foreign born, moved into the country's burgeoning cities, they experienced pressures and problems unknown in rural areas or in the relatively small cities of the colonial period. The century between 1820 and 1920 was in many ways a period of adjustment, a time in which urban Americans learned to live in large cities and to cope with the intricacies of their cramped environment. . . . This process of adjustment produced equally profound changes in urban recreation. Many features of city life, such as long, highly regimented workweeks, the remoteness of the countryside (particularly before improvements in transportation), and the temporary loss of any sense of community that affected many new arrivals in America's metropolises, rendered the simpler, unorganized, and often spontaneous diversions of rural America unsatisfactory or inaccessible to many residents of the city. As urban centers grew, it quickly became apparent that old patterns of leisure, like other aspects of the country's rural background, had to adapt to the new requirements of an urban society. (Somers, 1971, p. 126)

Somers (1971, p. 127) goes on to suggest that the urban residents responded to the recreational and social void in several ways: They joined social clubs and other voluntary associations; they listened to lectures or visited public libraries; some took to the taverns (see Alt, 1976), but the major response to the quest for newer forms of recreation lay in the spectacular growth of *commercialised* amusements and sports. Schlesinger (1933, p. 308) aptly noted in the latter realm that many had 'to take their most strenuous forms of exercise by proxy.' Redlich offers a similar argument:

> The separation of thousands from that relaxation to which they had been accustomed either in America or abroad gave by the middle of the nineteenth century rise to the so-called spectator sports practised for the sole purpose of being watched and of making money from being watched. The onlookers enjoyed vicariously what they would have liked to do themselves, and the excitement which they worked up released emotions pent up by the drabness of their lives. . . . It was the sudden large demand for a new kind of passive 'leisureship' which opened the door through which business could enter the field. (1965, p. 18)

Thus, Schlesinger, Betts, Somers, and Redlich concur that the privations created by the urban-industrial environment paved the way for the emergence of organised sport as an economically conditioned component of popular culture. Nevertheless, even though the exclusion of traditional pastimes and the resulting void in participation opportunities were *necessary* conditions for the creation of commercial sport, they were not *sufficient* for the integration of sport into the market.

The inclusion of sport in the American market system was aided and abetted by several technological innovations. Although these innovations were not conceived for sport per se, they encouraged the 'audience habit' (Schlesinger, 1933, p. 308). That is, several technological innovations not only stimulated a greater enthusiasm for commercialised sport, but also played a key role in expanding commercialised sport's market.

The initial impact of the technological revolution upon the inclusion of sport in the marketplace was related to the areas of transportation and communications. In general terms, improvements in transport assisted the geographic spread and 'primary consumption' of commercialised sport while improved and expanded systems of communication built 'secondary' and 'tertiary consumption'[6]. As might be expected, the expansion and improvement of the systems of transport and communications— partly alongside of and partly the result of industrial expansion—initially increased the vicarious involvement in those sports that had already generated a following (e.g., thoroughbred racing and trotting; see especially Betts, 1974, p. 30). Later, the railroads played a pivotal role in the inclusion of baseball, prize fighting, professional cycling, and intercollegiate athletics into the marketplace.

It should be noted that the role played by the railroads in stimulating the primary consumption of sport was not restricted to the transportation of spectators to an event. The railroads also helped to stimulate spectator appeal by enabling various sports to become supralocal in scope and, thereby, to take on a *representational* flavour. In a sense, the railroads aided those who would market sport for profit by providing sport entrepreneurs with a symbol that met the urban masses' search for some collective identity. Also, in aiding sport to become supralocal, the railroads played a major role in improving the quality of a sporting event, for they allowed the better performers (animal and human) to have a greater degree of geographic mobility. Here, the improvement in the quality of the event was clearly a boost to those in the business of promoting spectator sport, for it differentiated their product from the local product. Finally, the railroad companies stimulated the primary consumption of organised sport by actively promoting sporting events to increase the volume of passenger traffic. To increase profits, the railroads advertised sporting events and catered to the sporting crowds.

At the same time that transportation improved, the telegraph spread across the country. Telegraphy, like the railroads, was encouraged by the expansionist dynamics of industrial capitalism—both were related to the industrial capitalist drive to extend the market and to 'annihilate space with time' (Marx, 1973, p. 539). Although the telegraph was initially costly, the later, more general use of telegraphy played a significant role in the spread of sporting news (see Betts, 1953b, pp. 238-239). Telegraphy reduced the time necessary to report the outcomes of sporting events. Also, it facilitated an activity that provided an added allurement for secondary consumption in sport: gambling. Poolrooms and saloons were often equipped with receiving sets to keep their customers abreast of the odds and the results (see Betts, 1974, pp. 72-73). Prior to the radio, telegraphy was the main mechanism that stimulated secondary consumption.

Telegraphy not only expanded the ranks of the secondary consumers but also was instrumental in promoting sport at the level of tertiary consumption. Although the post-Civil War sporting magazines anticipated the newspapers in capitalising upon the growing spectator interest in sport (see Betts, 1953a, p. 51), the rise of sporting journalism was closely related to the development of a national telegraphic network (see Betts, 1974, p. 73). When coupled with other inventions, such as those that facilitated the mass publication of the daily paper, telegraphy enabled the metropolitan newspapers to make their great bid, beginning in the 1880s, to capture and capitalise upon the sport-minded public (see Betts, 1953a, p. 53). No doubt encouraged by the success of Richard Kyle Fox's sensationalistic *National Police Gazette*, publishers such as Bennett, Dana, Pulitzer, and Hearst[7] regularly featured sporting news as a part of the reading fare and thus contributed to the vicarious popularisation of sport.

In the 1880s, the invention of the incandescent light bulb aided the marketability of sport as well as inaugurating a new era in the recreational life of the cities. Betts (1974, p. 77) argues that the appeal of 'six-day bicycle races, basketball games, and prize fights was directly attributable to the revolution which electric lighting made in the night life of the metropolis between 1880 and 1920'. Lighting, however, was not the only amenity that benefited from electrification. Electrification aided in the development of more rapid, inner-city transit systems. Around the turn of the century, the electric trolley aided in the commercialisation of sport, for it played a significant role in acquainting large numbers of city dwellers with the racetrack and the ballpark (see Betts, 1974, pp. 77-78).

The arguments overviewed thus far that link industrialisation to accelerated urbanisation and participatory deprivation also relate to our concern for instrumental rationality and valorisation in several ways. The urban environment created an expanding cash nexus between individuals, which gave calculating entrepreneurs the potential to stimulate consumable entertainment needs in the urban population. If profit was one's objective there was now a possible calculated decision as to how it would be made—selling consumer goods like boots and coats or selling entertainment services. The urban workers, whose work lives extended over a large part of the day, still had some nonwork time to fill, and the entrepreneurs endeavoured to turn that leisure time into a source of value. Time became valorised in both labour and leisure—what Marcuse would refer to as 'surplus repression'. Spatiality, in turn, would become subjected to bourgeois values (see Soja, 1989, 1985).

Nevertheless, stated in only the terms covered thus far, the arguments are one-sided. They assume that accelerated urbanisation pushed out many traditional pastimes and created a void to be capitalised upon by the profit-hopeful sport entrepreneur. Presented in this fashion, the arguments seem to imply that had there simply been a change in the forms of games and/or the development of newer types of sports suited to the conditions of urban-industrial life, then commercial sport might not have been established. While it might be asserted that, with the possible exception of baseball (which had begun to attract participation from within the ranks of lesser-status professions and skilled labour) no such change in the older game forms or the development of newer forms had occurred in the decades immediately preceding the Civil War, it is difficult to sustain this claim for the decades following it. Yet, the commercialisation of sport and the disproportion in the process of popularisation (vicarious prior to actual) persisted. This paradoxical state of affairs deserves an explanation and one such explanation can be derived from an appreciation of the distributive and relational aspects of the class structure of America.

The Role of Class in Commercial Sport Development

Beginning in the 1840s and continuing throughout the second half of the nineteenth century, changes in the traditional forms of sport had begun, and newer types of sport were emerging. As Dunning (1975) characterised it, sport was becoming incipiently modernised. That is, it was becoming more formalised, codified, organised, and limited territorially and temporally. Interestingly, these developments were initially seen in the most urbanised and industrialised country in the world, England. It is necessary to understand the social context in which these developments occurred in England so that the subsequent modifying influence of the English 'Athletic Revival' upon the one in the United States can be examined.

In England, especially in the 'reformed' Public Schools, an uneasy compromise was being effected between the aristocratic and bourgeois conceptions of culture (i.e., the nonutilitarian and the utilitarian)—a compromise that presumably was intended to fuse the heirs of these two cultures into a more uniform ruling elite. It is by no means certain that this compromise represented a victory for the bourgeoisie within the confines of education or within the political realm at large (see Arnstein, 1973, 1975). Rather, it would appear that the resolution of the two cultures' conflict entailed some 'bourgeoisification' of the aristocratic worldview and a considerable 'aristocratisation' of bourgeois interests. Thus, while the 'reformed' Public Schools tended to reject the chivalric components of the aristocratic attitude because it fostered a sense of honour rather than a sense of duty (see McIntosh, 1968, p. 32), they continued to emphasise the classical curriculum, to de-emphasise science, to ignore applied science, and to neglect all forms of purely vocational training. Their curriculum stressed continuity and tradition. It inculcated acceptance of social hierarchy, fostered the cult of the amateur, and attempted to turn out country gentlemen, army officers, imperial administrators, civil servants, and members of Parliament rather than merchants and businessmen (see Arnstein, 1975, p. 220; Wilkinson, 1964, chap. 6). In short, it might be suggested that the 'reformed' Public Schools, albeit unwittingly, were the instruments of a subliminal, 'extraordinary strategy' by which bourgeois talent was captured in the promotion of gentry class power (see Wilkinson, 1964, p. ix). The compromise effected in the 'reformed' Public Schools thus did not result in the thoroughgoing 'bourgeoisification' of aristocratic culture. Rather, it produced a peculiar interpretation of high culture—it was what the less affluent middle class and the proletariat lacked (see Birnbaum, 1969, p. 138). And, while compromise produced some modification in the conception of the gentleman, it preserved the distinctions long associated with this label (see Morford and McIntosh, 1993).

The arguments of Arnstein and Wilkinson cause us to reconsider the argument often put forth that the changes in sport forms were part of a more general concession that the aristocrats made to middle-class criticisms and demands. Indeed, the concessions appear to have been made by middle-class headmasters as a price to be paid for the cooperation of the gentry class boys in maintaining discipline and effecting 'reform' (see McIntosh, 1968, p. 33). Also, it should be remembered that many middle-class headmasters conceded quite willingly to the sporting desires of their students because they believed that athletic involvement (especially in team games) promoted precisely those qualities of character—manliness, vigour, self-restraint, courage—that were requisites of gentlemanly status.

The changes that occurred in sport (i.e., formalisation, codification, spatial and temporal limitation) thus took place within the social parameters set by gentry conceptions of propriety and the amateur ideal, and within a society where cultural cleavages were neatly matched. As a result, sport's institutional arrangements were coloured by class imagery and, on the part of the elite, an orientation to corporate group closure—an orientation that reflected a desire both to maintain the quality of their social relationships and to preserve the distinctions of social rank. Hence, while the changes created in the 'reformed' Public Schools eventually assisted the vertical spread of sport throughout the class structure (most notably in the case of association football), they were not initially conceived for this purpose. That is, despite the 'class integrationist' sentiments of some of the Muscular Christians (e.g., Charles Kingsley and Thomas Hughes), such changes were not originated with a view to incorporating the masses into the cult of the athletic. Indeed, some middle-class authorities (particularly physical educators) were of the opinion that the 'non-utilitarian' sports and games of the Public Schoolboy were inappropriate activities for the masses. What the masses needed, they thought, was the kind of physical activity that would promote work and military efficiency, health, discipline, and obedience. To these ends, they proposed various systems of rational gymnastics and drill—precisely those activities which were deemed to be of little value in the character training of prospective gentlemen (see McIntosh, 1968, chaps. 1 and 6).

In sum, the English 'athletic revival' did not represent (with the exception of association football) the *vertical* diffusion of sport and the resurgence of participation throughout the English class structure, but rather the *horizontal* spread of organised sports and games within the ranks of the gentry and the more affluent members of the bourgeoisie. And it seems that the ascriptive aspects of English organised sports and games appealed to the upper echelons of American society, thus leading to their reproduction when the 'athletic revival' initially arrived in the United States. That is, class imagery was one of the modifying influences that the English 'athletic revival' had upon its counterpart in the United States. As a result, the American athletic revival represented one more contradiction to the rhetoric of 'nonegalitarian classlessness' (see Ossowski, 1963, chap. 7) contained within the American Dream.

The organised sports and games of the English 'athletic revival' entered the United States primarily in the northeast following the termination of the Civil War (see Dulles, 1965, p. 184). Upon arrival, they were taken over, for the most part, by 'high society', the members of which were susceptible to English culture, manners, and customs (see Vondracek, 1932, p. 46). And as Dulles (1965, p. 184) has observed, not only did society's leaders take over these activities but an attempt was also made to monopolise them: 'Again and again the complacent statement may be found in contemporary articles in the better magazines that such and such a sport—whether tennis, polo, or bicycling—does not offer ''any attractions to the more vulgar elements of society'' '.

The fact that the sports and games of the English 'athletic revival' were taken over and monopolised by the urban upper classes (traditional, then *parvenu*) affected the development of such activities in American society during the decades following the Civil War. That is, 'American athleticism was promoted by coteries of enthusiastic individuals who banded into clubs in every organized sport' (Betts, 1974, p. 98); coteries of individuals who generally were members of the Protestant patriciate (see Baltzell, 1964, chap. 5) or of the world of fashion. Thus, it seems fair to state that the American athletic revival, like its English counterpart, initially represented the more or less horizontal diffusion of organised sports and games within the ranks of the privileged and also among those with elite pretensions. It also appears that amateur sports organisations, which emerged during the last three decades of the nineteenth century (see Lewis, 1969a), were not conceived initially for the purpose of promoting mass participation. Their purpose was to assist and regulate competition between the athletic clubs of the privileged few. Moreover, it should be remembered that the majority of amateur sports organisations were inaugurated at the precise time when the members of the Protestant patriciate were becoming actively engaged in the social defence of their 'caste' (see Baltzell, 1964, chap. 5). One might ask if these organisations were not tainted by the social snobbery that had become a feature of the patriciate's social relationships and of the relationships between those who comprised the *arriviste* New York 'four hundred'? That is, since these amateur sports organisations were comprised of representatives of clubs that had become elite protective associations, could it have been the case that their policies reflected the interests of exclusion?

In sum, the elite concern with ascriptive particularisms and their tendency to organise sport within the protective confines of socially exclusive metropolitan, suburban, and student athletic clubs were contributing factors to the disproportion found in the process of popularisation (see Willis & Wettan, 1976, pp. 53-56). Their membership policies and the practice of screening spectators at some athletic events excluded the 'common man' from both actual and vicarious participation in many of the sports and games that were the products of the English 'Athletic Revival'.

This exclusion likely provided added incentive for those engaged in the commercial/valorisation of sport, for it reduced the common man's opportunity to participate directly or vicariously and, as argued earlier, left him susceptible to, indeed dependent upon, the devices of the profit-hopeful sport entrepreneur. Such exclusionary practices continued until certain of the clubs (most notably the student athletic clubs) became 'contaminated' by the crass commercialism and meritocratic principles of the 'lower status', *parvenu* elite (see Earnest, 1953, chap. 7; Lewis, 1972; Sack, 1973; Scott, 1951, chap. 3; Westby & Sack, n.d.).

So far, two possible explanations for the valorisation of sport have been suggested. The first explanation stressed the idea that urban-industrialism pushed aside many of the traditional, popular sporting pastimes. As a result, the urban proletariat was forced to satisfy their sporting desires vicariously, and this group of consumers permitted the emergence of the sports entrepreneur. The second explanation stressed the idea of elite control. That is, new or changed sports that conformed to the urban-industrial conditions had become available, but these activities were generally viewed through the English notion that they should be the exclusive property of gentlemen. Thus, the urban proletariat continued to lack sporting opportunity, which helped create the conditions for commercial sport. This second explanation, like the first, is not without its shortcomings. While it is quite understandable that the urban proletariat could not take over those newer or changed forms of sport that required elaborate facilities, 'cultivated' tracts of land, expensive equipment, or considerable amounts of discretionary income and time, it does seem reasonable to assume that they could have engaged in those activities that were within their means. The fact that they did not obtain reasonable access to many of the newer and/or changed forms of sport until quite late in the nation's history deserves some consideration. Here we would propose that, in addition to the objective and subjective circumstances of class closure, the physical and demographic conditions of the industrial city, the slow and cautious response of public officials to improving the environmental and cultural conditions of the urban proletariat, and the recessions of the 1870s and 1890s (which, even if there had been the inclination, would have impeded any large-scale, 'welfare status' type transfers from the private to the public sector) ought to be taken into account.

Social Reform Movements and Commercial Sport

After the Civil War, the growth of the cities had been rapid and chaotic (see Boyer, 1978, chap. 8; Faulkner, 1959, p. 23). In the period between the Civil War and the turn of the century, many of the cities doubled and trebled in size—a trend that was accompanied by a flight of the wealthier residents from the old urban centres and a concentration of immigrants into the increasingly impoverished inner-city ethnic enclaves (see Boyer, 1978, p. 124). And because there was only marginal support for enlightened urban planning or for alleviating the social problems that arose in conjunction with urban growth, middle-class uneasiness and fear of the urban menace did not immediately translate into an official response to the fundamental sources of poverty, ignorance, squalor, violence, and vice. As Faulkner (1959, p. 23) states, 'Streets went unpaved; garbage and sewage removal were left to accident and time; water supplies were allowed to become polluted; and conditions in the slums sank to appalling depths of human degradation'. In addition, law enforcement agencies oftentimes were as corrupt as the municipal authorities that employed them and could not be depended upon to enforce the law. Urban middle-class uneasiness, easily transformed into a moral panic concerning the survival of the social order, would result in a variety of 'environmentalist' rather than 'individualist' interventions (via their voluntary associations and charity organizations) as the century progressed, but the point is that such interventions were initially tied up in the self-serving interests of power-broker politicians and the callousness of the industrial capitalist class. Not until the 1890s would the urgency of the moral reformers coalesce with that of the political/municipal (see Boyer, 1978, p. 168; Hofstadter, 1955a, b).

Within the ranks of the industrial capitalist class, the fundamental disregard shown for the problems that confronted the urban poor (especially those perceived as degenerate) had, in the period following the Civil War, been given an ideological sanction in the form of *Social Darwinism*. Social Darwinism corresponded to the political mood of the industrial capitalist class and, as a reaction to the political agitation of the period preceding the Civil War, was a manifestation of their desire for the unhindered pursuit of power and wealth (see Hofstadter, 1955a, p. 5). Specifically, Social Darwinism was seized upon by the *laissez-faire* 'conservatives' not only because it fit into their experiences but also because it aided in the defence of the political status quo and of a political economy that advanced their class interests. Social Darwinism thus imparted a 'moral' explanation for economic success and failure—indeed, for the industrial capitalist class, human progress and moral progress came to be defined in economic terms (see Hofstadter, 1955a, p. 61). In addition, its evolutionary determinism supported the *absence* of political action that would improve the environment of the urban masses. Such policies, the Social Darwinists proclaimed, would not only be 'unnatural' but would be doomed to failure, for the social structure of inequality was the product of a gradual evolutionary process of the social survival of the fittest. In short, among the ranks of the industrial capitalist class, Social Darwinism and laissez-faire entrepreneurial capitalism combined to encourage a callous resignation to the questions on injustice, inequity and suffering—these were inherent in the race to survive.

In the Gilded Age, then, those with the objective power to reform the urban environment expended little energy (notice we do not say no energy; it is a matter of scale, after all) to solve the problems confronted by the unskilled working class and the poor. And, in the context of current concerns, if the industrial capitalist class and the power-broker politicians were unwilling to confront the objective sources of vice, squalor, disease, ignorance, and poverty, why should they have been concerned with providing a broad access to the means of sports participation? This relative failure on the part of those who controlled the political and material resources of the city provides a third explanation for the disproportion that existed between the vicarious and actual participatory popularisation of sport. To paraphrase Cozens and Stumpf (1953, pp. 34-35): It was not the commercialisation of sport that created a nation of spectators but rather the modern city and the restricted opportunities for participation that were the real cause of 'spectatoritis'.

Given the slow response of public officials and the indifference of the industrial capitalist class to the issues of social reform, it is not surprising that the impetus for the latter and for the provision of recreational services of a noncommercialised nature was derived from other sources—that is, from those heirs of the traditional, metropolitan elite who were shocked by the consequences of urban-industrialism and who retained a sense of *noblesse oblige* in the form of paternalism (the compassionate conservatives), from certain of the professions (e.g., the clergy, the medical, and those oriented to the *new* social sciences), and from those of the urban middle class who viewed the problems of the city in *initially* religious and moral rather than political-economic terms (see Baltzell, 1964, chaps. 6 & 7; Boyer, 1978, chaps. 8-10; Faulkner, 1959, pp. 26-29; Hofstadter, 1955b, chap. 4). In the absence of any solid working-class movement (see Faulkner, 1959, p. 26; Hardy, 1980), it was largely through the efforts of these groups that steps were taken to refute the more rapacious, individualistic, and invidious components of *laissez-faire, laissez-seule* ideology; to alleviate poverty, disease, and vice, and to prepare the way for the masses to achieve citizenship rights through education, welfare, and moral training. In combination, they would contribute to the development of that sense of urgency that would so characterise the Progressive Era and also to the breeding of a utilitarian consciousness about the potential of sport (and leisure) that would lead to sport's sociopolitical instrumentalisation. Thus, it was, in part, through the efforts expended by these purportedly ideal interest groups that many of the new or changed sports and games would become popularised at the level of actual participation. That is, in providing facilities and organisational knowledge, they played an instrumental role in the growth of working-class athletic clubs and in the formation of working-class athletic leagues (i.e., the settlement house leagues, the Sunday School Athletic Leagues, the Church Athletic Leagues, the Catholic Athletic Leagues, the Public School Athletic Leagues, etc.) during the first decades of the twentieth century.

Given the important role that the socioreligious, moral, and educational reform groups played in the sociopolitical instrumentalisation of sport, they deserve something more than a passing mention. What, for example, was their mission, and how did sport aid in the prosecution of such? We think it is fair to state that it is not possible to provide an adequate response to this question without briefly focusing attention on the Progressive Movement and especially its *corporate* imagery[8].

Progressivism arose out of the social and political dislocations of the late nineteenth century. It was the visible response to a search for order (see Weibe, 1967) and a quest for social justice (see Faulkner, 1931). At its heart, Progressivism was an effort to realise familiar and traditional ideals under novel circumstances (see Hofstadter, 1955b, p. 215). That is, it was a liberal democratic response to the conditions of anomie and the absence of authority that resulted from the *laissez-faire* underpinnings of entrepreneurial capitalism. To use Hofstadter's words:

> Toward the turn of the century it became increasingly evident that all this material growth had been achieved at a terrible cost in human values and in the waste of natural resources. . . . What had happened, as a great many men of good will saw it at the beginning of the Progressive era, was that in the extraordinary outburst of productive energy of the last few decades, the nation had not developed in any corresponding degree the means of meeting human needs or controlling or reforming the manifold evils that come with any such rapid physical change. The Progressive movement, then, may be looked upon as an attempt to develop the moral will, the intellectual insight, and the political and administrative agencies to remedy the accumulated evils and negligence of a period of industrial growth. Since the Progressives were not revolutionists, it was also an attempt to work out a strategy for orderly social change.

In short, Progressivism represented a desire to resolve the crises resulting from entrepreneurial capitalism, to instil a sense of civic responsibility, and to regulate the potential excesses of both finance capitalism and restless labour *within the capitalist framework* (see Hofstadter, 1955b, pp. 238-240; Kolko, 1963).

Because Progressivism had a diffuse following (e.g., some of the Protestant patriciate, Mugwump intellectuals, some corporate magnates, muckraking journalists, the *petit bourgeoisie*, labour leaders such as Samuel Gompers, etc.), not everyone viewed the social question from a similar vantage point (see Kelly, 1977, p. 549; Weibe, 1967, p. 176). Yet, as Hofstadter (1963, p. 4) has stated, 'For all its internal difficulties and counter-currents, there were in Progressivism certain general tendencies, certain widespread commitments of belief, which outweighed the particulars'.

For Hofstadter (1963, pp. 4-6) these general tendencies and widespread beliefs were *activism* (social evils would not take care of themselves, so people had to be stimulated to work for social progress using the positive powers of government), optimism (no problem was thought to be too difficult to overcome), and *democratism* (democracy could be revived if, through information and exhortation, people would make wise use of the ballot to find new and vigorous, popular leaders). Taken together, these would be the antidotes for elite ignorance, corruption, civic indifference, and extortionistic materialism.

For Weibe (1967, pp. 145-154) the central characteristic of urban Progressivism is to be found in the bureaucratic/civil service mentality of the new middle class. Although divided into two broad categories—the professions and the specialists in business and labour—it embraced the values of continuity and regularity, of administration and management in order to cope with the problems of urban-industrial development. Properly managed, urban-industrial development could lead to rationality and peace, decent living conditions, and an equalization of opportunity. Thus, while the idealism and optimism identified by Hofstadter supplied most of urban Progressivism's superstructure, bureaucratic thought filled its interior (see Weibe, 1967, pp. 162-163). The good society, then, not only would be one of prosperity and rationality, but also one that would be a highly organized and smoothly functioning corporate structure—it would be the utopian product of social engineering.

Finally, the fact that the Progresssive mind was largely a Protestant one should not be overlooked, for at the heart of Progressivism was the most important aspect of the Protestant personality—the ethos of responsibility. This ethos gave Progressivism its moral urgency (see Hofstadter, 1955b, pp. 204-205).

The religiously based reform groups' particular mission might be viewed in terms of a three-part, temporal sequence. First, the religiously based reform groups had the traditional, ecumenical mission of saving souls. Second, they appear to have believed that a good society was one comprised of 'civilised' individuals, and this could not be achieved if large segments of the population were beset by problems of brutality, inhumanity, ignorance, squalor, poverty, and vice. Thus, the 'civilising' mission could not be brought to fruition merely by exposing such segments of the population to, for the most part, Protestant precepts. In addition to evangelism, then, there would have to be a caring for the 'whole man' and an attempt to civilise the urban environment per se (see Baltzell, 1964, p. 161). Third, it seems reasonable to speculate that the socioreligious reform groups joined the moral reform groups (e.g., the playground movement) and the political socialisation agencies (e.g., the public schools) in an overall attempt to integrate the urban proletariat functionally into the increasingly corporate, capitalist state and thereby diminish the threats posed by the rising strength and militancy of the working class and the increasing size of the ethnic population.

In order to achieve some measure of success for all three missions, the socioreligious reform groups had to wage a war on three fronts. That is, they had to raise the social conscience of those who were responsible for the creation and continuation of the chaotic, brutal, and squalid urban environment. At the same time they had to divert the urban masses, particularly the urban poor, from their 'vulgar' pastimes to more elevating forms of cultural activity. And third, they had to build a corporate, integrationist value system among the potentially conflicting segments of the urban proletariat. While it was the case that the socioreligious effort to reform the culture and environment of the urban proletariat was a compassionate mission to enlist the urban proletariat in a collaborative quest for self-improvement, historians have only recently begun to consider fully the extent to which this effort was aimed at achieving value-consensus through an indoctrination of the working and 'under' classes in the corporate image of society, or was designed to control socially the urban proletariat by policing their nonwork activities—a hegemonic agenda that really involved coercion rather than consent (see Goodman, 1979).

Irrespective of actual content, the socioreligious reform groups first had to attract into their fold those whom they wished to convert and improve. And in the face of declining religiosity, this entailed the finding of vehicles other than the evangelical with which to make initial contact. While 'welfare' services were one approach to the problem, it was increasingly perceived that the provision of leisure services and of facilities and programmes for legitimate sports and games would be another. Thus, the provision of welfare, leisure, and sport services became an integral part of the Social Gospel, and they became the means of attracting members and of exercising social control over the non-working-time behaviour of the urban proletariat. The Gospel was not just a Social Gospel but, in many respects, a Muscular Gospel too. It became the gospel of both the rational recreationists and an ideology of an emergent professionalism in physical education.

The impoverished urban-industrial existence, urban intemperance (in the broad meaning of the term), the progressive secularisation of urban life, and the need to find 'drawing cards' thus combined to effect a change in the programmes of various religious agencies. Evangelism, by itself, had been proclaimed as insufficient in the fight against brutality, inhumanity, ignorance, and vice. Social work, the caring for the 'whole man', and 'environmentalism' had to be added to the concern for the state of mind and soul. Convinced by the arguments of medical, educational, and social science professionals that sport had mental, physical, and moral redemptive qualities, religious missionaries came to view sport not only as a 'drawing card' by which to attract the urban proletariat into the fold but also, *when properly supervised*, as an agency of enculturation (see Richardson, 1913, p. 191). Many of the social work extensions of the 'institutional Church' (e.g., the settlement house, the YMCA, the Boy Scouts, the Boys' Brigade) thus incorporated the duty of sponsoring recreational games and organised sports into their civilising mission. And once they had accepted this duty they wasted no time in establishing large and well-maintained programmes, especially for children and youth. Here, it seems legitimate to propose that organised sport was viewed instrumentally as a way of instilling Christian and corporate capitalist truths into the ranks of the urban proletariat and as a means of saving the youth from juvenile delinquency, juvenile gangs, and the base attractions of urban life that led away from the industrious Christian life. Sport, now conceived of as physical and moral training, was one way the Church attempted to establish a proper standard of recreation for the community and help maintain a proper balance between work and play (see Atkinson, 1915, p. 259). Indeed, so strong was the idea of redemption (secular as well as religious) *via* sport that 'in the theological schools a new generation of ministers was being indoctrinated with the philosophy that to minister to the bodies as well as the minds and souls of men was a part of their work' (Cozens and Stumpf, 1953, p. 96).

Although we have emphasised the important role that the socioreligious reform movements played in the sociopolitical instrumentalisation and subsequent participatory popularisation of organised sport, there may be a danger in exaggerating their accomplishments. The majority of the socioreligious reform movements not only were Protestant sponsored but were also in the business of promoting a Protestant way of life. On the other hand, the urban poor were recent immigrants of Catholic persuasion. Hofstadter (1955b, p. 181) has pointed out that the typical Progressive and the typical immigrant were very different, and the gulf between them was not usually bridged with much success in the Progressive era. Finally, it is hard to imagine that the socioreligious reformers found many converts among the 'toughened' segments of the exploited proletariat. Hofstadter (1955b, p. 182) argues that more often than not the settlement worker or the agent of Americanisation was rebuffed by the most exploited sector of the urban population.

The Playground Movement and Commercial Sport

As we noted earlier, the socioreligious Progressive reform groups were not the only ones engaged in the attempt to civilise and socially control the urban proletariat. They were accompanied in their so-called humanitarian quest by Progressive professionals in the parks and playground movement and the educational reform movement—the positive environmentalists. Within the realm of play, games, and sport, it is difficult initially to separate the parks and playground movement from the educational reform movement. Their respective leaderships tended to interlock and to view their missions as conjoint and also tended to share the same theoretical assumptions concerning environmental manipulation and the utilitarian functions of play, games, and sport in promoting the moral, physical, and intellectual welfare of children and youth (see Cavallo, 1976; Spring, 1974). That is, their respective leaderships assumed that properly supervised and correctly organised play, games, and sport would

1. provide moral rescue and social control of the urban masses;
2. be ways of filling the disciplinary void created by the dislocations of modern life;
3. play a major role in curing and compensating for the ills, monotony, and drudgery of an urban, technological society;
4. channel adolescent sexual and social impulses to constructive purpose;
5. mould sentiments of corporate solidarity and thereby promote social unity; and
6. create the proper democratic character of loyalty, self-sacrifice, and self-devotion to the great national ideals.

With specific reference to the playground movement, it reached fruition during the last decade of the nineteenth century as part of a more widespread concern for children's rights (see Boyer, 1978, chap. 16; Faulkner, 1931, chap. 8)[9]. No doubt stimulated by a fear that the political order might be undermined by a growing immigrant population susceptible to boss-style politics, by the lurid pictures painted of the working conditions endured by child labour, by the high rates of infant and child mortality, by depictions of slum life such as that offered by Jacob Riis (1971) in *How the Other Half Lives*, and by the perception of a rising tide of juvenile delinquency and crime, concerned citizens instituted programmes to Americanise immigrant children, to improve public health and sanitation, to combat delinquency and crime, to alleviate overcrowding, to prevent cruelty, and to provide wholesome play facilities (see Weibe, 1967, p. 169).

In the opening decades of the twentieth century, then, a new dream alien to the later nineteenth century began to take shape. 'Instead of molding youth in a slightly improved pattern of their fathers, like cyclically reproducing like, the new reformers thought in terms of fluid progress, a process of growth that demanded constant vigilance' (Weibe, 1967, p. 169). And why not propose a new dream? After all, the Progressives of the new middle class were by no means sure that they approved of the parental pattern in which the children and youth of the 'unrespectable' urban proletariat had, thus far, been moulded; a parental pattern that, in the case of the immigrant, had been viewed stereotypically throughout the latter half of the nineteenth century as a mixture of poverty, crime, and political corruption and, simultaneously, as a tendency to extreme discontent, subversion, and ideologies antagonistic to American society.

Although the concern for the physical and moral welfare of children and youth had been manifested much earlier than the Progressive era, it was this era that witnessed the widespread growth in the number of organisations that had the sole function of rescuing children and youth through 'positive environmentalism' (see Boyer, 1978, chap. 15). The Playground Association of America, formed in 1906, was the first of many nationwide organisations sponsoring sports and games that was devoted to the protection, nurturance, and social control of children and youth. Others included 4-H, Boy Scouts, Camp Fire Girls, Girl Scouts, and Boys' Club of America. Like the socioreligious reform groups that preceded them—and out of which some of these child and youth organisations sprang—they accepted that organised sports and games not only were drawing cards but also were invaluable in 'properly' channelling the instinctual impulses of children and youth. That is, organised sports and games were not simply recreational but were viewed both as antidotes and as means of preparing the corporate, democratic character in accordance with the Progressivists' vision.

Spring has encapsulated the views of Gulick, the first president of the Playground Association, who set the movement out on its missionary path:

> Without giving consideration to economic and social power, Gulick firmly believed that economic and social exploitation could be ended in modern society by creating a new corporate conscience on the playing fields of America. Out of this corporate conscience would be built a concept of freedom that was not based on exploitation but upon the good of the corporate whole. This type of freedom found in play would be 'conditioned by the rules of the game. . . . It is for this freedom and this control that play gives preparation and training'. (Spring, 1974, p. 488)

In short, Gulick and others of his ilk saddled organised sports and games with specific sociopolitical objectives, and in doing so provided an ideological rationale that has remained in vogue up to the present time.

The School System and Sports Development

During the opening decades of the twentieth century, the public schools also embraced the Progressives' corporate image of society (see Bowles & Gintis, 1976, chaps. 2 and 7; Spring, 1972). In characterising Progressive education, Bowles and Gintis (1976, p. 43) state: 'The leitmotif of the day was "taking the lid off kids"', and the aim was to sublimate natural creative drives in fruitful directions rather than to repress them'. Unfortunately, there seem to have been some differences of opinion as to which directions were fruitful. That is, there appear to have been two countercurrents; one that saw the mission of the public school in terms of democracy and creative, developmental education, and one that saw the mission in terms defined by instrumental rationality and valorised activity. And, if we have interpreted the critical theses of Bowles and Gintis and of Spring correctly, there is little doubt that the debate between these Progressive worldviews was won by the business ideology. Spring clearly characterises the effects that the importation of valorised motives and instrumental rationality in the pursuit of upward mobility had upon educational reform:

> Education reacted to this image in two major ways. On the one hand education adopted the goal of training the type of man required by this organization [i.e., the hierarchical, functionally differentiated corporation]. This meant teaching the students how to cooperate with others and work in groups. This resulted in class and school programs designed to socialize the student and prepare him for a life in the corporation. On the other hand, education was viewed as one institution working with others to assure the progress and efficient operation

of the social system. This meant that the schools trained pupils in the specialized skills required by the new corporate organization. Ideally the students would be able to leave school and directly enter a social niche. To a great extent children became a form of natural resource that was molded by the schools and fed into the industrial machine. (Spring, 1972, p. xii)

Public education, then, would no longer be simply a matter of academic training, but would be the instrument used for social cohesion, system integration, stability, and vocational placement.

The institutional moulding of the integrative, corporate conscience, however, would involve more than a manipulation of curricular activities—it would extend to the extracurriculum as well. Hence, it was during the Progressive era that athletics and other extracurricular activities were brought under the umbrella of the school (see Spring, 1974, pp. 491-492). And it was during the Progressive era that the fusion of athletics and physical education, initiated in the colleges, percolated down to the schools; a fusion legitimated on the basis that sport would not only promote, as had gymnastic exercises, the traditionally valued goals of health, physique, and fitness, but would also be invaluable in the fulfilment of important social objectives, namely socialisation, social cohesion, social solidarity, and the worthy use of leisure (see Lewis, 1969b; Spring, 1974).

The fusion of sport and physical education in the period 1906 to 1916 had interesting consequences. First, the once extracurricular tail began to wag the curricular dog; second, as had happened in the colleges (see Lewis, 1972), the recreational became the commercial. Operating under the banner 'athletics are educational', the physical education curriculum became a sports skills curriculum, the sports skills curriculum became a feeder system for interscholastic athletics and this, in turn, became not only a source of revenue but also a form of public relations used to sell the school to the community (see Spring, 1974, p. 495). And in the case of professional physical educators, while they were forming various associations to promote professional autonomy, they (particularly the men) paradoxically were accommodating to the demands of commercialised sport by developing the skilled labour force needed to provide wageworkers for this emergent enterprise. By 1916, sport within the schools no longer reflected the sociopolitical ideals of such people as Gulick, Adams, and Curtis—ideals that had legitimated its *participatory* popularisation among children and youth—but rather had come to reflect the meritocratic principles of corporate capitalism and the language of budget and boosterism. In short, sociopolitical instrumentalisation gave in to the valorisation of sport as a spectator pastime and the development of the 'skilled workers' needed to produce the product that now had abundant consumers. In the words of Spring:

One major concern about athletics by the 1920's was its growing commercialism and the rise of spectatorship over participation. While athletics was promoted as a cure to technological society, that very society turned it into a commercial enterprise. Athletics became big business. The naivete that led to the belief that athletics could cure society's problems overlooked the fact that without any fundamental change in the social and economic structure athletics would be turned into a business enterprise. This occurred in public school and college athletics as well as professional sports. (Spring, 1974, p. 495)

And, although efforts would be made after the First World War to compensate the nonelite performer by expanding the programmes of intramural sports, to this day it has remained the case that within the schools and colleges the recreational and the educational-instructional programmes have remained subservient to the commercial and representational. Thus, despite the original intentions of the more democratically minded Progressives, sport in the schools and colleges, like the schools and colleges themselves, capitulated to the business values of instrumental rationality and were structured like the rapidly expanding corporate capitalist system (see Bowles & Gintis, 1976, p. 44).

It is, of course, entirely possible to develop many more arguments that will show how sport became an instrumentally rational activity organised chiefly to produce profits. Attention could be focused on the role played by the military in the promotion of sport as a morale and fitness builder; the instrumental value of sport for the fighting of ideological wars; sport's use as a means of diluting political consciousness; the mutually beneficial relationship between sport and the mass media; the use made of sport by corporate capital to improve employer-employee relations (see Vincent, 1981), worker morale, public relations, and the sale of commodities; the use of sport as means of gainful employment—that is, the transformation of sport from an avocation into a 'service occupation' (see Becker, 1951, p. 136); the economic exploitation of the public's free time by those in the sporting goods industries; the use of athletes in the manipulation of public taste and opinion—the list could go on. However, to analyse each of these trends would only supply more detail to our thesis that industrialisation created the material and ideational conditions conducive to the valorisation of sport and the use of instrumental rationality to mould consciously sport for profit and/or political gain. Industrialisation marked the point at which a significant change in people's perception of sport and game-contests began to come into being. It was in response and in reaction to the critical conditions of urban-industrialism that the expressive was made instrumental, use-values inherent in play were subordinated by the exchange-values of the commodity market, and the embodied became subject to abstracted market values. With industrialisation, the intrinsically irrational ends (e.g., fun, festivity, sociability) of traditional elite and folk sporting pastimes were transformed into the achievement of extrinsically valued goals—profit, performance, and social control (see Marcuse, 1955, chaps. 2 and 4). The organic community was transformed through several processes: (1) valorisation, (2) rationalisation, and (3) bourgeois conceptions of civility that truly are anchored in possessive individualism and property.

The 'Inevitable Thesis': Some Problems

While we have stated our intention not to discuss all the nuances of instrumentalisation, no analysis of the industrialisation, instrumentalisation, and popularisation of sport would be complete without some mention of what Lewis (1977, p. 129) has termed the 'inevitable thesis'—that is, that the popularisation of sport was a natural consequence of increased affluence and free time. Lewis, in his evaluation of the 'inevitable thesis', does not question the validity of its materialistic assumptions. That is, he does not object to the idea that following the widespread rationalisation—or Taylorisation—of the work process there has been, with the notable exceptions of the economic crises of the 1930s and 1970s and the political crisis of war, an increase in real income and discretionary time. Rather, he takes issue with the idea that the widespread popularisation of sport was a logical drive of the new age of affluence and leisure and its consumptionist ideology. If we have interpreted Lewis's unstated premise correctly, it would appear that its essence is that while affluence, free time, and an increased emphasis upon consumption led to the growth in all forms of non-work-related activities, one still has to account for the forces governing the directions of choice and, especially, for the decision on the part of the American people to devote much of their money and time to sport.

In his attempt to account for the forces that propelled the American people into sport, Lewis suggests that the 1920s not only mark the point at which money and free time had become more readily available to a larger segment of the American population but also marked the onset of the 'fun morality' of the twentieth-century worship of the retention of youth. In combination, these material and ideational factors supposedly allowed a greater number of Americans to turn to sport as a way of embracing conventional morality within the context of the new. Sport, for Lewis, thus represents an apparent sphere of value continuity operating within an era of changed cultural and moral values—that is, despite the changed basis of values originating in the 1920s, the instrumental and moral rationales (e.g., constructiveness and wholesomeness) put forth initially by the medical professionals and the Muscular Christians, and later by the Progressive sociopolitical reformers, have remained in vogue (see Ingham, 1985).

Having made the case that sport has continued to be linked with conventional morality, Lewis focuses his attention on the relationship between conventional morality and the tremendous increase in the enthusiasm for sport that began to be seen during the 1920s. Lewis argues that the increase in enthusiasm for sport did not necessarily represent—with certain exceptions—an absolute, normative commitment to the values of conventional morality. Rather, the increase in the enthusiasm for sport derived from the realisation that the proclaimed goodness of sport could overshadow the morally questionable activities that were gaining in popularity in conjunction with the fun morality and the fetish for the retention of youth (see Hepworth & Featherstone, 1982). In short, when the immoral was combined with the moral, the former now appeared more legitimate. And, states Lewis (1977, p. 137), it was this combination of the moral and immoral that accounts for the rising popularity of sport during the 1920s and thereafter. Thus, and paradoxically, it has been the case that those normatively committed to the moral elevation of sport have provided a 'purity blanket' for those who would use sport as a vehicle for the release of repressed urges of an antisocial character.

While we would not take issue with Lewis's hypothesis—that the upsurge in enthusiasm for sport stemmed from the fact that sport was a haven for those fun-seekers whose values rhetorically remained with the conventional view of morality—as a partial explanation of the rise of modern sports, we would question the extent to which sport's purity blanket was responsible for its popularisation in the strictest meaning of the term. That is, we would argue that the Lewis hypothesis is, in essence, an interpretation that nicely characterizes middle-class behaviour and life-style. It presents in broad relief the ambivalence of the middle class, the class that was the original carrier of conventional morality and which, since the 1920s, has been tempted to savour increasingly the 'forbidden fruits'. To use the words of Brohm (1968, p. 55), we would claim that it has been the middle class that historically has had the most trouble coping with 'la dialectique de la sublimation et de la desublimation' (see Ingham, 1985).

Even if one limits the Lewis hypothesis to the middle class, we think it is reasonable to argue that its emphasis upon the ideational tends to overlook the point that it could have been the expansion of the white-collar labour force per se that created the fetish of things corporal. That is, it could be argued that the Taylorisation of the administrative means of production and the bureaucratisation of federal, state, and local government increased by leaps and bounds the number of those employed in an occupational sector that makes few physical demands. Hence, the increased popularity of sport within the ranks of the middle class may have been one consequence of the 'demuscularisation' of work—a release of the repressed. If one descends from the dizzy psychoanalytic heights, however, the expansion of the white-collar labour force may have led to sport's increased popularity on other grounds; namely, because the expansion of the white-collar labour force augmented the importance of credentials. And since credentials are obtained through prolonged education, many more people were exposed to an institutional sector that placed a heavy emphasis upon sport. In a sense, high schools, colleges, and universities not only socialised their students into work but also into the consumption of sport. And with the expansion of intramural sports programmes that followed the First World War and the widespread trend to make physical education compulsory, many more students were enticed or coerced into taking their bodies seriously.

To claim that the Lewis hypothesis is limited in viability primarily to the middle class is also to claim that the hypothesis is, by and large, irrelevant to an understanding of how sport became popularised within the ranks of the working class. In the case of the working class, we would suggest that the 'inevitable thesis' deserves to be reconsidered. However, as an explanation of the popularisation of sport, we would agree with Lewis (1977, p. 129) that its obviousness is deceiving. Other than the fact that, as a simplistic, materialistic explanation, it does not deal successfully with its own internal contradictions (e.g., how to account for the zeal for sport during depressions and recessions), it also fails to take into account the change in the views of labour with respect to what they would do with their leisure and the forces that engineered such a change. In short, while the Lewis hypothesis ignores the fact that, when it came to a debate as to what constituted a worthwhile use of leisure, labour leaders and middle-class reformers were not always speaking the same language (see Spring, 1974, p. 493)[10], the 'inevitable thesis' overlooks the idea that an increase in affluence and leisure per se does not intrinsically determine the ways in which they are spent. Thus, the 'inevitable thesis' fails to take into consideration the point that the popularisation of sport may have been one consequence of the depoliticisation of labour's leisure and the subsequent institutional manipulation of labour's cultural tastes. Or to state it differently, the popularisation of sport may have occurred as a result of an historical shift in working-class consciousness—that is, a shift from a focus on work to a focus on consumption and the adoption or acceptance of American culture, especially sport—rather than opposition to it.

Taken at face value, the 'inevitable thesis' with regard to the working class has some validity for the following reason: Increased affluence and (especially) free time allowed workers vicariously (and to some extent directly) to reclaim that which has been a part of both the folk tradition and working-class tradition. That is, prior to the rapacious days of entrepreneurial, industrial capitalism, game-contests had been a feature of the rural unity of labour and leisure. It was one of the ways in which family, friends, and neighbours could reaffirm the bonds of social solidarity through collective activity. And even during the period of entrepreneurial, industrial capitalism, there is evidence to suggest that sport continued to function in this role for the members of the occupational communities (see Alt, 1976; Rader, 1977). That is, despite long hours of work and harsh labour discipline, sport and game-contests were means of enjoyably reproducing in leisure the relationships that were formed in the workplace. Sport, like the tavern and the lodge, was a way of reaffirming the group cohesion developed during the performance of labour (see Alt, 1976, pp. 58-59). In addition, it was a way of preserving the commonalities of ethnicity (e.g., the Scottish Caledonian Clubs, the Turner societies) and, perhaps, aided in the defence of ethnicity itself. Thus, even prior to the so-called age of affluence and leisure, and despite the impediments posed by urban-industrialism, sport may have been anchored in working-class culture as a legitimate expression of working-class collectivism.

As a result, there was likely no need for the Progressive missionaries to direct the working class into sport. The working class would—and in some cases did (see Kidd, 1981; Wheeler, 1978)—organise sport activities to meet its own needs and demands (Hardy & Ingham, 1982). But sport in general has not been a working-class domain in America to the extent that it has been in Britain, for example, and this requires a brief explanation. Why the difference?

We would put forth three points that, when fully developed, would explain the absence of strong working-class control of sport in America. First, the valorisation of spectator sport in America took on a much more aggressive and culturally compartmentalised form than in Britain. Entrepreneurs did not try to sell sport events that had some traditional meaning and significance to workers; they sold a spectacle, which happened to be athletic, to consumers in need of entertainment (partly a real need and partly a created one). Second, the instrumental rationality of entrepreneurs in the sports market was centred fully on profit. Sport entrepreneurs were interested in profit ahead of any community service or responsibility (see the work of Reiss, 1980 and Ingham et al., 1987 for detailed analysis of these points). This differs considerably from the case of British soccer, for example (see Taylor, 1971, 1976, 1981). Because of this extreme calculated approach to profit, entrepreneurs moved quickly to form monopoly conditions in the marketplace through the development of athletic cartels (Vincent, 1982). With the complete control of spectator sport assured, owners would move teams out of smaller markets to the large commercial markets where they could cash in on more broadcast and print-media dollars (Vincent, 1982). Finally, the labour movement in America itself has had a far different history and character than that in Britain.

This last point is tremendously broad and complex in scope. Its full elaboration would include a study of the rise of the capitalist state and its role in shaping the worldview of the population as a whole and how the state has become so strongly involved in the ideological realm of social life. However, these issues cannot be discussed fully here, although we can overview some important events within the class structure per se that explain the ambivalent attitude of labour in America to sport.

In general terms, it has been suggested that, since the 1920s, social cohesion in the United States has not come about because of value consensus but because of a lack of a consistent commitment to general values of any sort and because subordinate social groups have pragmatically accepted the existing corporate capitalist order in the absence of concrete alternatives (see Livingstone, 1976, p. 243; Mann, 1970, p. 423). This pragmatic accommodation on the part of subordinate social groups has been facilitated not only by the system's capacity to deliver the goods but also by the manipulative socialisation of such subordinate groups—a process made possible by the privatisation of the subordinate groups' social relationships and the mediation of class consciousness by consumer goods (see Alt, 1976, p. 55; Livingstone, 1976, p. 247). In short, the pragmatic acceptance of the political-economic order has been to some degree dependent upon commodity fetishism eclipsing the radical and syndicalist sentiments of wage-labour—an eclipse aided and abetted by the tactics of labour's own leaderships (see Aronowitz, 1973, chap. 4). States Aronowitz:

> One hundred years ago workers fought desperately for the right to form unions and to strike for economic and social demands. Unions arose out of the needs of workers. In the period of the expansion of American capitalism they were important means for restraining the bestiality of capital. Even into the twentieth century, long after the labour movement as a whole stopped reflecting their interests, workers fought for unions. But their hope was not to become new agents of social transformation. Industrial workers joined unions seeking a share in the expansion of American capitalism, not its downfall. (Aronowitz, 1973, p. 257)

The co-optation of labour—its deradicalisation and desyndicalisation—was accelerated in the 1930s. With the death of the Industrial Workers of the World, labour's genuinely radical wing, the trade unions evolved into a force for integrating wage-labour into the corporate capitalist system. Where militancy remained, it was in response to the company's refusal to recognise the union. Since the 1930s, the trade unions have narrowed their orientation to the economic side of bargaining—that is, to delivering goods in terms of wage benefits and pensions. This orientation to collective bargaining has at the same time encouraged labour leaders to assume the responsibility of providing a disciplined labour force for the employer; the concession for tangible benefits. Out of such collective bargaining and despite occasional rhetorical exercises in militancy, labour leaders and employers have formed an alliance against the ignorant and undisciplined rank and file (see Aronowitz, 1973, p. 219). Hence, ' . . . radical ideologies and organizations [have] played virtually no independent role in the trade unions after 1935' (Aronowitz, 1973, p. 257).

The deradicalisation and desyndicalisation of labour was not just the result of the co-optation of the union leadership into the corporate capitalist system; it was also related to the Taylorist reorganisation of industrial production. That is, the deradicalisation and desyndicalisation of working-class consciousness resulted from the reduced salience of work within the working-class consciousness. What Taylorised production did was to remove the collectivist forms of work and to substitute specialised functions within a machine process that isolated workers and their tasks from each other (see Alt, 1976, p. 71). In the long run, then, the Taylorised, machine-dominated production process would break down the bonds of social solidarity formed in the performance of labour, and in so doing it would eventually break up the occupational cultures that had been prominent in earlier forms of industrial organisation (see Alt, 1976; Berger et al., 1973).

Labour accepted (although not initially) the Taylorist rationalisation of production because it promised that wage-labour would be granted a share of their increased marginal productivity. 'Mass consumption, as the necessary otherness of Taylorised mass production, was itself offered as the ultimate justification for the rationalisation of labour' (Alt, 1976). Such consumption would be enhanced by another of Taylorism's 'payoffs', reduced work time. Thus, in the period of transition from entrepreneurial to corporate, monopoly capitalism, an ideology was created that was rooted in the idea that production and consumption reproduce and justify domination (see Marcuse, 1955, p. 91)—an ideology that apparently was bought by the trade union leaderships. It was during this period of transition that the authentic popular culture of the occupational community became transformed into the mass-consumer culture of the modern industrial labourer (but see Willis, 1990). This is the full impact of valorization upon all social relationships when it becomes the focus of instrumentally rational decisions. The leisure of labour no longer would be autonomously produced within the collectivist setting but would be externally organised for consumption within the private setting. Alt expresses the change in the following way:

The point is that the class experience of work no longer contributes to the constitution of most employees' consciousness as it did for the early industrial pre-Taylorized worker. With respect to leisure, work has lost its former centrality and what employees do in their free time is generally unrelated to the nature of their employment. One of the great cultural transformations of the twentieth century is the disappearance of traditional forms of industrial working class leisure and the emergence of socially-privatized leisure related to the products of the consumer industries. This transformation began in the 1920s and 1930s and is only now reaching its completion. For instance, in the 1930s, Lundberg concluded from his survey of the leisure activities of suburban Westchester County, New York, that 'Leisure and recreation are indeed to a large extent coming to be regarded as commodities to be purchased rather than as experiences to be lived'. While this applied more to the middle class and skilled workers than to the larger stratum of unskilled workers, it indicated the beginnings of a trend which would eventually encompass the entire working class, once their traditional occupational communities had broken up and they had the financial means and time to participate in the new national consumer culture. (Alt, 1976, pp. 75-76; but see Clarke, 1993 for an analysis of current trends)

In short, since the 1930s there has been a qualitative change in the cultural character of the working class and an absence of traditional conceptions of class consciousness (see Alt, 1976). We would claim that it has been this reordering of working-class priorities—orchestrated by corporate capital and trade union leaderships alike—that facilitated the popularisation of sport. It was not that the relative increase in income and time directed the working class into sport, but rather that the relative increase in income and time, when coupled with the rise of the consumptionist ethic and the deradicalisation of political consciousness, allowed the working class's traditional interest in sport to be diversified and capitalised on in a way that previously had not been possible. Baseball was no longer the only game in town.

While it is probably premature to state that Veblen's leisure class has become the leisure mass—the distribution of the 'good things' in life continues to be disproportionate—the working class' pragmatic acceptance of their subordination has been aided by the corporate capitalist system's capacity to deliver tangible benefits and by its promise to deliver more. Thus, it has been the case that the working class can increasingly partake in the material comforts and sporting privileges that were once the prerogatives of the elite—a trend programmed by the monetary aims of those in the commodities and leisure industries and the sociopolitical aims of those who stood to benefit from the depoliticisation of working-class consciousness. In sum, the working class's pragmatic acceptance of its relatively improved lot has encouraged the popularisation of sport as but one of the tangible benefits and compensations for the performance of rationalised and alienated labour. Since advanced industrial capitalism has not succeeded in making people excited about work, it has tried to make them excited about consumption. And sport has become an orchestrated component of this latter form of excitement. While increased affluence and free time have created illusions of more freedom and spontaneity, the whole work world and its recreation have become a system of animate and inanimate things—equally subject to administration (see Marcuse, 1955, p. 93). In loosening the living links between the individual and his/her culture, the corporate capitalist system has succeeded in making sport and other forms of leisure into instruments of social control and effective legitimation (see Clarke & Critcher, 1985; Clarke, 1993).

CONCLUDING REMARKS

We have tried to indicate a number of changes in game-contests and their place in American (also other so-called first world nation states) social life by employing two key concepts—instrumental rationality and valorisation. We have shown that as America industrialised, it provided the material conditions that allowed the emergence of new sport forms that could be instrumentally developed for profit. The bulk of our analysis focused upon the creation of a consumer market for valorised sport, which was a key ingredient for the capitalisation of sport in America. The market was created partly by physical deprivation from direct sport participation, partly from class-based privation, and partly by a number of reformist interventions that had various impacts in working-class life and the worldview of workers. While the development of wageworkers for sport progressed slowly throughout this phase of American history, by far the greatest impact upon their conditions of existence came following the Second World War. Since the transformation of private athletic labour into social/productive labour has been treated in varying degrees by others, we have not really examined the production side of valorisation in this essay at all (see, for example, Beamish, 1982, 1988; Ingham, 1975; Ingham et al., 1987; Terkel, 1974).

The essay has closed with a frank analysis of the possibilities for popular reclamation of sport in American life. On the basis of the material presented here, and the numerous studies we have cited throughout that take up this question from other vantage points, we are thoroughly pessimistic that popular control is even a remote possibility at this moment in American history. Nevertheless, we know that history is an open-ended process and that it is not necessary or inevitable that sport and leisure will remain the subject of profit rationality or a fetishised obedience to commodity production and the market economy. To paraphrase Max Weber—whose own pessimism is often misunderstood—who knows what collective action may release us from the iron cage of rationality?

NOTES

1. As the editors have noted in their postscript, the production of this anthology has taken a long time. But time *per se* does not deteriorate ideas. Given our subject matter, conjunctural time is not of *the* issue. We have added certain references that we deemed important. We could have added more, especially in our theorization of the subject matter. But neither of us believe that fashionable thinking is terribly important—being *au courant* is important but it is not substitutable for a reasoned, self-reflexive viewpoint that has taken years of our lives to develop. Thus, we have changed since our original submission of this chapter in 1981. But we have not changed in any epistemological sense from our materialist lens of analysis.
2. The actual development of the scientific worldview is a complex and significant area of enquiry. Some writers have explored this area of human achievement

quite well, although most tend to treat the development of science in an idealist fashion. Among the better accounts are Borkenau (1934), Koestler (1990), Mandrou (1978), and Sohn-Rethel (1978). While retaining his oft-made distinction between economic *determination* and economic *conditioning*, Weber (1958, p. 24) notes: 'The development of these [natural] sciences and of the technique resting upon them . . . receives important stimulation from these capitalist interests in its economic application'.

3. The basis of this discussion comes from Marx's detailed commentaries in *Capital*, I (1976, pp. 270-307), *Capital*, II (1973, pp. 109-144), and *Grundrisse* (1973, pp. 88-100, 253-325, 471-514).

4. Needless to say, the valorisation and rationalisation of American games and traditional frontier activity, as well as the integration and imported game/sport forms, involved a considerable expanse of time. We have had to telescope the series of events involved and deal mainly with the highlights, due to space limitations (see Gorn, 1986; Ingham, 1978; Riess, 1989).

5. Capitalism is a broad term referring to an economic system in which wage-labour is employed in a production process that is based on abstract value creation for the purposes of creating profits that generally accrue to privately held capital. It presupposes the existence of a market in which commodities are bought and sold according to standards of monetary exchange (see Giddens, 1973, p. 142). Industrial capitalism, on the other hand, is something more specific. It represents a particular variant of the capitalist mode of production in which capital is increased primarily through the production moment (as opposed to surplus generated through circulation—profit upon alienation) via increased marginal productivity through the increasing use of fixed (or constant) capital.

6. These categorising concepts are defined by Loy (1968, pp. 13-14) as follows: ' ''Primary consumers'' are those individuals who become vicariously involved in sport through ''live'' attendance at a sport competition. . . . ''Secondary consumers'' consist of those vicariously involved in a sport as spectators via some form of mass media. . . . ''Tertiary consumers'' are those who become vicariously involved with sport other than as spectators. Thus an individual who engages in conversation related to sport or a person who reads the sport section of the newspaper would be classified as a ''tertiary consumer'' '.

7. William Randolph Hearst deserves a special mention. When he bought the New York *Journal* in 1895 he outdid his publisher rivals in the reporting of sporting news. He signed up sports champions to write for his paper and began the practice of publishing a Sunday sports section. Overall, Hearst should be credited with inventing the modern sports section (see Betts, 1974, p. 67; Cozens and Stumpf, 1953, p. 114).

8. Perhaps the most comprehensive treatment of the moral reform movements is Boyer's *Urban Masses and Moral Order in America, 1820-1920* (1978). The motives and consequences of the reformers' instrumentalisation of play are discussed in some detail in Hardy and Ingham (1982).

9. For a detailed, though partisan, history of the play movement, see Curtis's *The Play Movement and Its Significance* (1917) and Rainwater's *The Play Movement in the United States* (1922). For an assessment of social historians' view of the playground movement and an evaluation of the cross-class alliances and class oppositions that were formed around the issue of supervised 'play' see Hardy and Ingham (1982).

10. Spring (1974, p. 493) states:

> Nowhere in the labor literature can one find a union or union spokesman arguing that a worker could best use the leisure time gained through the shorter working day by participating in or watching an athletic event. For the labor movement this would hardly be considered a 'worthy use of leisure time'. From the Knights of Labor in the nineteenth century to the AFL in the twentieth century there has been a steady advocacy of labor lyceums, nightschools, study groups, colleges, summer camps, chatauauquas and libraries.

> To say that labor thought of worthy use of leisure as studying and preparing for social change is not to say that those who thought of it in terms of athletics were reacting to labor's philosophy. In fact, those who advocated athletics and recreation tended to view social unrest and social problems as things that could be solved through institutional manipulation and the proper molding of character. Athletics and recreation would channel the instinctual unrest and create the proper democratic character. They did not see the problems in the same terms as labor nor speak the same language.

11. When we wrote this essay, we anticipated but could not really apprehend how the Thatcherite and Reaganite re-formation of 19th-century classical liberalism would perform or malfunction. Our anticipations were correct concerning how supply-side economics have malfunctioned in nearly all of the liberal-democratic, "first-world" nation states. Providing for the 2% who control 70% of a nation's wealth has contributed to under-employment and chronic unemployment in the nation-state. Capital moves to the global economy and seeks out the cheapest labour force. World 'free-market' trade policies are used by capitalists to undermine legitimate claims made by the domestic labour force. Collective bargaining has also been undermined and the right to health care has now been made into privileged access (always was in the USA). Consumerist, commodity-relations policies have confused both the middle and subordinate class groupings—particularly the 'respectable' working class and the lower-levels of the middle-classes. It would seem that 'possessive individualism' (see Macpherson, 1973) has once again become naturalized in a way that the gene and sociality have become conflated. In the process ethnophobia and racism have been resurgent, and neo-fascism (read ethnocentric coalitions) have been resurrected.

    We have refrained from citing post-modernist, fashionable thought. As historical materialists, we would not re-write our paper in accordance with the Parisian 'philosophes' whose eccentricity removes us from the lived experience of everyday life. Neither of us suffer from what E.P. Thompson (1978) has called 'The peculiarities of the English'; but we do reject nihilistic theory as the animadversion of reason and of political praxis.

REFERENCES

Adelman, M. (1986). *A sporting time: New York City and the rise of modern athletics, 1820-70.* Urbana: University of Illinois Press.

Alt, J. (1976). Beyond class: The decline of industrial labour and leisure. *Telos, 28,* 55-80.

Arnstein, W.L. (1973). The survival of the Victorian aristocracy. In F.C. Jaher (Ed.), *The rich, the well born, and the powerful,* pp. 203-257. Urbana: University of Illinois Press.

Arnstein, W.L. (1975). The myth of the triumphant Victorian middle class. *The Historian, 37* (2), 205-221.

Aronowitz, S. (1973). *False promises: The shaping of American working class consciousness.* New York: McGraw-Hill.

Atkinson, H.A. (1915). *The Church and people's play.* Boston: Pilgrim Press.

Baltzell, E.D. (1958). *Philadelphia gentlemen: The making of a national upper class.* New York: Free Press.

Baltzell, E.D. (1964). *The Protestant establishment: Aristocracy and caste in America.* New York: Vintage Books.

Beamish, R. (1982). Sport and the logic of capitalism. In H. Cantelon and R.S. Gruneau (Eds.), *Sport, culture and the modern state.* Toronto: University of Toronto Press.

Beamish, R. (1988). The political economy of professional sport. In J. Harvey and H. Cantelon (Eds.), *Not just a game.* Ottawa: University of Ottawa Press.

Berger, P., Berger, B., & Luckmann, T. (1973). *The homeless mind.* New York: Vintage.

Berger, P., & Luckmann, T. (1966). *The social construction of reality.* Garden City, NY: Anchor Books.

Betts, J.R. (1953a). Sporting journalism in nineteenth century America (1819-1900). *American Quarterly, 5:* 39-56.

Betts, J.R. (1953b). The technological revolution and the rise of sport, 1850-1900. *Mississippi Valley Historical Review, XL* (Sept.), 231-256.

Betts, J.R. (1974). *America's sporting heritage: 1850-1950.* Reading, MA: Addison-Wesley.

Betts, J. (1984). *America's sporting heritage: 1850-1950.* Reading: Addison-Wesley.

Birnbaum, N. (1969). *The crisis of industrial society.* New York: Oxford University Press.

Borkenau, F. (1934). *Der Uebergang vom feudalen zum burgerlichen Weltbild.* Paris: Felix Alean.

Bowles, S., & Gintis, H. (1976). *Schooling in capitalist America*. New York: Basic Books.

Boyer, P. (1978). *Urban masses and moral order in America, 1820-1920*. Cambridge, MA: Harvard University Press.

Brohm, J-M. (1968). La civilisation du corps: Sublimation et desublimation. *Partisans Revue*, *43*, 46-65.

Cavallo, D. (1976). Social reform and the movement to organize children's play during the progressive era. *History of Childhood Quarterly*, *3* (4), 509-522.

Clarke, A. (1993). The reformation of corporal corporatism: Victorian ideology in the "lifestyle crisis" of the 1990s—the civic ideology in the public domain. (tentative). In A. Ingham and J. Loy (Eds.), *Sport in social development: Traditions, transitions, and transformations*. Champaign: Human Kinetics.

Clarke, J., & Critcher, C. (1985). *The devil makes work: Leisure in capitalist Britain*. London: Macmillan.

Conzen, M.P. (1977). The maturing urban system in the United States, 1840-1910. *Annals of the Association of American Geographers*, *67* (1), 88-108.

Cozens, F.W., & Stumpf, F.S. (1953). *Sports in American life*. Chicago: University of Chicago Press.

Curtis, H.S. (1917). *The play movement and its significance*. New York: Macmillan.

Dulles, F.R. (1965). *A history of recreation: America learns to play*. New York: Appleton-Century-Crofts.

Dunning, E. (1972). The development of modern football. In E. Dunning (Ed.), *Sport: Readings from a sociological perspective* (pp. 133-151). Toronto: University of Toronto Press.

Dunning, E. (1975). Industrialization and the incipient modernization of football. *Stadion*, *1* (1), 103-139.

Dunning, E., & Sheard, K. (1979). *Barbarians, gentlemen and players: A sociological study of the development of rugby football*. New York: New York University Press.

Durkheim, E. (1938). *The rules of sociological method*. (G.E.G. Catlin, Ed.; S.A. Solovay & J.H. Mueller, Trans.). New York: The Free Press.

Earnest, E. (1953). *Academic procession: An informal history of the American college*. Indianapolis: Bobbs-Merrill.

Faulkner, H.U. (1931). *The quest for social justice, 1889-1914*. Chicago: Quadrangle Books.

Faulkner, H.U. (1959). *Politics, reform and expansion, 1890-1900*. New York: Harper and Row.

Giddens, A. (1973). *The class structure of the advanced societies*. New York: Harper and Row.

Goodman, C. (1979). *Choosing sides: Playgrounds and street life on the Lower East Side*. New York: Shocken Books.

Gorn, E. (1986). *The manly art: Bare-knuckle prize fighting in America*. Ithaca: Cornell University Press.

Gruneau, R.S. (1981). *Class, sport and social development: A study in social theory and historical sociology*. Unpublished doctoral dissertation, University of Massachusetts.

Hardy, S. (1980). 'Parks for the people': Reforming the Boston park system, 1870-1915. *Journal of Sport History*, 7 (3), 5-24.

Hardy, S. (1982). *How Boston played: Sport, recreation, and community, 1865-1915*. Boston: Northeastern University Press.

Hardy, S. (1990). Entrepreneurs, structures, and the Sportgeist: Old tensions in a modern industry. In D. Kyle and G. Stark (Eds.), *Essays on sport history and sport mythology*, pp. 45-82. College Station: Texas A & M University Press.

Hardy, S., & Ingham, A.G. (1982). Games, structures, and agency: Historians on the American play movement. *Journal of Social History*, 17 (2), 37-67.

Heller, A. (1976). *The theory of need in Karl Marx*. London: Allison & Busby.

Hepworth, M., & Featherstone, M. (1982). *Surviving middle age*. Oxford: Basil Blackwell.

Hofstadter, R. (1955a). *Social Darwinism in American thought*. Boston: Beacon Press.

Hofstadter, R. (1955b). *The age of reform*. New York: Vintage Books.

Hofstadter, R. (Ed.) (1963). *The progressive movement, 1900-1915*. Englewood Cliffs, NJ: Prentice Hall.

Ingham, A.G. (1975). Occupational subcultures in the work world of sport. In D.W. Ball and J.W. Loy (Eds.), *Sport and the social order: Contributions to the sociology of sport*, pp. 333-389. Reading, MA: Addison-Wesley.

Ingham, A.G. (1978). *American sport in transition: The maturation of industrial capitalism and its impact upon sport*. Unpublished doctoral dissertation, University of Massachusetts.

Ingham, A.G. (1979). Methodology in the sociology of sport: From symptoms of malaise to Weber for a cure. *Quest*, 31 (2), 187-215.

Ingham, A. (1985). From public issue to personal trouble: Well-being and the fiscal crisis of the state. *Sociology of Sport Journal*, 2, 43-55.

Ingham, A., & Hardy, S. (1984). Sport: Structuration, subjugation and hegemony. *Theory, Culture & Society*, 2 (2), 85-103.

Ingham, A., Howell, J., & Schilperoort, T. (1987). Professional sports and community. *Exercise and Sport Sciences Reviews*, 15, 427-465.

Kelley, R. (1977). Ideology and political culture from Jefferson to Nixon. *American Historical Review*, 82 (3), 531-562.

Kidd, B. (1981). *'We must maintain a balance between propaganda and serious athletics': The workers' sports movement in Canada, 1924-1940*. Paper presented at the 9th biannual Conference of the Canadian Association of Ethnic Studies, Edmonton, Alberta, October 14-16.

Koestler, A. (1990). *The sleepwalkers*. Harmondsworth, Middlesex: Penguin Books.

Kolko, G. (1963). *The triumph of conservatism*. New York: The Free Press.

Lewis, G.M. (1969a). 1879: The beginning of an era in American sport. In 72nd *Proceedings* of the Annual Meetings, pp. 136-145, National College Physical Education Association for Men, Durham, North Carolina.

Lewis, G.M. (1969b). Adoption of the sports program, 1906-1939: The role of accommodation in the transformation of physical education. *Quest*, 12, 34-36.

Lewis, G. (1972). Enterprise on the campus: Development in intercollegiate sport and higher education, 1875-1935. In B.L. Bennett (Ed.), *The history of physical education and sport*, pp. 53-66. Chicago: The Athletic Institute.

Lewis, G.M. (1977). Sport, youth culture and conventionality 1920-1970. *Journal of Sport History, 4* (2), 129-150.

Livingstone, D.W. (1976). On hegemony in corporate capitalist states. *Sociological Inquiry, 46* (3-4), 235-250.

Loy, J.W. (1968). The nature of sport: A definitional effort. *Quest, 10*, 1-15.

Lucas, J. (1968). A prelude to the rise of sport: America, 1850-1860. *Quest, 11*, 50-75.

Macpherson, C.B. (1973). *Democratic theory: Essays in retrieval.* Oxford: Clarendon Press.

Mandrou, R. (1970). *From humanism to science, 1480-1700.* Harmondsworth, Middlesex: Penguin Books.

Mann, M. (1970). The social cohesion of liberal democracy. *American Sociological Review, 35* (3), 423-439.

Marcuse, H. (1955). *Eros and civilization: A philosophical inquiry into Freud.* New York: Beacon Press.

Marx, K. (1973). *Grundrisse.* (M. Nicolaus, Trans.). Harmondsworth, Middlesex: Penguin Books.

Marx, K. (1976). *Capital*, Vol. 1 (B. Fowkes, Trans.). Harmondsworth, Middlesex: Penguin Books.

Marx, K. (1978). *Capital*, Vol. 2 (B. Brewster, Trans.). Harmondsworth, Middlesex: Penguin Books.

McIntosh, P. (1968). *Physical education in England since 1800.* London: Bell.

Metcalfe, A. (1982). *The emergence of modern sport in Canada, 1867-1914.* Toronto: McLelland and Stewart.

Morford, W.R., & McIntosh, M. (1993). Sport and the Victorian gentleman. In A. Ingham and J. Loy (Eds.), *Sport in social development: Traditions, transitions, and transformations.* Champaign: Human Kinetics.

Mutch, R.E. (1980). Colonial America and the debate about the transition to capitalism. *Theory and Society, 9* (5), 847-863.

North, D.C. (1966). *The economic growth of the United States, 1790-1860.* New York: Norton.

Ossowski, S. (1963). *Class structure in the social consciousness.* London: Routledge and Kegan Paul.

Rader, B.G. (1977). The quest for subcommunities and the rise of American sport. *American Quarterly, 29* (4), 355-369.

Redlich, F. (1965). Leisure-time activities: A historical, sociological, and economic analysis. *Explorations in Entrepreneurial History, 3* (Fall), 3-23.

Richardson, N.E. (1913). *The religious education of adolescents.* New York: Abingdon Press.

Riess, S. (1989). *City games: The evolution of American urban society and the rise of sports.* Urbana: University of Illinois Press.

Riis, J. (1971, 1901). *How the other half lives.* New York: Dover.

Sack, A.L. (1973). Yale 29—Harvard 4: The professionalization of college football. *Quest, 19*: 24-34.

Schlesinger, A.M. (1963). *The rise of the city, 1878-1898*. New York: New Viewpoints.

Scott, H.A. (1951). *Competitive sports in schools and colleges*. New York: Harper.

Sohn-Rethel, A. (1978). *Intellectual and manual labour*. (M. Sohn-Rethel, Trans.), London: Macmillan.

Somers, D.A. (1971). The leisure revolution: Recreation in the American city, 1820-1920. *Journal of Popular Culture, 5* (Summer), 125-147.

Spring, J.H. (1972). *Education and the rise of the corporate state*. Boston: Beacon Press.

Spring, J.H. (1974). Mass culture and school sports. *History of Education Quarterly, 14*, 483-499.

Terkel, S. (1974). *Working*. New York: Avon.

Thompson, E.P. (1961). *The making of the English working class*. Harmondsworth, Middlesex: Penguin Books.

Thompson, E.P. (1978). *The poverty of theory and other essays*. New York: Monthly Review Press.

Turner, R.E. (1940). The industrial city: Centre of cultural change. In C.F. Ware (Ed.), *The cultural approach to history*, pp. 228-242. New York: Columbia University Press.

Vincent, T. (1981). *Mudville's revenge: The rise and fall of American sport*. New York: Seaview Books.

Vondracek, F.J. (1932). The rise and development of athletic sports in the United States: 1860-1900. *Quarterly Journal, 23* (Fall), 46-58.

Weber, M. (1958). *The Protestant ethic and the spirit of capitalism*. (T. Parsons, Trans.), New York: Scribner's.

Weber, M. (1974). Subjectivity and determinism. In A. Giddens (Ed.), *Positivism and sociology*, pp. 22-23. London: Heinemann.

Weber, M. (1978). *Economy and society*. (G. Roth and C. Wittich, Eds.) Berkeley: University of California Press.

Weibe, R.H. (1967). *The search for order, 1877-1920*. New York: Hill and Wang.

Westby, D.L., & Sack, A. (n.d.) *The rationalization and commercialization of college football in the late nineteenth century*. Department of History, Pennsylvania State University.

Wheeler, R.F. (1978). Organized sport and organized labor: The workers' sport movement. *Journal of Contemporary History, 13*, 252-265.

Wilkinson, R. (1964). *The prefects: British leadership and the public school tradition*. New York: Oxford University Press.

Willis, J., & Wettan, R. (1976). Social stratification in New York City athletic clubs, 1865-1915. *Journal of Sport History, 3* (1), 45-63.

Willis, P. (1990). *Common culture*. Boulder & San Francisco: Westview Press.

American Football, British Society, and Global Sport Development

Joseph Maguire

In 1987, James Connelly, the National Football League's International Marketing Director, commenting on the rapid development of American football in Britain in the 1980s, noted:

> What you now have in the UK is a microcosm of the US NFL market with one major difference: business that took almost 20 years to develop in the USA has taken a fraction of that time in Great Britain. It is obviously a very receptive market for new ideas and products. (Connelly, 1987a, p. 24)

In this chapter, I want to examine the 'figurational dynamics' and cultural significance of this emergence of American football on the landscape of British sports culture (Elias, 1978; Maguire, 1988b). In order to accomplish this task, it will be necessary to place this development within the context of the more general debate concerning the Americanisation of British culture (Bigsby, 1975; Hebdige, 1981; White, 1983; Chambers, 1986; Collins, 1986; Webster, 1988). It will also be necessary to examine how such changes in 'sports culture' are intertwined with broader cultural changes. Once these preliminary discussions have been concluded, a substantive account of the making of American football in Britain between 1982 and 1989 will be provided. The chapter will conclude with a 'figurational' perspective on Americanisation, focusing on both the 'political economy' of and the 'mimetic' functions performed by American football in British society (Elias, 1982; Elias & Dunning, 1986).

AMERICANISATION AND THE CULTURE DEBATE

In analyses of the alleged Americanisation of British culture, especially popular culture, little or no attention has been paid to the question of sport. Perhaps this is not surprising given the evident inability of researchers to emancipate themselves from the dominant value system in which sport is considered 'nonserious', separate from other cultural activities, and not in need of critical evaluation. Instead, attention has focused on the Americanisation evident in areas such as films, records, TV programmes, clothes, advertising, and consumer products. A number of competing explanations have been put forward in this regard and it is to these that attention will now be directed.

Concern over Americanisation is nothing new. From as early as the 1890s, conservative social critics began to make disparaging remarks regarding the visits of American tourists to Europe (Bigsby, 1975). Significantly, such observations were occurring in a more general climate of concern regarding what conservative social critics, such as Spengler and Eliot, saw as a threat to 'high culture', namely the emergence of mass society (Bennett, 1982).

Equating mass society with mediocrity and the atomisation of the masses renders them susceptible to manipulation by those who control the mass media; it is perhaps not surprising that, following the First World War (when American cultural products began to appear on the British scene), this development was seen by mass society theorists as symptomatic of a 'levelling down' of standards. Americanisation was the symbol of mediocrity (Hebdige, 1982). As Chambers (1986, p. 151) put it: 'America . . . clearly dominated images of leisure from the 1920's onwards'. American influence was thus evident in several areas of popular culture, notably film, music, and dance. During the late 1940s and 1950s, this 'foreign contamination' of popular culture in general was enhanced by the adoption of its more public manifestations by Britain's emerging youth subcultures. American rock'n'roll, in particular, was perceived to be a source of corruption and as embodying all that was 'trash' in American culture (Chambers, 1986, pp. 152-158).

Significantly, criticism of Americanisation in the 1950s and 1960s was not confined to conservative cultural critics who saw such trends as a threat to high culture. Writers such as Hoggart viewed Americanisation as a threat to the texture of authentic working-class culture as well. Here, American television programmes and consumer products were the source of concern (Hebdige, 1982, pp. 198-199). During the 1960s, such concerns of the left began to be reinforced by the work of the Frankfurt school. Writers such as Adorno, Marcuse, and Horkheimer launched powerful critiques against popular culture, equating it with consumerism and holding that it engendered 'false aspirations' and satisfied 'false needs'. At the heart of such critiques, however, is a strand held in common with mass society theories, namely that the users of popular culture are 'cultural dupes'.

Critical analysis of the culture industries has not overlooked the global impact of Americanisation on the mass media and popular cultural forms. Subsequent work has argued that the media are American (Tunstall, 1977) and that this Americanisation constitutes a form of cultural imperialism (Ang, 1985). By the late 1980s, what Collins describes as a 'moral panic' appears to have developed regarding the dominance of American programmes on European television schedules (Collins, 1986, p. 67). The ikon of this dominance, to which the European Commission drew attention when criticising the impact of non-European television, is 'Dallas'.

At this stage, I do not wish to prolong discussion of the contemporary scene. More extensive discussion of this will, in fact, form the context in which to place the substantive concerns of this study. Nor do I wish to detail at this stage an alternative to both mass society theory and critical theory. Attention will be paid to this in the conclusion. It is perhaps appropriate, however, to provide some preliminary guidelines by which to locate the 'touchdown' of American football on the landscape of British sports culture.

To what does the concept of Americanisation refer? White, commenting on the Americanisation of Australian society, captured a number of the elements usually referred to in the debate. For White:

Americanisation most usefully refers to the fundamental reference points of a culture, and the extent to which they can be located in the United States rather than in the culture itself; not just cultural change, but what it has transmitted; not just the measure of American content, but its impact, (if any) on behaviour and ways of thinking. In this sense the examination of Americanisation should embrace not just the impact of Americanisation on popular culture, but also its effect on the culture as a whole. (White, 1983, p. 110)

The perspective adopted here is in broad agreement with White. It is accordingly essential to document not only the extent of Americanisation within the context of the commodification of British sport forms generally, but also to gauge its impact, as manifested by American football, on the behaviour and ways of thinking of British culture as a whole. The task will be to avoid both cultural elitist and cultural imperialist positions. Instead, there is a need to maintain both a radical critique of the impact of American popular cultural forms on the landscape of British culture and yet also to grasp how such forms provide a source of pleasurable excitement (Maguire, 1988a; Elias & Dunning, 1986; Rojek, 1985). It is to these substantive concerns of the present study that attention will now be turned.

THE DEVELOPMENT OF AMERICAN FOOTBALL IN BRITAIN, 1982-1989

Prior to the early 1980s, American football was virtually unknown on the British cultural landscape. The game was infrequently reported and when it was, the reports tended to be short and related to the annual end-of-season Super Bowl. In fact, a content analysis of *The Times* Index for the five-year period prior to the first televising of American football in 1982 revealed only seven brief reports. American football was also hardly played in Britain, except by United States Air Force personnel, and, even in this instance, games usually took place within the confines of their air bases. The same held true as far as spectatorship was concerned. When audiences did view the game prior to 1982, it was on closed-circuit television at cinemas in London with, for example, only some 2,500 people, mainly American, in attendance (*The Times*, 27 January 1981). Radio coverage was also virtually nonexistent except on the American Forces network (*Sunday Times*, 18 January 1987). But during 1982, the initial stages in the making of American football as a significant cultural form within the culture of sections of British society were evident.

In tracing the main features of this transformation, a number of key elements have to be identified. These include the decision of Channel 4 to screen American football in a particular style and on a regular basis, the marketing strategy of the NFL, and the involvement of Anheuser-Busch, the producers of Budweiser beer.

In 1982, the newly created Channel 4 began to screen American football on a regular basis. Why was this decision to screen 75 minutes per week of highlights of regular-season fixtures taken? The Commissioning Editor of Channel 4 Sport, Adrian Metcalfe, had been faced with both limited funds and limited airtime

(Whannel, 1987). The importing of American football and the coverage of British basketball appear to have been perceived as one means to solve the problems faced. More crucially, however, it was not simply the decision to cover American football that was to prove important, but the programme style and presentation. This requires spelling out.

The sports department of Channel 4 appears to have made the decision that the traditional form of British sports coverage was no longer appropriate. Channel 4 decided to take the American television footage and commentary from the main networks (CBS, ABC, and NBC) and then to use a British production company—Cheerleader Productions—to package the game via edited highlights, popularist presenters, rock'n'roll title music, and colourful graphics. Derek Brandon, Cheerleader's Executive Producer, noted in this connection:

> The televising of sport in America is simply stunning. They make it fun, they make it stylish, and they make it a family occasion. These are the things that we've lost from British sport. If LWT had done American football . . . they'd have been back to the presenter in the blazer with the glass of water. (*The Observer*, 5 October 1986)

This shift towards an American style of coverage with the emphasis on 'entertainment' and away from a British 'journalistic' style has also been commented on by Goldlust (1987) with reference to Australian television broadcasting. Before we consider how this coverage of American football dovetailed with both the NFL and the Anheuser-Busch marketing strategies, it is perhaps best to give some indication of the growth in coverage and in viewing figures of the sport since 1982.

In 1982 American football, along with the basketball, was the only sport shown by Channel 4. Showing 75 minutes of edited highlights of the previous week's NFL action, this programme has continued to occupy a central slot in the sport schedules of Channel 4 during the 1980s and early 1990s. In 1983 and 1984, it accounted for some 20% of the sports broadcasting of the station. In 1985, despite diversification into other sports, American football still ranked in the top three of Channel 4's sports output (Whannel, 1987). In fact, along with horse racing and snooker, American football still made up over 50% of the channel's output in 1985 and 1986 and this, in turn, constituted 8% of the total output of the station (Channel 4, 1987). From 1982 to 1986, the amount of time devoted to coverage of the regular season had remained the same, though this was complemented by increased live broadcasts of the playoffs and Super Bowl, the first live Super Bowl being broadcast in January 1983. In 1984, *The Times* felt it appropriate to publish the radio wavelengths of American broadcasts of live games being played in the United States and claimed that 'several thousand' stayed up into the early hours to listen to them (*The Times*, 21 January 1984). During 1987, coverage of American football was further increased with an additional one-hour programme being broadcast on Tuesday evenings, and it now makes up 12% of the total sports output of Channel 4 (Whannel, 1987). But how many people watched these programmes?

Table 1 documents the growth in audiences watching American football between 1982 and 1988. As can be seen, in that period a substantial increase in audience numbers occurred.

During 1987/88, figures as high as 4.7 million were achieved during weeks 11 and 12 of the regular NFL season and, for Super Bowl XXII, an audience high of 6.1 million was recorded (Gallup Polls, 1988). It is important to grasp that while these figures are dwarfed by ratings in the United States, Britain soccer's premier event of the year, the F.A. Cup Final, draws 8 million on BBC and 4 million on ITV and that approximately 400,000 attend Football League matches at weekends. But attention must also be paid to the social composition of this audience.

Analysis of the audience profile of viewers of American football appears to have been considered essential to Channel 4, NFL marketing, and their existing and prospective clients. Based on market research conducted on their behalf, data are available for the seasons 1985/86 to 1987/88 (see Table 2).

The significance of this audience profile will become clearer when attention is switched to examining how this trend has been utilised by specific groups involved in the development of American football in British culture. It is sufficient at this point to note that the viewing audience appears to have an affluent profile with a high proportion of AB and C1 viewers evident. The audience also appears to be disproportionately male and weighted towards the younger age groups.

This general picture of a rise in viewing figures and of a primarily young, male, and affluent audience is borne out by other indices of the development of American football in Britain. Between 1982 and the early 1990s, for example, there emerged a number of magazines devoted exclusively to the gridiron game, namely *Touchdown, Firstdown/Quarterback*, and *Gridiron*. *Touchdown* is reported to sell 25,000 copies per issue. (*The Times*, 20 January 1984) and *Gridiron* had sales of over 29,000 per issue in 1987 (Audit Bureau of Circulations, 1987). A national newspaper, *The Daily Telegraph*, publishes a weekly magazine, *The Daily Telegraph American Football Magazine*, with a readership peak during the 1989-1990 season of some 100,000. Marshall Cavendish, a specialist publisher of magazine collections, produced an 18-part series timed to coincide with the NFL season. The series was heavily advertised on television, including Channel 4, and Part 1 achieved a sale

Table 1   Channel 4's American Football TV Audience Profile 1982/83-1987/88

Year	Average audience	Year	Average audience
1982/83	1.1 million	1985/86	3.1 million
1983/84	1.5 million	1986/87	2.9 million
1984/85	2.3 million	1987/88	3.7 million*

*Two broadcasts per week.

Source: AGB/BARB cited in NFL Merchandise Catalogue 1988.

Table 2   Channel 4's American Football TV Audience Profile in Terms of Social Class, Age, and Gender: 1985/86-1987/88

	Overall population	1985/86	1986/87	1987/88
Social class*				
AB	19	13	18	20
C1/C2	50	57	56	54
DE	31	30	26	26
Age				
4-15	19	19	22	24
16-35	29	40	39	36
35+	52	41	39	40
Gender				
Men	49	61	63	64
Women	51	39	37	36

*Based on the Registrar General's classification, which assumes that occupation is the most useful indicator of social class. Class A = professionals (e.g., lawyers, doctors, managers); Class B = intermediate professionals (e.g., shopkeepers, farmers, teachers); Class C1/C2 = manual and nonmanual workers (though their incomes are similar, there is a wide gap between them in values and lifestyles); Class D = semi-skilled workers (e.g., bus drivers, farm workers); Class E = unskilled occupations.

Source: AGB/BARB. C4 cited in NFL Merchandise Catalogue 1988.

in the region of 275,000 copies (Marshall Cavendish, 1989). The series sold, in total, in excess of two million copies (Connelly, 1987b, p. 53).

Not surprisingly, the readership of this range of magazines appears to be similar to that which watches American football on Channel 4. As part of the launch of the Cavendish series on American football, a questionnaire was sent out with Part 1; analysis of its findings revealed that at least half of the respondents were in their teens, that the vast majority were male and that their social class origins tended towards the C1 and AB groupings (MIL Research Ltd, 1986, p. 2). Over 50% of the respondents had purchased copies of magazines such as *Touchdown* and 91% viewed American football on Channel 4 every week, though two-thirds had never attended a 'live game' (MIL Research Ltd, 1986, p. 13). Given data such as these, it is perhaps not surprising that a writer in the *Sunday Times* could claim in January 1987 that:

> Cheerleader have clearly found the advertisers' nirvana—a young, rich and enthusiastic audience . . . It's almost as if the yuppies of the world were waiting for a spectator sport they could feel was theirs—something that was at its best when watched on the small screen in the warmth of their home. (*Sunday Times*, 18 January 1987)

In catering for this young, affluent, and predominantly male group, American football yearbooks have been published since 1983, and other publishers such as Queen Anne Press have produced a range of titles that are carried in most major book chains. This dissemination of American football literature is not confined, however, to journals and books. In 1987, *The Daily Telegraph* put together a series of eight guides to the game and distributed them free with the newspaper around the London area. Readership increased by between 5% and 10% each Friday it was distributed, and 30,000 readers outside the London area subscribed for special postal delivery of the magazines (Licensing Management International, 1989).

Significantly, *The Daily Telegraph* not only underwrote the production costs of Cheerleader Productions's editing of American football for Channel 4, but the newspaper title was carried on caption when the programme broke for advertisements. While this example is revealing in terms of demonstrating the interweaving of media interests in the televising of American football, the underwriting of Cheerleader's production costs of American football is, in fact, nothing new. The production costs of the programmes broadcast in the first year of Channel 4's coverage of American football were underwritten by Anheuser-Busch. Coca-Cola is the programme's current sponsor. Having provided some indication of the growth in American football as a cultural phenomenon in Britain, it is perhaps appropriate at this stage to turn attention to how this development was interwoven with the marketing strategies of Anheuser-Busch and the NFL.

Anheuser-Busch has played a significant role in the development of American football in Britain in a number of key areas. The investment of £100,000 in the production costs of televising American football in the UK (*The Times*, 23 December 1985) was combined with direct advertising during slots in the programme. Significantly, Budweiser advertisements sometimes included American footballers. One notable example, where reality and fantasy arguably meshed, involved the meeting within a Western saloon of players of the Washington Redskins and the Dallas Cowboys!

In 1986 the marketing strategy of Anheuser-Busch also involved them in establishing the Budweiser League. This league attempted to pull together several rival leagues that had mushroomed in the three years since the first Channel 4 broadcasts. It was only in the summer of 1983 that the first team, the London Ravens, was formed. In all, 72 teams joined the Budweiser League, in which Anheuser-Busch owned a 51% shareholding (Budweiser League Yearbook, 1987, p. 7). By 1987, the Budweiser League had expanded to 105 teams with the member clubs nominally owning the league. A rival British Gridiron Football League was also formed in this period and, by 1988, it, too, had 72 teams. The main stumbling block to amalgamation of the various leagues appears to have been Anheuser-Busch's 51% share of the Budweiser League. The European Football League refused to recognise the Budweiser League unless such ownership was dropped (*Gridiron UK*, May 1986, p. 19). By late 1988, formal ownership had passed to the clubs but the involvement of Anheuser-Busch had not ceased, for the company had agreed to sponsor the Budweiser League for the following two seasons. Each season was planned to culminate in the playing of the Budweiser Bowl. In 1986, this involved an 18,000 sellout crowd at Crystal Palace. By 1988, it was reported that there were 198 senior teams and 16,000 registered players in the United Kingdom (Algar, 1988, p. 58). In this situation, unification of the game was perceived to be crucial to further commercialisation. Take the following comments made by a writer in *Gridiron UK* in February 1987:

> The unification of the British game will help to make our American football more attractive to the sponsor . . . Budweiser's own investment should help to convince other potential sponsors that British American football is a game worth backing. (*Gridiron UK*, February 1987, p. 55)

The development of this league structure and of the Budweiser Bowl by Anheuser-Busch was combined with the development of the American Bowl at Wembley Stadium. Held in the preseason period of the NFL, and played between two NFL teams, the first American Bowl was played in August 1986 between the Dallas Cowboys and the Chicago Bears. The event was sponsored by a combination of TWA, American Express, and Budweiser (*The Times*, 11 April 1986). The 1986 game was a sellout. 80,000 tickets were sold in seven days, with seat prices as high as £20. Television coverage ensured an even wider audience (Connelly, 1987, p. 54). Following the success of this venture, in December 1986 Anheuser-Busch announced that they were planning to increase their spending on American football in Britain over the next two years to more than 1.5 million pounds (*The Times*, 20 December 1986). An indication of the success of this marketing strategy is that sales of Budweiser have risen considerably in this period.

These developments also relate to and were reinforced by the marketing strategy of the NFL. The NFL is not simply the administrative arm of the game of American football but is also a trade association that directs the operations of NFL Properties and NFL Films, the revenue producing companies for American Football. The activities of these companies in the home market centre on TV rights, retail licensing, publishing, and corporate sponsor development. These companies have proved to be highly effective. Their products appear in over 40% of all United States households involving 250 million dollars of annual retail business. The publishing activities of the NFL involve a diverse range of magazines and books, and each year between 30 and 40 business categories are selected and NFL promotion rights are granted that allow the companies involved to promote, advertise, and merchandise their own products endorsed with the NFL logo. It would appear, however, that the NFL is aware of limitations developing within their own market, especially with respect to TV revenues (Harris, 1987, p. 605). In this regard, they are not unlike other United States transnational companies that have sought to diversify their operations on a global scale (Gilpin, 1976). This trend was highlighted by James Connelly when he addressed a British audience on the subject of 'Influencing Your Customer' in 1987:

> The League now recognises that international marketing is the key area of future growth potential for the sport and has pledged its resources accordingly including the League Office, respective ball clubs, NFL Properties and NFL Films. (Connelly, 1987b, p. 52)

But who exactly do the NFL regard as their customers? Three main groups are identified: the NFL fan/consumer, NFL licensees, and NFL corporate clients. The marketing strategy for the United Kingdom was therefore clear. According to Connelly, the strategy was to 'create, develop and influence a whole new customer base in the U.K.' (Connelly, 1987b, p. 46). In order to achieve this aim, the NFL sought to meet four main objectives. These were:

1. to promote the game abroad on a long-term sustained basis;
2. to create and then educate a new fan base;
3. to establish and protect the NFL trademarks on a worldwide basis for commercial application; and
4. to generate revenues. (Connelly, 1987b, p. 52)

The following section will attempt to detail how the NFL achieved these goals in the United Kingdom and how their efforts were interrelated with the activities of Channel 4 and Anheuser-Busch. The first crucial step in the NFL strategy has been to achieve television and media coverage. Again Connelly addressed this issue when he argued:

The key . . . to building this marketing business is successful television placement. Once you are successfully able to place your product on television with a strong programmed package, and an advantageous viewing hour, you can generate the initial awareness, interest and exposure . . . for your product. Once that has been established you can then go in and develop the resulting licensing businesses. (Connelly, 1987b, p. 52)

This strategy meshed with the programming policy of Channel 4. That is, as was established earlier, Channel 4 sought to distance themselves from the conventional style of British sports broadcasting. Taking their coverage from the main U.S. networks, and with the reediting provided by Cheerleader Productions, a 'strong programme package' was achieved. In addition, given that the actual programme was broadcast on a Sunday evening when the BBC and ITV were showing religious programmes, an advantageous viewing hour was achieved. The fact that the programme was shown early in the evening also ensured that a potentially young audience could be attracted. The importance of the initial screening of American football in 1982 was not overlooked by either the television companies or the NFL. In 1984, Andrew Croker, marketing director of Cheerleader Productions, commented:

The high level of interest in the game is television led. The point is that this is the best-covered sport in the world in terms of television technology and cash. That makes it a very strong product, and one that had had very limited exposure here. And it is very much a television sport . . . the packaging of the game into highlights tends to allow the game to gain pace, in the way that soccer highlights lose pace. (*The Times*, 20 January 1984)

Significantly, Croker described American football as a television sport. This has not happened by chance. Sewart (1987) has noted how American football was regarded in its home market in the early 1970s as 'boring' and television ratings dropped to an all-time low. The NFL Rules Committee responded with a series of rule changes that were designed to speed up the action and increase the potential for high-scoring games (Sewart, 1987, p. 172). The effect of these rule changes was reinforced in Britain by the packaging by Cheerleader, which, Croker notes, allowed the game to 'gain pace'. The role of Channel 4 and Cheerleader was acknowledged by Connelly in 1987 when he remarked:

> We were very fortunate in that . . . there was a Channel 4 and a 'Cheerleader' production who put together a dynamically packaged programme at a good viewing hour . . . that created the initial exposure and awareness of our sport. That has helped trigger all of the successes we have enjoyed in the resultant licensing areas. (Connelly, 1987b, p. 53)

This strategy of promoting the game dovetailed with the attempt to 'create and educate a fan base'. Here, the operations of the NFL in other areas of the media reinforced the exposure received on Channel 4. NFL Films and NFL Properties, working through a local agent, Licensing Management International, reached publishing agreements with a number of companies. As noted earlier, Marshall Cavendish launched an 18-part magazine series devoted to the game, timed to coincide with the 1986 coverage of American football. NFL licenses have also been agreed with other media organisations including Queen Anne Press, Mediawatch International, and Ladybird Books. These companies have produced publications such as *American Football Annual Yearbook*, *Who's Who in American Football?*, *Quarterback*, and *American Football Book*. Other licenses have been granted to companies to produce American football fact packs, calendars, stickers, diaries, posters, jigsaw puzzles, painting-by-numbers games, and playing cards (NFL Merchandise Catalogue, 1988, p. 23). *The Daily Telegraph*, which, as noted, gave away free to its readers an American football magazine, received its materials from NFL Films. Given the data cited earlier regarding the extent of the consumption of these products, it would appear that this part of the NFL marketing strategy had been achieved, but this strategy had, as noted, other objectives.

The need that the NFL perceived to be essential in their operations was to establish and protect their trademark on a worldwide basis for commercial applications. In Britain, this was to be achieved through the operations of Licensing Management International. Beginning in the 1983/84 season, this licensing operation has grown to a point where over 70 companies are involved. The motivation behind this aspect of NFL strategy in the United Kingdom was not only to increase profits in the short term. The concern appears also to have been to increase awareness of the NFL logo in the marketplace. This is what Connelly had to say about this issue:

> If they [the corporate client] . . . by using an NFL theme promotion . . . increase their sales and, at the same time, expose our trademarks in a quality promotional context, then we have achieved mutual objectives. (Connelly, 1987b, p. 49)

A diverse range of merchandise and companies has been involved. The merchandise licensed under the NFL franchise includes but is by no means exhausted by the following: Huddles children's clothing, replica NFL helmets, shirts, satin jackets, knitwear, underwear, nightwear, caps, coffee mugs, skateboards, rollerskates, bean bags, key rings, fun beds and seats, easter eggs, watches, and clocks! The companies involved range from specialist leisurewear manufacturers (e.g., Charterhouse Textiles Manufacturing), small sports retailers and outlets, and larger and more well-known companies such as Marks and Spencers, Mothercare, Asda, and British Home Stores.

The scale of this merchandising operation has been matched by the product endorsements that have been secured. These include products such as Marathon chocolate bars (Snickers), Wagon Wheel biscuits, and Leaf bubble gum. An indication of the 'success' of these operations is that during the period of their promotion, sales of multipack Marathon bars went up by 40% and Wagon Wheels by 30% (Licensing Management International, 1989, p. 2). The NFL understands why this occurred. Connelly, in commenting on NFL operations in the United States, remarked:

> We allow them to trade on the equity of the NFL trademarks to enhance the sale of their products or services and/or to embellish their advertising or promotion programme. (Connelly, 1987b, p. 47)

But why should this association with the NFL have proved so attractive, and how has it applied to developments in Britain? In order to answer this, one has to keep in mind the audience profile of Channel 4 American football outlined earlier. In recent work conducted by Gallup Polls for the NFL, it was claimed that the NFL market was becoming 'younger and more affluent' (NFL Merchandising Catalogue, 1988, p. 3). This finding corresponds to the general profile of the television audience outlined earlier. More particularly, the findings of the market research showed that 38% of all households with children between 4 and 15 years old were interested in NFL football; over 50% watched it regularly on Channel 4; 33% owned some NFL-branded merchandise; and 50% of households with boys aged 10 to 15 years old were interested in the game (Social Surveys, Gallup Polls, 1988).

Significantly, this market research also revealed that 77% of the British households that view NFL football considered that products carrying the NFL shield would be of equal or higher quality than most products; 91% of 16 to 25 year olds, 75% of 25 to 44 year olds, and 86% of those in social class AB considered that products with the NFL shield are of equal or higher quality than most other products (Social Surveys, Gallup Polls, 1988). In fact, the licensing programme adopted reflected the audience profile reported by the market research (Licensing Management International, 1989, p. 1). This strategy is similar to the one adopted by the NFL in their home market. In considering the United States, Connelly observed: 'We have worked within this licensing sector to target ourselves and market to a specific customer profile' (Connelly, 1987b, p. 47).

It would appear, therefore, that the NFL strategy for their franchising and corporate client arrangements in Britain has been to target specific groups identified as being interested in American football, and this identification stems from the audience profile of Channel 4's programme. This strategy not only allowed for the possibility of greater profits to be generated in the short term but allowed for the NFL logo to penetrate deep into the cultural terrain of British society. This dissemination followed the cultural terrain that the products endorsed by the NFL then covered. An example of this process is the development of the Wagon Wheels biscuit. Having reached agreement over NFL endorsement of their product, Burton Biscuits then arranged a media schedule in autumn 1986 that involved placing advertisements in a range of children's comics, including *Buster, Whizzer and Chips, Eagle*, and *Roy of the Rovers* with a combined circulation of 378,734. On this basis, perhaps it was no surprise that media commentators believed that an advertiser's nirvana had been found.

This penetration of the cultural terrain of British society is also evident in other areas. Linking with the marketing strategy of Anheuser-Busch, the American Bowl would not have been possible without NFL approval and cooperation. In fact, Licensing Management International appears to have played a significant part in arranging the sponsorship package that underpinned the 1986 American Bowl involving American Express, TWA, and Budweiser (Connelly, 1987, p. 54). In addition, the NFL provides equipment and instructional advice for Budweiser League teams and allows limited use of the NFL logo on their jerseys. Channel 4's live coverage of Super Bowl XXI was complemented by the release of the official NFL programme, the only difference being that it carried British advertisements. In the three days prior to the screening of the game on Channel 4, over 150,000 copies were sold.

In adopting this strategy, the NFL has also met its fourth objective. An indication of this can be gained from the fact that while in 1983/84 £125,000 worth of merchandised goods were sold at retail, by 1988/89 a figure of £24 million was forecast (Licensing Management International, 1989, p. 1). The success of this operation can also be gauged in other respects. In 1982, 60% of NFL overseas business came from Canada and Mexico. By 1987, 80% came from Europe, of which, as Connelly has noted, 'the UK is by far our leading and most successful market' (Connelly, 1987, p. 53). Two points are of interest in this connection. One should not be surprised by the fact that the satellite broadcasts of Sky Television (Murdoch owned) and Screensport to a wide range of European countries contain a significant proportion of American football and American sports coverage in general (*The Guardian*, 1 February 1989). For a transnational company believing that 'international marketing is the key area of future growth', gaining a place on such satellite broadcasting is essential. Indeed, according to Licensing Marketing International, NFL football is 'well established in the British high street as a family sport with good opportunities for growth in licensing, publishing, and marketing programmes' (Licensing Management International, 1989, p. 3). The success of these operations has been such that in March 1989, NFL Commissioner Pete Rozelle proposed to the NFL Long Range Planning and Finance Committee that a 'Spring League' be established in Europe, from 1990, involving NFL reserve team players and European teams (*The Daily Telegraph*, 8 March 1989). This strategy has been formally agreed to by the NFL and a 'Spring League' will operate in Europe. The league was formally launched in the early 1990s and operates as the World League of American Football. The league has had mixed fortunes. While it has proved popular in Europe, especially in the cities where teams are based (Barcelona, Frankfurt, and London), it has not proved as successful in North America. In that context the crucial test is with regard to television ratings. Unfortunately for the National Football League (NFL), audience ratings have proved disappointing. The league operated at a loss in its first two seasons. NFL owners have yet to make a decision regarding its future. Given this backcloth, the question thus arises of how we are to make sense of the making of American football in British society in the 1980s and early 1990s.

TOUCHDOWN ON BRITISH CULTURE: 'SCORE ONE FOR THE GIPPER'?

In order to provide some explanation of the manner and form of the development of American football in British society, it is necessary to examine three main issues. Attention must be paid to the broader cultural terrain in which this development took place. A reconsideration of the issue of Americanisation must also be undertaken and a more general analysis of sport, cultural change, and popular culture must be provided.

While a detailed study of the broader cultural context lies outside the scope of the present paper, some assistance can be provided by the work of Webster (1988). In his survey of British culture in the relevant period, Webster seeks to steer a line between the need to examine popular culture critically while at the same time avoiding the adoption of the cultural elitism of mass society theorists or the overly simple conspiracy theories of some Marxist writers. More particularly, he argues that 'the link between critiques of popular culture and opposition to U.S. foreign policy works to block effective political analysis' and that 'it is necessary to separate conservative worries about the national cultural heritage from political opposition to American policies' (Webster, 1988, pp. 245-246).

In demonstrating how effective political analysis has so far been blocked, Webster points to how both ends of the political spectrum have analysed popular culture in the 1980s. The right have associated 'video-nasties', with their alleged gratuitous celebration of sex and violence, with Americanisation and the perceived threat to British values. The left regard television series such as 'Dallas', 'Dynasty', and 'Falcon Crest' as a threat to British, indeed European, national identity and as a form of cultural imperialism. Fast-food chains, tourism to the United States, and the development of Britain as a theme park for wealthy yet 'uncouth' Americans have also been the foci for criticism in the last decade.

Criticism of American cultural imperialism was conjoined with several key political debates in Britain in the 1980s. Threats to the sovereignty of the nation were seen as posed by the American nuclear bases in Britain, especially in the deployment of Cruise missiles. This perceived undermining of British sovereignty was reinforced by the British need to seek American approval to retake the Falklands and by the launching from British bases of the American raid on Libya. Threats to the economic sovereignty of Britain were raised by the Westland helicopters affair, in which a key defence firm was, in effect, taken over by an American transnational. The spectre of Americanisation loomed large indeed on the cultural and political map of the 1980s!

In some instances, political and cultural concerns over Americanisation have overlapped. The criticism levelled at films such as 'Rambo', 'Red Dawn', 'The Delta Force', and 'Top Gun' are examples of this trend in Britain in the 1980s (Webster, 1988). Criticism of President Reagan's 'Star Wars' programme has also been matched by suspicion of satellite broadcasting. With its expected diet of American movies, sports, and films, one critic described satellite broadcasting as 'tripe from outer space'. Webster notes in this connection that:

> What is noticeable is the way that Anglo-American cultural relations and political/military/industrial relations act as metaphors for each other . . . American cultural products are often marketed around masculinity, and those models of masculinity are . . . used as images for American military power. Britain's relative 'impotence' provides the corresponding term. (Webster, 1988, p. 245)

If the drawing of enforced connections between American cultural wares and U.S. foreign policy has served to confuse rather than clarify the attempt to understand changes and continuities in popular culture, what is the alternative? Indeed, how do we locate the development of American football within this cultural matrix? Some assistance can be provided in this regard if we reconsider both the concept of the Americanisation of popular culture and the issue of cultural change in sport.

It was suggested at the beginning of this chapter that the perceived Americanisation of British society and culture have tended to be conceptualised in terms either of the discourse of the mass society theorists or that of the Frankfurt school. While, clearly, there are important differences between these approaches, what they have in common is an assumption that Americanisation has an entirely negative impact on popular culture. Mass society theorists have argued that Americanisation reinforces and reflects the general massification of society. Popular culture, associated with mediocrity and poor taste and with its consumers subject to external control and manipulation, is perceived to be a threat to 'high culture'. Critical and orthodox Marxist theories also tend to portray the consumers of popular culture as 'victims' subject to influences outside their consciousness or control. Americanisation is seen to be eroding 'authentic' popular culture and, in consuming America's cultural wares, the 'children of Albion are selling out their birthright' (Webster, 1988, p. 211).

Neither perspective can be viewed as satisfactory. The trick is to maintain a radical critique of culture but to avoid both the cultural elitism of mass society theory and the blindness of critical theory to the fact that 'insider' consumption can involve active appropriation of meaning and not just passive surrender to the meanings imposed by powerful 'outsider' groups (Elias and Scotson, 1965; Elias, 1982, pp. 251-258). Let us consider the difficulties that are arguably inherent in these approaches in a little more detail.

The alleged effects of Americanisation have been challenged by a number of writers. Kaplan (1986), for example, argues that the Americanisation thesis contains within it an undifferentiated and oversimplified view of popular culture. The receptivity of popular culture to American cultural wares, she maintains, is both active and heterogeneous. Indeed, according to Webster, since these cultural wares contain no 'fixed ideological message', they can be reacted to by different national audiences (Webster, 1988, p. 179). Similarly, Hebdige rejects the idea about the 'homogenising influence of American culture'. In contrast, he argues that 'American popular culture offers a rich iconography, a set of symbols, objects and artefacts which can be assembled and re-assembled by different groups in a literally limitless number of combinations' (Hebdige, 1982, p. 216).

The work of Bigsby reinforces this position. He argues that, in the process of cross-cultural diffusion, American culture 'suffers a sea-change', it 'assumes a new identity', and becomes, in effect, a 'superculture, a reservoir of shifting values' (Bigsby, 1975, p. 27). In arguing for the possibility of the emergence of a 'new identity', Bigsby is allowing for the capacity of individuals to reinterpret the American cultural product into something distinct. He further argues that Americanisation is an 'emblematic' and not a causal source of change.

One further point regarding this reassessment of Americanisation needs to be made. It is that insufficient attention has been paid in the literature so far to the pleasure experienced in consuming American popular culture. That is, when distinctions are made between 'personalised consumption' and 'mass consumerism', the pleasure gained in the latter is seen as inauthentic and as in some way serving to endorse the system that produced it. In contrast, Webster correctly notes that the 'pleasure of the consumer is not exhausted in his or her contribution to record company profits' (Webster, 1988, p. 210). According to Ang, indeed, the images of American films and television programmes have become 'signs which no longer indicate something like Americanness but visual pleasure as well' (Ang, 1985, p. 18). Webster similarly remarks that American images do not just give pleasure: They signify pleasure.

Despite these useful observations, the experience of pleasure remains untheorized in this debate. That is, while it is important to note that American images may signify pleasure, what is also needed is an analysis of pleasure per se. It is here that the experience of American cultural products, be they films, sports, or novels, needs to be placed within a broader analysis of the mimetic functions of leisure activities (Elias & Dunning, 1986). This reassessment of Americanisation will be returned to in the concluding section of this chapter.

The question arises whether the arguments that Kaplan, Hebdige, Ang, and Bigsby present regarding Americanisation and popular culture in general also apply to the development of American sport forms, particularly insofar as they have diffused to Britain (Maguire, 1988b). These arguments may have provided a useful corrective to a crude Americanisation thesis, but this should not lead one to the conclusion that the consumer is sovereign, that there are no power differentials involved in the provision of cultural forms and that this provision cannot be explained in terms of 'figurational dynamics'. These points will be returned to in due course. For the moment, some aspects of the emergence of American football in British society that have already been documented need to be explained with reference to the prevailing balance of power between the 'providers' and the 'consumers'. Furthermore, nowhere in the work of these writers is attention paid to sport. In order to provide a more adequate analysis, consideration must also be given to the issue of cultural change in sport.

The study of sport, cultural change, and popular culture has received some analysis in the sociology of sport (Donnelly, 1985). Given the concerns of the present chapter it is ironic that the first such analysis investigated the cultural diffusion of football to America itself (Riesman & Denney, 1981). In the present context, the work of Kidd (1981) is especially pertinent and deserves consideration.

Kidd's study of sport in Canada is located within a broader analysis of the development of Canadian national culture. Noting the potential importance of sport in the strengthening and enunciation of national identity, Kidd observes that the commodification/Americanisation of Canadian sport has served to undermine this potential. Focusing on the National Hockey League as a 'critical case' in this regard, he highlights how both the ideological marketing strategy of the NHL and the overall process of commodification in between the two world wars served to 'accelerate the disintegration of beliefs and practices which had once supported and nurtured autonomous Canadian institutions' (Kidd, 1981, p. 713). Leaving aside the issue of whether such institutions were ever autonomously 'Canadian', for Kidd, an explanation of these processes lies not in Americanisation per se but in a critique of capitalism. He writes in this regard:

> Explanation lies neither in U.S. expansion nor national betrayal, but in the dynamics of capital. Once sport became a sphere of commodity production . . . then it was almost inevitable that the best Canadian hockey would be controlled by the richest and most powerful aggregates of capital and sold in the richer and more populous markets of the U.S. The disappearance of community control over Canadian hockey strengthened a much larger process—the centralization of all popular forms of culture. (Kidd, 1981, p. 714)

While there are several parallels with recent sports developments in Britain, there is reason to believe that Kidd's substantive concerns are in some ways more relevant to the emergence of basketball in this country than to American football (Maguire, 1988b). That is, concomitant with the commercialisation of basketball, the meaning of the game and the social composition of the playing and coaching personnel became increasingly American. What Kidd's Marxist analysis does sensitise one to is the need not to lose sight of the essential role of capital in the transplantation of American football to British society. Although the reassessment of Americanisation by the writers referred to above has value, particularly in acknowledging the capacity of people in other cultures to reinterpret American products, this should not obscure the power realities in the provision and production of this consumption. However, there are also dangers in pointing to the role of capital to the exclusion of all else. If that is done, the problems associated either with economic determinism or with the 'cultural dupe' thesis associated with the Frankfurt school reappear. So, how are we to understand the making of American football in British society?

CONCLUDING REMARKS:
AN EVALUATION OF THE CULTURAL SIGNIFICANCE
OF THE MAKING OF AMERICAN FOOTBALL

In order to make sense of the making of American football in Britain in the 1980s, analysis of its 'figurational dynamics' and cultural significance must be attempted. Three main issues require attention in this connection: The figurational dynamics of Anglo-American relations; the 'political economy' of American football; and the place of this game within the broader 'mimetic sphere'. This requires spelling out.

The term figurational dynamics is derived from the work of Elias (1978). Figurational sociology is concerned with examining the multiple networks of interdependence that both constrain and enable the actions of people. The integration and dynamics of figurations cannot be understood simply in terms of the plans and intentions of individuals but must be explained in terms of the whole network of unintended interdependencies within which intentional actions take place and the unintended consequences that tend to result from the interweaving of an aggregate of intentional acts (Elias, 1978). In addition, Elias is concerned with moving away from the idea of social structures as comprised of separate or only loosely connected spheres and of attempting to assess the relative 'causal weights' of these spheres.

Figurations thus refer to the totality of relationships that, created by interdependent people as a whole, undergo different magnitudes of development over time. The concept of development is used in contrast to the term change because it more adequately captures the complexity of figurations in flux. A developmental approach allows the possibility of capturing both the processes that involve movements towards higher or lower levels of differentiation and integration and the connections between stages in such processes (Dunning, 1987). Use of this concept allows scope for probing an issue that is essential for developmental and figurational sociologists, namely, that of tracing 'movements' over time and of explaining how later social formations arise out of earlier ones. The study of Americanisation is no exception to this.

That is, in order to capture the dynamics of Americanisation, or indeed globalisation, there is a need to think processually. In order to understand Americanisation, one must avoid 'today-centred' analyses that probe the issue in a nonrelational manner. Instead, it is important to recognise that Anglo-American relations, in their totality, are deeply rooted in the histories of these countries. In addition, there has always been a balance of power in this relationship, which, while early on, favoured the English, still allowed scope for the development of indigenous American cultural forms and for the exchange of cultural styles and values.

In the early development of what Lipset has termed 'The First New Nation', the British, especially the English, were dominant. This domination, however, was not complete. Significantly, as Lipset remarks, 'although colonial subjects, Americans were also Englishmen and were thus accustomed to the rights and privileges of Englishmen' (Lipset, 1964, p. 93). But despite these 'new Americans' shaking off their status as a colony, eighteenth- and nineteenth-century American intellectuals had not lost, according to Lipset, a sense of 'inferiority' relative to their European counterparts (Lipset, 1964, p. 71). The diffusion of American ideas to Europe in this period demonstrates that there was a cultural exchange, albeit contoured by an uneven power ratio, which, at this stage, continued to favour the English.

Given that the substantive concerns of the present chapter involve the development of American football in Britain, recognition of the role of American intellectuals and the exchange of cultural forms in the nineteenth century is particularly relevant. That is, it was in the late 1860s that the English game of rugby spread to American universities. According to Riesman and Denney, it was Harvard and Yale that 'served as the culturally receptive importers of the English game' (Riesman & Denney, 1982, p. 681). While the details of their analysis need not concern us here, they note that, in the context of university sport, a distinctively American game emerged: American football. It was this dissemination of English rugby to America that provided the antecedents for the game that has now appeared on the British cultural landscape in the 1980s. But despite Britain being, in the 1870s, relatively dominant, Americans still had the cultural power to remake the game of rugby in their own image.

Though America has, during the course of the twentieth century, become relatively more dominant in its relationship with Britain, and this, as noted, has manifested itself in the spread of American cultural wares, this cultural exchange has not been all one way. In sport, we can observe that during the mid-1970s the game of Association football, arguably *the* world sport, became increasingly popular in the United States. A large number of Britons went to the United States as players and coaches. Though not successful at a professional level, despite attempts by corporate business to 'package' the game for television (Sewart, 1987), soccer has become a significant participant sport at the high-school and collegiate levels. What impact hosting the 1994 World Cup will have on American culture remains a matter of speculation. In the arts and the theatre, the British influence on sections of American culture is also evident. An illustration of this is the East Coast cable channel ESBN, which has a predominantly Anglophile intellectual audience, and which carries a significant proportion of British productions on its schedules. The struggle for cultural hegemony is not confined to Britain! Moreover, although the United States remains, at present, the world's leading power, its dominance, at least in the industrial and financial spheres, has been challenged in recent years by the Japanese. One cultural consequence of this is the virtual disappearance of uniquely American cars from U.S. streets and a proliferation of Hondas, Toyotas, etcetera. This 'Japanisation' of American society also involves the purchase of prestigious real estate developments. Furthermore, the dominance of Anglo-Americans is also under threat from the Hispanicisation of American society.

What these examples indicate is that Anglo-American relations need to be understood in terms of interdependence and that America itself is caught up in a whole set of figurational power balances. Anglo-American interdependence is contoured and shaped by power differentials, but these differentials are by no means fixed. In this context, power needs to be understood as a structural characteristic of interdependencies. For figurational sociology, attention focuses on the potential for interdependencies to move in different directions. That is, power refers to a capability that is not primarily the quality of an individual but a structural property of all social relationships, which is both relational and processual. This conception of power is closely related to the problem of teasing out how unintended interdependencies can be used by human beings as a basis for intentional interventions in ongoing social processes (Bogner, 1986). People on both sides of the Atlantic have had, and continue to have, a fluctuating ability to interpret and change the cultural wares diffusing, more or less, between these two countries. But they are, nevertheless, no less caught up in long-term unintended global interdependency chains.

This observation links to a more general issue. Figurational sociology is critical of work that sees the economy as universally the key determinant of other aspects of human relations. From this perspective the development of political and economic structures is seen, in fact, as two quite inseparable aspects of developing webs of interdependence (Elias, 1978, pp. 140-142). Elias, in rejecting the primacy given to the economic dimension and to the 'material-ideal', 'base-superstructure' dichotomy inherent in some forms of Marxism, attempts to get away from the compartmentalisation of social life that tends to be involved (Elias, 1978, pp. 138-145). Instead, attention is given to the 'immanent dynamics of developing social figurations' and to the processes of increasing or decreasing differentiation and integration that occur within them. The task is to reveal interdependencies through which the development of particular social processes can be grasped as part of the development of a whole network of functions within and between societies. Elias's analysis of the commercialisation of French court society is a powerful example of this approach (Elias, 1983, pp. 160-161).

This is not to suggest that the Marxist approach is without value. The work of Kidd (1981), as noted, and indeed of Donnelly (1985) and Sewart (1987), contains a number of insights that will have to be incorporated into any synthesis that lays claim to provide a fuller account of the commercialisation of sport forms. Although critical, the present analysis has drawn, to an extent, on their and other Marxist work. Thus it is argued here that while the making of American football in British society cannot be reduced solely to an economic dimension, capital investment and entrepreneurial activity played an important role in this process. Globalisation processes are the key to understanding sport development in the late twentieth century (Maguire, 1992).

In considering the rise of television as a mass leisure form, Rojek (1985, p. 163) seeks to outline the web of interdependency involved. These interdependencies engender structural tensions, conflicts, and struggles. Crucially, however, the development of the figuration in question was not, according to Rojek, subject to the will or power of any single individual or group. Those who owned and produced the programmes could not control the overall figurational dynamics. The task is to grasp what these figurational dynamics are. Similarly, no one group had a monopoly over the making of American football. No matter how hard the NFL sought to further their marketing strategy, they too were caught up in figurational dynamics that they could not control. That is, the interdependency chains that have formed the main focus of this essay lay outside of their control. But this is not to suggest that they, along with Channel 4 and Anheuser-Busch, have not been the most powerful players in seeking to create a global market for the consumption of their product. In this regard they have achieved not a little success. Whereas the consumers are no less caught up in this unfolding figuration, they do have the capacity, as Bigsby notes, to reinterpret the American cultural product into something distinct. In fact, as Hebdige observes, the receptivity of popular culture to American cultural wares is both active and heterogeneous. The idea about the 'homogenising influence of American culture' is overstated and overlooks the possibility of the emergence of a 'new identity'.

Two additional points need to be made about the figurational approach. In examining the more general issue of sport, one of figurational sociology's leading exponents, Eric Dunning, makes a number of observations that are pertinent to the present enquiry. First, he argues, certain British sports retained an amateur ideology, which had consequences for their approach to the financing and organising of sport at least until the late 1960s. The result of this was that British sports exhibited a lower level and, in many ways, different forms of commercialisation than that exhibited in American sports. Second, he suggests that during the early 1970s this previously established system of amateur control was breaking down and professional sport was becoming increasingly commercialised (Dunning, 1975). By the early 1980s, this process had arguably gathered momentum (Maguire, 1988b). It is in the context of this broader commercialisation of British sport and British society more generally that the emergence of American football needs to be located. With regard to this broader context, Thatcherite Britain, with its emphasis on an 'enterprise culture', has provided a highly favourable climate for the spread here of American cultural forms. In turn, these are interwoven with broader globalisation processes.

It is also necessary, however, to locate the making of American football within what Elias and Dunning have termed the 'mimetic sphere'. That is, it is in terms of the mimetic sphere that the pleasure derived from American football, and, as Ang notes, from American popular culture in general, needs to be considered. Reference to this moves one decisively away from some crude form of economic determinism and towards both an understanding of the pleasurable excitement engendered in consuming American cultural goods and of the possibility of the emergence of a 'new identity', with individuals reinterpreting this American cultural product into something distinct. This needs spelling out.

The details of what Elias and Dunning (1986) term the 'spare-time spectrum' need not concern us here. Rather it is important to note that leisure activities are seen by them to fall into three spheres. These are what they call 'purely or mainly sociable activities', 'activities involving motility', and 'mimetic activities'. Mimetic activities vary considerably in terms of their structural properties and the degree of excitement they generate. Nevertheless, they have certain basic structural characteristics in common. That is, they provide a 'make-believe' setting that allows emotions to flow more easily and that elicits excitement imitating that produced by 'real-life' critical situations, yet with the dangers or risks inherent in these situations restricted by external control and self-control. Mimetic activities also allow, within certain limits, for socially permitted self-centredness. Excitement is elicited by the creation of tensions: This can involve imaginary or controlled 'real' danger, mimetic fear and/or pleasure, sadness, and/or joy.

This controlled decontrolling of emotions lies, for Elias and Dunning (1986), at 'the heart of leisure sport'. The different moods evoked in this make-believe setting are the 'siblings' of those aroused in real-life situations. This applies whether the setting is a tragedy enacted at the 'Old Vic' or an American football match watched on Channel 4 or at Wembley stadium. Such leisure activities involve the experience of pleasurable excitement that, Elias and Dunning argue, is at the core of most play needs. But whereas both involve pleasurable excitement, in sport (especially in 'achievement sport') struggles between human beings play a central part. Indeed some sport forms, such as American football, resemble real battles between hostile groups (Elias & Dunning, 1986; Maguire, 1988a).

Reference also needs to be made to several other key features of the Eliasian perspective on leisure, sport, and the emotions. The mimetic sphere, though creating highly specific settings, forms a distinct and integral part of social reality. It is no less real, according to Elias and Dunning, than any other part of social life. The manner in which this 'quest for enjoyable excitement' finds expression in social institutions and customs varies greatly over time and space. Nevertheless, the mimetic sphere does contain elements that are integral to all leisure forms, namely sociability, motility, and imagination. There is no leisure activity where all of these elements are absent; usually two or three elements combine in varying degrees.

In studying the problems of leisure, therefore, attention must focus on two inter-dependent questions: What are the characteristics of the personal leisure needs developed in the more complex societies of our time, and what are the characteristics of the specific types of leisure events developed in societies of this type for the satisfaction of these needs? This does not blind the present analysis, however, to the fact that the taste for American football is socially constructed and that issues of style and distinction reflect and articulate existing power relations (Elias, 1982, pp. 311-312; Bourdieu, 1984).

As Rojek has argued, contemporary leisure practices reflect and reinforce four deep-rooted historical tendencies: privatisation, individuation, commercialisation, and pacification. These trends represent the increasing emphasis on the self as the focal point of action and experience. They have 'projected the self, the individual body, to the forefront of leisure action and experience' (Rojek, 1985, p. 181). Given this, perhaps the receptivity of groups of British people to American football is less surprising. That is, the cult of individualism evident in the ideology of American sport finds a cultural resonance with British society of the 1980s and early 1990s, and it is this, combined with the part played by capital, entrepreneurs, and transnational corporations, within the broader context of globalisation processes, that provides a framework within which to understand the making of American football in British society over the past decade.

REFERENCES

Algar, R. (1988). American football. *Leisure Management, 8*, 6, 58-60.

Alt, J. (1983). Sport and cultural reification: From ritual to mass consumption. *Theory, Culture and Society, 1*, 3, 93-107.

Ang, I. (1985). *Watching Dallas: Soap opera and the melodramatic imagination.* London: Methuen.

Audit Bureau of Circulations (1987).

Bigsby, C. (Ed.) (1975). *Superculture: American popular culture and Europe.* London: Ezek Books.

Bogner, A. (1986). The structure of social processes: A commentary on the sociology of Norbert Elias. *Sociology, 20*, 3, 387-411.

Bourdieu, P. (1984). *Distinction. A social critique of the judgment of taste.* London: Routledge and Kegan Paul.

Budweiser league yearbook (1987). London: Mildman.

Chambers, I. (1986). *Popular culture: The metropolitan experience.* London-Methuen.

Collins, R. (1986). Wall-to-wall Dallas? The US-UK trade in television. *Screen, 27*, 3-4, 66-77.

Connelly, J. (1987a, March/April). Touchdown. *Sport and Leisure*, p. 24.

Connelly, J. (1987b). *Influencing your customer. Recreation management: The sports council's national seminar and exhibition.* Harrogate, March 1987, pp. 46-58.

The Daily Telegraph (1989, 8 March).

Donnelly, P. (1985). *A preliminary examination of dominant, residual and emergent aspects of culture in sport.* International Committee for the Sociology of Sport (ICSS) Symposium, Prague, August 1985.

Dunning, E. (1975). Theoretical perspectives on sport: A developmental critique. In Parker, S. et al. *Sport and leisure in contemporary society.* Central London Polytechnic.

Dunning, E. (1987). *Sport in the civilising process: Aspects of the figurational approach to sport and leisure.* Unpublished paper, University of Leicester.

Elias, N. (1978). *What is sociology?* London: Hutchinson.

Elias, N. (1982). *The civilising process: State formation and civilisation.* Oxford: Blackwell.

Elias, N. (1983). *The court society.* Oxford: Blackwell.

Elias, N., & Dunning, E. (1986). *Quest for excitement: Sport and leisure in the civilising process.* Oxford: Blackwell.

Elias, N., & Scotson, J. (1965). *The established and the outsiders.* London: Cass.

Gallup Polls (1988). *Social surveys: Textile market studies*, May 1988.

Gilpin, R. (1976). *U.S. power and the multinational corporation.* London: MacMillan.

Goldlust, J. (1987). *Playing for keeps: Sport, the media and society.* Melbourne: Longman.

Gridiron UK (1986, May).

Gridiron UK (1987, February).

The Guardian (1989, 1 February).

Gurevitch, M., Bennett, T., Curran, J., & Woolacott, J. (1982). *Culture, society and the media*. London: Methuen.

Harris, D. (1987). *The league: Inside the NFL*. New York: Bantam Books.

Hebdige, D. (1979). *Subculture: The meaning of style*. London: Methuen.

Hebdige, D. (1982). Towards a cartography of taste 1935-1962. In Waites, B., et al. *Popular culture: Past and present*, pp. 194-218. London: Croom Helm.

Hoskins, C., & Mirus, R. (1988). Reasons for the US dominance of the international trade in television programmes. *Media, Culture and Society, 10*, 499-515.

Kaplan, C. (1986). The culture crossover. *New Socialist, 43*, 11, 38-40.

Kidd, B. (1981). Sport, dependency and the Canadian state. In Hart, M., & Birrell, S. *Sport in the sociocultural process* pp. 707-721. Iowa: Brown.

Licensing Management International (private correspondence) 1989.

Lipset, S. (1964). *The first new nation*. London: Heinemann.

Maguire, J. (1988a). *Eliasian and figurational perspectives on a theory of the emotions, sport and leisure*. Paper presented at the 2nd International Leisure Studies Conference, June-July 1988, University of Sussex.

Maguire, J. (1988b). The commercialization of English elite basketball 1972-1988: A figurational perspective. *International Review for the Sociology of Sport, 23*, 4, 305-323.

Maguire, J. (1992, July). *Hired corporate guns: Elite sports migrants in the global arena*. Paper presented at the Olympic Scientific Congress, Malaga, Spain.

MIL Research Ltd. (1986). *American football national launch: Report prepared for Marshall Cavendish*.

NFL merchandising catalogue (1988). London: NFL.

The Observer (1986, 5 October).

Riesman, D., & Denney, R. (1981). Football in America: A study in cultural diffusion. In Hart, M., and Birrell, S. *Sport in the sociocultural process* (pp. 678-693). Iowa: Brown.

Rojek, C. (1985). *Capitalism and leisure theory*. London: Tavistock.

Sewart, J. (1987). The commodification of sport. *International Review for the Sociology of Sport, 22*, 3, 171-192.

Sunday Times (1987, 18 February).

The Times (1981, 27 January).

The Times (1984, 20 January).

The Times (1984, 21 January).

The Times (1985, 23 December).

The Times (1986, 20 December).

The Times (1986, 11 April).

White, R. (1983). A backwater awash: The Australian experience of Americanization. *Theory, Culture and Society, 1*, 3, 108-122.

Webster, D. (1988). *Looka yonder! The imaginary America of populist culture*. London: Routledge.

Whannel, G. (1987). *Sport on 4*. London: Windsor Press.

Conclusion to Part II

SUGGESTIONS FOR ESSAYS AND CLASS DISCUSSION

A number of questions were raised in the introduction to this section that can serve as stimuli for discussion and debate centred around the contributions of Guttmann, Heinemann, Arbena, Ingham and Beamish, and Maguire. In addition, it seems to us that questions such as the following might prove fruitful as essay subjects and foci of class discussion:

1. What parallels, if any, are detectable between the patterns of 'ludic diffusion' observable in the Ancient World and the international spread of sports and games today?
2. What are the principal causes and consequences of the spread of Western sports to third world countries?
3. How would you account for the spread of modern sports to Latin American countries? What have been the principal social consequences of this spread?
4. Why, when sports diffuse from one country to another, do they sometimes change and sometimes not?
5. Why, when soccer and many of the athletic events have become global sports, have sports such as cricket, baseball, rugby, and gridiron football spread mainly only within the 'spheres of influence' of the countries where they originated?
6. Compare and contrast a Marxist account of the development and spread of modern sport with the account provided by a different sociological perspective.
7. Comment on the contention that it is only in combination with Weber's theory of rationalisation that Marxist theory can provide a viable explanation of the development and spread of modern sport.
8. What criticisms might a Marxist make of the chapter by Guttmann?
9. Develop a figurational critique of the chapter by Ingham and Beamish.
10. How might a Marxist respond to the arguments and analysis proposed by Maguire?
11. In what way, if at all, might *either* a figurational sociologist *or* a Marxist seek to criticise and extend the analysis offered by Heinemann of sport in developing countries?
12. Has Maguire been successful in his attempt at wedding figurational sociology and Marxism in his exploration of 'the making' of American football in Britain?

RESEARCH TASKS

Project One: Patterns of Structural Continuity and Cultural Variation in the Spread of Modern Sports

Choose a sport that has spread to a number of different countries and explore the pattern of similarities and differences in its meanings and functions in *any two* of them (e.g., soccer in England and Brazil; baseball in America and Cuba; cricket in Australia and the West Indies; rugby in New Zealand and France; gridiron football in the United States and Britain). What effects, if any, do such cultural variations as you identify have on the playing of matches between teams from the two countries? What, if any, are the effects on the interaction of spectators from the two countries when their club or international sides meet?

Project Two: The Spread of Soccer to Latin America

Explore the spread of soccer to Latin America and account sociologically for the success of teams such as Argentina, Brazil, and Uruguay. Why have these countries emerged as dominant 'soccer powers' in Latin America and the world? Has their socioeconomic development generally been helped or hindered by their relative soccer success? Why do they 'export' so many of their soccer stars to countries such as Italy and Spain? What are the effects, domestically, of this pattern?

Project Three: The Spread of Soccer to the United States

Using secondary sources, examine why soccer has so far failed to develop as a major sport in the United States. Why did most of the professional leagues begun there in the 1960s and 1970s fail to take root? Is the 'grassroots' spread of soccer occurring now in the United States likely to be a more permanent development? Is the holding of the 1994 World Cup Finals in the United States likely, on balance, to be a positive or a negative factor in the development of soccer in that country? (Students in the United States, of course, could be encouraged to use primary sources in carrying out this project. Also, after 1994 it will be possible for students to analyse retrospectively what the effects were of staging the 1994 World Cup Finals in America).

Project Four: The International Spread of American Sports

Using Maguire's analysis as a model, provide a sociological account and explanation of the spread of *any one* American sport beyond the shores of the United States (e.g., the spread of baseball to Japan, Cuba, Mexico, or any other Latin American country; the spread of basketball or volleyball around the world). Alternatively, test Maguire's explanation of the spread of gridiron football to Britain, either by tracing the diffusion of that game to a different country (i.e., a country other than Britain) or by tracing the spread of another American sport, for example basketball, to Britain.

Project Five: Patterns of Resistance to the Spread of Modern Sports

Using primary sources if possible (e.g., newspapers, books, diaries, club records), trace any attempt that there may have been in your country to promote national sport forms in an effort to prevent the encroachment of sporting forms from abroad (e.g., the 'Turner' movement in Germany; the Highland Games in Scotland; Catalan and

Basque sports in Spain; the martial arts in Japan). Attempt to determine how success-ful this attempt has been and account sociologically for the pattern of relative success or failure that you discover.

Project Six: The Spread of Modern Sports to Africa

Using available secondary sources, trace the spread of Western sports to one or more African countries. Show which non-African groups (e.g., traders, missionaries, colonial administrators) were primarily responsible for this process and which African groups (e.g., members of the urban middle classes, tribal people from rural areas) were most receptive. Document the major consequences of this process of diffusion for traditional indigenous pastimes and sports. Account for the relative success of some African nations in selected sports (e.g., Kenyans in long-distance running or the Cameroons in soccer). Explore why, relatively speaking, American sport forms have so far failed to spread to African countries.

PART III

Comparative and Developmental Studies of Modern Sports Cultures

One of the potentially most fruitful insights that can be obtained from adopting a comparative and developmental perspective on human societies and cultures is an understanding of the fact that they differ according to their locations in space and time. Another—perhaps simpler—way of putting it would be to say that such a perspective can help one to see that human societies and cultures vary both geographically and historically. Such variations basically result from the fact that, because they are fundamentally dependent on the biologically inherited and therefore universal human capacity for learning, human societies and cultures have an inbuilt capacity for and tendency to change. Indeed, since sociology first began to emerge some 200 or so years ago, it has become increasingly evident that—however bewildering it may be to the individuals caught up in it and pushed hither and thither in its throes—social change is not random or chaotic but patterned and structured. It is patterned and structured, for example, in the sense that particular changes always occur in a given sociocultural context, which implies that human societies always reveal a particular balance between continuity and change. What is true of societies and cultures generally is, of course, *ipso facto* also true of particular aspects of them such as sports and games.

For most of the history of humanity, the pace of social change has been relatively slow. For several centuries now, however—since at least the Renaissance—Western societies have been changing at a faster rate than was ever experienced in the past. It was in the context of such accelerating changes that the scientific, industrial, and what one might call the 'sporting' revolutions took place. It was in that context, too, that Western countries established forms of colonial and postcolonial hegemony over vast tracts of the rest of the world, providing the context for the processes of diffusion of and resistance to Western sport-forms that were examined in Part II of this volume. And it was also in that context that the three great ideologies of the twentieth century—the competing, secular ideologies of capitalism, socialism, and nationalism—began in their various forms and permutations to be forged and increasingly to replace the religious and charismatic ideologies that had been predominant hitherto[1].

Capitalist, socialist, and nationalist ideologies—together with variants and amalgams of them such as communism, fascism, and racism—figure centrally among the sources of struggle in the twentieth-century world. Such ideologies and the ways in which they have affected the practice and development of sport are the main subjects of this third section of *The Sports Process*. It was our original intention, formed in the early 1980s when the Cold War was still at its height, to start this section by contrasting Eastern and Western perspectives on the development of sport. However, our Eastern contributor, Andrzej Wohl of the University of Warsaw, a man who played a pivotal role in the development of the sociology of sport (not least through his editorship of the *International Review of Sport Sociology* for many years), understandably felt that, with 'glasnost', 'perestroika', the weakening of the Soviet 'empire', the dismantling of the USSR, and the apparent global triumph of capitalism, the piece that he had prepared for us was ideological and outdated. As a result, Wohl withdrew his chapter. We regret Wohl's decision for several reasons. His proposed contribution was of considerable historical interest, providing us with a clear example of the sorts of things that could be seriously argued about sport in capitalist and socialist societies at the height of the Cold War. More importantly, however great the discrepancies between sporting rhetoric and sporting practice may have been in the former Soviet Union and its satellites, the progressive ideology that informed Wohl's thinking remains, in our opinion, of considerable value as a basis on which to build an understanding of how and why such disparities between ideals and realities could have come to prevail. An understanding of this kind is urgently needed at the moment in a context where the collapse of communism and the apparent triumph of capitalism have given rise to an ideological void in the Western world—a kind of 'ideological anomie'. And yet, the pathologies of capitalism, many of which were successfully diagnosed by Marx and Marxists, continue to produce and reproduce negative consequences for society and for sport. Think of the problems of class, racism, sexism and sport, and the problems that are posed by the apparently unstoppable processes of commodification and commercialization that are taking place in this sphere. It is for reasons such as these that we very much wanted to keep Andrzej Wohl's chapter in *The Sports Process* and we hope he will forgive us if we provide a summary of what he said. That, of course, is less satisfactory than publishing his chapter in full. But, at least it provides the reader with the flavour of what he wrote and will enable discussion to take place on such issues as why the gap was so wide between sports rhetoric and sports practice in the former Eastern Bloc, and whether Marxism does or does not continue to provide a basis on which to forge more adequate means of coping with the manifold problems that continue to beset society and sport in the world today.

What Andrzej Wohl argued was this. Modern sport first arose in the West, he suggested, in conjunction with the emergence of industrial capitalism. However, the inherent inequalities and contradictions of capitalism are obstacles to the realisation of its full potential. More particularly, Wohl argued, the class and other inequalities of capitalist societies permit the development of 'mass sport' but this nevertheless involves systematic discrimination against workers, women, and ethnic minorities and the continued existence of elitist and exclusionist practices. Sport in capitalist societies also continues to develop in a largely spontaneous manner and is not systematically planned and controlled from the centre, that is, by the state. It continues to be involved in the unfettered and therefore harshly competitive market. As a result, it inevitably comes to develop an equally harsh competitive character.

All this was very different in the Soviet Union and the societies of Eastern Europe, according to Wohl. In these countries, although most of them were relatively underdeveloped industrially at the time of their socialist revolutions, a uniquely socialist pattern of sports development took place. It was a pattern, Wohl said, in which the chances for realising the 'true potential' of sport were maximised. State planning and central control of sport, for example, fit in perfectly with local initiative, autonomy, and self-government by sportspersons. Successful efforts were also made to orientate sport towards workers and peasants and females as well as males. As Wohl saw it, starting in almost all cases from a very low base, sport in socialist countries rapidly developed the character of mass sport.

After the 1960s, planned efforts were also made to develop 'universal sport', that is, to arrive at a situation where all groups—the old as well as the young, females as well as males, the disabled as well as the able-bodied—had an equal opportunity to participate. By the time of his writing, the goal of universal sport had not yet been reached, but neverthless, said Wohl, strong developments in that direction had occurred. Along with such things as universal state-provided education, a state health service, social insurance, a five-day work week, social justice, security for all, a stress on cooperation, and opportunities for the development of individuals, universal sport would form, Wohl predicted, one of the integral features of the 'developed socialist society'. The 'universal sport' of 'developed socialism', said Wohl, would remain competitive, but it would be purged of the pathological features that mar and distort sport under capitalism. In that context, sport would be placed on a par with other aspects of culture such as literature, music, theatre, and the arts.

Western readers will probably readily agree with many aspects of Wohl's critique of the inequalities and contradictions of sport in capitalist societies. However, they will probably want to question parts of his analysis of socialist sport. In particular, they may want to probe issues related to the fact that, although socialism is an egalitarian ideology, there is evidence to suggest that the former Soviet Union and the countries of Eastern Europe that came under its sway developed forms of inequality that are today unknown in the West. This is not to deny the massive inequalities that exist in and are constantly recreated in capitalist societies. It is simply to point out that—although this may now be changing in conjunction with the processes set in motion by *perestroika*—the former Soviet Union and the formerly socialist countries of Eastern Europe were based politically on forms of one-party rule and that, until recently, ideological deviance from the tenets of Marxism-Leninism was not publicly permitted. It is also to point to what Milovan Djilas as early as 1957 called 'the new ruling class', which dissident intellectuals more recently named the *nomenklatura*; that is, a party-based 'political bureaucracy' that, according to Djilas, came to exercise 'monopolistic ownership' and 'totalitarian authority'[2]. Members of this class even had access to special shops that were reserved for them alone. The *nomenklatura* also showed signs of developing as a closed, hereditary, 'caste-like' class. Andrzej Wohl may have written enthusiastically of the development towards 'universal sport' and the emergence of nonpathological forms of sporting competition in the socialist countries, but it is difficult to believe that facts such as one-party rule and the existence of the *nomenklatura* and its equivalents elsewhere did not come to be reflected in their sports. That in fact they did is suggested by Riordan when he points out that recent events in the former USSR and Eastern Europe 'have demonstrated that sport in such countries has been identified in the popular consciousness with privilege, coercion, hypocrisy, distorted priorities, and, in the case of non-Soviet states, with an alien Soviet-imposed institution'.

However, as Riordan also shows, that does not represent the whole story. There are elements of truth buried in Wohl's panegyric. To see them, sport in the USSR and the other formerly socialist countries must be looked at in the cold light of day. It is precisely such a dispassionate analysis that Riordan attempts to provide in his 'Sport in Capitalist and Socialist Countries: A Western Perspective'. Riordan shows, for example, that it is essential as a starting point to take account of such facts as that some 80% of the Russian population were peasants when the revolution occurred in 1917. In other words, at that time the USSR had many of the hallmarks of an underdeveloped country. Its emergence for a period of 50 or so years as a major world power was a very rapid process. According to Riordan, account also has to be taken of the fact that, in the twentieth century, the Russian people experienced 'two world wars, three revolutions, a civil war, rapid industrialisation and urbanisation, the forced collectivisation of agriculture, purges, and mass terror'. That is, their history in the present century has been one of recurrent turmoil and violent commotion, and neither their social development generally nor the development of their sport can be understood independently of such facts. The same holds true for most of the countries of Eastern Europe with the obvious addition that, for 40 years after the end of World War II, they lived under the shadow of Soviet power. When one takes account of all this, it is difficult to believe in the existence of the sporting and general utopias depicted by Wohl.

Because he starts out from a basis of solid fact, Riordan is able to provide a more balanced and realistic picture. He shows how, in the 1920s, there was widespread adherence in the former Soviet Union to the idea of *mens sana in corpore sano*, the belief that physical culture could be of use in combatting socially undesirable phenomena such as crime, delinquency, alcoholism, and prostitution. He also shows how sport came to be viewed as a useful modernising agent, an activity that could help former peasants adjust to an urban-industrial environment, playing a part in weaning them from their dependency on what were, from the standpoint of the revolutionary regime, such 'pathological' practices as religion and the 'cult of the individual'. He also points out how, in that context, sport was believed to form a useful means of military training, and, in a multinational, multicultural society, of promoting the social integration of the USSR as a whole.

The 1930s in the Soviet Union were, as Riordan shows, a decade of rapid industrialisation. They also witnessed the collectivisation of agriculture and the consolidation of Stalin's rule. In that period, sport came to be seen as a means of linking people into the Communist Party and of binding them to their leader. As such, says Riordan, it came more firmly under party and state control and began to be used more and more as an instrument for attempting to secure such ideological aims as the enhancement of national prestige. In that context, too, it began to be dominated by the security police and the armed forces. The systems for discovering and nurturing talent, long the envy of many people in the West, also began to be developed in that period.

In his stimulating account, Riordan sheds fresh light on these developments and on how Soviet sportspersons and physical educationalists grappled with the contradiction between their commitment to the socialist value of cooperation and the inherent competitiveness of sport as it had developed in the 'bourgeois' West. He concludes by expressing the hope that, in the era of *glasnost* and *perestroika*, sportspersons in the former Soviet Union will not rush headlong into copying market-orientated sports practice. If they do, he suggests, they may place in jeopardy some of the real gains that socialism made possible in the sporting sphere. Central among them, for Riordan, is an avoidance of the extremes of hooliganism, corruption, and commercialism that, he feels, have disfigured so many sports in the West. The reader may want to consider in this connection whether Riordan underestimated the incidence of hooliganism and the prevalence of corruption in the sports of the former Soviet Union and the Eastern Bloc. It is also arguable that, despite his attempted disavowal towards the end of his essay, he underestimates the extent to which sporting policies and practice in those countries departed from official egalitarianism, with mass participation being sacrificed for growing and sometimes excessive elitism.

The subject of Jarvie's chapter is another of the sources of the disfigurement of sport and, hence, of major struggle and conflict in the contemporary world: the South African crisis and the part played in it by sport. The chapter is written not only as a contribution to the understanding of how sport developed in the racist South African context, but more generally as a contribution to the politics of sport. Like Gruneau in his contribution to Part I, Jarvie adopts a basically 'Gramscian' stance towards his subject. However, he eschews a 'cultural studies' approach because, he says, the proponents of such an approach in the field of sports studies have often in the past 'either marginalised or misinterpreted the work of Gramsci'[3]. It follows that Jarvie's own first task has to be that of summarising what he takes to be the core features of Gramscian Marxism in order to show where, in his opinion, earlier users of such a theory have gone astray. He seeks to accomplish this objective through a brief review of the general literature on the politics of sport.

According to Jarvie, much recent work on the politics of sport is characterised by what he calls 'a violence of abstraction'. It also prematurely dismisses earlier descriptive and empirical work in the field, much of which, says Jarvie, retains its value. He next reviews Marxist contributions to the sociology of sport and suggests that, while the 'Althusserian' approach[4] represented an advance relative to 'reflection' (correspondence) theory, it is overly deterministic and unable to account adequately for subjective experience, agency, and struggle. Hence, it is unable to account for the way in which ideology is 'generated and sustained in lived experience'. The great merit of Gramsci's work, suggests Jarvie, is precisely that it emphasises the fact that 'the dominant ideology' is 'never given but always struggled with, challenged, and the object of intense negotiation'. The value of such an approach as applied to sport, he says, 'lies in its attention to historical context, its treatment of sport as culture, its avoidance of determinism and class reductionism, and its sensitivity to the tensions and contradictions that exist within and between cultural forms'. The cultural studies proponents of such an approach have produced valuable work. However, they tend, Jarvie argues, to assume that nationalism is at odds with Marxism and socialism, an error that Gramsci was at pains to redress. According to Jarvie, moreover, sociologists of the cultural studies 'school' also tend to lose sight of such key Gramscian concepts as the 'organic' and 'conjunctural' elements of a crisis, that is, those elements that grow out of the inherent 'faultlines' of a socioeconomic system and those that result from ad hoc, short-term attempts to resolve the basic, underlying contradictions.

Turning his attention to South Africa, Jarvie goes on to suggest that a unique social formation emerged in that country in conjunction with racism, capitalism, and Western imperialism. He suggests two main features of this social formation: The mass of the population was denied ownership of the means of production, and the black majority was denied civil and political rights. The recent concessions made by the white regime, he maintains, are 'conjunctural' responses to an underlying 'organic' crisis that revolves around two key dimensions: the way in which the process of capital accumulation has increased the dependency of the white minority on African labour, and the increasing—and increasingly violent—resistance of the black majority. An important part of the state's conjunctural response, Jarvie suggests, was the establishment in the 1970s of a 'multinational sports policy', which he describes as 'attacking down the right'. It was opposed, outside as well as inside South Africa, by people who 'attacked down the left' as part of a struggle to secure fully nonracial sport in that country.

In the face of mounting black resistance, the conjunctural response of the South African state since 1989 has been to dismantle more and more aspects of apartheid legislation and to create mechanisms that will allow all Africans to participate in the making of political decisions. However, as Jarvie notes, the white minority is not willing to countenance black majority rule and the sort of representation of black opinion that is envisaged involves the creation of channels for the expression of group rather than individual opinions and needs. It is this conjunctural response against which the opposition needs to mobilise, suggests Jarvie, and for a variety of reasons sport is likely to be of considerable importance in this regard. It is likely to be of importance, he argues, because South Africa appears to be unique in the degree to which sport there became an object of civil struggle and because, when other avenues of protest have been closed down by the state, the sporting avenue has tended to remain relatively open. Furthermore, partly on account of the success of the international boycotts and the expulsion of South Africa from the Olympic movement, the importance of sport in the struggle to end apartheid is recognised by the African National Congress (ANC).

The South Africans, of course, were allowed to enter the 1992 Olympics in Barcelona, and other avenues of international sports participation were reopened for them around the same time. It also seems likely, following the concessions granted by the de Klerk regime, that some form of majority rule will emerge in South Africa, perhaps along lines similar to those in Zimbabwe–Rhodesia where whites were guaranteed special parliamentary representation for a limited transitional period. However, at the time of writing it is too soon to say what the outcome of current developments in South Africa will be. In the summer of 1992, expressions of white nationalist/racist sentiment were strongly in evidence at rugby matches between South Africa and New Zealand. They were roundly condemned by the ANC. However, the ANC did not demand an immediate renewal of the boycott, though that remains a strong possibility. South Africa at the moment is a powderkeg and it is impossible to predict what the outcome of the present struggles will be. One of the few things that can be said with any certainty in this connection is that sport will be central to the struggles, whether they take a more violent and bloody outturn or not.

The struggle over apartheid and its aftermath, and over such issues as whether there can be 'normal' sport in an 'abnormal' society is an ongoing process. In his chapter, Jarvie sheds new light on it and contributes to political sociology more generally through his use of Gramscian theory and his critique both of more orthodox forms of Marxism and of some of the work on sport of the 'cultural studies' school. In our view, however, the reader might fruitfully question the scope of Jarvie's analysis of the South African crisis, privileging, as it does, imperialism and the capitalist nature of the South African economy but failing to take into account such further complexities as the dual colonisation of that country by settlers of English as well as Dutch descent and the multiplicity of tribal groups that live in the country. In short, although Jarvie rightly points to some of the similarities there are between the Gramscian and the figurational approaches to sociology, there is reason to doubt whether his analysis takes sufficient account of the figurational complexities of South African society and the myriad ways in which they impact on sport. It remains true nevertheless, that Jarvie has provided us with an insightful *analytical* essay. It advances knowledge in his field and will, we are sure, provide the reader with a basis for developing an empirical understanding of the part played by sport in the South African crisis.

Rigauer's stimulating and thought-provoking chapter on 'Sport and the Economy: A Developmental Perspective' is written largely from the perspective of the 'Frankfurt School', the brand of critical (neo-) Marxian sociology initiated at the University of Frankfurt's *Institut fur Sozialforschung* by Theodor W. Adorno and Max Horkheimer in the 1920s and continued by scholars such as Erich Fromm, Herbert Marcuse, and, more recently, Jurgen Habermas[5]. In the weight that he attaches to cultural processes such as the drive towards 'rationalisation' and not simply to 'economic factors' and the 'relations of production', Rigauer's analysis can be said to follow in the tradition of the Frankfurt school in that his analysis represents an attempt to wed or synthesise the sociological approaches of Marx and Weber.

According to Rigauer, all human societies have their play-forms. However, sport, he suggests, is distinctively Western, a product of the process of rationalisation that has accompanied the development of market-orientated capitalist-industrial societies.

Taking up the analysis proposed in his classic, *Sport and Work*[6], Rigauer argues that, like the forms of work and scientific training in societies of this type, sport is characterised by a 'logic' of competition and intensifying struggle for 'achievement'. Just as in the industrial and scientific spheres, increasingly in the world of sport nothing is left to chance but planned and calculated scientifically. Sport has its own economy—its own 'material base'—but, at the same time, this is articulated with the economy of the wider society. The fact that sport has its own economy—in the form of revenues generated through membership subscriptions, for example, or through money taken at the gate—allows it to enjoy a degree of cultural and political autonomy. However, to the extent that it becomes dependent on outside economic and political interests, this autonomy is threatened. Precisely this, Rigauer argues, has been happening with growing frequency in recent years as commercial and advertising interests have come to recognise that—along with the fields of leisure and entertainment generally—sport represents a potentially lucrative and hitherto untapped market, a market for the production and advertising not only of sports goods, but, on account of the mass popularity of sport, of industrial products and services more generally as well.

Not only does sport have its own economy, Rigauer contends, it also has—although these overlap empirically—what he calls an 'external' economy and an 'internal' one. The former coincides with the term 'economy' as it is generally understood. The latter refers to the learning or 'internalisation' by sportspersons over time of what Rigauer calls 'rationalised forms of movement'. So deep has been the penetration of the rationality principle into sport, he argues, that movements are judged to be 'right' or 'wrong' in terms of whether they are executed 'economically', that is, in the most efficient manner possible. Industrial societies, Rigauer next observes, are characterised by a 'logic' of increasing material growth. This yields benefits such as greater material comfort, but it simultaneously poses dangers, for example, to the natural environment. Both these trends, Rigauer suggests, are replicated in sport. Thus the 'logic' of material growth is paralleled by the drive for records and results, and this leads to dangers to the body through the use of drugs and increases the chances of injury, stress, and mental breakdown. What is needed, argues Rigauer, are new forms of sport that are intrinsically enjoyable, mutually enhancing, and not orientated towards competition and achievement. Indeed, he suggests, some such forms are becoming visible already (e.g., jogging and 'fun runs').

In his chapter, Rigauer has brilliantly brought together areas such as 'sport and the economy' and 'sport and the body', which are traditionally thought of as existing in separate compartments. He has also identified some key trends in the development of modern sport. Top-level sport has undoubtedly become heavily dependent on commercial and industrial interests, and this results in pressure for change in terms of a commercial and industrial 'logic' rather than a sport-specific one. Taken to extremes, such a trend could well result in the destruction of sport as we know it. It is also undoubtedly the case that the pressures of competition and towards achievement-orientation in sport—pressures that have ramifications from top-level sport down to the lowest levels—produce 'pathological' effects that give the lie to the ideology of *mens sana in corpore sano* (i.e., the idea that sport is unquestionably 'good', always and everywhere beneficial for physical and mental health). Neverthe-less, despite its brilliance and the new insights that it makes available, there are aspects of Rigauer's analysis that the student may wish to question. Is it really the case, for example, that jogging is an example of a new sport-form that has arisen entirely independently of the 'logic' of the market? Is its emergence not connected, at least partly, with ideals and images of the body that are promoted by advertising in the pursuit of commercial goals? Perhaps more importantly, if the elements of fun, play, and mutual enhancement have disappeared from 'normal' sport to the extent that Rigauer implies, why is it continuing to spread around the world as a *largely* voluntary movement? In other words, is there not a suspicion that Rigauer's analysis involves treating the players and consumers of sport as 'cultural dopes'? Moreover, however intrinsically valuable and enjoyable they may be, are jogging and fun runs really sport? Is not competition one of its integral elements, a chief source of the pleasure and excitement that can be generated in connection with sport? If that is so, may it not be the case that what is needed are not so much noncompetitive replacements for modern sport as serious efforts—locally, nationally, and on a worldwide scale—to bring sports competition under stricter control in order to reduce the impact of its more dangerous and destructive aspects? However, whether the reader agrees with Rigauer's diagnosis or thinks that our critical observa-tions may have some substance, one thing is certain: Through his rigorous analysis of sport and the economy in all its permutations and ramifications, Rigauer has added considerably to our critical understanding of modern sport and its develop-ment. Above all, he has extended—in ways that will undoubtedly generate further research and debate—the analysis that he began in the 1960s with the publication of *Sport and Work*.

NOTES

1. For a discussion of these developments, see Norbert Elias, *What Is Sociology?* London, Hutchinson, 1978.
2. See Milovan Djilas, *The New Class: An Analysis of the Communist System*, New York: Praeger, 1959.
3. A primary source for Gramsci's work is Antonio Gramsci, *Selections from the Prison Notebooks*, New York. International Publishers, 1971.
4. The 'Althusserian approach' is that form of structuralist Marxism that was influenced by the writings of the French philosopher Louis Althusser (see especially his *For Marx*, Harmondsworth: Penguin, 1969).
5. The approach of the 'Frankfurt school' is also known as 'critical theory'. Among their most important books are: Max Horkheimer, *Critical Theory: Selected Essays*, New York: Seabury Press, 1972; Herbert Marcuse, *One Dimensional Man*, London: Abacus, 1964.
6. Bero Rigauer's book was originally published in German in 1969 under the title *Sport und Arbeit*, Frankfurt: Suhrkamp.

REFERENCES AND
SUGGESTIONS FOR FURTHER READING

Allison, L. (Ed.) (1986). *The politics of sport.* Manchester: Manchester University Press.

Coakley, J. (1990). *Sport in society* (4th Ed.). St. Louis: Mosby.

Cantelon, H., & Gruneau, R. (1982). *Sport and the modern state.* Toronto: University of Toronto.

Deem, R. (1986). *All work and no play? The sociology of women and leisure.* Milton Keynes: Open University Press.

Donnelly, P., & Theberge, N. (1984). *Sport and the sociological imagination.* Fort Worth: Texas Christian University Press.

Eitzen, S. (1989). *Sport in contemporary society* (3rd Ed.). New York: St. Martin's Press.

Goldlust, J. (1987). *Playing for keeps: Sport, the media and society.* London: Longman.

Gruneau, R., & Albinson, J. (Eds.) (1976). *Canadian sport: Sociological perspectives.* Reading, MA: Addison-Wesley.

Gruneau, R. (1983). *Class, sports, and social development.* Amherst: University of Massachusetts Press.

Hargreaves, Jennifer (Ed.) (1982). *Sport, culture and ideology.* London: Routledge and Kegan Paul.

Hargreaves, John. (1986). *Sport, power and culture.* Oxford. Polity.

Hart, M., & Birrell, S. (Eds.) (1981). *Sport in the sociocultural process* (3rd Ed.). Dubuque, IA: Brown.

Harvey, J., & Cantelon, H. (1988). *Not just a game: Essays in Canadian sport sociology.* Toronto: University of Ottawa Press.

Lapchick, R. (1986). *Fractured focus: Sport as a reflection of society.* Massachusetts: Lexington Books.

Rigauer, B. (1981). *Sport and work* (A. Guttmann, Trans.). New York: Columbia University Press.

Riordan, J. (Ed.) (1978). *Sport under communism.* London: Hurst.

Snyder, E., & Spreitzer, E. (1989). *Social aspects of sport* (3rd Ed.). Englewood Cliffs, NJ: Prentice Hall.

Wimbush, E., & Talbot, M. (1989). *Relative freedoms: Women and leisure.* Milton Keynes: Open University Press.

Sport in Capitalist
and Socialist Countries:
A Western Perspective

James Riordan

Any comparative analysis of sport runs the risk of comparing like with unlike. No development of sport can be fully understood apart from a country's size and traditions, climate and culture, military and international considerations, social and economic needs, as well as the ideals of a political order. There is therefore no *single* model of capitalist or socialist sport, however similar many of the structural features may be. It would be as mistaken to posit the British and Soviet models as representative of capitalist and socialist development as it would be to export them unadapted. Both of course have been tried.

That is not to say that certain fundamental characteristics are not common to sports development in the West and the East: in countries like Britain, the United States, and Canada on the one hand, and the former USSR, China, and Cuba on the other. In liberal capitalist development, sport came to be regarded typically as the concern primarily of the individual; in state socialist development, it came to be regarded as the concern primarily of the state. The distinction is important because it provides an insight into the role of sport in social development and into conflicting conceptions of sport as a 'cultural-universal' or 'developmentally-specific modern phenomenon'. It is important, too, for an understanding of the place of sport not only in capitalist and socialist societies, but in those that follow—for example, in the modernising societies of Africa, Asia, and Latin America.

This chapter examines sports development largely on the examples of Britain and the USSR, with which the author is familiar. But be warned: The unsuspecting reader nurtured on Weberian 'objectivity' should not be lulled into a sense of false security in the hands of a 'Western sociologist' on the inside looking out. The author is a far from dispassionate viewer of sport anywhere. Sport and sociologists are not always what they seem.

SPORT IN WESTERN DEVELOPMENT

In the development of liberal Western society, whose prevailing ideology was that of 'individual' decision making and 'free' contracting between 'equal' social atoms, sport came to be regarded as the concern solely of the individual, a feature of life unconnected with the social order, classes, economics, politics, or the state. In Britain, it was individual enthusiasts from the 'leisured' classes who pioneered the development of certain organised sports, gave them their rules and conventions, and initially made them exclusive to their own social, racial, or sexual group. There were thus established single-sport clubs, governing bodies for individual sports separate from one another based for purposes of control and finance largely on their members. So there evolved voluntary, independent organisations based on a particular social group with a particular social outlook. It was from this firmly entrenched social base that there emerged such hostility to government 'interference' and control, professional players and coaches, or anything else that implied sport becoming a profession or career. In some other Western states that started their industrialisation later, however, the organisation of and ideology surrounding sport developed somewhat differently. The basic unit came to be not the private single-sport club, but the mixed or multi-sport club open to local enthusiasts and linked to local and central government. This happened largely because in these countries—for example, Spain, Portugal, Italy, and most of Latin America—sport developed in step with the Olympic movement and Olympic committees.

These differences notwithstanding, the emergence during the Industrial Revolution of a radically new pattern of sport for an industrial and urban population was a common feature of West European development (as, too, was the disintegration of feudalism and the rise of a new privileged class of property and leisure). The new ruling class—denoted variously as the 'bourgeoisie', 'capitalists', 'middle class', and 'Philistines'—usurped the more casual field sports of the aristocracy and altered the entire mode of playing games. The transition to the new dominant pattern of sport in Britain was completed by the end of the nineteenth century. As McIntosh has put it:

> The middle classes had produced their own team games such as football and hockey, their own form of track and field athletics, their own swimming competitions and their own racket game of lawn tennis. Rowing and cycling they organised, and into cricket they infiltrated in such numbers that they made it almost a middle-class game. Of all these activities only lawn tennis was invented by the middle class for the middle class. The other sports were discovered in an embryonic state and were developed and organised by the Philistines. The successful sports were all those that could be practised in or around the growing towns and cities, in suburban gardens, on quite small grass fields, in public parks, on rivers, in public swimming baths and on the public highway[1].

Western sports as we know them today, competitive and disciplined, were thus almost entirely developed and shaped by the industrial bourgeoisie over the centuries of its rise to power. What is more, the sports were developed not only or even primarily as leisure pursuits, but as means of moulding character and conditioning behaviour, as well as of acquiring physical skills and social accomplishments. In Britain, this took place at the public schools. As two British members of Parliament have written:

> As the scene of the first industrial revolution, Britain had, by the nineteenth century, a prosperous middle class and good communications. These basic

conditions allowed seven schools and two universities—Rugby, Eton, Harrow, Charterhouse, Westminster, Winchester, Shrewsbury, Oxford and Cambridge— to exercise a considerable influence in Britain, on the continent of Europe, and throughout the expanding empire. In these schools and universities, international sport was born. Most of the games that are now played across the world and which command such earnest attention from kings and presidents were invented by a few hundred wealthy young Victorian Englishmen[2].

The training of so-called middle-class (i.e., ruling class) boys in such character traits as self-control, self-discipline, initiative, loyalty, competitiveness, and leadership, ensconced in an unwritten code of sporting ethics, was intended to prepare them for their future careers principally in laissez-faire capitalism or as agents of colonial development. As both Tawney and McIntosh have reminded us, the moral code of the builder of capitalism and of the British Empire equally applied to and was reinforced by the business-house, the Church, and the playing field—although it was industrial organisation and the drive for overseas profits that determined the 'ethics' of both sport and Protestantism[3].

If the new games were instrumental in producing a recognised type of self-confident, cooperative, and loyal public administrator and industrialist, they were also expected to perform the specific function of training an officer class for the army; the public school playing fields became associated with the imperial battlefields. It is worthy of note that there were as many as 11 wars fought by the British Army all over the world in the period from the accession of Queen Victoria in 1837 up to 1860—a period in which many national sports associations in Britain were founded. More direct military training for wider sections of the population took place outside the public schools and became systematised in a form of physical training (PT) adopted by the elementary schools. This PT had its roots in military drill and gymnastics.

The link between sport and military combat was particularly evident during the period of rising nationalism and imperialism in the latter part of the nineteenth century (when, not coincidentally, the first international sports-contests took place between select national teams drawn from the bourgeois and aristocratic strata of society). The rational gymnastics that were (and still are) the core of school physical education in many countries originated in Germany as part of preparations for the 'war of liberation' against Napoleon. Friedrich Jahn, founder of the German *Turnen* gymnastics movement, defined his intention as 'protecting young people from softness and excess in order to keep them sturdy in the coming struggle for the Fatherland'[4]. Elsewhere, systems of gymnastics were introduced through similar motives of national rehabilitation from the Napoleonic Wars. In Denmark in 1804, King Frederick VI established a national Military Gymnastics Institute and appointed Franz Nachtegall its director; 10 years later a royal decree made gymnastics a compulsory subject in Danish elementary schools 'as an immediate contribution to national defence'[5]. In Sweden, the monarchy supported the proposal of P.H. Ling to open a Central Gymnastics Institute in 1814 and his system of therapeutic gymnastics was introduced at all Swedish schools—inspired 'more by military needs (to revive the ancient vigour of the North as described in the sagas) than by the needs of the schools'[6]. In Russia, gymnastics were made compulsory for the senior classes of all schools and colleges in 1864 with a stress on parades, weapon-handling drills, and field training; the first training courses for gymnastics instructors were, under the direction of Pyotr Lesgaft, established for army officers in 1877[7]. And when the Russian sports movement began to take shape, it was 'inspired by defeat in the Russo-Japanese War of 1904-05'[8]. In France, Baron de Coubertin, the celebrated founder of the modern Olympic Games, saw sport chiefly as a means of reinvigorating the French nation to regain France's lost glory: He 'sought to convince the ruling elites that sport for the masses had paramilitary value'[9]; indeed, 'why should not France succeed in recapturing its old splendour through the new Olympics?'[10]

The ideas of Jahn, Ling, de Coubertin, and others gradually gained currency among American educators and military personnel after the American Civil War: Within 5 years of the War's end, the first professional baseball league was formed in America, to be followed, 5 years later, in 1876, by the National League. The late 1860s and 1870s also saw the first college football games and the first tennis exhibition[11]. In England, the introduction of a foreign amalgam of gymnastics into the elementary schools was argued for on the following grounds during the debate on the 1870 Education Bill: 'Rational gymnastics . . . would increase work and military power . . . they would also save money by the diminution of the Poor Rates, the Police Rates and the expenses of criminal machinery'[12].

Furthermore, at the turn of the century, the authorities in most Western states gave encouragement to the formation of units of Boy Scouts with a distinctly military-religious-patriotic stamp. The Boy Scout movement had been founded by a British army officer, Robert Baden-Powell, during the Boer War: 'My idea of training boys in scouting dates from 1897 when I applied it to young soldiers in the 5th Dragoon Guards, having for years previously found the good of developing a man's character before putting upon him the dull routine of training then considered necessary for a soldier'[13]. Baden-Powell thus developed his paramilitary organisation to provide character training through troop games and above all through physical activities like camping, hiking, climbing, and other outdoor activities.

These 'educational' institutions and organisations therefore developed to meet social as well as physical needs. By today they have become so well entrenched and, sometimes, modified, that their original *raison d'etre* is frequently forgotten. In fact, sports fields and gymnasiums have traditionally been regarded as training grounds for building the kind of men needed to police an empire—whether in pre-World War II India or postwar Vietnam. However, insofar as the maintenance of a strong military apparatus is still regarded as essential by Western governments, sport and physical education are seen as important in contributing to a physically fit nation of potential soldiers—as was spelled out in the recommendations of such bodies as the Wolfenden Committee in Britain, President Kennedy's national fitness council, and the Task Force on Sports for Canadians.

At the turn of the century, the requirements of monopoly capitalism and the Empire for fit, obedient, smart, and orderly workers and soldiers increasingly brought the extension of organised sports and physical training to boys and girls of working-class background. Until then (and up to the present in some sports), social distinction had found its reflection in the social exclusiveness of organised games, expressed in the regulations that distinguished 'gentlemen' from 'players' and, as in rowing and athletics, excluded anyone who was 'by trade or employment a mechanic, artisan or labourer'. The amateur-professional distinction was without doubt first made by the English ruling class 'not so much from idealism as to keep the inferior masses out of their private pleasure garden—sport'[14]. In fact, in the early stages of capitalist development, it was practically impossible for the mass of the population to engage in sport simply because of their lack of free time. As Marx wrote of free time and the working man:

Time for education, for intellectual development, for the fulfillment of social functions and for social intercourse, for the free-play of his bodily and mental activity, even the rest-time of Sunday . . . are sheer moonshine! In its blind unrestrainable passion, its were-wolf hunger for surplus labour, capital oversteps not only the moral, but even the merely physical maximum bounds of the working day. It usurps the time for growth, development and healthy maintenance of the body. It steals the time required for the consumption of fresh air and sunlight[15].

The extension of sports to the working class took place during the transition from laissez-faire to monopoly capitalism; in Britain, this 'democratisation' of sport began in the last third of the nineteenth century. There were three main reasons for the change.

First, the campaigns by workers for shorter hours reached such proportions that factory owners and the governments that shared their outlook were compelled to make concessions. For the first time, sections of the working people gained a period of free time over and above that necessary to re-create themselves and their energies for work; men (and some women) were able to devote part of this 'leisure' time to sporting activities. It was when first clerks and then manual workers received Saturday afternoon off that the great proliferation of sports clubs took place in Britain. This occurred in the 1870s. It did not spell ruin for the firms partly because they were able to make concessions at home on the strength of their enormous profits abroad, and partly because they were able to 'control' the leisure activities of their labour force so as to boost productivity and keep down labour unrest.

Second, once the working class had leisure time, it was important for the continued existence of 'civilised society' to channel workers' energies into relatively 'safe' areas, into sports imbued with just the right type of values and norms—obedience, self-discipline, teamwork—that would divert them from the 'idle use of leisure' and from sedition, and would train them to accept 'polite society's' ideology and, therefore, the status quo. Sport became an important means of social control. The working class was, therefore, accepted into some sports on condition that it conformed to bourgeois ethics and conduct of play. Once the value of sport as a distraction from various 'evils' was fully appreciated, some industrialists and like-minded ideologists in the Church even went so far as to introduce sports to working people with a missionary zeal. Several well-known English soccer clubs, for example, owe their origin to eager young 'men of the cloth' (e.g., Aston Villa, Southampton, Everton, Wolverhampton Wanderers, and Bolton Wanderers). As Dennis Molyneux found in his research into the Birmingham district, a survey of football clubs that had come into existence by 1880 'shows that of 344 clubs, 83, or 24%, are known to have been connected with church, chapel or religious organisation. Many more whose origin is obscure were almost certainly similarly connected. The comparable figure for cricket clubs is 21%'[16].

To play games with one's workmates and superiors was seen as creating feelings of togetherness that helped disguise the conflict of interest between labour and capital. When these same entrepreneurs took their businesses abroad, they often introduced team games for the same purpose as they had at home—as a means of consigning any dissatisfactions on the part of their work force into the oblivion of the 'safe' sphere of sports and of obtaining trouble-free cooperation. A similar motivation lay behind the introduction of sports by colonialists and missionaries in their imperial possessions—with the added intention of implanting their values in the new soil.

Third, in the last third of the last century, changes were taking place within the capitalist system that had serious repercussions for sport. Middle-class sports were extended to the working class as a means of training body and mind not only to get the masses to accept their alienated and passive status but to adapt them to the new demands of industry. The rationalisation of production techniques in order to increase the intensive use of labour was projected onto the playing field to the extent that organised sports, especially those played professionally for paying spectators, became a branch of production.

Thus, with economic change, rising living standards, and the beginnings of leisure for wider sections of the community, many sports were extended to the urban populace, some being taken over almost completely by them (except in their running). The process was uneven and incomplete: Several 'middle-class' sports (e.g., golf, tennis, squash, sailing, fencing, badminton, and, in some parts of Britain, rugby) are still confined by convention or design to private clubs and associations and controlled by their committees (or to high-priced middle-class dominated 'public' sports centres). In the course of these changes, many sports became commercialised and adapted for mass consumption and diversion, dominated by the profit motive, and emasculated by the needs of a 'sports industry'. This process has continued throughout the twentieth century with fewer and fewer sports and sports clubs being closed to workers, with the amateur-professional distinction being removed or circumvented in many sports and with the increasing intervention of the state in sports organisation and investment—paralleling a similar process in the Western economy. Moreover, the internationalisation of capital has had its corollary in the internationalisation of sport, with the result that sport was said (between 1945 and the late 1980s) to be a weapon employed not only in the contention between rival Western states, but in 'the battle for men's minds' between the capitalist and state-socialist systems.

All this is not to say that all the sporting activities engaged in by all sections of the community are invariably commercially or politically manipulated—or shaped solely by the 'ethic' of the ruling class. More or less autonomous popular pursuits exist (pigeon fancying, whippet and greyhound racing, darts, snooker, fell walking, coarse fishing, crown green bowling)—games often based on cooperation and solidarity rather than society's dominant values of individualism and competition. The authorities would not wish to, nor indeed could they, control all popular leisure pursuits. This notwithstanding, the dominant pattern of sport in Western society would still seem to be a microcosm of that society; indeed, the erosion of deference reveals even more nakedly the 'cash-nexus' relations of capitalist production. Western sport is a source of profit, something to package and sell (a medium for football pools, betting shops, cigarette advertising, and the sportswear and equipment industry) as well as being a distraction for the populace, an opiate of the people, selling a vicarious and largely fantastical experience, thereby helping to ensure conformity with the consensual status quo.

It was the less sophisticated forerunner of this Western 'sport', the competitive commercial simulacra of play, that Anatoly Lunacharsky, the early Soviet political leader, declared unsuitable to the new socialist society: 'Bourgeois sport has a clearly-defined class character. . . . It cannot have far-reaching social significance, insofar as it leads to a fetishism of sport and downright commercialism'[17]. As we shall see, it was the firm intention of the early Bolsheviks (and later the Chinese communist leaders) to develop a qualitatively new pattern of sport or, rather, physical culture.

SOME THEORETICAL CONSIDERATIONS ON SPORT AND SOCIALISM

At the time Marx was writing, metaphysics was in the grip of a dualism that separated mind from matter and, under the influence of Christian theology, often exaggerated a distinction into an antagonism; in such a worldview, body and soul were seen as warring parties with the body cast as the villain of the piece[18]. Marx rejected the dualist philosophy and stressed that not only was there an intimate relationship between matter and mind, but that the former largely determined the latter. In his view, political and social institutions and the ideas, images, and ideologies through which people understand the world in which they live, their place within it and themselves, all ultimately derived from the 'economic base' of society—the class relations into which people had to enter with one another in order to produce. This fundamental Marxist tenet contains certain implications for sport.

First, since the human psychosomatic organism develops and changes under the influence of external conditions including the social environment, subjection to physical exercise not only develops that part of the body to which it is directed, but also has an effect on the body as a whole—on the personality. A strong bond exists between social and individual development and between the physical and mental development of the individual. Societies are likely to seek to shape this development. Marx himself had looked forward to the education system of the future, which would 'combine productive labour with instruction and gymnastics, not only as a means of improving the efficiency of production, but as the only way to produce fully-developed human beings'[19]. This would seem to imply that physical culture should be treated on a level with mental culture in socialist society both for the all-round development of the individual and, ultimately, for the health of society.

Second, sport being part of the social superstructure and therefore strongly influenced by the prevailing relations of production (not something 'in itself' and so divorced from politics)—though with some temporal independence from the economic base—a society's pattern of sport will ultimately depend on the specifics of that society's socioeconomic foundation, its class relationships. Moreover, says Marx, 'with a change in the economic foundation, the entire immense superstructure is more or less rapidly transformed'[20]. The nature of sport can, therefore, be expected to alter with any change to a new socioeconomic foundation. Figure 1 is an attempt to portray a Marxist view of the component parts of sport and their interrelationship.

Third, the acceptance of a dualist metaphysic, a sharp separation of body and mind, had often led to a concern with things of the mind at the expense of bodily activities. Marx emphasised that practical activities have a decisive impact on all human development in the broadest sense. None more so than work, through which people could change themselves as well as Nature:

Labour is, in the first place, a process in which both man and Nature participate, and in which man of his own accord starts, regulates, and controls the material reactions between himself and Nature. He opposes himself to Nature as one of her own forces, setting in motion arms and legs, head and hands, the natural forces of his body, in order to appropriate Nature's products in a form adapted to his own wants. By thus acting on the external world and changing it, he at the same time changes his own nature[21].

This proposition implies a strong link between work and such other bodily activities as physical exercise and games-playing.

Whether games-playing contained its own justification within itself or whether its value was to be sought in ulterior ends was not a question specifically raised by Marx. The Marxist vision of the future, however, does seem to imply that work and physical recreation will merge, or that work will be elevated to the plane of recreation by the removal of the yokes of specialisation and compulsion. But Marx evidently did not envisage recreation under communism as simply games—rather as a fusion of worklike activities with play. In this, he affirmed a principal criterion of playful activities, namely, that they are freely chosen and are pursued for their inherent pleasure rather than for practical results. This is a view that was later to be reiterated by Trotsky, who maintained: 'The longing for amusement, diversion, sight-seeing and laughter is the most legitimate desire of human nature. We are able, and indeed obliged, to give the satisfaction of this desire a higher artistic quality, at the same time making amusement a weapon of collective education, freed from the guardianship of the pedagogue and the tiresome habit of moralising'[22].

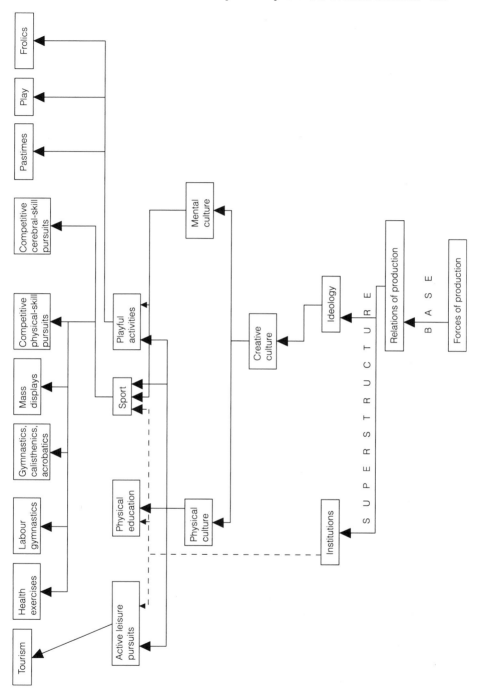

Figure 1.   Sport in society: A Marxist view.

To sum up, Marx provided few clear-cut guidelines on sport or physical culture. On the one hand, he stressed the interdependence of work and physical recreation and, on the other, he saw the playful use of energy as contributing to the enrichment of the personality, or self-realisation. The same might be said of Lenin. That is not to say, of course, that there is no consistency in the writings of Marx or Lenin, no *Marxism* or *Leninism*. A Marxist-Leninist interpretation of culture, mental and physical, including a belief in the interdependence of the mental and physical states of human beings, provides a general framework within which physical and mental recreation has been viewed in all socialist states. It should, however, be noted that aphorisms drawn from and myths about Marx, Lenin, Mao, etcetera, in regard to physical culture have been taken to justify policies at particular stages of development and need not be taken as creative Marxist thinking (indeed, they have sometimes replaced it).

SPORT IN SOCIALIST DEVELOPMENT

It was thought natural by some after the Russian Revolution of 1917 that a fundamentally new pattern of recreation would emerge, reflecting the requirements and values of the working people and the new socialist state. In the melting pot of ideas and theories that existed in the USSR during the 1920s, many influential people sharply contrasted the new 'proletarian physical culture' with competitive sport.

The strongest proponents of physical culture were the 'hygienists', who were mainly medical personnel concerned about the need to raise health standards to eliminate disease and epidemics. The extent of their influence may be judged from their virtual control over the government's Supreme Council of Physical Culture, the Health Ministry, the institutes of physical culture, and the 'sporting' press.

To the hygienists, sport implied competition, games that were potentially injurious to mental and physical health. Such pursuits as weightlifting, boxing, and gymnastics were said to be irrational and dangerous, and encouraged individualist rather than collectivist attitudes and values. They frowned upon the 'record-breaking mania' of contemporary sport in the West, and they favoured noncommercialised and nonprofessional forms of recreation that dispensed with grandstands and spectators. Doubts were cast upon the social value of competitive sport—above all, on attempts to attain top-class results. As future Soviet President Kalinin was to put it, 'Sport is a subsidiary affair and should never become an end in itself, a striving to break records. . . . Sport should be subordinate to communist education. After all, we are preparing not narrow sportsmen, but citizens of communist society who ought to possess primarily a broad outlook and organisational ability as well as strong arms and a good digestive system'[23].

Not all supporters of the hygienists, however, were opposed to every form of competitive sport. Nikolai Semashko, Chairman of the Supreme Council of Physical Culture, who was himself a doctor and concurrently also People's Commissar for Health, argued against restricting physical culture to narrow medical confines and against banning competitive sports: 'If you feed the populace on the stodgy porridge of hygienic gymnastics, physical culture will never gain wide currency'. Competitive sport was, he believed, 'the open door to physical culture. . . . It not only strengthens the various organs, it helps a person's mental development, teaches him attentiveness, punctuality, precision and grace of movement, it develops the sort of will-power, strength and skill that should distinguish Soviet people'[24]. Moreover, although he wrote the following lines before the full-scale campaign for 'socialist competition' had been launched to accompany the industrialisation drive, he clearly anticipated the regime's support for competition: 'Competition should serve ultimately as a means of involving people in building socialism. That is how I look upon competitive sport and competition generally'[25].

Another widely influential group in 'sport' during the 1920s was the 'Proletarian Culture Organisation' (*Proletkul' t*). The Proletkultists demanded the complete rejection of competitive sport and all organised sports that derived from bourgeois society as remnants of the decadent past and emanations of degenerate bourgeois culture. A fresh start had to be made through the 'revolutionary innovation of proletarian physical culture', which would take the form of 'labour gymnastics' and mass displays, pageants, and excursions. Gymnasiums and their 'bourgeois' equipment would be replaced by various pieces of apparatus on which young proletarians could practise their 'labour movements'.

While the hygienists had admitted the possibility of the usefulness of some bourgeois sports, the Proletkultists made no such concessions. To many Proletkultists, the recourse to 'bourgeois' institutions such as sports seemed a compromise, a withdrawal from already conquered positions. Lenin criticised them, pointing out the need to draw on the cultural heritage of the past and to base further development on everything valuable that had been accumulated by humankind up to the Russian Revolution: 'What is important is not the *invention* of a new proletarian culture, but the *development* of the best forms, traditions and results of *existing* culture from the viewpoint of Marxist philosophy'[26]. Other critics maintained that there were no such separate entities as bourgeois and proletarian sports; there was, rather, a bourgeois and a proletarian *attitude* to sport, a bourgeois and proletarian *spirit* of competition. Sporting attainments were, they asserted, necessary for inspiring young people to fresh successes in sport—-which were, in some way, a measure of the country's cultural and technical development. This point of view was given the official stamp of approval in the Party's famous resolution on physical culture in 1925, which stressed that:

Physical culture must be considered not simply from the viewpoint of public health and physical education, not only as an aspect of the cultural, economic and military training of young people. It should also be seen as a method of educating the masses (inasmuch as it develops will-power and teamwork, endurance, resourcefulness and other valuable qualities). It must be regarded, moreover, as a means of rallying the bulk of workers and peasants to the various Party, Soviet, and trade-union organisations, through which they can be drawn into social and political activity. . . . Physical culture must be an inseparable part of overall political and cultural education, and of public health'[27].

The years of experimenting and searching in the 1920s reflect a contradiction fundamental to the period: between the subjective desires to shape society according to ideological preconceptions and the objective lack of the material conditions for implementing ideals. There can be little doubt that because they were not based on the reality of the USSR's situation some immediate aspirations, including those of the hygienists and Proletkultists, were utopian and unrealistic. Even so, the questions they raised are important and relevant to any assessment of the role of sport in socialist society for, as the actual development of sport showed, sport became geared far more to practical needs than to ideological considerations.

It was against the background of world and civil war, economic and political breakdown that the Bolsheviks had to introduce a new system of sport after 1917. The first steps to be taken were by no means obvious, for there was no pattern to follow; the changeover from criticism of capitalist institutions and the sports of Western industrial states to practical action in an 80% peasant, overwhelmingly illiterate society presented immense problems and dilemmas. In fact, like everything else, sport during the first few years came to be subordinated to the needs of the war effort. All the old clubs and their equipment were commandeered and handed over to the military training establishment *Vsevobuch*, whose main aim was to supply the Red Army with contingents of trained conscripts as quickly as possible. One means of achieving this was to carry out a crash programme of physical fitness for all people of recruitable and prerecruitment age.

In line with the policy of combining military drill and weapon handling with political and general education in elementary hygiene, it was also decided to coordinate the activities of *Vsevobuch* with those of the commissariats of Education and Health. In the opinion of the head of *Vsevobuch*, Nikolai Podvoisky, it was impossible to bring the Civil War to a successful conclusion or to start to build socialism without a large-scale campaign to improve physical fitness and health. A second major consideration then (after military training) was *health.* Having inherited a country with an inclement climate, whose population was more than three-quarters illiterate, where disease and starvation were common, and where most people had only rudimentary knowledge of hygiene, the Soviet leaders appreciated that it would take a radical economic and social transformation to alter the situation substantially. But time was short, and able-bodied and disciplined men and women were vital, first for the country's survival, then for its recovery from the ravages of war and revolution, for industrial development and defence against further attacks.

Regular participation in physical exercise was to be one relatively inexpensive but effective means of improving health standards rapidly and a channel by which to educate people in hygiene, nutrition, and exercise. One indication of the health policy being pursued was the campaign during the Civil War under the slogans 'Help the Country with a Toothbrush!', 'Help the Country by Washing in Cold Water!', and 'Physical Culture 24 Hours a Day!'. With the influx of masses of peasants into the cities (bringing with them rural habits), the significance of health through physical exercise took on a new dimension. The ignorance that was the cause of so much disease, starvation, and misery—and which hampered both military effectiveness and labour productivity—was to be combated by a far-reaching pro-gramme of physical exercise and sport. And if the material facilities were lacking, then people were urged (by Podvoisky) to make full use of 'the sun, air, water and natural movement—the best proletarian doctors'[28]. The therapeutic value of sport was also widely advertised in the intermittent three-day antituberculosis campaigns of the late 1920s. It was, further, not thought incongruous to put out a poster ostensibly advertising sports, yet featuring a young man with a rifle and toothbrush above the slogan 'Clean your Teeth! Clean your Rifle!'.

But sport was not confined to improving physical health; it was regarded as important in combating antisocial and anti-Soviet behaviour in town and country. If urban young people, especially, could be persuaded to take up sport and engage in regular physical exercise, they might develop healthy bodies *and* minds. Thus, the Ukrainian Party Central Committee issued a resolution in 1926 expressing the hope that 'physical culture would become a vehicle of the new life . . . a means of isolating young people from the evil influence of the street, home-made alcohol, and prostitution'[29]. The role assigned sport in the countryside was even more ambitious: It was 'to play a big part in the campaign against drunkenness and uncivilised behaviour by attracting village youth to more sensible and cultured activities. . . . In the fight to transform the village, physical culture is to be a vehicle of the new way of life in all measures undertaken by the Soviet authorities—in the fight against religion and natural calamities'[30]. Sport, then, stood for 'clean living', progress, health, and rationality and was regarded by the Party as one of the most suitable and effective instruments for implementing its social policies.

The far-reaching aims envisaged for sport may be illustrated by the early concern that physical culture should make some contribution to the social emancipation of women—in Soviet society generally, and especially in the Muslim areas where women were effectively excluded from all public life. The bodily liberation and naked limbs (and faces!) along with the self-acting, competing 'image' associated with sport were not accepted without a struggle: 'I would call our first sportswomen real heroines. They accomplished great feats of bravery in liberating women from the age-old yoke of religion and the feudal-bey order'[31]. Even in the European areas of the country, the women's emancipation through sport policy was presented as both feasible and effective. For example, in a letter to Podvoisky through the medium of *Pravda* in 1922, the first women graduates from the Central Military School of Workers' Physical Culture wrote: 'You understood how important physical culture is for women and you tried to impress its importance upon us women, among whom there is so much passivity and conservatism, the results of age-old servitude, both economic and social'[32].

The physical culture campaign could only catch on, in the view of the authorities, if the emotional attraction of *competitive sport* were to be utilised to the utmost. Contests began to be organised during the 1920s from the lowest level upwards, culminating in the All-Russia Pre-Olympiads and the First Central Asian Olympics of 1920. Sports were taken from the town to the countryside, from the European metropolis to the Asiatic interior, as an explicit means of involving as many people as possible in physical exercise and organised sport. A third explicit function of sport then was *integration*. The significance of the First Central Asian Olympics, held in Tashkent over a period of 10 days in early October 1920 (before the Civil War was over!), may be judged by the fact that this was the first time in history that Uzbeks, Kazakhs, Turkmenians, Kirgiz, and other local peoples, as well as Russians and other European races, had competed in any sporting events together (as many as 3,000 participants altogether). As was made clear later, the authorities regarded sport as an important means of integrating the diverse peoples of the old Russian empire into the new Soviet state: 'The integrative functions of sport are very great. This has immense importance for our multinational state. Sports contests, festivals, spartakiads and other types of sports competition have played a major part in cementing the friendship of Soviet peoples'[33].

To sum up, there existed during the 1920s a widespread adherence to the notion of *mens sana in corpore sano*, a feeling that physical culture could somehow be used, along with other policies, to combat socially and politically undesirable phenomena. It was also a valuable means of promoting national integration and military training.

By the end of the 1920s, the scene was set for the implementation of an industrial-isation programme that was to hurl the whole of the country into a gigantic campaign to 'build socialism', then to lead to the forcible collectivisation of agriculture and to transform the USSR from a backward agrarian into an advanced industrial economy—all on the nation's own resources. The implications for the sports move-ment of these processes were extremely important, for it was in the 1930s that the pattern of Soviet sport (and of most other socialist states) was basically formed and its main role and functions set. By the end of the 1930s, the main organisational pattern had already been established—with its sports societies, sports schools, national fitness programme (the *GTO*) and the uniform rankings system for individual sports and proficient athletes. The Soviet society of the 1930s differed from that of the preceding period in seeing the flourishing of all manner of competitive sports (soccer, basketball, volleyball) with mass spectator appeal and the official encourage-ment of leagues, stadiums, cups, championships, popularity polls, cults of sporting heroes—all the appendages of a subsystem designed to provide general recreation and diversion for the fast-growing urban population.

Millions of people, uprooted from centuries-old traditions, were pitched into new and strange environments; the newcomers to industry joined factory clubs and looked to them for the recreation they had previously enjoyed in an open-air rural setting. Since urban conditions were spartan and deteriorating, sports served many townsfolk as an escape from the drudgery of their domestic and work environments. The many sports contests of the 1930s were intended, too, to create and reinforce a 'togetherness', to evoke feelings of patriotism, and to demonstrate to people at home as well as abroad how happy and carefree life was under socialism. It is significant that sports rallies often accompanied major political events or festivals (May Day, Anniversary of the Revolution Day, Constitution Day). In this way, sport became a means of linking members of the public with politics, the Party and, of course, with political leaders.

Furthermore, a relatively close link was reestablished in the 1930s between sport and the military. It stemmed partly from the conviction of the need for a state surrounded by unfriendly powers to be strong militarily and constantly on the alert. This conviction became widespread in the 'besieged fortress' atmosphere of the 1930s, encouraged by the rise of fascism in Europe. Sport openly became a means of providing premilitary training and achieving a relatively high standard of national fitness of men and women for defence. Several sports with potential military application—for example, shooting, skiing, gliding, and mountaineering—came to be dominated by servicemen. The two largest and most successful sports clubs in the USSR were those run by the armed forces and the security forces: the Central House of the Red Army (subsequently the Central Sports Club of the Army—*TsSKA*) and *Dinamo*, respectively. And, after 1931, the *GTO* national fitness programme was expressly intended to train people, through sport, for work and military preparedness—the Russian acronym *GTO* standing for *Gotov k trudu i oborone* (Prepared for Labour and Defence).

The war years (1941–1945) cannot simply be seen as a wasted interlude that retarded the Soviet sports movement. They had certain consequences, some intangible, but nonetheless far-reaching, whose effect was evident for many years ahead. For a start, the war convinced the authorities that they had been absolutely right to 'functionalise' sport, to control it from the centre, and to make countrywide physical fitness a prime target.

With the conclusion of the war and the setting of a new national target—to catch up and overtake the most advanced industrial powers (and that included catching up and overtaking in sport), the Soviet leadership felt it possible to demonstrate the preeminence of sport in socialist society. Given the limited opportunities elsewhere, sport seemed to offer a suitable medium for pursuing this goal. This was an area in which the USSR did not have to take second place to the West.

With the central control of sport and the utilitarian-instrumental role assigned it, it is natural that the pattern of foreign sports competition involving the USSR should follow the course of Soviet foreign policy and display clearly differentiated contours in regard to the geopolitical situation of different countries. With the completely new balance of power that developed after World War II (the creation of a group of socialist states, the emergence of newly independent Afro-Asian countries, and the nuclear stalemate), the Soviet leadership assigned sport such tasks as winning support for the communist system, encouraging friendly, commercial, and good-neighbourly relations with the USSR, and achieving unity within the socialist bloc. It evidently considered that sports emissaries can sometimes do more than diplomats to recommend a political philosophy and way of life to the outside world.

To sum up, the leaders of the former Soviet Union would seem to have opted for the following in developing forms of sport, particularly since the late 1920s:

First, using sport as a means of obtaining the fit, disciplined, and cooperative work force needed for attaining economic and military strength and efficiency—in particular:

1. to raise physical and social health standards—and the latter meant not simply educating people in the virtues of bodily hygiene, regular exercise, and sound

nutrition, but also overcoming unhealthy, deviant, antisocial (and therefore anti-Soviet) conduct: drunkenness, delinquency, prostitution—even religiosity and intellectual dissidence;

2. to socialise the population into the new establishment system of values. Character training, advanced (so the Soviet leaders seem to have believed) by sport in such values as loyalty, conformity, team spirit, cooperation, and discipline, may well have encouraged compliance and cooperation in both work and politics;

3. to encourage a population, in transition from a rural to an urban way of life, to identify with wider communities, all-embracing social units such as the workplace, the town, the district, the republic, and, ultimately, the entire country. By associating sport (like other amenities) organisationally with the workplace, the Party leadership and its agencies could, moreover, better supervise and 'rationalise' the leisure-time activities of employees.

Second, linking sport ideologically and even organisationally with military preparedness; the reasons for this 'militarisation' of sport must be sought in:

1. the leadership's fear of war and its conviction of the need to keep the population primed to meet it;

2. the all-pervasive presence throughout society of military and security forces, necessitated by the imposition from above, should enthusiasm from below flag, of 'socialist construction' on a tired public. This 'presence' had been the norm in Russian society before the Revolution in sport as elsewhere;

3. the fact that, in a vast country with problems of communication, lukewarm (at best) popular attitudes towards physical exercise and few sports facilities for most of the Soviet period, military organisation of sport was actually an efficient method of deploying scarce resources in the most economical way and using methods of direction that were, perhaps, more effective coming from paramilitary than from civilian organisations.

Third, in a vast multinational land that witnessed disorientingly rapid change, sport extended to and united wider sections of the population than probably any other social activity. With its broad relevance to education, health, culture, and politics, and its capacity to mobilise people (predispose them towards change), sport uniquely served the state as a vehicle of social change and national integration. Moreover, it served a public that, in a short span of time, lived through such shattering events as two world wars, three revolutions, a civil war, rapid industrialisation, forced collectivisation of agriculture, purges, and mass terror. In this society, hard work, discipline, self-censorship, and periodically necessary acute readjustments may well have needed a counterpart in sport, offering as it does a particularly rewarding area of relaxation, diversion, and recreation.

Many of the processes described above in relation to the development of the USSR were experienced in other socialist countries, and their sports organisation showed several similarities with that in the USSR. One reason for the latter is, of course, that they have all (including China) been strongly influenced by the USSR in their attitudes to and organisation of sport: Sport was state controlled, encouraged and shaped by specific utilitarian and ideological designs (it was certainly not a matter merely of 'fun and games' or the 'garden of human activities'). A more fundamental reason for the similarity of sports development in the former and current socialist countries, however, is likely to be that, with few exceptions (Czechoslovakia, German Democratic Republic), they were all modernising, developing countries based at least initially on a mainly peasant population. No leisure class existed to develop sport for its own sake; in any case, sport (with its potential for social change) was regarded as too important to be left to the whim of private clubs with restricted entrance, commercial promoters, circus entrepreneurs, and foreigners (as it was in China, Cuba, and Russia before their revolutions). Thus, in China, sport has been employed quite explicitly to help build up a backward nation: for health, hygiene, and defence. It would seem to be an integrating factor in a multinational country and to contribute to the promotion of patriotism. In the former German Democratic Republic, where other channels were closed, sport would seem to have helped attain a measure of recognition and prestige at home and abroad for the regime. In Cuba, success in international sport has helped nurture and satisfy patriotic pride in the face of boycott and subversion; it has also helped divert potential popular discontent with declining living standards, rationing, and austerity[34].

SOME CONCLUSIONS ON SPORT IN CAPITALIST AND SOCIALIST DEVELOPMENT

The state-centralised control of sport in socialist states prevented commercial exploitation of mass spectator sports for private profit and the playing of particular sports in which actual or simulated violence predominates; it also inhibited the extremes of hooliganism, corruption, and commercialism associated with a number of sports in the West.

All the same, there were features of organised sport strikingly common to both socialist and capitalist societies. There were, of course, the very sports themselves. Together with these sports went an elaborate system of government sports departments, giant amphitheatres, officials, trainers, semiprofessional and full-time professional players, sports journalists, and so on—even gambling establishments (for horse racing, for example). A similar sports ideology in East and West cultivated irrational loyalties and ascribed similar prominence to the winning of victories, the setting of records, and the collecting of trophies. Indeed, the 'citius, altius, fortius' design had nowhere such an elaborate supporting system as in the socialist countries for spotting, nurturing, and rewarding sports talent, with the aim of establishing world sporting superiority.

Despite these practices, communist leaders consistently affirmed their allegiance to Marxism-Leninism in general, and their adherence to a number of Marxist goals in respect to recreation in particular, emphasising the provision of sport for all and the need specifically to enable all citizens to be harmoniously developed, to combine 'spiritual wealth, moral purity and perfect physique'[35]. Such affirmations notwithstanding, official practice would seem to have diverged from official theory and the forms of recreation that developed in socialist societies did not coincide with the predictions of Marxist writers about playful activities in the society of the future.

As far as the former Soviet Union was concerned, reasons for the divergence may be assumed to parallel those in other areas of life. In the early postrevolutionary period, genuine efforts were made by certain future-oriented groups to move in the direction foretold by Marx and Lenin, but civil war and national poverty made them impossible to bring to fruition. From the late 1920s, command over the repressive apparatus, disposal of material resources, and sources of information were in no real sense under popular control but in the hands of members of the leading group in the ruling party, which, in the absence of help from a revolution in the industrial West, was pursuing a policy of building a strong nation-state power-base, using these instruments of power.

Some Marxists might argue that the fetishisation of recreation in the form of competitive sport (which, as we have seen in East and West, offers vast opportunities for manipulating people's minds) in the socialist states was one of a number of temporary 'defects' of a society *in transition* to communism, 'still stamped with the birth-marks of the old society from whose womb it emerges'[36]. Such 'defects' might be regarded as inevitable as long as the individual still remains subordinate to the division of labour, as long as labour is primarily a means of livelihood, as long as the forces of production are at too low a level to permit the all-round development of the individual—that is, as long as the socialist states remain 'at the first phase of communist society'[37].

Whereas in Western society, the fetishisation of sport was a consequence of this field of human endeavour (like almost all others) offering the possibilities of profit making—and turning out to be a highly appropriate means of distracting the populace from class-conscious politicisation, in socialist society, it characteristically resulted from centralised planning and administration designed to subordinate areas of social life such as sport to the political, economic, and social tasks of building a strong state. The distinction is important in terms of an understanding of the two systems. That state socialism throughout Eastern Europe rapidly disintegrated as a result of the 1989 revolutions should not detract from attempts to comprehend its essence and intentions, or those of countries like China and Cuba, or indeed any future society which takes a socialist road.

NOTES

1. McIntosh, P., *Sport in Society*, Watts, London, 1966, p. 64.
2. Goodhart, P., & Chataway, C., *War Without Weapons*, W.H. Allen, London, 1968, p. 22.
3. See Tawney, R.H., *Religion and the Rise of Capitalism*, John Murray, London, 1948, pp. 230-231; McIntosh, *op.cit.*, p. 107.

4. *Geschichte der Körperkultur in Deutschland, 1789-1917*, (History of Physical Culture in Germany, 1789-1917), Limpert, Berlin, 1965, p. 63.

5. McIntosh, P., Dixon, J., Munrow, A., & Willetts, R. *Landmarks in the History of Physical Education*, Routledge & Kegan Paul, London, 1973, p. 84.

6. *Ibid.*, p. 91.

7. See Riordan, J., *Sport in Soviet Society*, CUP, 1977.

8. Legostaev, F., *Fizicheskoye vospitanie i sport v SSSR*, Munich, 1951, p. 7.

9. Mandell, R., *The Nazi Olympics*, Macmillan, New York, 1971, p. xii.

10. Senay, A., & Hervet, R., *Monsieur de Coubertin*, Paris, 1956, p. 3.

11. See Dulles, F., *A History of Recreation*, Appleton-Century Crofts, New York, 1965, Chap. 11.

12. Quoted in McIntosh, P., *Physical Education in England since 1800*, G. Bell & Sons, London, 1972, p. 108.

13. Reynolds, E.E., *Baden-Powell*, OUP, 1942, p. 137.

14. Meisel, W., 'The Importance of Being Amateur', in Natan, A. (Ed.) *Sport and Society*, London, 1958, p. 129.

15. Marx, K., *Capital*, Vol. I, F.L.P.H., Moscow, 1961, p. 265.

16. Molyneux, D.D., *The Development of Physical Recreation in the Birmingham District, 1871-1892*, Univ. of Birmingham, 1957, p. 24. See also Walvin, J., *The People's Game*, Allen Lane, London, 1975, p. 57.

17. Lunacharsky, A.V., 'Mysli o sporte'. *Fizkul'tura i sport*, 1928, No. 2, p. 5.

18. For a more detailed study of Marx and Lenin on sport, see Riordan, J., 'Marx, Lenin and Physical Culture', *Journal of Sport History*, 1976, No. 3., pp. 152-161.

19. Marx, K. *Capital, op. cit.*, pp. 483-484.

20. Marx, K., *A Contribution to the Critique of Political Economy*, in Feuer, L.S., *Marx and Engels. Basic Writings on Politics and Philosophy*, Fontana, 1969, p. 85.

21. Marx, *Capital, op. cit.*, p. 177.

22. Trotsky, L., *Problems of Everyday Life*, Monad Press, New York, 1973, p. 32.

23. Kalinin, M., *O kommunisticheskom vospitanii*, Moscow, 1962, p. 17.

24. Semashko, N.A., 'Fizicheskaya kul'tura i zdravookhranenie v SSSR', *Izbrannye proizveniya*, Moscow, 1954, p. 264.

25. Semashko, N.A., *Puti sovetskoi fizkul'tury*, Moscow, 1926, p. 14.

26. Lenin, V.I., *Leninsky sbornik*, vol. XXXV, Moscow, 1945, p. 148.

27. *Izvestiya tsentral'novo komiteta RKP (B)*, Moscow, 20 July 1925.

28. Podvoisky, N.I., *O militsionnoi organizatsii vooruzhonnykh sil Rossiiskoi Sovetskoi Federativnoi Sotsialisticheskoi Republiki*, Moscow, 1919, p. 41.

29. *Teoriya i praktika fizicheskoi kul'tury*, 1972, No. 12, p. 13.

30. *Ibid.*

31. *Fizkul'tura i sport*, 1970, No. 6, p. 5.

32. *Pravda*, 22 June 1922.

33. *Teoriya i praktika fizicheskoi kul'tury*, 1975, No. 9, p. 9.

34. See Riordan, J. (ed.), *Sport Under Communism. Sport in China, Cuba, Czechoslovakia, German Democratic Republic and USSR*, C. Hurst, London, 1978.

35. *Programme of the Communist Party of the Soviet Union*, in *The Road to Communism*, Moscow, 1961, p. 567.
36. Marx, K. 'Critique of the Gotha Programme', in McLellan, D. (Ed.), *Karl Marx, Selected Writings*, Oxford University Press, Oxford, 1977, p. 569.
37. *Ibid.*, p. 568.

Sport, Politics, and South Africa (1948-1989)

Grant Jarvie

Something that has always struck me about the *early* literature on the politics of sport in general, and more specifically on South African sporting issues, has been the comparative absence of any attempt to locate the politics of sport within the broader political, economic, and social forces operating at any particular point in time[1]. This is not to say that writings concerning the political or ideological assumptions about the nature of sport do not exist but that far too often sport is viewed as an independent object of study rather than a mediated cultural form situated within a set of social relations. It is not enough merely to recognise that sport in any society does not take place in a social vacuum or indeed that it is influenced by and at times influences political and economic relations; it needs to be grasped as an aspect of all social relations and consequently as an arena, for example, of conflict and struggle.

One response to this early malaise was from Marxists, neo-Marxists, and various cultural radicals who have relied heavily upon the theoretical and practical notions of ideology, hegemony, class conflict, and cultural reproduction to ask core questions about the nature and practice of power and domination in state socialist and capitalist liberal democracies[2]. At risk of considerable simplification, it can be said that when placed within this wider context sporting practices are capable of providing a great deal of information about the patterns, arrangements, tensions, conflicts, and various webs of interdependence inherent in any particular social formation.

While this paper specifically concerns itself with sport, hegemony, and problems of popular struggle in South Africa, at a more general level I shall make a number of remarks about some of the early literature in the politics of sport area. With these two considerations in mind, this paper has been divided into two parts. As a means of developing various theoretical points of departure for an analysis of South African sport, the first part of the paper comments upon some of the strengths and weaknesses of some of the politics of sport literature. The second part provides an analysis of South African sport that is located within the broader patterns of social relations that characterised the South African social formation until the late 1980s.

THE POLITICS OF SPORT

In the late 1960s and early 1970s a great deal of descriptive material emerged attacking the ideal of sport as an essentially voluntary and political institution. For instance, Natan in discussing sport as a tool of politics showed how nationalism was reflected through sport and how international competitions had become an arena for competing ideologies; Riordan succinctly pointed out the five broad political aims of Soviet International sporting relations while Lapchick bravely commented that after 23 years the forces opposing apartheid in sport may have achieved their ultimate goal of the total isolation of South African sport[3]. While different authors paid particular attention to different social formations, the themes that emerged from this body of literature tended in many ways to be similar: the use of sport as political propaganda, increasing nationalism in sport, an analysis of the various interventionist policies of both state-supported countries and capitalist liberal democracies, the assertion held by some that sport had the capacity for being a great social leveller and, therefore, provided a greater degree of equality of opportunity than that found in the economic sphere, the effects of various sporting boycotts, and the increasing demands made on the state under welfare capitalism for the provision of sporting facilities.

The conventional wisdom on the politics of sport has been widely reviewed by a number of critics, and I certainly do not intend to expand upon a commentary that is already somewhat extensive[4]. However, there is a very real danger in dismissing much of this earlier work because of its atheoretical or descriptive nature. While recent theoretical discourses have in some instances become popular, it is wrong, I believe, to dismiss studies at a lower level of abstraction. I shall limit myself to making several broad remarks concerning this politics of sport literature. In agreement with Cantelon and Gruneau the problem with many of the previously mentioned cases is that sport is invariably reduced to an independent object of study as opposed to a 'mediated cultural form located in an ensemble of social relations'[5]. As mentioned earlier what is missing from this bulk of literature is any serious attempt to tackle those issues so central to political theory, namely power and domination. On the other hand the strength of this literature is that it provides a wealth of empirical, concrete data that is often missing from many theoretical polemics on the politics of sport.

In the late 1970s a great deal of attention was paid to the influence of structural Marxism on sporting analysis. In particular the work of Brohm, although not exclusively, attempted to demonstrate the crucial role that various sporting ideologies have played in the legitimation of the capitalist order[6]. Sport, the argument goes, is an instrument of bourgeois hegemony; that is, sport, like education, the media, and the church, is one of those secondary arms of the state that enables one social group to exercise its hegemony over national society as a whole. This ideology, argues Brohm, hides the true nature of class relations by turning the relations between individuals within sporting institutions into material relations between scores, machines, and records, which contributes to an overall commodification process[7].

The work of Brohm is informed throughout by the work of the French theorist Louis Althusser. One of the major advances made by this tradition was to reject simplistic reflection theory and conceive of the various dimensions of superstructure—arts, law, education, and so on—as having a relative autonomy and operating, in the first place, in terms of their own diverse modes and practices while, in the last analysis, being determined by the relations of production in the economic base[8]. The Althusserian approach to ideology contains at least two crucial elements. First, it has a material existence that in this instance would structure the rituals, practices, and processes inherent in sport; second, while ideology neither produces consciousness nor a willing compliance for Althusser, it functions as a system of representations, carrying meanings and ideas that would structure the false consciousness of athletes[9]. These two interrelated processes induce athletes into an imaginary relationship to their real material conditions of existence.

This position had important implications or consequences for the analysis of culture by producing work that was firmly grounded in the Marxist concern with the operation of ideology but that went about it in a way that respected the specificity of various cultural modes and practices. The most substantial limitation of the Althusserian position was that it had no place for struggle, negotiation agency, and subjective experience[10]. In the last analysis, its determinism, its posing of culture as unambiguously the site of dominant ideology, negates the idea of cultural institutions and forms, including sport, as sites of contention and struggle. The structural Marxist position, therefore, does not really provide us with an adequate theory of ideology or culture.

A similar problem might be attributed to the more recent work by Hoberman entitled *Sport and Political Ideology*[11]. The task that Hoberman undertakes is to interpret the major twentieth-century sporting ideologies as distinct expressions of a particular doctrine or doctrines. Hoberman deals mostly with the Soviet Union, East Germany, and China as examples of the left ideology, while the right is represented by Germany and Italy. American sport is dismissed because, according to Hoberman, American sport has no official ideological status on the left or the right. The strength of the text lies in its breadth of content and depth of historical material.

Yet a limited usage of the core concept, namely ideology, detracts from the text. As Hargreaves points out: 'If the analysis of political ideology is restricted to examining its formal constituents in abstraction from everyday usage and social practice it is impossible to make sense of how it works'[12]. Like the structural Marxists, Hoberman's approach to ideology leaves no appreciation for the fact that ideology is generated and sustained in lived experience. As such, it is constantly the focus of struggle and negotiation with the essential outcome always being problematic and uncertain. In short, what is being said is that ideologies, while they may represent various social ideas that guide the political practice of various social groups, including sporting groups, the dominant ideology is never given but struggled with, challenged, and the object of intense negotiation.

It is the great merit of Gramsci's work that it reinstates and centralises precisely this point. Inside Gramsci's concept of hegemony are the ideas of negotiation and consent, not of imposition from above[13]. The idea of hegemony involves understanding how particular classes reach positions of dominance through constant and repeated struggles in particular sites: culture, in particular popular culture, being one of the most important. Gramsci was interested in a whole range of cultural forms and institutions, although even he was tardy in recognising the importance of such cultural forms as sport or the cinema. However, what sets Gramsci apart from his counterparts is his grasping of culture as a fundamental site of conflict within which ideological hegemony is contested and his having a total theoretical framework (historical materialism) that relates this to political struggle[14].

Gramsci's notion of hegemony relied heavily upon forms of ideological processes operated through cementing and unifying the existing social order. In other words, the ideological subordination of the working class by the dominant class enabled the dominant class to rule by negotiated consent. If a social transformation was to come about, Gramsci argued that a counter hegemony would have to break the ideological bond between the ruling class and various sectors of the general population[15].

As a general rule, hegemony works through ideology, but it does not always consist of false ideas, perceptions, and definitions. It often works primarily by inserting members of the dominant class into key institutions and structure that support the power and social authority of the dominant order. Yet, these forms of mobility are often little more than simple incorporation. While society opens up for a few individuals, class power, expressed as the capacity to define economic and cultural standards, remains unchanged. This type of power is referred to by Lukes as:

> The power to define the agenda, to shape preferences, to prevent conflict from arising in the first place or to contain conflict when it does arise by defining what sorts of resolution are reasonable or realistic within the existing order[16].

While accepting Gramsci's contribution, it is important to realise that hegemony itself is rarely sustained by any one class or group. The content of any hegemony is partially determined by those subcultures, countercultures, and oppositional class fractions that form a hegemonic bloc. Hegemony or a hegemonic society is not simply class rule. As Hall points out, it requires at least some degree of consent from the subordinate classes, which, in turn, has to be won and secured[17]. While the dominant culture retains power, its repertoire of control is continuously challenged in complex and subtle ways. As a result, this repertoire of control is often weakened and transformed. Hegemony, as Williams describes it, is always an active process, a process that can never be taken for granted but has to be continually fought for[18].

In sport, a number of writers have made valuable contributions to the sport/hegemony debate[19]. Sport, Hargreaves contends, cannot be dissociated from the context of class relations and specific hegemonic patterns. In order to understand how sport forms part of the totality, the relevant processes must be analysed in dialectical terms and characterised by conflict and consent, coercion, and struggle. If the role that sport plays in hegemony, writes Hargreaves, is to be properly understood, the relevant processes have to be elucidated in their concrete detail[20].

Almost all of the arguments made by Hargreaves are powerful, penetrating, and provide useful points of departure. Indeed Hargreaves has gone to some length to show how a Marxist analysis of sport might proceed. While I agree with Hargreaves that in order to understand the role that sport plays in hegemony the relevant processes have to be grounded in concrete detail, it is precisely this concrete detail that is missing in this instance. I certainly do not wish to rationalise empiricism, nor indeed do I wish to rationalise a withdrawal from epistemology. However, it is not necessary to retreat into epistemology as a means of sidestepping the necessity for empirically grounded and theoretically guided observations. We need eventually to ask a number of empirical questions.

A second point is raised by Parry, who calls for the use of the term hegemony to be addressed in a more thorough fashion[21]. Like many others Hargreaves believes it suffices merely to mention the now infamous definition of hegemony used by Williams[22]. While I agree with the position adopted by Williams, Parry suggests that due attention has not been paid to the notion of hegemony as it was originally used by Gramsci. Gramsci's theory placed a particular emphasis on the role of organic intellectuals whose precise task it was to develop counter-hegemonic struggles by virtue of their critical understanding. The way in which sport might be used in terms of counter-hegemonic struggle is a peculiar silence in many discussions concerning sport and hegemony theory.

My purpose in this initial brief discussion has been to make a number of general comments about the development of the early politics of sport literature. In moving from the general to the specific the second part of this paper limits itself to an analysis of one particular strand in the politics of sport area, namely South African sport. The analysis draws upon some of the theoretical concerns already mentioned and locates sport within the broader patterns of social relations inherent within the South African social formation between 1948 and 1989.

SPORT IN SOUTH AFRICAN SOCIETY

Over the last two decades there has been considerable interest in the patterns and policies of South African sport. The expulsion of South Africa from the Olympics, the 1984 Zola Budd affair, and the crisis concerning the threat to the 1986 Commonwealth Games as a result of the English Cricket tour to the West Indies with players who have in the past maintained South African connections have all served to focus international attention on South African sporting practices. On the one hand, a number of writers argued that South African sport had been liberalised; on the other, some suggested that sport remained a mechanism for the extension of apartheid policy in general[23]. Most of these writers tended to focus their evaluations purely on the question of race and thereby missed the complex interaction between racial and class dynamics as a background for understanding the South African sporting way of life.

The complex interaction of racial and class dynamics in South Africa has often been concealed by the appearance of social realities under apartheid. Race and racial discrimination appear to be the dominant consideration determining and affecting all aspects of social life. Black people, regardless of class position, are still systematically denied equality of opportunity in political, economic, and cultural spheres. Yet what this overlooks is the fact that South African racism has not evolved in a social vacuum. Rather, it has developed in conjunction with very significant relations of colonisation, capitalist development, and western imperialism.

It is along these lines that the South African Congress of Trade Unions ruled in 1962 that:

> It must never be forgotten that apartheid and racial discrimination in South Africa, like everywhere else, has an aim far more important than discrimination itself; the aim is economic exploitation. The root and fruit of apartheid and racial discrimination is profit[24].

The argument was that South Africa could be understood with regard to the production process and the social relationships formed around the mode of production. The main characteristics of South African society can be summarised as follows. First, it is a capitalist social formation in which the mass of the population have been separated from the means of production and where the production of commodities is greatly dependent upon cheap labour, foreign exchange, and western investment. Second, the overwhelming majority of the population, including most of the industrial working class, were denied both in law and practice many civil and political rights on the grounds of colour. In the 1970s and 1980s, however, many Africans have enjoyed a less stringent implementation of several petty apartheid rules[25]. To understand these concessions in the context of the historical process, it is necessary, I believe, to consider what Gramsci referred to as the organic and conjunctional dimensions of crisis[26].

The current living crisis in South Africa might be referred to as an organic crisis:

> A crisis occurs sometimes lasting for decades. This exceptional duration means that incurable structural contradictions have revealed themselves (reached maturity), and that despite this, the political forces, which are struggling to conserve and defend the existing structure itself, are making every effort to cure them, within certain limits, and to overcome them. These incessant and persistent efforts . . . form the terrain of the conjunctural and it is upon this terrain that the forces of opposition must organise[27].

At the core of Gramsci's model of transformation is a dual perspective involving the organic and conjunctural dimensions of change. By conjunctural Gramsci meant the passing and momentary period of crisis during which the contesting political forces struggle for state power. As Hall points out, the conjunctural must be seen in terms of a lived historical bloc in which new political figurations, new programmes, and new policies point to a new settlement[28]. The organic, on the other hand, must precede the conjunctural. A crisis occurs when structural contradictions occur within the organic. As such the conjunctural must not be seen as a reflection of the crisis but as a response to it.

It is entirely appropriate to see much of this as directly applicable to the situation in South Africa. The process of capital accumulation that has evolved historically in South Africa entered a period of crisis during the 1970s with the emergence of a skilled white labour shortage and a periodic slump in the price of gold[29]. Yet such events alone were not enough to term the crisis facing the South African social formation as organic. A transformation of this nature resulted from the dramatic escalation in resistance to apartheid rule from a number of oppressed cultural groupings. In short, the organic crisis revolved around two key dimensions: first, the structural contradictions that emerged from the process of capital accumulation and an increased dependency of the white minority culture upon the African culture in terms of labour needs, and second, the increase in resistance as exemplified by events leading up to Soweto in 1976 and exemplified by the intense period of struggle and violence that erupted in South Africa in 1985 and has continued through to the present[30].

The conjunctural dimension of the crisis referred to the attempts made by policy decision makers to introduce a number of new programmes and policies aimed at maintaining important features of the status quo. If transformation of a broader nature was going to take place, it was precisely this dominant cultural response that the forces of opposition had to organise against. In any case, accounts of social change in general must not only allow for structural limits to change but also the ways in which such limits are dealt with by subordinate groups and cultures. Related to this is the important issue of how subordinate groups try to penetrate and resist dominant cultures.

Although pressure from foreign investors and sectors of the ruling class for major reforms within the existing system had been in evidence for some time, it was only after Soweto in 1976 that major changes in South Africa policy were actually implemented. Both Botha and then Foreign Minister Koornhof consciously tried to present new measures as proof of the regime's willingness to modify and cater to black aspirations[31]. A significant part of this conjunctural response was the establishment of a 'multinational' sports policy, which finally emerged in September 1976. Yet it is important to realise that the success of South Africa's multinational sports policy rested upon a degree of confusion being perpetuated by the terms multinational, multiracial, and an antiracial sports policy. Internationally, sport under apartheid had been marketed as multiracial while internally sport for the majority of Africans was controlled through a number of economic and political factors that, in effect, mitigated against the free playing of multiracial sport, never mind a truly nonracial sports policy[32].

In terms of economic expenditure, facilities, and sponsorship, a gross inequality still exists between the different racial groups. A major reason for this lies in the fact that sport in South Africa is not primarily determined by sporting legislation but by general economic conditions and government policy. It was the unique interaction of apartheid law with the social relations of South African capitalism that served to institutionalise the inequalities in sporting practice. When we talk of sporting change in South Africa we are therefore talking about socioeconomic and political changes. Yet, the emergence of the conjunctural response must not give rise to the idea that attempts were not made to dismantle this ideology, nor indeed should the emergence of a multinational sports policy give rise to the idea that such a development evolved without a struggle. It is this struggle and resistance over white sporting hegemony, which lasted until the late 1980s, that the remainder of this paper briefly addresses.

SPORT, HEGEMONY, AND PROBLEMS
OF POPULAR STRUGGLE

South Africa is unusual and perhaps unique in that sport has become an overtly open object of civil struggle. Various white sporting policies have met with considerable internal and external resistance. Aiming to create sporting practice free from all forms of racism, including the racism inherent in multinationalism, black sporting resistance internally was expressed during the 1980s through the South Africa Council on Sport (SACOS). While a number of sporting organisations have historically compromised their demands, the strength of SACOS as a sporting mode of resistance lay in its refusal to separate sporting demands from broader demands for social change.

The level of sporting consciousness expressed by SACOS affiliates has evolved historically through a number of internal sporting struggles. African sporting resistance originally found solidarity in the South African Sports Association (SASA) and the South African Non-Racial Olympic Committee (SAN-ROC). The creation of SASA in 1958 marked the beginning of the nonracial sports movement. By providing a source of unification in purely sporting terms SASA permitted black sporting culture to support the broader struggle against apartheid. While SASA provided a source of solidarity, the same could not be said of the broader liberation forces, which experienced a major split during the second half of the 1950s.

Historically, the African National Congress (ANC) exemplified many of the contradictory tensions that the revolutionary movement in South Africa is currently facing. While the initial ANC strategy was essentially reformist, there was within it a more militant approach stemming from the Trade Union Movement under the leadership of Clements Kadalie. Only after the 1946 'Mine Workers Strike' did the National Movement, represented by the ANC, and working-class groups represented by the South Africa Congress of Trade Unions (SACTU), begin to link up more effectively[33]. On 26 June 1955 SACTU and the ANC formed an alliance that immediately increased the impact of the South African Communist Party (SACP) in drawing the ANC movement towards a more proletarian line of action. The coalition between the philosophically opposing forces found its expression in the Freedom Charter adopted in 1956. The main points of the charter, write Karis and Carter[34], were:

1. All national groups shall have equal rights.
2. All national groups will be protected by law against insults to their race and national pride.
3. All people shall have equal rights to use their own language and to develop their own folk culture and customs.
4. The preaching and practice of national, race, or colour discrimination and contempt shall be a punishable crime.
5. All apartheid laws and practices shall be set aside.

For the militant national faction of the ANC the Freedom Charter marked a shift in policy. The charter marked a noticeable swing towards a more socialist approach and stressed the need for unity among the African majority with regard to the nature of the liberation process. Although the ANC declared that South Africa belonged to all who lived in it, Mandela took care to explain that support for the Charter was by no means a blueprint for a completely socialist state[35].

By the end of the 1950s both the ANC and SASA succeeded in extending resistance to apartheid into a number of areas. The tactics used by SASA in extending black resistance into sport were similar to those by the ANC. As Archer and Bouillion note:

The tactics of civil disobedience adopted by sportsmen were also those used by the ANC. . . . Furthermore, because it was played by the petty bourgeoisie and by the urban workers . . . sport provided a particularly favourable ground upon which to attack apartheid[36].

As a result of the dominant cultural response to the Sharpeville riots, SASA remained one of the few avenues for protest against apartheid during the 1960s. It is all the more significant, therefore, that at the time when the leaders of the broader liberation forces were arrested, SASA created a further militant sporting organisation, namely SAN-ROC. The formation of SAN-ROC in 1962 stemmed from SASA's continual failure to win support from the International Olympic Committee (IOC). Under the leadership of Denis Brutus, SAN-ROC emerged as a symbol of struggle for nonracial sport in South Africa. The movement's specific policy was to expose racial domination wherever possible in sport and to force the IOC to expel South Africa from the Olympic Movement.

SAN-ROC's existence within South Africa, notes Brutus, was relatively short-lived, since within two years of its creation, its leading members 'had been exiled and its activities suspended within South Africa'[37]. Yet it was during this period of repression that SAN-ROC scored its first major victory in that the IOC in 1964 banned South African athletes from participating in the Olympic Games in Tokyo. As Brickhill records, the shock to the white public, accustomed to free participation in world sports, was considerable[38]. More shocks were to come.

The broader, relatively trouble-free time of the 1960s was not to last for long. During the 1960s and early 1970s the initiative lay primarily with the groups of black students who found expression through the leadership of Steve Biko. The student organisations gave birth to a number of militant organisations. Their message, 'black man, you are on your own', articulated for many the frustrations of a generation of young blacks whose sole experience was that of apartheid. While the Black Consciousness Movement (BCM) ideologically laid the roots for the Soweto uprising of 1976, it subsequently bore the brunt of the repression that followed and culminated in the shooting of Steve Biko.

However, the resistance movement was not forced entirely underground. In May 1978 the BCM sought to regroup with the Azanian African People's Organisation (AZAPO) with the aim of specifically organising black workers to take militant action through strikes. Despite the emergence of a number of internal resistance movements during the 1970s and 1980s the then exiled ANC movement was still viewed as the major mobilising force on the liberation front. According to Saul and Gelb there are two basic reasons for the ANC having this sort of gravitational pull[39]. One important reason was the ANC's growing military capacity. The dramatic acts of sabotage at the Sasolburg oil storage facilities in 1980 forced the Minister of Police to proclaim that ANC forces were everywhere in South Africa. A less tangible factor, but equally important, was the movement's depth of history and involvement with the liberation struggle since its inception in 1912.

Just as the ANC continued to function from exile, so did SAN-ROC. By 1965 SAN-ROC had again become the dominant force within the nonracial sports movement. Operating from London, the group continued to agitate against white sporting federations and white South African society in general.

With SAN-ROC in exile, the nonracial sporting movement in South Africa was not only deprived of a means of solidarity but was subjected to a campaign waged against them by the white associations and coordinated by the government. This campaign formed the basis of what was later to become multinational sport. It revolved around three axial principles: (1) to create separate Indian, Coloured, and African associations; (2) to finance and promote the emergence of a small black sporting elite; (3) to force this black elite to support the status quo and official apartheid policies. This move effectively deprived the nonracial sports movement inside South Africa of finance, facilities, and unification.

Yet, the move to form nonracial sporting organisations as opposed to black sporting organisations proved to be significant in that it greatly increased the strength of the sporting resistance movement. Up until that point, the only political weapon available was a plea for the expulsion of the white sporting federations. The removal of a discriminatory policy against white subjects meant that the black sporting organisation could now expand its demands in calling not only for the expulsion of white sporting federations but also for the international recognition of nonracial sporting federations.

While the policy of nonracial sport in principle was adhered to by the black oppressed sporting culture, in practice it meant the near cessation of nearly all sporting activity. Despite major problems facing the movement in theory, nonracial sport as a political weapon was preserved[40]. The position of the nonracial bodies was very much in line with the position adopted by the nonracial South African Amateur Swimming Federation:

> Our goal is complete non-racial swimming at every level in the country adminis-tered by a single, truly non-racial swimming organisation, not the useless, ineffective, and misleading body like the Amateur Aquatics Federation of South Africa[41].

With SAN-ROC in exile, the primary task of the nonracial movement was simply to survive against the push for multinational sport. Despondent with the lack of progress towards the nonracial sport, representatives from a number of national sports organisations gathered in Durban during September 1970 to form the South African Non-Racial Sports Organisation (SASPO). The formation of SASPO again brought a degree of internal solidarity to the nonracial movement. However, while continually denouncing South African sports policy, the organisation was willing to collaborate with white organisations on a number of issues. It is of no small significance that during the same period the BCM was calling for the reestablishment of black identity and for an end to black recognition and relations with white culture. As Biko argued:

> The biggest mistake the black world ever made was to assume that whoever opposed apartheid was an ally. For a long time the black world has been looking at the governing party and not so much at the whole power structure as the object of their rage. In a sense the very political vocabulary that the blacks have used has been inherited from the liberals[42].

The awakening of black consciousness strongly affected the direction of the nonracial sports resistance in that black athletes called for a more aggressive approach to multinational sports. In March 1979 the formation of the South African Council on Sport (SACOS) provided black sporting culture with a more militant resistance movement. As already mentioned, the appeal of SACOS lay in its policy of no negotiations and a declaration of solidarity among nonracial sports organisations until all the symbols of apartheid had been removed, not only from South African sport but also from South African society. Indeed, the aggressive approach adopted by SACOS worried some of its own members, who felt that the inflexible approach to radical policies might sever the movement from the mass of African sports participants.

The resistance to multinationalism from SACOS revolved around four key issues. First, the movement took issue against the permit system, which requires nonwhites to be in possession of sporting permits if they are playing any form of multinational sport. Any sports event that is not multinational (i.e., government endorsed) is refused a permit. If a black sports body wished to defy government policy and hold a mixed sports event, its officials were politely warned about the consequences. In a pamphlet issued to all black athletes in 1978, SACOS not only called for athletes to shed their slave mentality but to refuse to play sport under permit conditions, since it deprives athletes of their human rights as South Africans.

Second, SACOS stood firm around the 'Double Standards Resolution', which served as a means of maintaining cohesion among truly nonracial organisations. The resolution banned black individuals who collaborated with multinational sport in any form from becoming SACOS members. This meant that any affiliate to SACOS in one code or sport could not belong to a racial unit in another code or sport (e.g., multinational organisations). The policy of noncollaboration must be seen within the broader context of the liberation struggle. In both cases, other forms of recourse—negotiation, protest, and critical cooperation—have been frustrated or crushed by the authorities. Blacks have consistently been pressed by the multinational sporting organisations to concede the principle of racial equality, over which they refuse to make concessions.

Third, SACOS took issue over the unequal distribution of sponsorship money in sport. This was very much in line with SACOS's policy of nonnegotiation with the apartheid system in any shape or form. Since the major sponsorship companies derived their profits from black labour, sponsored sport served only to support the apartheid formation. SACOS's policy in this area has been confined to a negative criticism of unequal sponsorship distribution within the tripartite sports system.

Fourth, SACOS called for a complete ban on international sporting relations with South Africa until the existing social formation is abolished and nonracial sporting practice universally accepted. The commitment of nonracial sports participants is highlighted by SACOS resolutions that banned all tours by nonracial as well as racial associations. The position taken by SACOS over international sporting relations was strengthened by the international backing of its policies. For instance, the United Nations ban on sporting contact with South Africa issued on 24 October 1980 included the compilation of a list of all those countries who maintained sporting contact with South Africa. According to a United Nations Press Release:

The director of the centre against apartheid . . . announced today that in accordance with the decisions made by the special committee, the centre has initiated a compilation of a register of sportsmen, sports administrators and others who flagrantly violated the sports boycott against South Africa[43].

The success of the international boycott revolved around several influential pieces of legislation, none more so than the Gleneagles Agreement signed by all the heads of Commonwealth countries on 15 June 1977. However, while the international boycott served to bring pressure to bear on South Africa and provided SACOS members with a certain degree of security from repression, sporting literature, I believe, has tended to overemphasise the part played by the international boycott at the expense of the struggles waged by the sporting proletariat within South Africa.

While the importance of the international boycott should not be underestimated, the futility of sporting sanctions alone could be criticised on a number of grounds. First, as already pointed out, while the international boycott provided the nonracial movement with some degree of political leverage, it also tended to undermine the efforts of the international resistance movements in forcing change in South Africa. Second, although a number of Western and Eastern countries implemented sporting sanctions, the same countries (such as Britain, America, Japan, and West Germany) continued to enter into political and economic trade negotiations with South Africa. Finally, if the liberation from apartheid was going to materialise or even capitalise on the organic crisis, it resulted not from the isolated efforts of sporting resistance movements but from a total strategy involving the broader liberation forces. To reiterate Archer and Bouillon:

Sport and sporting policy is marginal in that relatively few Africans play sport, which means that even if sport were completely integrated, it would have little effect on the well-being of the majority, who would still be confined to the compounds, townships and bantustans[44].

CONCLUSIONS

This chapter has revolved around three major themes. In reviewing some of the early politics of sport literature I have argued that much of the conventional wisdom in this area is capable of providing a great deal of empirical, concrete data upon various political sporting processes. The strength of much of the early politics of sport literature lies in this wealth of empirical data, which is often missing from many of the recent theoretical polemics on the politics of sport. Yet empiricism without any theoretical grounding is just as lacking as theoretical grounding without any attempt to tackle empirical considerations. Furthermore, I have argued that in agreement with a number of authors it is unsatisfactory to view sport, and indeed the politics of sport, as an independent object of enquiry as opposed to a mediated form of cultural practice located within an ensemble of social relations. In order to understand how sport forms part of this totality, the relevant forces and processes need to be analysed not only in abstract terms but also concrete detail.

Bearing these points in mind the final theme in this chapter has specifically concerned itself with sport, hegemony, and problems of popular struggle in South Africa. In attempting to locate the politics of sport within a broader framework involving the political, economic, and cultural forces inherent in South African capitalism, I have argued that various indicators have suggested that South African capitalism had entered a phase of deep crisis in the 1980s, a crisis that might be termed organic. The conjunctural response to this crisis was for the dominant white culture to introduce various concessions in an attempt to maintain the status quo. A major aspect of this conjunctural response revolved around the politics of South African sporting practice.

Yet the conjunctural response did not merely emerge, it was the object of intense civil struggle. An examination of the different revolutionary and cultural struggles present within the South African social formation underlines the fact that it was not necessary to speculate about revolutionary change in South Africa; it was always there. Yet the destruction of apartheid required a coordinated struggle not only through armed struggle, or national or class struggle, or through cultural struggle, but through the convergence of various forms of resistance and struggle, including sport[45].

NOTES

1. For examples of this work see Krotee, M. and Schuick, L., 'Impact of Sporting Forces on South African Apartheid', in *Journal of Sport and Social Issues*, Vol. 3, No. 1, 1979; and Lapchick, R., *The Politics of Race and International Sport*, Connecticut, 1975.
2. Cantelon, H. and Gruneau, R.S. *Sport, Culture and the Modern State*, Toronto, 1982.
3. Natan, A., 'Sport and Politics', in Loy, J. and Kenyon, G. (Eds.), *Sport, Culture and Society*, New York, 1969; Riordan, J. 'Soviet Sport and Soviet Foreign Policy' in *Soviet Studies*, No. 26, 1974; Lapchick, R., *op. cit.*, 1975.

4. For an example of this commentary see Cantelon, H. and Gruneau, R.S., *op. cit.*, 1982, pp. vii-xiv.

5. Cantelon, H. and Gruneau, R.S., *op. cit.*, 1982, p. ix.

6. Brohm, J.M. 'Theses Towards a Political Sociology of Sport', in Hart, Marie and Birrell, Susan (Eds.), *Sport in the Sociocultural Process*, Iowa, 1981.

7. Brohm, J.M. *Sport: A Prison of Measured Time*. London, 1978.

8. Althusser, L. 'Ideology and the Ideological State Apparatus', in *Lenin and Philosophy and Other Essays*. (B. Brewster, Trans.). New York, 1971.

9. On this point see Brohm, J.M., *op. cit.*, 1978, pp. 52-64.

10. A concise summary of the Althusserian position and its lack of sensitivity to the notion of agency can be found in Anderson, P., *Arguments Within English Marxism*, London, 1980, pp. 16-58.

11. Hoberman, J., *Sport and Political Ideology*, London, 1984.

12. Hargreaves, J., 'Body Politics: A Review Essay of John Hoberman', in *Sociology of Sport*, Vol. 2, No. 5, 1985, p. 249.

13. Gramsci, A., *Selection from Prison Notebooks*, New York, 1980, p. 39.

14. Gramsci, A., *op. cit.*, 1980, p. 45.

15. Gramsci, A., *op. cit.*, , 1980, pp. 40-42.

16. Lukes, S., *Power, A Radical View*, London, 1974, p. 23.

17. Hall, S. 'Moving Right', in *Socialist Review*, 1981, No. 55.

18. Williams, R., *Marxism and Literature*, Oxford, 1977.

19. See Whitson, D. 'Sport and Hegemony: On the Construction of the Dominant Culture', *Sociology of Sport*, Vol. 1, No. 1, 1984.

20. Hargreaves, J. 'Sport and Hegemony: Some Theoretical Problems', in Cantelon, H. and Gruneau, R., *op. cit.*, 1982, p. 104.

21. Parry, J. 'Hegemony and Sport', *Journal of the Philosophy of Sport*, Vol. X, 1983.

22. Williams, R., *op. cit.*, 1977, p. 110.

23. For an insight into the number of competing definitions of the South African issue see Lapchick, R., *op. cit.*, 1975; Archer, R., and Bouillon, B., *The South African Game*, London, 1982; and Ramsany, S., *Apartheid: The Real Hurdle*, London, 1982.

24. Jarvie, G., *Class, Race and Sport in South Africa's Political Economy*, London, 1985, p. 3.

25. For instance, the removal of laws forbidding interracial marriages, recognition of the black Trade Union movement, the development of an interracial parliamentary system (except for Africans), and moves to eradicate the passbook system of identity.

26. Boggs, L., *Gramsci's Marxism*, London, 1980, p. 114.

27. Gramsci, A., *op. cit.*, 1980, p. 178.

28. Hall, S., *op. cit.*, 1981, pp. 116-117.

29. Saul, S. and Gelb, S., *The Crisis in Southern Africa*, London, 1981.

30. On the aftermath of the 1976 Soweto Uprisings see Callinicos, A. and Rodgers, J., *Southern Africa After Soweto*, London, 1977.

31. Jarvie, G., *op. cit.*, 1985, pp. 53-61.

32. Jarvie, G., *ibid.*, pp. 78-82.
33. Lukhardt, K. and Wall, B., *Organise or Starve*, London, 1980.
34. Karis, T. and Carter, G., *From Protest to Challenge*, Vol. 3, 1972, p. 205.
35. Mandela, N., *The Struggle Is My Life*, London, 1978.
36. Archer, R. and Bouillon, B., *op. cit.*, 1982, p. 192.
37. Brutus, D., 'The Sportsman's Choice', La Guma, A., in *Apartheid: A Collection of South African Racism*, London, 1972, p. 156.
38. Brickhill, J., *Race Against Race*, London, 1976.
39. Saul, S. and Gelb, S., *op. cit.*, 1981, p. 139.
40. During 1979 assassination attempts were made on the lives of SACOS members M. Pather and Morgan Naidoo, president of the nonracial swimming federation.
41. United Nations Centre Against Apartheid, *Report 8/80*, London, 1980.
42. Biko, S., *I Write What I Like*, London, 1979, pp. 63-64.
43. United Nations Centre Against Apartheid, *Report 5/80*, London, 1980, p. 62.
44. Archer, R. and Bouillon, B., *op. cit.*, 1982, p. 307.
45. This paper has limited its focus to a discussion of South African sport up until the late 1980s. The paper was written *prior* to both Marxist theoretical shifts and the reforms introduced by President F.W. deKlerk on February 2, 1990.

Sport and the Economy: A Developmental Perspective

Bero Rigauer

No matter where one's eye strays, one sees flourishing everywhere activities that function according to capitalist principles, trapped between rational economism and the magical game. (Ludwig Harig [writer], on football)

We all stand under the intense pressure of public opinion. Only the better tomorrow counts, not the even better day after tomorrow. Schools and football are still only reflections of our competitive market society. There is no peaceful continuity any more. Only success counts. The game is no longer a source of joy. Everyone has been bludgeoned by our times through and through. (Jupp Derwall, one-time manager of the former West German football team)

A FEW PRELIMINARY REFLECTIONS

Sport and the economy are not strangers. Sport has 'its' economy and the economy 'its' sport. In the first case, the economy serves to maintain and develop what was once a private affair, in the second sport serves as the impetus for the opening-up of a commercial market (which can also be a private concern!). It has to be pointed out in this connection that the particular as well as the general features of sport and the economy can be conceptualised as the interlacing of specific human attitudes and ways of behaving. My central assumption is already contained in these preliminary reflections: Sport and the economy are interrelated in a variety of ways. In a reciprocal normative interpenetration, they utilize generally applicable economic methods and, at the same time, reveal specific economic meaning-orientations and social forms. It is a question of the cultural effects of an historical process that has to be seen in connection with the rationalisation of European life[1]. This process of rationalisation has contributed to the fact that 'sport', in the present meaning of the term, first arose in the phase of the industrial-capitalist social order[2]. Sport reproduces a model of physical and social relationships in terms of which human motor behaviour is developed according to rational principles. This occurs in the context of a logic of competition and intensifying achievement, which can be seen in industrial work and scientific training, and which finds one of its technical-organisational expressions in sport. People working and playing sport act rationally in the sense that they seek as far as possible to achieve specific goals with the maximal use of given capacities and means. It is in this that the 'economy' of their behaviour lies.

It seems to me that such an historical-sociological limitation of the concept of sport is necessary because, with the universalising application of the term to include past and present non-European systems of physical education and motor practice, an illegitimate ideological levelling of different cultural origins and foundations is presupposed. Hidden behind it is a form of Eurocentric thinking and a corresponding arrogance. By 'sport', then, I shall mean in what follows the European model of physical movement and behaviour, a model that is oriented towards the goals of physical education, development, health, higher achievement, leisure satisfaction, and so on. It stands in an ideological, though, of course, not exclusive, relationship with the development of the economic principles of our rationalistic culture.

Terminological Clarification

In German, the title 'Sport and the Economy' yields a double meaning. By 'the' economy, the social institution of the 'political economy' (*Volkswirtschaft*) is understood[3]. I am signifying terminologically with the term 'political economy', the cultural-historical process of appropriating nature for purposes of sustaining life and, beyond that, the expansion of individual and social existence. Within the concept of economy (*Ökonomie*), however, a further meaning is contained: It signifies a particular human attitude in terms of which methods of materially appropriating nature become raised into a principle of human life and differentially applied. I call this the 'economy principle' (*Ökonomieprinzip*).

Now, as far as the history of European economic behaviour compared with that of other cultures is concerned, there is something typical to be observed. The development of our economic forms and the application of the economy principle in that context has been increasingly subjected to the principle of rationality. We no longer leave the economy, whether as an action-context or as an attitude to life, simply to natural, spontaneous, and chance events but plan it more and more consistently with the help of causal thinking (the formal logic of mathematics and the natural sciences). Seen in this way, the 'economy' forms part of the idea of more calculating and technological planning as it is expressed in industrialism. In the European model of a rationalised economy, natural and unplanned forms of economic behaviour are being conquered but at the same time suppressed.

Sport and the Economy—A Sociological Theme

Various authors have already written in sociological publications on the question of the reciprocal relationship between sport and the economy[4]. I shall not repeat here the facts and relationships investigated by them. Rather, I shall give a short overview of what seem to me to be the most important thematic orientations. There has been a series of expositions on the mediation of sport and the economy via the social medium of generalised economic values[5]. Closely related to this line of analysis is the question of a specific economy of sport[6]. In both cases, the common core consists of a focus on the relationship between sport and work[7]. An empirical interlacing is assumed in this connection, which is expressed both in specific modes of sporting action and organisation and in the modelling of these according to economic principles and methods—for example, in the training technology of sport.

Closely connected with that is the sociological research interest in the description, classification, and explanation of sports-specific forms of professionalisation, especially in connection with their changes and adaptations as an occupational activity[8]. Another continuing theme consists of enquiring into the politico-economic interrelationships between the level of economic development of a society (measured by its gross national product) and the level of development of its so-called top-level sport in terms of the production of records and achievements, including the material and scientific preconditions for this. The higher the level of industrial productivity, the higher, as a rule, is the level of 'sports production'[9].

Another direct relationship between sport and the economy has been taken up in the sociology of sport through a concern with sports consumption. That has to be understood in two ways: First, as 'active' sports consumption (individuals and groups take up commercial sports offers in order to take part in sport themselves); second, they take part as spectators in spectacular sports performances[10]. Another structural relationship can be seen in the area of industrial or occupational sport. Here, too, a form of sports consumption can be identified that is satisfied by the occupationally organised offer of sport. At the same time in this connection, however, whether consciously or unconsciously an economic correlation is produced in such a way that human labour power can be regenerated via economic subsidy by the firm[11]. Seen from a sociopolitical point of view, many forms of sports activity contain such reproductive moments.

As studies of sports teams and sports associations have shown, the organised sports movement secures its existence economically by means of financial and other forms of payment from its members. In this way, the latter take on a supporting function and play a part in shaping a portion of the economy of sport[12]. Also pointing in the same direction are the other state and social institutions that contribute to the economic basis of sport (e.g., government, administration, political parties, foundations, sponsors).

In this introductory overview, I want to point out that, in relation to the theme of sport and the economy, there has been sociological research and the construction of sociological theories about which way these two spheres are structurally and functionally interrelated. If we sum up what has been discussed so far, it can be said that, on the one hand, organised sport produces its own economic basis and value-principles, and, on the other, partly because the use-interests of the economy are implicated in it, that it requires the economic basis of society at large to sustain and to develop it. In order to add to knowledge of the relationship between sport and the economy, we shall have to think through sociologically the correspondence and contradictions that arise in this connection.

SPORT, THE ECONOMY PRINCIPLE, AND THE ECONOMY

A many-faceted relationship exists between sport and economy. Developed sports have organised themselves in such a way that they have become factors within the larger economies in which they operate; consequently sport becomes an entity to be interacted with and to be acted upon by other portions of an 'external' economy. Sport, however, also contains an 'internal' or 'inner' economy in which elemental economic thinking influences how the sport itself is further developed and played. In this part of my essay, I shall explore the nature of sport's external and internal economies.

Sport and Its External Economic Basis

Sport is based upon economic principles in pragmatic and aesthetic ways. Pragmatically, sport must establish itself as a viable economic entity, often using its sportspeople and its spectators as a means of production and sustenance. Aesthetically, the nature of sporting games and competitions increasingly admits economically sound technologies and strategies in order to play out sports contests in the most productive manner possible.

On the Economic Organisation of Sport.   If the social forms of organised sport wish to adapt and survive in a society that conceives itself historically as an industrial and above all 'economic' one, they have to create their own economic base. That is because, seen in systems-theoretical terms, the part systems of an economic society can only realise their ideas and values to the extent that they are in a position to generate economic (i.e., material and financial) preconditions. In order to achieve this aim, the sports movement has introduced specific institutional models by means of which it becomes possible economically to control the systems-connection referred to. This can be illustrated with the example of the sports association and the sports club[13]. In the course of the sports history of European industrial societies, people interested in sport have themselves produced the economic conditions for the pursuit and administration of sport. Via their own economic efforts, they have provided the material and organisational preconditions for, for example, the building and financing of stadia, sports halls, etcetera and their technical requirements (sports equipment, special floor coverings, etc., the appointment of trainers and sports teachers, the setting-up of offices for administering the sport and coping with its ongoing economic transactions). It is a question here of creating sports-related and therefore also economic values and services, which doubtless leads to a situation where we can speak of 'rich' and 'poor' sports associations and sports clubs. Seen from a sports-economic standpoint, there are, connected with these distinctions, also distinctions that relate to the political and power relationships of clubs and associations[14].

The process of striving for a secure economic existence in the sports movement is distinguished by the fact that specific rules and methods can be isolated that prescribe and control the need for a thrifty approach to means and conditions. Following the economy-principle, which is generally adhered to, physical and material resources will be managed at any given time with a view to securing their optimal use. The association and club statutes will secure such management by means of precise rules regarding decision making and organisation, and selected designated representatives (experts) will see to it that the economic rules are adhered to[15]. In this context, a specialised body of knowledge has been formed that consists of a collection of models of sports-economic praxis. Such knowledge is based on the economy-principle and specifies the functional forms and ways of carrying out sports-economic action; for example, the rules governing economic cooperation between the different role players in a sports association. It reveals a series of possibilities regarding sports-economic performance. Probably the earliest form of such a relationship is where club and association[16] members pay a 'subscription'. In the meantime, an extensive catalogue of ways of subsidising sport have arisen: the performance and provision of voluntary work and services by participants in the organised sport; the provision of services by sports associations and sports clubs in the form, for example, of practice and training opportunities (sometimes these are available for unorganised sportspersons, too); sports spectators as paying participants (spectacular sport); contributions and irregular gifts from nonsporting institutions, mostly political or connected with the state (ministries, political parties, etc.); donations and bequests from persons, groups, institutions (patrons, sponsors); promotional initiatives (promotional associations, supporters' clubs, etc.); consumption earnings, for example, from entry charges levied on sports halls but increasingly also from shirt advertising and personal endorsements; and financially, income from radio and television broadcasts. That the sources by means of which organised sport is economically supported have become many sided can be seen generally in the nonstate areas of culture and leisure. A central aim of the methods enumerated here lies in the fact that, with successful economic stabilisation, the sports movement as a part social system is able to achieve a degree of cultural and political autonomy. Yet the more it falls economically into the clutches of political and economic interests, the smaller this autonomy becomes. The historical experiences of sports organisations confirm this relationship[17].

The Organised Sportsperson as an Economic Factor. I wish to return once more to the historical starting point at which the economic supporting of sport began and to describe more precisely the socioeconomic model of behaviour that has arisen in that connection. We can start from the fact the people (groups) interested in sport make the decision to participate in regulated sport. They understandably seek to realise this goal through existing models of cultural and social organisation, which cannot in any case be established without economic preconditions; not, at any rate, as formal structures. Two real possibilities offer themselves to the initiate in this situation. In the one case, no opportunities for organised sport can be found. In order to satisfy his/her expressed interest under these conditions, only one solution is possible—to create the conditions necessary for sports-participation themselves. They have to found a sports club (or else some analogous social form) and support it economically by financial contributions as well as by voluntary organisational work and services. In the other case, people interested in sport find communal, commercial, or associationally promoted sports opportunities and participate in them as paying consumers or club members. We can therefore establish that, in the historical framework of western industrial societies, the purposive accomplishment of individual and group interests in this sphere has led to the development on a political and economic basis of club and associated forms. To wish to take part in organised sport, therefore, always necessarily involves the simultaneous production of an economic performance. The people interested in sport and the demand for sport are involved in an exchange relationship that, besides its formal and normative framework, is originally and fundamentally based on a direct human decision. This relationship points to both its subjective and objective sides. Such an exchange relationship in no way exclusively constitutes a form of utilitarianism but equally involves motives of social contact, emotional needs for movement, and so on, which push the production of economic performances into the background[18].

The exchange relationship between sports-practitioners and organised sport can be conceptualised as part of an 'inner economy'; it consists, besides its 'monetary moment', of specific kinds of so-called 'honorific' activities. Even these contain economic aspects, though they are not always intended. Similar to the amateur principle of active sports involvement, there is a principle of voluntary and unpaid participation in the organisational and educational areas of sport. Sports functionaries carry out various administrative tasks; sports teachers and trainers help to raise the level of sporting achievement; club members undertake maintenance and repair work. On the basis of such honorifically provided services, the sports movement guarantees the economic preconditions of its organisational effectiveness. Beyond this can be mentioned such productive labour services as the building of a club house, a sports hall, the manufacture of sports equipment, and so on, which are likewise produced voluntarily and without financial reward. In the former West Germany, empirical findings show that, without these economic performances, organised sport would hardly be realisable in its existing social form[19]. Summarising, we can conclude that ideally based motives for action produce internal economic effects; to put it another way, people who practise sport become in a direct way the economic subjects of sport.

Sports Spectatorship as Economic Behaviour. Without defining themselves as sports participants in a formal sense, sports spectators take on a direct economic function as supporters of sport. This role has a political as well as a cultural-historical past, whether in the form of mass psychological demonstrations of political power, in its social psychological effects on the motives of sporting actors, or in its influence on the construction of rules regarding tension-producing sports situations. It is further implicated in the production of a significant reciprocal sports-economic effect: As we have seen, the organisation of sport gives rise to material costs. I have already described some methods of meeting these costs. Another way consists of staging sports competitions in a manner similar to theatrical productions and of getting paying customers to visit them. The entrance monies raised flow into the coffers of the organisers and serve both to pay the expenses that have arisen and to produce a profit. To this degree, sports spectators take on a function of economically reproducing sport. The material security of top-level amateur and professional sport in particular depend, among other things, on the numbers of paying spectators they attract. The voyeuristic motives of the sports public, it is reasonable to suppose, lie less in this reproduction relationship than they do in needs and interests, the psychical and social genesis of which need not concern us here.

The 'Economised World' of Sports Practice. The sportspersons do not only enter an 'economised' field of experience and action; at the same time, they create it for themselves. The 'world' of sport in many of its aesthetic aspects resembles a material expression of economic principles[20]. In order to underpin this thesis, two specific historical characteristics of the sports movement in industrial societies have to be kept in mind, namely its orientation towards competition and records. From these two attitudes, a form of sporting rationality has developed that consists in the fact that at least two persons or teams stand in competitive opposition to each other in order to reach a common aim. It is a question, for example, of obtaining more goals, points, seconds, metres, etcetera than one's opponents, or of securing as high a number of goals, points, metres as possible or in the shortest possible time. In order to realise this aim, sport has invented its own economy, that is to say, economising, results-optimising ways of behaving, together with the appropriate material and social conditions. At the centre of such endeavours stand such considerations as: how one can measure, evaluate and compare performances, records and competitions; how one can standardise their preconditions and effect the production of them. From this, there arises consequentially a sports-economic logic and a variety of attempts at developing an effective material and formal framework for achieving this. Let us look at some examples.

Standardised systems of evaluation and measurement facilitate the objective establishment and comparison of sports performances; for example, 'centimetres' and 'metres' for distances travelled, 'seconds' and 'minutes' for times conquered, 'grams' and 'kilograms' for weights lifted, 'points' for movements compared with ideal-typical movement-patterns, 'goals' for achieving aims, and so on. Performances measured in this way are scaled (sequences, tables, record lists) and thereby made checkable and communicable at any time. Particular rules of competition and evaluation specify times and determine the methods of measurement to be used (e.g., the number of rounds and their duration in boxing, the formulae for measuring the long jump). We can also characterise these facts through the concept of the standardisation of sporting action. It facilitates, among other things, the achievement of the goal of economising time and effort in the practice and organisation of sport. It would be a waste of time to measure each performance by arbitrary, different, and always newly defined evaluative procedures. Economically and socially facilitating standardisation of that type comes very clearly and graphically into our field of vision through standardised race tracks, sports equipment, lines of playing fields, heights of hall roofs, prescribed forms of surface, and so on. With such standardisation, which is heading finally to the universalisation of the action-situations of sport, there goes hand in hand a kind of economising technisation of the material conditions of sport. Industrial innovations and developments are taken up by or initiated in sport, for example the sports-related application of plastics, measuring instruments, the increasing technisations of sports equipment, sports halls, and sports arenas. The pole vault can illustrate what I mean. Through the construction and use of a highly elastic plastic pole, not only can the power released by the vaulter be more effectively used but, at the same time, the catapulting power of the bent pole. The process of pole-vaulting has been economised.

For some time now, models of sports-learning and training have shown similar regularities and effects. No longer do roundabout methods count as worth striving for in sports pedagogy but, on the contrary, the rational, time-saving, learning- and training-intensive and therefore successful way. Methods of motor, cognitive, and psychosocial conditioning dominate the new sports-praxis[21]. While traditional movement education used to be oriented towards a 'holistic' and fantasy-ridden way of looking at activity in physical education, sport today is pursued by means of increasing specialisation and objectification following an ideal of economised learning and behaving. It means, within given temporal and psychophysical preconditions, striving to produce a maximal level of sporting skill and performance.

The Foundations of the Economy of Amateurism.   The world of sport does not only appear externally as economised behaviour but, in this sense, it influences the people taking part the longer and more persistently they engage in it. We can clarify this putative relationship through the role of the amateur in top-level sport[22]. Bound up with the rationalised demand in industrial societies for improving performance and the breaking of records there are constantly rising costs for the organisation and realisation of sporting goals[23]. In order to produce high-level sports performances, the sports-practitioner has to intensify his/her training and take part in a large number of qualifying competitions. Besides this, he/she has to spend money on sports equipment and sports clothes, save for long-distance travel, hotel accommodation, and so on. That has a number of consequences: high time, material, and financial expenses (i.e., economic costs), which also have to be 'paid for' psychically and physically. For that, sports-economic solutions are necessary; for example, indirect financial gifts (educational assistance, stipendia, release from occupational duties, etc.) or direct, illegal ('sham' amateur) monetary and material payments (money or material prizes, honoraria, endorsements, income, etc.). We can conclude from the relationships described that the development (under the conditions of an industrial society) of a form of sport that is ideologically defined as 'playful' and 'nonmaterial' has economic effects as a consequence. The practice of sport under such conditions is transformed into a kind of double existential struggle: on the one hand for the production of sporting achievements and records and on the other for the reproduction of the economic conditions necessary for sustaining human life. Both struggles stand in an interrelationship and condition one another mutually; without sporting success, no material security. In Germany, for example, the financial payments to top amateur sportspersons are lowered or even discontinued when strictly defined levels of achievement ('norms') are not met. In this regard, amateur and professional sport are becoming structurally closer and closer.

I now come to my first thesis: The sports movement, formed under the conditions of an industrial market society by people with an interest in and who practise sport, is organisationally based on economic principles and its own economic products. There arise the forms of an internal economy of sport. Through standardised and technicised forms of appearance, and through the application of economic models, the world of sport reveals itself as an economised field of experience and action. I call these characteristics the structures of an 'external' economy of sport because they are of a more formal and factual kind.

The 'Inner' Economy of Sport

Let us recall the example of the economisation of the learning of and training for sport. It is not only the case that learning and training processes in sport are growing more intensive, accelerated, and rational in their forms but also that they have consequences for socialisation. There arise processes of internalising (sport-) economic patterns of behaviour.

On the Physical- and Movement-Economy of Sport.   What the type of sporting bodily movement characteristic of industrial societies signifies is an increasing formalisation that is manifested paradigmatically in sports-specific movement 'techniques' and 'tactics'. Based on the European machine model[24] of the human being, the movement of the body in sport is investigated from a biomechanical standpoint and explained in terms of biomechanical laws. A thrusting movement of the arm appears in sports understanding as a self-closing and self-opening hinge, consisting of two levers (laws of leverage). The bodily extremities, trunk, and head, all the parts of the body in their motor coordination form a self-moving or moving system that behaves rationally. Movements thus result in optimal performance (lifting a weight, executing a balanced movement, throwing a ball, etc.) when, in the context of the sporting goal to be reached (moving fast, jumping as high as possible), the causal laws of bodily physics are followed, producing a form of movement-economy. This pattern does not only hold for the single bodily movement in sport and the individual human body but also for collective play. In the sport-games, tactics are developed that are like spatiotemporal planning models. Here, it is a question of reaching a game-specific goal (goal, basket, finishing point, etc.) with the greatest economy of effort, that is, by the 'shortest route', and more successfully than the opposing team. On this basis, every player, every team reflects on how they can cooperate rationally. Game-tactics are drafted and (to the extent that the opponents permit it), collectively tested in offensive and defensive game-situations. In sports-tactical behaviour we encounter a model of 'social economy' in which the most successful spatiotemporal organisations of bodies make a decisive difference. Over time and in its general application, this model, a declared goal of sports-praxis, becomes internalised and optimalised as a type of action so that one can speak of effort- and time-saving sports techniques and tactics.

The Consciousness of Sport as 'Economised' Knowledge.   The techniques and tactics of bodily movement applied at any given time do not remain simply an internalised economy of practical behaviour, that is, expressed in actual movement, but further lead with people who pursue sports to the foundation of a deeper-lying consciousness of movement. To the extent that clear ideas of movement have been physiologically imprinted, sporting body movements become thought of and anticipated as technical and tactical images in connection with the purposively rational (*zweckrational*) setting of goals; that means correspondingly expected and judged in one's own performance as well as that of others. Just as with motor techniques in the fields of handicraft and industrial work, we encounter in sport highly formalised ideas of movement, perhaps concerning whether a movement is 'right' or 'wrong'. The rightness or wrongness of a sporting movement has its deeper foundation, not in some aesthetic idea, but in the idea that a sporting movement can only be right when it is executed economically in terms of the defined goals. Bodily movements that are time-wasting, fanciful, or conducive to losing are prohibited on that account and, in practice situations and competitions, even negatively sanctioned. Imagine the judgment that would be passed on a runner who, while running, turns completely round, runs a few metres backward, and then remains temporarily at a standstill. In terms of successful goal-achievement (time-reduction), he/she is behaving 'uneconomically' and uneconomic movements in sport are the 'wrong' ones to the extent that achievement-orientation dominates.

My second thesis is: There is in sport, besides an 'external' economy, an 'inner' economy—though the boundary between the two is empirically fluid. This inner economy manifests itself in movement techniques and tactics, and in their internalisation as rationalised movement-consciousness. In sport—viewed historically—a model of the 'economic body' characteristic of an industrial society has arisen: People who practise sport communicate the generally adhered to economy principle in the form of sports-specific movement and bodily knowledge[25].

Economic Interests and Sport

The economy of an industrial society follows the maxim of increasing material growth. Correspondingly, it involves a continuous search for commercialisable social areas, which are developed as markets through the awakening and enlarging of needs with a view to realising economic gains. If, at one time, this strategy was pursued in sectors of necessary consumption, today less necessary areas such as, for example, 'leisure' and entertainment are being laid claim to. We speak, significantly, of the leisure and entertainment 'industry' and it is an industry into the economic relationships of which the organised sports movement is integrated.

The Economy Discovers the Utility of Sports.   The preliminary remarks above do not refer to a chance or contingent relationship but to the fact that particular branches of the industrial economy have discovered sport—both its practice and organisation—as a vehicle for their economic aims. In the course of the last 30 years they have (particularly in Western Europe and North America) created a sports-related market with gradually increasing 'sports consumption'[26]. With such a practical aim in mind, the sports goods industry produces sports equipment and sports clothes. Special industries produce measuring instruments for the objectification of sports performances. Building concerns, with the help of industrial and standardised construction methods, erect stadia and sports halls. Commercial service firms offer a variety of sport courses with different themes such as 'sport holidays' that are spent in specially erected 'sports centres'[27]. In short, the field of possible sports activities with all its material and organisational preconditions has been 'marketised'. With continuing development, one can observe a refinement of the methods used. That is, not only are sports goods produced and sold but, at the same time, publicity for the producer is obtained. Symbols on sports clothes signify to the onlooker that they were produced by a particular firm; measuring instruments disclose on television the trademarks of their producers; so-called ribbon advertising and mobile advertising in sports halls and stadia convey to the consumer sports goods that he or she might use; professional and amateur sportspersons advertise the trademarks of their sponsors on their sports gear.

Although the publicity methods described here emanate primarily from industry, nevertheless a mutuality of interests can be discerned. Industry produces sports goods along with other aids and equipment for the practice of sport and, at the same time, advertises these products in the market. On the other hand, the idea of involvement in sport is spread through industrial products and advertising, and not only that: Organised sport, as a carrier of industrial advertising—not only for sports goods—receives financial and material contributions to the 'sports industry'[28].

It is possible to find out, at any rate indirectly, about the direct reciprocal relationships between the economy and sport, especially those that take the form of propagandistic expressions on an ideological level. Thus, both sports and economic functionaries in industrialised societies maintain that there is a cause and effect relationship between productive success in the economy and in sport. Generalised, this means that the most productively efficient societies should be the most highly 'developed' in respect of cultural values! This self-estimation hardly stands up to strict examination. To return, however, to the central theme: Economic and sporting achievements have been brought into a symbolic political-economic relationship. This ideological standpoint is not unfounded. I pointed at the beginning[29] to the accepted correlation between gross national product and success in international sport. According to this, there is an obvious economic foundation for the production of sporting achievements and records. How seriously this thesis is taken is shown by the financial investment in top-level sport that is commonly undertaken today by the state and economic institutions. Both are engaged in a form of sports-economic investment politics[30].

Sport as Show Business. Sports activities are other-directed. They seek and need spectators—even in the case of informal sports groups and at the lowest levels of sporting achievement. There are many reasons for this. One is that sports activity involves an element of external comparison and measurement of bodily measurement; in other words, it facilitates valorisation through 'visible' motor expression. Sporting achievements are also admired, by their producers as well as spectators. Historically, a trend towards spectacular presentation and sensation in sport has spread. The signs of this may arise by chance but they can also be planned for and staged just as in the theatre or the circus. This task is being taken over today, on the one hand by the institutions of organised sport (sports associations, clubs, etc.) and, on the other—as is highly developed in the United States—by commercial spectator sports enterprises and other sections of the leisure and entertainments industry. That costs money but it is also possible to earn money in this way. Attractive and qualified 'show-sport' persons receive wages for their performance. The spectators pay entrance money. Likewise, funds flow into the coffers of the promoters. If their economic calculations are correct and their income exceeds their costs, they skim off the profits. In commercialised spectator sport, we find a practical model of economically valorised sport. It is a model that, nevertheless, cannot be understood solely from that standpoint.

Professionalisation in Sport.   If we look at the material introduced so far, it is clear that representation of an important aspect of economised sport is lacking, namely the professionalisation of its organisers and occupational actors. The latter can be counted as so-called 'professionals' because they earn a living from sports-performances. The degree of this professionalisation increases with the degree to which sport can be commercialised, but it is also dependent on its consumption—or spectacular value—and is subject to the market economic mechanisms of supply and demand. Similar relationships can be supposed for the organisers and promoters of sport. With the trend towards institutional enlargement and growing complexity that goes hand in hand with the economisation of organised sport, the need arises for qualified experts, functionaries, managers, trainers, and sports teachers. This expertise can only grow in a market society when it is freely applicable to sports-related activities and is thereby able to compete for material conditions of existence. That happens, at least with the quantitative growth of leisure (leisure-management as an occupation). In the process of becoming professionalised, the two functional groups referred to represent an exemplary personalisation of sports-economic relationships. They are 'professionalised sportspersons' and act as the elite of a special sector of the leisure and entertainment industry.

My third thesis is: Some sectors in the economy of an industrial society discover and develop sport as a specific market in which sports-related products and services can be bought and sold. The advertising of products and services via sport, commercialised spectator sport, and the opening-up of formal sport as an occupational sphere permit the establishment of a kind of 'sports industry', which creates economic advantages for both the economy and sport. This mutual economic effect is not specific to sport alone but holds for wide areas of socialised leisure and entertainment.

ATTEMPT AT A THEORETICAL SYNTHESIS: SPORT, THE ECONOMY PRINCIPLE, AND THE ECONOMY

I have tried in the first two parts of this essay to describe factual connections that characterise the relationship between sport and the economy—perhaps not in complete detail but nevertheless paradigmatically. In the next part, it is a question of bringing these factual relationships together in a theory that presents a scientific programme of conceivable sociological research into the area of 'sport and the economy'.

Sport in Industrial Societies: A Model of Some Correlations

From the discussion up to now, a number of functional relationships can be worked out. People who are interested in sport wish to take part in it. For that, special organisational preconditions are required and created in the social form of sports associations and sports clubs. The pursuit of active sport would hardly be possible without a material, technical, and personnel base. We can also say that the rationally organised industrial societies of Europe have separated practically all human activities into types that are consigned to their own spatiotemporal spheres. Describing it from the standpoint of socially defined conditions, that is the case with the pursuit of sport. Such conditions have to be worked for, since they are not forthcoming as 'natural' givens. Once they are produced, their material and organisational maintenance has to be secured and, with growing needs, enlarged upon and differentiated. People with an interest in sport seek in this connection for practical principles and methods for realising their sporting goals. Since their means and power are limited, they devise economic ways for reaching and consolidating these goals and preconditions. But, within the historical framework of European economic forms, that can only mean handling themselves, with the given financial (capital) and direct services (work), in such a way that optimal and need-satisfying conditions for the pursuit of sport can be created. The results of such efforts manifest themselves in a practical 'economy of sports'. It consists basically in the fact that sportspersons produce their own financial means and services and, beyond that, realise income from the sale and arrangement of sports-performances, programmes, and so on. In addition, all 'costs' as well as 'gains' are administered according to the economic rules of 'running a business'. Knowledge of this kind and of the methods used gives rise to a model of the economic behaviour that is typical of sport and, with rising expectations regarding the shape that organised sport should take, it undergoes a further differentiation[31].

As we have seen, the sports movement is implicated in a reciprocal cause and effect relationship with the general political economy. It is involved in mutual relations with it and uses it materially, technically, methodologically, and even ideologically. In this respect, a reverse direction of use and valorisation has arisen: Specific industrial sectors discover and build up sport as a market, use it as a publicity medium, buy professional spectator sports enterprises in order, themselves, to produce spectacular sports performances and obtain financial returns. In this case, economic rules and methods are consistently applied: To make a profit means further investment; to sustain a loss means sale of the sports enterprise, including its employees. Finally, today, even traditional sports clubs act according to this law to the extent that they are commercially active in spectator and professional sport.

Each of the two models of economic behaviour introduced above links the 'economy principle' of industrial societies ideologically with the western 'rationality principle'. The latter demands from us an attitude that should possibly lead to the optimisation of behaviour. The principle holds here that a given potential has to be aligned with the goal of maximal effect. An offence against it constitutes 'irrational' behaviour. So, in this sense, not only is the uneconomic running of a sports club or association negatively valued but also the poor play of a footballer, the inefficacy of a training programme, or a laborious and clumsy movement in the context of a sport. Historically, the industrial economy-*qua* rationality-principle that is realised in sport finds its normative expression above all in the orientation towards competition and achievement, in the reciprocal attitude of always having to outdo the other. That leads necessarily to what we call today the ideology of 'economic growth'.

My fourth thesis is: The 'megaeconomy' of the economy and sport obeys the rationality principle of an industrial society. It leads to a one-sided understanding of economic behaviour (capitalism). The characteristic moment of the 'economic' (household maintenance) is ideologically foreshortened into the formula of maximising 'rational' behaviour and results.

Sociological Levels and Perspectives on an Economy of Sport

In the next step of our reflection, we take up again the categories introduced earlier of an 'external' and an 'internal' or 'inner' economy of sport. By 'external' economy of sport, I understand the historical-social development and institutionalisation of sports-specific forms of economic behaviour: ways of running businesses in organised sport; models of cooperation with specific industrial sectors (including commercial advertising, mass media) as a mutual exchange of interests and material goods; the discovery and practice of patterns of physical movement as rationalised models of motor behaviour; the undertaking of professionalised economic roles by sports experts; the collection and application of sports-economic knowledge in the form of the pragmatic rules of experience (everyday theories) and legal principles (statutes) of a formal sports business. We should not understand these forms exclusively as things that are socially pregiven and objective. Behind them people interested in sport are working as 'economic subjects' with their material expenditures and voluntary or paid labour services. These examples may help to clarify the concept of an external economy of sport, though it seems to me that it has not yet been sufficiently explained. That is the task of our next step. It is possible to locate conventions regarding sports behaviour through which, with the help of the principles and methods of the rationality principle, the ideas and praxis of sport are influenced and provided with the formal framework and conditions for sports behaviour. It is a question of the purposively rational (*zweckrational*) coordination of interests and actions with the aim of generally optimising both them and the conditions for their maximal realisation. We can also speak of the economised transformation of sports-related experiences, which, in the last instance, are conjoined with learnable techniques of behaviour. One can manage them, use them, and shape them into such social forms as sports association, sports clubs, professional sports, and so on but also as rationalised physical and movement techniques. This is revealed very clearly in the human-machine models of shot putting and weight lifting. The level of the economy of sport reflected in all this appears above all as an external and observable form. It manifests itself as a 'social fact'[32].

Nevertheless, it does not exist simply as an external appearance: The 'external' economy of sport is also connected with an 'inner' economy. Take the example of motor learning in sport. To wish to pursue a sport actively has as its precondition the learning of sports techniques and tactics that—as has been described—represent economised patterns of movement. These techniques and tactics ('nominal values' in the language of cybernetics) are internalised and made automatic by the learner in the course of an assimilation process. He/she learns specific types of movement and, at the same time, the fact that, as 'sporting' physical movements, they fulfill the purpose of realising defined aims such as shooting at goal in football, hanging from the vertical bar, throwing the javelin in the most time- and effort-saving manner possible. As learning and experience progress, there can occur what we might call an internalised economy of bodily movements. A whole series of further examples could be cited in order to underpin this—for example, the organisation of a sports club, the conception of a training system, the planning of competitions. If only from the standpoint of a particular social perspective, people learn and internalise rules of economic behaviour even in the context of such sport-related activities. Nevertheless, further precision is still necessary: The economic rules and methods encountered in the social exchanges of sport are not something abstract but are, rather, primarily grasped as 'sport-specific' ('unique', 'characteristic'), that is, probably no longer seen or understood in their structural correspondence to the industrial or general economy. That is what is meant by the concept of an 'inner' economy of sport.

The fact that the internalisation of the economic dimension of sport is mainly externally caused should not be mistaken for or lead to the deduction of the idea that there exists a complete external correspondence. We may all be collectively subjected to economic constraints but nevertheless we remain capable of transcending such socially pregiven facts in our ideas and we can draw up and anticipate counter-models. Accordingly, the internalised structure of the sports economy can be reflected on and changed by the people concerned. Even more: The people who practise sport make sporting 'discoveries' that can easily be expressed in technical terms ('Fosbury flop', 'Ali shuffle', etc.). To that extent, the external and internal economies of sport can hardly be separated empirically[33]. Nevertheless, such a separation seems to me to be analytically meaningful because, with its help, greater clarity over the connections between the subjective and objective levels and effects of the sport-specific economy can be obtained. Up to now, to my knowledge, the subject of sport and the economy has been handled too economistically and sociologistically, that is, centrally as an external form or else as a formal structural model. It is my intention to counter this with the reflections articulated here.

My fifth thesis is: The practical transposition and development of the economy-*qua* rationality-principle of industrial societies in organised sport yields, looked at analytically, two levels: an outer level, rather in the sense of an objectified and formal-technical economy; and an inner level, or rather, a psychic and social economy. Empirically the two dimensions are not separate: They condition one another mutually. They form a particular kind of 'economic aesthetics' of sport in such a way that specific moments of sport and physical movement can be meaningfully experienced and thought of as a syndrome comprising such qualities as: economizing of space, time, and effort; economic; lucrative; optimizing/maximizing; and purposively rational (*zweckrational*)[34].

Sport and the Economy: A Qualitative Comparison

I have tried to describe and analyse some of the interrelations between sport, the economy principle, and the economy. The qualitative moments of so-called economic rationality involved in this, however, have so far been neglected. An enquiry into them forms the last step of this investigation.

The Ideological Contraction of the Concept of the Economy and the Economy Principle in Sport.   At the beginning, I defined political 'economy' (*Wirtschaft*) as the social appropriation of nature for purposes of sustaining existence, and 'economy' (*Ökonomie*) as an effort-conserving, thrifty method of appropriating nature. What has followed from this in the historical phase of industrial-social development? The motive of self-preservation has remained: The fusion of the economy principle and the rationality principle in European history has led to a logic of unlimited growth (capitalism). On the one hand, creative and productive consequences make their appearance, for example a general rise in standards of material comfort, technical discoveries (even though, geopolitically, they are not equally shared) and on the other, harmful results such as an increasingly destructive exploitation of natural resources and human beings themselves. Economic and rational action are visibly endangering our existential base. The mistake, however, is not that we act economically but rather that we one-sidedly limit our economic understanding, our practical application of the economy principle; that is, we align it exclusively towards continual economic growth. The essential moment of the 'economic' ('household maintenance') is forgotten and abandoned. 'Economy' in its moral and ethical sense means the maintenance and development of the conditions for existence, not, however, their destruction[35].

Such considerations can also be applied to and thought through in respect of formal sport. Doubtless, the economic organisation of sport does not destroy its own existential preconditions. On the contrary, it facilitates the achievement of sporting goals and ideals. However, in its direct interlocking with economic interests and sectors one can find tendencies that at least influence the ideal and social conditions of the sports movement in a dangerous or change-provoking way. With financial dependence on industrial sponsors and advertising revenues[36], sports clubs, for example, become subjected to a one-sided economic logic: Only when they sustain or improve their sporting performances are they able to remain in business with their economic partners. However, 'relegation' from the highest level of sports competition (league) has as its consequence the withdrawal of commercial advertising contracts. This and comparable examples, nevertheless, do not seem to me to be the central problem in relation to economic development but rather the uncompromising internalisation of the economy or rationality principle in sport. In professional and top-level amateur sport this leads, as has been shown, to an inhuman logic of maximising records and achievements under the dictates of which neither biological nor psychological manipulations have so far been discouraged. In this way, however, the psychophysical and social conditions of life are endangered if not perhaps wholly destroyed[37]. Beyond that, it has been known for some time that, with uncontrolled and overly achievement-oriented mass participation, physical injuries including fatal heart attacks have in some cases already occurred. That can be related to the ideological absolutism of the model of top-level sport. Even the mass sportsperson orientates him/herself normatively to that model and develops his/her sports-related attitudes and values in that context. I am describing with this observation an economic development in specific areas of the sports movement but not its empirical totality. That is because more complex tendencies can be identified right up to the possibility of life-enhancing individuation or socialisation. I have only intended to clarify the problem of the internalisation of one-sided and life-endangering rationalistic value-orientations in sport.

We can also seek to illuminate this problem area in the following way. The person who engages in sport is the economic subject of sport and remains such, together with being the economic subject of an industrial society. He/she initiates transactions and is subject to the process of economic enculturation in which he/she learns to behave economically[38]. The *homo economicus* pursues, among other things, sport. Why should he/she behave there uneconomically? The socially accepted model of acting and thinking economically is given a generalised but at the same time modified application in sport. Structurally, it works differently in different areas of human activity.

Towards 'Another' Economy of Sport.   It remains to be shown that economic praxis and realisation of the economy principle in sport produce specific forms and methods. Sectors of the economy use sport in order to realise their interests and, in that way, influence structural developments in the realm of sport. Nevertheless, the complexity of sport can in no way be explained exclusively in economic terms. On the contrary, many observable forms of sports behaviour and organisation rest upon other causal moments. How else can one explain that a cyclist in training brakes at the bottom of a hill and loses his momentum in order then to be able to attack the next hill with greater power[39]? On the one hand, we can assume in this case the economy of a training plan and on the other, for example, joy in putting strain on and testing the body. With this example, it becomes clear that uneconomic behaviour is also possible in sport. It would certainly be possible to find similar examples in the organisation of sport, its methods, and its normal praxis.

It is nevertheless worth reflecting on the fact that the present development of formal sport bears witness to an economistic trend that even—as has already been shown—brings sport-reducing (or -destroying) consequences in its train. In its broader workings, this trend gives rise to a critique of sport from the standpoint of its effectiveness, as well as its material and nonmaterial gains. In this, the rationalistic encroachment of the economy principle that was mentioned earlier is reflected. However, against all this, in so-called 'free-time' activities, the search for and testing of an 'alternative' economy should be offered. By that, I understand a sports praxis that includes various possibilities of appropriating and developing physical move-ments, perceptions of the body, and bodily knowledge, together with, based on all that, the construction of psychically and socially sensible forms of interhuman relationships. For me, such an 'economy of sport' means conducting ourselves economically in such a way that we learn to experience our bodies meaningfully as an 'economic' precondition of sporting and above all human action in its many-sidedness. In its social aspects, it means pursuing sport not only as an achievement-orientated and competitive activity but openly and, above all, in a mutually enhancing way. That demands a regaining and further development of a long-known form of human sport—think for a moment of the utopian unity of work and play[40]. I shall illustrate these programmatic statements by means of two examples. Sports running, which is today widespread through personal initiative (e.g., jogging), is pursued less in conjunction with the purposively rational (*zweckrational*) goal of improving bodily performance, of comparison, of (personal) records, and supported by special training methods, machines, and laboratory tests, but primarily for the rediscovery of meaningful bodily capacities whose formation is increasingly hampered by civi-lisational developments[41]. Running through woods, over fields, and through towns (except through traffic and smog); collecting impressions and digesting them in-wardly (e.g., reactions to different types of surface, changes of motor-coordination with tiredness, forms of breathing), getting to know and appreciate the biological constitution of one's own body and to influence it according to one's own require-ments. It is a question here of the discovery of 'my' or else 'our' economy of running. In this, there exists yet another economy of running, that is, sport pure and simple. Or, as anticipated through the example of the economy of learning sport: no longer learning exclusively in terms of the rationality principle but equally via detours, methods found and tested by oneself in a free unfolding of meaningful and social experiences with the aim of overcoming the monofunctional industrial socialisation of the human body.

My sixth thesis: Sport and the economy are mutually interrelated. Both are characterised by peculiarities but also by correspondences that become clear espe-cially in the practical application of the economy cum rationality principle. The alternative proposed by me does not demand a sport without economic ideas and foundations but rather the sketching out and testing of an ecologically grounded economy of sport. Only by means of an open theory and praxis of progressive economies in many social spheres can the dominant, life-threatening economy of the industrial social system be overcome.

CONCLUSION

It is not news that current events proceed much more rapidly than books. In the interval between this chapter's original submission and its publication (see the editor's postscript), both sport and economics have continued to change. However, I have not found it necessary to update my text because the cultural and social interaction between sport and economy has not turned to another direction. Indeed has become more economised than ever. The economic basis has spread out, and it affects structural and functional consequences for the evolution of sport. At present, I would say sport has reached an advanced stage of external economisation. The 'old' sport disappears and a 'new' sport is born. All sports—fun or serious, low or top level, amateur or professional—are being transformed into big business in an increasingly commercial market. Active and receptive participation in sport means nowadays to consume sport. The classic sport values are converted into economically influenced values. I define this as a change from sport to sportindustry. The sociology of sport should observe, investigate, and reflect upon this described process and its consequences, one of which could be a future of totally commercialised sport. The central ideas and aims of sport then will be functionalised by an external system. Sport will lose its specific and autonomous status as a self-grounded and self-referring cultural and social praxis. An authentic human activity will perhaps be integrated into mechanisms of the capitalist economy[42]. I do not hope so—but we will see!

NOTES

1. For the process of rationalisation in European cultural history and its psychological and social effects, see, above all, M. Weber (1964) and N. Elias (1976).
2. Cf. here, e.g., H. Eichberg (1973, esp. 89-140).
3. Another meaning of the concept of economy (*Ökonomie*) is the study of political economy or else the scientific theory of the economy.
4. On the general and particular aspects of our theme, see: R. Andreano (1970, 164-174); T. Dytschewa (1964, 20-33); H. Edwards (1973, 273-316); B. Gilbert (1970, 175-186); S. Güldenpfennig (1974, 11-59); J. Habermas (1970, 56-74); K. Heinemann (1984); P. Hoch (1976, 42-51); R.G. Kraus (1970, 187-198); H. Lüdtke (1972, 23-47); J. McMurtry (1976, 51-56); O. Model (1955); T.J. Murray (1970, 157-163); W.C. Neale (1975, 204-219); A.D. Novikov and M. Maksumenko (1972, 156-167); F.R. Pfetsch et al. (1975); A. Wohl (1973).
5. Here it is a question principally of economic socialisation into sport. Cf. B. Rigauer (1969; 1972, 60-74; 1979) and K. Rittner (1976).
6. On the specific economy of sport, see e.g., H. Lüdtke (1972, 23-47); O. Model (1955); P.W.C. Neale (1975, 204-219).
7. See note 5. See also S. Güldenpfennig (1974, 11-59); J. Habermas (1970, 56-64); H. Plessner (1966, 18-32).
8. To my knowledge, no comprehensive theory of sports professionalism has yet been constructed, only some approximations, e.g., H. Edwards (1973, 273-316); G. Hortleder (1974, 9-55); W.C. Neale (1975, 204-219); P. Weiss (1973, 192-211); and A. Wohl (1973, 166-172).
9. See A.D. Novikov and M. Maksumenko (1970, 156-167). The investigation by F.R. Pfetsch et al. goes into this relationship in great detail. In their empirical research, France, the former German Democratic Republic, and the 'old' German Federal Republic are compared.
10. A general theory relating to the problem area of sports consumption is, so far as I know, lacking. Some aspects have been looked into by, e.g., G. Eichler (1972, 47-59); P. Hoch (1976, 42-51); G. Hortleder (1974, 55-104; 1978, 57-92); R.G. Kraus (1970, 187-198); H. Lüdtke (1972, 23-47); J. McMurtry (1976, 51-56); H. Meyer (1973, 59-78); and B. Rigauer (1979, 95-105).

11. On the politico-economic value-relations between sport and the reproduction of labour power, see S. Guldenpfennig (1974, 11-59; 1978, 64-204).

12. On the economic situation and organization of sports associations in the former West Germany, see the still most-relevant research of W. Timm (1979, 133-146).

13. The concepts 'sports association' (*Sportverband*) and 'sports club' (*Sportverein*) are used here paradigmatically and are terminologically equivalent to the organisational forms of sport in countries outside the German-speaking area (e.g., sports club, committee, federation, association, etc.).

14. These are national and international level sports organisations, which, on account of their economic potential, assume a high political status. It is a question mainly of associations that administer popular sport-forms—e.g., in Europe and South America, football (soccer); in North America, baseball, basketball, American football, ice-hockey. Most are sport-games rather than individual forms of sport, with the exception of sports that involve competition between two persons. (Two-person sports played with a ball, e.g., tennis and table tennis, are sport-games. The author was thinking here of sports such as boxing, wrestling, and judo. Eds.)

15. In the traditional type of German association and club, one can distinguish between the plenary session as legislature, the board of directors (president, directors, section leaders, etc.), as well as the whole association/club and its part-units (sections, divisions, etc.) and finally the specialist advisers (experts). The economy of a sport, too, to the extent that it is responsible for formal tasks, is organised according to this democratic, self-ruling model.

16. In the German forms of association there are in terms of civil law both 'natural' and 'legal' members. The latter are separated from the former and treated legally as abstract persons.

17. The loss spoken of here, and also the unperceived autonomy or the autonomy asserted against better judgement, is clear in the political and economic utilisation of professional sport and the Olympics. See, e.g., H. Harder (1970); U. Prokop (1971); and H.J. Winkler (1972); up-to-date: V. Simson and A. Jennings (1992).

18. On the sports-specific need- and motivation-structure of members of West German sports associations, see K. Schlagenlauf (1977, 57-184); G. Pilz.

19. Without this form of voluntary service the economic basis of sport would be endangered. That is true at least for the type of organisation of sport in the former West Germany. See W. Timm (1979, 159-60).

20. That is not a peculiarity of the 'sports world' alone but can be established for other social spheres as well. At any rate, the 'economisability' of an action-field increases to the extent that forms of behaviour can be subjected to rational principles of optimisation/maximisation, measurement, and comparison.

21. In the training technology of modern sport, just as in the science of work, it is a question in the last instance of searching for 'a best way' (Taylorism) of increasing performance and production.

22. By 'amateurism', I am referring to the development of high-achievement or top-level amateur sport right through to 'sham' amateur sport (industrial, university, and state-supported amateurs).

23. On this and the economy of amateurism, see, e.g., F.R. Pfetsch et al. (1975, 100-108).

24. On the genesis and continuation of the European 'man-machine model', set in motion as early as the Renaissance by Leonardo da Vinci's philosophical-scientific reflections and sketches with their metric, mechanical representation of the human body, see M. Herzfeld (1906, 103, 113-114, 115); R.z. Lippe (1974, Vol. 1, 278-285). While Leonardo still had a totalising vision of the human body, his followers in modern engineering and the science of work have narrowed this down to a mechanistic-biological theory of the human body as an organic-machine system.

25. My reflections in this connection are based on M. Foucault (1977, 36-39, 173-292), who introduced the concept of 'the political economy of the body' and who, in his investigation of the history of European prisons (with special reference to France), worked out the moments in the politicisation and economisation of the human body. A goal of such socialisation consists in the 'correction' and 'adjustment' of the human body (discipline) which only becomes a 'usable power' 'when it is both a productive and subjected body' (M. Foucault, 1977, 37). In sport, bodily discipline in the process of learning and executing movement techniques and tactics takes on an important function: here, too—paradigmatically in top-level sport—only the 'subjected' body is finally 'productive'.

26. In a press communication (September 1979), a spokesperson for the sporting goods industry imparted that, in 1979, this branch in West Germany expected to increase its returns by 5% to around 4.2 milliard DM. Meanwhile, in 1992 its returns climbed over 20 milliard DM.

27. The commercialisation of skiing can serve as an illuminating example of this. In the European Alps, this development began with the construction of 'ski-centres' (cable cars, ski-lifts, starting pistes, cross-country ski-runs, toboggan runs, ice stadia, sport hotels, etc.). The places where winter sports championships are decided (national right up to the level of the Winter Olympics) use such sports events to advertise their qualities as places for sports holidays. This model is also applicable to regional and urban areas that are situated near to sports- and leisure-centres.

28. For example, according to information published in the West German press (September 1979), somewhere in the region of 5.2 million DM per playing season flow into the coffers of the amateur clubs in the German Football Association (DFB) from income from shirt advertising. Another example: the German Skiing Association (DSV) has set up, together with the ski-manufacturers, a so-called 'material pool' from which top skiers are fitted out free of charge in return for advertising the manufacturers' products.

29. On this, see my amplifications in the section titled 'Sport and the Economy—A Sociological Theme' and note 9.

30. On the comparative financing of top-level sport in France and the former Democratic and Federal Republics of Germany, see F.R. Pfetsch et al. (1975, esp. 58, 80-88, 164-167, 174-187, 196, 199-204).

31. These considerations apply only to private and not to state-organised sports businesses.

32. I am referring epistemologically in this connection (sport as 'social fact') to E. Durkheim's classic *Rules of Sociological Method* (1895) and to the 'Frankfurt School' of sociology. In both cases, it is a question of the 'objectification' (or 'reification') of social institutions and their effects on the behaviour of social subjects. It is the reverse of the problem of human resistance and the transformation of 'social facts' by people.

33. The epistemological position arrived at here represents a synthesis in which an attempt is made to conceptualise the subjective and objective moments of constructing social reality as an historical-empirical unity. See P.L. Berger and T. Luckmann (1974).

34. Compare in this context my attempt at constructing a sociological theory on the question of the 'structure of commodity aesthetics' in sport. B. Rigauer (1979, 87-146, esp. 95-105).

35. What the industrial societies widely lack and what will have to be developed (again) is a nature- and people-friendly 'economy of living' (cf. R. Lippe, 1978) of the kind found in the early history of European cultures but which was forgotten and suppressed with the advent of Western rationalism. Not only that; the Europeans (and the 'Europeanised' societies) are still today endangering and destroying nature and people-friendly economies outside their cultural sphere, for example, in the so-called 'developing countries'.

36. An example: In the German national leagues (*Bundesligen*), the member clubs are no longer able to raise their high costs for training, pocket money, performance premiums, players' wages, travelling, etc. unless they carry the shirt advertising demanded by their industrial sponsors.

37. Though this, of course, is not the rule, the biographies of retired top-level athletes (amateur as well as professional) point to mental, spiritual, and physical breakdowns and to identity crises. Isolated fragments of such incidents are taken up by the mass media. However, to my knowledge no scientific investigations of this problem area have been carried out or if they have, have not been publicised effectively.

38. On this, compare the 'theory of social exchange' as formulated in the works of P.M. Blau (1968, 452-457) and G.C. Homans (1973, 247-265) and critically developed in West German sociology by K. Ottomeyer (1977).

39. I have recently observed such behaviour. To my question (why he had broken his momentum by braking) a cyclist in training replied that he had intended to.

40. In European cultural history, a dualism of work and play has persisted. Against this, however, the false alternatives of this dualism have been repeatedly pointed out and above all the necessity of overcoming it through a unity of work and play (a 'humane' society). See, e.g., the investigation and theory of G. Eichler (1979).

41. We must pose the question of how an industrial society manages the body, what it makes of it, and we must think about how we can counteract it in the future. Sport, gymnastics, play, and movement therapies and many other forms of physical recreation, prophylaxis and rehabilitation will remain repair workshops so long as our industrial civilisation uses and misuses the human body primarily as an economic and political resource, and rationalises more and more its natural rhythms and elementary need for meaning. See R. Lippe (1978).

42. See in this context my essay on 'Sportindustry' (B. Rigauer, 1992).

REFERENCES

Andreano, R. (1970). Money and the folk hero. In G. Sage (Ed.), *Sport and American society* (pp. 164-174). Reading, MA: Addison-Wesley.

Berger, P.L., & Luckmann, T. (1974). *Die gesellschaftliche Konstruktion der Wirklichkeit*. Frankfurt.

Blau, P.M. (1968). Interaction: Social exchange. In *International encyclopedia of the social sciences: Vol. 7* (pp. 452-457). New York.

Dytschewa, T. (1964). Die körperkultur als dialektische einheit überbaulicher und nichtüberbaulicher seiten. In *Theorie und Praxis der Körperkultur* (pp. 20-33). Sonderheft.

Edwards, H. (1973). *Sociology of sport*. Homewood, IL: Dorsey.

Eichberg, H. (1973). *Der Weg des Sports in die industrielle Zivilisation*. Baden-Baden.

Eichler, G. (1972). Falsch getrimmt. Sport für alle? In J. Richter (Ed.), *Die vertrimmte nation oder sport in rechter gesellschaft* (pp. 47-59). Reinbek.

Eichler, G. (1979). *Spiel und Arbeit. Zur Theorie der Freizeit*. Stuttgart: Bad Cannstatt.

Elias, N. (1976). *Über den Prozeb der Zivilisation* (Vols. 1, 2). Frankfurt.

Foucault, M. (1977). *Überwachen und Strafen. Die geburt des gefängnisses*. Frankfurt.

Gilbert, B. (1970). Sis-boom-bah! for Amalgamated Sponge. In G. Sage (Ed.), *Sport and American society* (pp. 175-186). Reading, MA: Addison-Wesley.

Güldenpfennig, S. (1974). Erweiterte Reproduktion der Arbeitskraft—ein Ansatz zur Bestimmung des Verhältnisses von Sport und Arbeit. In S. Güldenpfennig (Ed.), *Sensumotorisches Lernen und Sport als Reproduktion der Arbeitskraft* (pp. 11-59). Köln.

Güldenpfennig, S. (1978). *Gewerkschaftliche Sportpolitik. Voraussetzungen und Perspektiven*. Köln.

Habermas, J. (1970). Soziologische Notizen zum Verhältnis von Arbeit und Freizeit. In J. Habermas (Ed.), *Arbeit. Erkenntnis. Fortschritt. Aufsätze 1954-1970* (pp. 56-74). Amsterdam.

Hammerich, K. & Heinemann, K. (Eds.). (1975). *Texte zur Soziologie des Sports*. Schorndorf.

Harder, H. (1970). *Unternehmen Olympia. Mustermesse. Pseudoreligion. Ersatzkrieg.* Köln.

Heinemann, K. (Ed.). (1984). *Texte zur Ökonomie des Sports.* Schorndorf.

Herzfeld, M. (1906). *Leonardo da Vinci. Denker, Forscher und Poet.* Jena.

Hoch, P. (1976). Who owns sport? In A. Yiannakis (Ed.), *Sport sociology: Contemporary themes* (pp. 42-51). Dubuque, IA: Kendall-Hunt.

Homans, G.C. (1973). Soziales Verhalten als Austausch. In H. Hartmann (Ed.), *Moderne Amerikanische Soziologie* (pp. 247-265). Stuttgart.

Hortleder, G. (1974). *Die Faszination des Fussallspiels. Soziologische Anmerkungen zum Sport als Freizeit und Beruf.* Frankfurt.

Hortleder, G. (1978). *Sport in der nachindustriellen Gesellschaft.* Frankfurt.

Kraus, R.G. (1970). Recreation for the rich and poor. In G. Sage (Ed.), *Sport and American society* (pp. 187-198). Reading, MA.

Lippe, R.z. (1974). *Naturbeherrschung am Menschen* (Vols. 1, 2). Frankfurt.

Lippe, R.z. (1978). *Am eigenen Leib. Zur Ökonomie des Lebens.* Frankfurt.

Lüdtke, H. (1972). Sportler und Voyeursportler. Sport als Freizeitinhalt. In J. Richter (Ed.), *Die vertrimmte Nation oder Sport in rechter Gesellschaft* (pp. 23-47). Reinbek.

Lüschen, G. & Weis, K. (Eds.). (1976). *Die Soziologie des Sports.* Darmstadt: Neuwied.

McMurtry, J. (1976). A case for killing the Olympics. In A. Yiannakis (Ed.), *Sport sociology: Contemporary themes* (pp. 51-56). Dubuque, IA: Kendall-Hunt.

Meyer, H. (1973). Der Hochleistungssport—ein Phänomen des Showbusiness. In *Zeitschrift für Soziologie 1* (pp. 59-78).

Model, O. (1955). *Funktionen und Bedeutung des Sports in ökonomischer und soziologischer Sicht.* Winterthur.

Murray, T.J. (1970). The big, booming business of pro football. In G. Sage (Ed.), *Sport and American society* (pp. 157-163). Reading, MA: Addison-Wesley.

Neale, W.C. (1975). Die eigenartige Ökonomie des Profi-sports. In K. Hammerich & K. Heinemann (Eds.), *Texte zur Soziologie des Sports* (pp. 204-219). Schorndorf.

Novikov, A.D. & Maksimenko, M. (1972). Soziale und ökonomische Faktoren und das Niveau sportlicher Leistungen. In *Sportwissenschaft 2* (pp. 156-167).

Ottomeyer, K. (1977). *Ökonomie Zwänge und menschliche Beziehungen.* Reinbek.

Pfetsch, F.R. *Leistungssport und Gesellschaftssystem.*

Pilz, G. (Ed.). (1986). *Sport und Verein.* Reinbek.

Plessner, H. (1966). Die Funktion des Sports in der industriellen Gesellschaft. In G. Klohn (Ed.), *Leibeserziehung und Sport in der modernen Gesellschaft* (pp. 18-32). Weinheim.

Prokop, U. (1971). *Soziologie der Olympischen Spiele. Sport und Kapitalismus.* München.

Richter, J. (Ed.). (1972). *Die vertrimmte Nation oder Sport in rechter Gesellschaft.* Reinbek.

Rigauer, B. (1969). *Sport und Arbeit. Soziologische Zusammenhänge und ideologische Implikationen.* Frankfurt. [Guttmann, A. (Trans.) (1987). *Sport and work.* New York.]

Rigauer, B. (1972). Leistungssport als Arbeitsleistung. In J. Richter (Ed.), *Die vertrimmte Nation oder Sport in rechter Gesellschaft* (pp. 60-74). Reinbek.

Rigauer, B. (1979). *Warenstrukturelle Bedingungen leistungssportlichen Handelns. Ein Beitrag zur sportsoziologischen Theoriebildung.* Lollar.

Rigauer, B. (1992). Sportindustrie. Soziologische Betrachtungen über das Verschwinden des Sports in der Markt—und Warenwelt. In R. Horak & O. Penz (Eds.), *Sport: Kult und Kommerz* (pp. 185-204). Wien.

Rittner, K. (1976). *Sport und Arbeitsteilung. Zur sozialen Funktion und Bedeutung des Sports.* Bad Homburg.

Sage, G. (Ed.). (1970). *Sport and American society.* Reading, MA: Addison-Wesley.

Schlagenhauf, K. (1977). *Sportvereine in der Bundesrepublik Deutschland. Teil I: Strukturelemente und Verhaltensdeterminanten im organisierten Freizeitbereich.* Schorndorf.

Simson, V., & Jennings, A. (1992). *Geld, Macht und Doping. Das ende der Olympischen Idee.* München.

Timm, W. (1979). *Sportvereine in der bundesrepublik Deutschland. Teil II: Organisations-, Angebots- und Finanzstruktur.* Schorndorf.

Weber, M. (1974). *Wirtschaft und Gesellschaft. Grundriss der verstehenden Soziologie* (Vol. 1, 2). Köln.

Weinberg, S.K., & Arond, H. (1976). Die Berufskultur des Boxers. In G. Lüschen & K. Weis (Eds.), *Die Soziologie des Sports* (pp. 253-260). Darmstadt: Neuwied.

Weiss, P. (1973). *Sport: A philosophic inquiry.* London/Amsterdam.

Winkler, H.-J. (1972). *Sport und politische Bildung.* Opladen.

Wohl, A. (1973). *Die gesellschaftlich-historischen Grundlagen des bürgerlichen Sports.* Köln.

Yiannakis, A. (Ed.). (1976). *Sport sociology: Contemporary themes.* Dubuque, IA: Kendall-Hunt.

Conclusion to Part III

SUGGESTIONS FOR ESSAYS AND CLASS DISCUSSION

Similarly to what we suggested for Parts I and II, some of the points we raised in our introductory commentary on this section can serve as foci for class discussion and debate. In addition, questions such as the following might be useful as discussion topics and essay titles in relation to the contributions of Riordan, Jarvie, and Rigauer.

1. What were the main similarities and differences in the organisation and practice of sport in capitalist and socialist societies? Pay particular attention in your discussion to the ideologies that grew up in this connection on both sides of the so-called 'iron curtain' and 'bamboo curtain'.
2. Consider the impact that the 'people's revolutions' of 1989 have had so far and are likely to have on sport in Eastern Bloc countries.
3. What are likely to be the effects of the movement of former Eastern Bloc athletes to the West on (a) these athletes themselves; (b) sports in their home countries; and (c) the sports of the countries to which they move?
4. Critically examine from a feminist perspective the experiences of elite women athletes from the former German Democratic Republic (East Germany) now that they are subject to the market forces of the Grand Prix athletics circuit.
5. Consider how and to what extent 'glasnost', 'perestroika', and the dissolution of the former Soviet Union have affected the organisation and control of sport. How are the demand for and the supply of sporting activities and opportunities likely to be affected by these processes?
6. What are the likely consequences for sport of the growth of nationalism and separatism in a number of the former USSR's constituent republics?
7. In what ways might *either* a cultural studies writer *or* a figurational sociologist approach the analysis and interpretation of the South African crisis? Pay particular attention in your answer to how you think they might approach the study of South African sport.
8. Comment on the contention that you cannot have 'normal' sport in an 'abnormal' society. In your answer, draw upon material from South Africa and *one other* society that can be said to have a 'racial problem'.
9. Using the conceptualisation developed by Rigauer, critically examine how the subject of 'Sports Science' contributes to a 'technologised' view of athletes.
10. How might a feminist criticise Bero Rigauer's chapter on 'Sport and the Economy: A Developmental Perspective'?
11. To what extent can sport be said to have grown dependent on 'outside' economic and political interests? What, in your view, are likely to be the

principal consequences of this process and how, if it is necessary, can they be remedied?

SOME POSSIBLE RESEARCH TASKS

Project One: Sport in Socialist Societies

Choose a sport in which a former Eastern Bloc country became internationally successful (e.g., Bulgaria—weight lifting; Rumania—gymnastics; Czechoslovakia— ice hockey) and attempt to establish whether there were any 'pathologies' specific to the sport of that country and to sport more generally in the former Eastern Bloc countries.

Project Two: The Migration of Sports Labour

Athletes from Eastern Europe are currently playing sports in a range of Western countries. Using in-depth interviews with a small sample playing in your country, examine their attitudes to and perceptions of the sports subcultures into which they were initially socialised and in which they now find themselves.

Project Three: Sport in Eastern Europe—the State versus the Market

Taking Riordan's arguments as a guide and using newspaper and journal articles as sources of information, assess the impact on sport in the former Eastern Bloc of the growth of Western, capitalist market influences. Try to establish in which specific areas of sport change is occurring. What are the ideological dimensions of these changes? Will the changes be elitist in the traditional socialist sense of a focus on winners, or will a market elitism develop in which top performers provide the backbone of financial, entrepreneurial, and bureaucratic elites? Or, conversely, will market forces stimulate development towards mass participation and wider leisure choice?

Project Four: Sport, the Media, and the South African Crisis

Using a Gramscian framework, critically consider the media coverage in your country of the readmission of South Africa to the Olympic Games in Barcelona in 1992. Compare the pattern you establish with the pattern of media coverage of racial issues in the Olympics in any year when South Africa was excluded. Attempt to specify in what ways, if at all, the approach of a non-Gramscian Marxist or a figurational sociologist to this issue might differ.

Project Five:
Sport and 'Race' in Historical/Developmental Perspective

Taking any two countries that can be said to have problems of severe inequality between racial or ethnic groups, examine historically the impact of patterns of racial inequality on the development of sport. What principal similarities and differences do you detect between their patterns of racial/ethnic inequality and in the development of their sports?

Project Six: Elite Sport, 'Sports Science', and 'the Body'

Using Rigauer's analysis as a guide, examine a range of sports and seek to establish whether elite athletes can be said recurrently to have the same or similar experiences. Did top-level athletes have such experiences in 'the age of amateurism' in the nineteenth and early twentieth centuries? Try to establish whether, in the twentieth century, a 'rationalisation' of performance and the body can be said to have taken place in top-level sports. Conduct a content analysis of 'sports science' journals and consider whether the research agenda of this subject area has become centred around a 'performance efficiency' model. In what ways and to what extent are these processes in sports and sports science interrelated? How can they be explained?

Postscript

Sociology and the Sociology of Sport in a Rapidly Changing World

It was at the beginning of the 1980s that we first had the idea of putting together the book of essays that has emerged as *The Sports Process*. Given its long period of gestation, some of the ideas that have affected our structuring of the book and its contents reflect one or two assumptions that now seem rather dated. The clearest example is our decision to commission chapters on sport in capitalist and socialist societies by an Eastern writer, Andrzej Wohl (who subsequently withdrew) and a Western writer, Jim Riordan. This decision reflected the cold war era, the 40 or so years after the Second World War during which the 'frozen clinch' (Elias, 1983, p. 274) or 'double-bind figuration' (Elias, 1987, pp. 49ff, 68-70, 96ff, 107ff) formed by the United States, the Soviet Union, and their respective allies seemed to be written in stone; a structure that, if it was not going to collapse in a nuclear holocaust, seemed likely to endure into the foreseeable future. However, the cold war is over; as the last decade of the twentieth century unfolds, people are being reminded, perhaps more forcibly than ever before in a period of relative peace, that social structures are products of human action and hence ephemeral. That is, they change. Even relatively enduring structures (such as those involved in and produced by the cold war) are no exception to this rule. They are products of human action in which the tendencies toward change are relatively opaque and work relatively slowly.

The Soviet Union may no longer exist; its empire may have crumbled; socialism may seem to be an ideology that has been confined by history to the garbage dump. Nevertheless, chapters such as Riordan's retain their value for at least three reasons. First, socialism/communism remains the ruling ideology in countries such as Cuba and North Korea, to say nothing of China, and Riordan's chapter can serve as a useful guide to sociological research into sport in those countries. Second, it illuminates an important aspect of the recent past and shows some of the ways that ideologies can affect human attitudes and actions. Third, it analyses structures and values that form important parts of the social nexus in which the future development of sport and society in the former Soviet Union and its satellites is going to take place. We do not mean this last point in some crude 'evolutionary' sense. It is our contention that the Soviet and socialist past will unavoidably influence the myriad individual decisions and actions affecting the future forms of sport and society in those countries. Whatever forms these changes take, the analysis of Riordan will be of value in understanding them as they unfold. That will be the case whether the changes incorporate aspects of socialist structures and values or whether they involve a complete reaction against them.

Even though the cold war has ended, it is by no means certain that we are about to enter a period of prolonged world peace. Nor is it entirely clear—even though large numbers of people seem to believe it—that Marxism, socialism, and communism are dead. Principal among our reasons for suggesting this are the massive social and economic problems faced by the capitalist countries of the West (those connected with recession, for example, to say nothing of racial, gender, and other forms of inequality), many of which are cogently, if not in all respects correctly, analysed by Marxist, neo-Marxist, and socialist theories. Given the continuation and perhaps the exacerbation of problems such as these, it is possible that we will witness a resurgence of socialist ideologies and values over the next decade or so. This swing of the ideological pendulum—if it occurs— will be facilitated by the absence of the socialist 'evil empire', which will make the imperfections of capitalism stand out in starker relief than was the case in the cold war years.

These worldwide changes have some implications for the sociological study of sport. The 1992 Olympics are just recently completed, and for the first time since the 1950s, the world's premier sporting spectacle was not a vehicle for the expression of cold war rivalry between East and West. Will future Olympics become a focus for the heightened expression of particular nationalisms? Will sources of rivalry emerge that have so far remained largely latent in an Olympic context (e.g., rivalries of a religious, ethnic, or economic nature)? Will the nations of the new 'commonwealth' that is emerging out of the former Soviet Union continue to compete under a single banner, or will they seek and be granted separate representation? And what about the reentry of South Africa? If there is delay in the process of democratisation or an increase in interracial and intertribal tension, how will that affect the attitudes and actions of South African athletes? How will it affect the attitudes and actions of officials and athletes from other countries towards their South African counterparts?

Similar questions may be asked about the countries of the European Community. If the process of growing economic and political integration continues, what will be the consequences for sport? Will a 'United States of Europe' enter athletes and teams into international competitions under a single European banner? Will the future of, for example, soccer in Europe see the emergence of a more powerful pan-European Football Association, the continued dominance of traditional national associations, or the construction of new controlling bodies that reflect the aspirations of nationalities that have been submerged up to now, such as the Catalans and Basques in Spain? Finally, what will be the consequences for sport of changes towards greater or lesser integration on a global level and of the struggles and conflicts associated causally and consequentially with these processes?

We hope you have found *The Sports Process*, with its historical/developmental and cross-cultural emphasis, the kind of book that is needed in the current situation. It may reflect the rudimentary state of knowledge at the moment, but, we believe, it is only through more and better studies of the kind represented here that we will stand any chance of obtaining the kinds of insights that will facilitate our understanding of how the sport we make is influenced by and sometimes in its turn significantly influences the societies in which we make it.

Eric Dunning
Joseph Maguire
Robert Pearton

Index